D0960963

Asphalt Nation

Also by Jane Holtz Kay

Lost Boston

Preserving New England

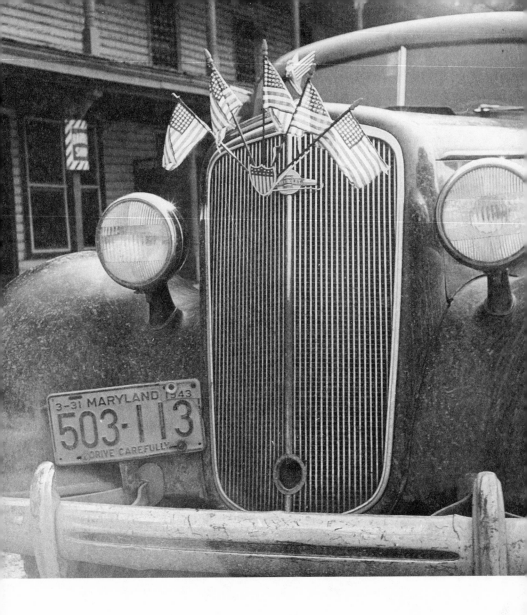

The motor vehicle embodied the American way of life long before the flag-waving World War II photo shown here. The imagery, if not the promise, endures, but the late auto age has erased the nation's dream of mobility. (Library of Congress)

Asphalt Nation

How the Automobile Took Over America,
and How We Can Take It Back

Jane Holtz Kay

CROWN PUBLISHERS, INC. • NEW YORK

Published by Crown Publishers, Inc., 201 East 50th Street, New York, New York 10022. Member of the Crown Publishing Group.

Random House, Inc. New York, Toronto, London, Sydney, Auckland
http://www.randomhouse.com/
CROWN is a trademark of Crown Publishers, Inc.

Printed in the United States of America

Design by Cynthia Dunne

LIBRARY OF CONGRESS CATALOGING-IN-PUBLICATION DATA
Kay, Jane Holtz.
    Asphalt nation : how the automobile took over America, and how we can take it back / Jane Holtz Kay.
        p.   cm.
    Includes bibliographical references and index.
        1. Automobiles—Social aspects—United States.   2. City and town life—United States.   3. Sociology, Urban—United States.
    I. Title.
    HE5623.K36   1997
    303.48'32—dc21   97-1605
                                                                          CIP

ISBN 0-517-58702-5

10   9   8   7   6   5   4   3   2

To Jacqueline and Julie

Contents

Acknowledgments

IT TOOK A village—a village of colleagues, friends, and family—to raise this book from conviction to finished work. Reporters, as news people were called before the more contemplative if less accurate name "journalist" was adopted, seldom thank those whose names appear in their works. In this case, the intellectual, political, planning, and grassroots activists who befriended this project at the start sustained it through a long journey. The people whose names appear in the text of this book are too numerous to cite here, but their talks and trips were essential.

A book written outside the professional or academic culture depends on an informal network to assure technical accuracy and scholarly fairness. I am in the debt of those who extended themselves quite beyond their daily chores to do so. Historians—some like-minded in recognizing the need to stress the automobile as an agent of destruction, others committed to no cause other than "getting it right"—join the list of those who read the manuscript and scored its pages with insights. Likewise, my thanks to the planners, conservationists, and economists who shared their thoughts and their science.

Among others who shared in disparate aspects of this book, thanks go to Steve Burrington, Donald Chen, Clifford Ellis, George Haikalis, Ann Hershfang, Charles Komanoff, Ruth Knack, Arleyn Levee, Josh Lehman, Charles Levy, Marcia D. Lowe, Todd Litman, Clay McShane, Carl Moody, Mark Rose, Robert "Rusty" Russell, Elliott D. Sclar, David Schuyler, and R. Stephen Sennott.

Many newspapers and magazines published my anti-auto sentiments and helped disperse the eccentric notion of design for people before cars long before a real constituency appeared. Thanks also to the *Nation,* my bivouac for two decades and the source of my first musings on the subject; to the professional magazines *Planning, Landscape Architecture,* and *Architecture,* and the newspapers the *Boston Globe,* the *New York Times,* and the *Christian Science Monitor.*

The Boston Athenaeum, the first of the breed, remained the source, foundation, and support for this book. Its gracious and scholarly staff members have my gratitude for their patience in fulfilling requests that must have seemed at once arcane and copious.

It also took friends and family to write this book. Mine offered everything from a clipping service to a critical reading. Chief among the early and repeated readers and supporters were Stanley Moss and Frederica Matera, joined by my other office friends and colleagues, Dorothea Hass, Pauline Chase Harrell, Mikki Ansin, and Anne Hafrey. Their daily help more than compensated for the noisy obstructions of street work outside our windows.

Dick McDonough, my agent, whose urban activism, acuity, and doggedness on my behalf helped generate this book, and Peter Ginna, my perceptive editor who scrutinized *Asphalt Nation* and helped shorten the extensions of its deadline, propped this project.

Beyond the "family" of anti-car crusaders and colleagues, my own family, my mother, Edith Holtz, and my aunt and uncle, Charlotte and Mike Alexander, gave constant support. The literacy and ideological enthusiasm of my daughters, Jacqueline and Julie, and my sister, Ellen Goodman, all of whom scoured this manuscript, made it worthwhile.

"What America drives, drives America."
—slogan of the American Automobile
Manufacturers Association

Introduction

The Late Motor Age: A Defining Decade

TWO DAYS AFTER May Day 1991, I began this odyssey into the auto age. Getting around on four wheels wasn't what it used to be, and, in the aftermath of what some were calling "the first petroleum war" in the Persian Gulf, Congress was debating whether to continue to make the world safe for America's major oil consumer, the automobile, or to adopt a new highway bill. With two-thirds of the nation driving through congested "carburbs," the system of moving Americans was clearly askew. Would the federal government continue covering the nation with asphalt or legislate a fresh approach? Would Washington still advance the policies that had produced dependence on the motor vehicle and assaulted the landscape and cityscape, the environment, and the quality of life, or would it tame the car?

And so, in order to gauge the late auto age, I decided to graph its extremes. On one side stood the advocates of "de-vehicularization," as the anti-auto activists had begun to call their goal, and on the other were the movers for more roads, more cars, more auto dependency. To see them, I would brave the separate worlds of foot power and horsepower: the road worriers versus the road warriors.

By a happy coincidence of events the polarities of what I would come to call the "asphalt nation" were holding conferences only days and miles apart. On May 3 and 4, the advocates for an auto-free America were meeting in Greenwich Village: on May 5 and 6, their adversaries, the traffic engineers, were assembling in Secaucus, New Jersey. In their own words, on their own turfs, each side would diagram the extremes of our motoring nation as it prepared to enter a new century.

The meetings couldn't have been staged in more appropriate locales. The car busters were gathering for the two days of their Auto-Free Cities assembly at Manhattan's New York University near Washington Square. A walk or train ride away from the most densely settled, well-railed pedestrian neighborhood in the United States, they were launching their joint crusade to curb the car. With equal symbolism, the Institute of Transportation Engineers, dedicated to molding the infrastructure of the motor vehicle, would gather a day later in the wasteland of Secaucus, New Jersey, a sprawling, auto-only, in accessible landscape.

Weeks after the nation's battle for the Middle East oil wells had ended in 1991 ("oil for the headlights of America," one commentator noted), mere months before highway legislation would hit Congress, the pedestrian-firsters and the highway-firsters would offer contrasting viewpoints. I would see the black and white of life on wheels: how the two ends of the spectrum would solve the congestion and chaos of motorized America. On the one hand, grassroots activists and advocates would argue that the car was the villain of the environmental age, the heavy in an era of anomie and isolation. On the other, the hard hat traffic bureaucrats, ready to pave their grandmothers to get home for Thanksgiving dinner, would argue for more asphalt.

My first stop, then, was with the anti-auto evangelists. In the academic environs of New York University's auditorium, they gathered for the First International Conference for Auto-Free Cities. The four hundred or so speakers and listeners had been summoned by Transportation Alternatives, a feisty group best known in the limited history of the anti-auto movement for their civil disobedience in stopping traffic on the Queensboro Bridge in protest of its closing to bicyclers and walkers. The "QB6" (Queensboro Six), *Newsday* had labeled the protestors. They succeeded. The bridge remained open for bicyclers and walkers.

Bearing the label "humanpower advocates," brandishing "Touch the Earth: Walk" buttons, and carrying bumper stickers for every environmental cause under the ozone, the conferencegoers were a legion. Passionate walkers, hardy bikers, and urban and environmental vigilantes disembarked from the dingy subway stops nearby and walked or parked their bikes outside the conference headquarters at 100 Washington Square East. How many had come without "benefit of car," a moderator asked. Three hundred hands shot up.

So it went throughout the day in the corridors and classrooms where the costumes of "radicalism" underscored the politics of the "radicalism" of scrapping the car. The footgear was a catalog of Birkenstock sandals, rainbow-colored sneakers, and trim boots. The rumpled assemblyman Jerry Nadler pounded the table before an audience that ranged from a toddler wearing a mini–bike helmet and T-shirt stamped "One Less Car" to adults in academic tweeds and jeans.

A hapless janitor had pulled down the shades on our surroundings in the columned auditorium. No matter. Within minutes, the energy savers were there, switching off the lights and pulling open the draperies. Daylight flooded the room as the listeners nodded in unison at warnings on the state of the planet ("all the indicators of the world's health are dim," said Lester Brown of Worldwatch Institute), cheered the closing of Manhattan's last GM dealership.

"Cars are filthy abominations," said Toronto bike activist Anne Hansen. Applause.

"Monstrous, dangerous, obtrusive," she went on. Applause.

"Abusive." Applause.

"Did I come to the right conference?" she asked with a laugh.

You bet she did.

Two days later, imbued with their anti-auto fervor and loaded with their pamphlets on every environmental cause on the planet, I headed to the engineers' conference.

Its site was a barren auto-bred wasteland. In the highway-wrapped environs of a Howard Johnson Executive Suites Hotel in Secaucus, New Jersey, sat the highway builders—with "their hearts in asphalt," as the conference organizer for the American Society of Civil Engineers and the Institute of Transportation Engineers put it.

The contrast between the two conferences was marked in every aspect. The anti-auto warriors had been replaced by an army of the auto age's status quo. No straphangers here. The Secaucus conferees came by internal combustion engine to discuss such topics as "Implementing Regional Mobility Solutions." They passed the placeless corporate boxes along Secaucus's highway, and many got lost en route. They looked out the hotel's front door on roads and parking lots as gray as the Executive Suites's gray garage, gray sidewalks' gray blank walls. Secaucus was the quintessence of nowhere and as far from its old landscape, the so-called Meadowlands, as bulldozers could make it. The land beneath the barren tundra of buildings and lonely parking lots possessed only enough link with nature to flood the new highway on wet days and make the route to the Newark airport an obstacle course.

From the stolid old New York University classrooms to the thin faux decor of the Howard Johnson restaurant was contrast indeed. The differences in the details of the conferences were equally striking. The anti-auto militants had lunched in Greenwich Village's Indian, Arab, or Greek cafés. They crashed overnight in friends' book-lined apartments lulled by the clamor of a Lower Manhattan Saturday night that didn't change decibel level as it slid into a raucous Sunday morning.

But it was eerie as a graveyard in auto-choked Secaucus. The administrators at the Secaucus sessions sat in the windowless world of the highway mall. They looked out their sealed windows at a glass box building poised on stilts above parked cars hard by the sign "Mill Creek Mall" (a body of water buried in the dozen or so lanes of traffic circling the hotel), then nodded off to sleep tranquilized by the white noise of the ten rooftop air conditioners and the whir of passing traffic.

Where the hard-pressed auto-free attendees had been asked to pay $35 or more if they were "doing all right financially" but not to worry if they couldn't ("This system is based on trust. . . . No one is turned away."), their opposites were well subsidized indeed. The members of the American Society of Civil Engineers and the Institute of Transportation Engineers handed institutionally stamped checks for their registrations, their spacious rooms, and notebooks smelling fresh as the first day of school.

But stop. The contrasts somehow began to seem too sharp, too forced, too simple. For, in the opening minutes, my script shredded as the first speaker, a man with enough graphics to map a NASA liftoff, launched the proceedings before the experts. His suit was gray, his accent moderate, his manner textbook professional. But his message did not come from the other end of the spectrum of the highway age at all. Word for word, syllable for syllable, it carried the import of the auto-free activists—and the same evangelical tone. Comments on congestion, concern with the way of life and the stress of the late auto age marked the speeches.

Card-carrying members of the transportation bureaucracy they might be, an audience of partisans to asphalt. Yet one thing was clear from their comments: the consensus of support for the auto age was fraying. The sentiments from either end of the transportation compass were so similar that, in the aftermath of the conference, my notes and quotes were almost indistinguishable. "What used to be rush hour traffic has become all day," I read. "I don't think our auto-controlled society has reached the ultimate in evolution." "A penny from the gas tax would get you a billion dollars a year; two would get you two."

But who had said what? Which advocate, pro or con, had uttered this or that? I could scarcely assign authorship: some anti-auto David? some former prohighway Goliath? "Crisis proportions . . . more cars than people . . . our roads did not come with instructions for how to work. . . ." Such criticism was scattered throughout my notes, and the attribution was sometimes uneasy, sometimes startling. "One of our states has completely disappeared," a confessed hardtopper quoted Russell Baker on the tarmac-ing of Florida.

Certainly, the transportation folks' hearts—and history—were in asphalt. But their solutions were in biking, in car pooling, in mass transit, in walking, and, to my delight, in an "incomparably thrilling land use revolution" that would end sprawl in favor of walkable, transit-based planning. "Balanced transportation" was the mantra: the need to balance the equation between the automobile and other modes of movement. Later, I would learn to question the conviction of their phrases. Notwithstanding, it was clear that the professionals were looking for what they called a "three-legged stool": the highway, public transit, land use. The balance was off, the stool was tilting, and, alike, these experts knew that the first leg—the highway—had been jacked so high that it had tipped the structure. Those most involved in moving the nation toward a new millennium were not convinced that we could do so by the motor vehicle. Not convinced at all. They were voicing a common concern and a common dislike of the way our driver-obsessed nation worked. It was a measure, but only one, of the growing distress of those who understood that the nation was reaching the end of that last frontier.

That summer of 1991, with the supposed last yards of the thirty-five-year-old interstate highway system in place and new legislation working its way through Congress, the question was even more visibly on the agenda. In Washington legislators were questioning our nation's auto dependency as a new highway bill started to roll through Congress. New York Senator Daniel Patrick Moynihan was proclaiming that "we've laid enough concrete." His words hit the news wires. Others shared his certainty that the interstate system was done. Quite done. "Suppose they said that 'we have won' and quit," one supporter of the highway bill, now known as the Intermodal Surface Transportation Efficiency Act (ISTEA), said borrowing the exit line offered by Senator George Aiken of Vermont to end the Vietnam War.

As the new year approached, the House and Senate passed the act, authorizing it with $151 billion. Congress's twelve-figure budget, for six years, was flexible. It would allow the states to use money not only for highways but for mass transit and other ways of moving America away from the four-wheeled vehicle as well. It was populist and planning oriented enough to insist that transportation systems must have community approval. It would encourage walking, bicycling, and transit taking to get us out of the car trap. In short, Congress seemed willing to let Americans explore a new way home.

But would they? Would—will—we?

This book addresses these questions. Part I, "Car Glut," begins where the anti-auto advocates did, showing how deeply enmeshed we are in the car culture. Part II, "Car Tracks," a history, traces the car from Henry Ford's mass-produced Model T in 1908 to the present to depict how this happened. It explores how a benign technology to mobilize Americans would transform a human-scaled landscape into the kingdom of the car. Part III, "Car Free," takes its

lessons into the future. It offers solutions, some new, some traditional, to show how we can relieve this dependence and destruction
and secure human and global well-being.

It is this book's conviction that we can find, create, and revive the
remedies, and that planning solutions depend, in the end, on land use
solutions—on mobility based on human movement and transportation beyond the private automobile. Above all, the book is written
with the conviction that we must and can end a late auto age in
which every transportation decision is a highway-based, driving-first
decision. It is written with the hope that human will and political action can become the engine to find ways to reduce the sway of the internal combustion machine.

Asphalt Nation argues that in the better part of the century since
the Model T set the nation on wheels and in the forty-one years since
the Interstate Highway Act of 1956 sprawled a vast network of highways across the continent, the nation has reached motorized stasis.
Our transportation is a tangle, our lives and landscape strangled by
the umbilical cord of the car. As we enter a new century, our vaunted
mobility is, in fact, obstructed by a car culture in which every at-
tempt to move is fraught with wasted motion, wasted time, wasted
surroundings, wasted money.

Looking at the long trail of that history, I believe that we are ap-
proaching the closing of a frontier. It is an ending and a dawning as
marked as the one that Frederick Jackson Turner made the cornerstone of a self-appraisal and shift in the American consciousness at
the turn of the last century. In his seminal essay "The Significance of
the Frontier in American History," Turner expanded the 1890 report
of the superintendent of the Bureau of the Census "that there can
hardly be said to be a frontier line" to establish a theory for the future. Turner's document recorded the end of the colonization of the
great West. Movement, once "the distinguishing feature of American
life," had defined the American character on an ever advancing frontier, he wrote. "This perennial rebirth, this fluidity of American life,
this expansion westward with its new opportunities, its continuous
touch with the simplicity of primitive society, furnishes the forces
dominating American character." An age ended. An era of regrets ensued, as Americans looked back to their founding myths and saw a

lost epoch. They pined for "the glory of movement, glory of change," contemporary historian William Cronon once observed.

Turner's emphasis on America's "advance"—its inexorable sense of movement and dominion over an environment deemed a commodity—characterizes how the motor vehicle ravished our continent thereafter. Today, however, more than one hundred years after Turner, the aggressive movement across the continent seems to be coming to a halt. Escape has become a wasteful and unsound exercise. The old consciousness is waning and with it confidence in our car-bound destiny. We are at the opening of a new frontier as well as a new century. *Asphalt Nation* maintains that, for all its pledges, the promise of the motorcar has been superseded by its problems, that we have reached the end of the age of the automobile viewed as an unredeemed good.

These, then, are the last days of a defining decade and century. They are the beginning of a millennium that will either transform the freewheeling, consumptive automobile and stop the asphalting of America—or propel us down a ruinous path. As in Turner's view, a route is closed, but new routes opened. There are negative implications to the closure. And yet, calling a halt to the notion of an endless frontier marks a more positive endorsement—the cultivation of a landscape that values place more than passage, that restrains auto mobility in the name of human mobility, that re-thinks the way we live.

In the annals of history, many recognize that we have moved as far as we can go on untamed wheels. A nation in gridlock from its auto-bred lifestyle, an environment choking from its auto exhausts, a landscape sacked by its highways has distressed Americans so much that even this go-for-it nation is posting "No Growth" signs on development from shore to shore. All of these dead ends make this a time for larger considerations. The future of our motorized culture needs change. It is the hope of this book not only to explore the origins and direction of that change but, above all, to instill an enthusiasm for creating a human and humane frontier in a new century.

The automobile's spatial greed invades cities and overruns green areas, if not so completely as Central Park is consumed by this Mazda. "Considering its size, it's remarkably easy to park," the ad notes, corroborating the swath of the automobile consuming seven parking spaces for every car. (Mazda)

PART I

Car Glut
A Nation in Lifelock

OPPOSITE: With travelers stuck in traffic and 80 million commuters facing ever more congested roads, this Labor Day greeting at the New Hampshire toll booth takes on a new irony. (Photo: Chris Fitzgerald. *New York Times* Pictures)

Bumper to Bumper

"You're not stuck in a traffic jam, you are the jam."
—German public transport campaign,
Urban Transport International

"It was the thing that I most regretted leaving behind."
—President Bill Clinton surveying a Mustang in Phoenix

"It's not a car. It's an aphrodisiac."
—Infiniti advertisement launched on the
twenty-fifth anniversary of Earth Day

THE NATION'S WAKE-UP call goes like this: "Some of the usual rough stuff out there." "It's a mess." "Don't even think of trying the expressway this morning." "You'll find a stack-up at the intersection, where a tractor trailer truck has turned over, so avoid. . . ."

It's morning in America and *avoid* is the imperative word. But avoiding is impossible. Traffic reports post warnings for specific locales, but why bother? The hits keep coming. At rush hour, A.M. or P.M., it's the usual: "heavy traffic in the *usual* places"; it's "the *usual* twenty-minute delay." The radio blares a chorus of stalled cars and jammed bridges, of car fires backing up interstates, of vapor lock bolting traffic into a motionless mass. Everywhere the commuters' clock ticks off the 8 billion hours a year Americans spend stuck in traffic.

The commuter's trip should jar us to a realization of the auto-bound life that penalizes both nondrivers and drivers of our 200 million motor vehicles. From the jammed tunnel under the Continental Divide to the Cross Bronx Expressway, movement is stymied on the nation's corridors. On the coasts that hold two-thirds of all Americans, the long-suffering "BosWash" and the newer "Los Diegos" freeways greet their share of the day's 80 million car commuters, and, with a screech of brakes, the love song of freedom and mobility goes flat. Freedom? Mobility?

We have heard these complaints before but never for so long a stretch of the day. A generation or so ago, in the complacent fifties, the motion was not so perpetual. The powerhouses of an earlier auto age rested between the hours of the commute. At midday roads emptied out. After darkness, too, there was respite as the steel chargers of the postwar boom, all those fin-tailed Buicks, those fang-grilled Chevies and Fords were corralled for the night in the nation's ranch houses.

Now, though, with four times the 50 million vehicles of that era and far more dispersed trips, the traffic never ceases. Highways become sealed chambers of isolation as commuters put in an average of ten forty-hour weeks behind the wheel each year. Back roads and arterials stall during our three-plus daily trips on errands. Steaming and waiting in traffic, we pay penance for the growth in cars and trips. Trading time behind the wheel for space in the exurbs, work-bound Americans travel from before daybreak to after dark to ever more sprawling homes.

No wonder aerial views show arteries that look like a chain of cabooses, bumper to bumper across the nation. In the last two decades we have doubled the mileage of the nation's highways and promptly filled these new roads by traveling twice as many miles. Seattle's traffic, for example, rising 121 percent in the past decade, matches most regions whose growing populations clog their roads. The chorus of complaints on congestion is hardly confined to any one place. A front-page Labor Day photo depicts a bulb-lit sign at a traffic jam near the tollbooth on the New Hampshire Turnpike. Its message emphasizes the irony: "ENJOY YOUR HOLIDAY!"

Generating Traffic

For decades traffic experts have observed the capacity of more highways to simply breed more traffic. "If you build it, they will come," the popular phrase, is the bleak truth confirmed by science and history. "Generated traffic" is the professional phrase used to describe the traffic generated by increased roads. "Triple convergence," another term, describes how more road space promotes more traffic in Anthony Downs's *Stuck in Traffic*, that is, if you have more road at peak hours, more cars will converge for three reasons: Some will converge for the improved roadway (spatial convergence), some for the more convenient time (temporal convergence), and some from public transportation (modal convergence). Equally glum and mathematical, the so-called Braess's paradox confirms that "by adding capacity to a crowded [highway] network you could actually slow things down." Add the experience of history, and you see why our road building prompts even some federal highway officials to predict that congestion will quadruple in the next twenty years.

And yet, the fact is slow to puncture the mythology of the traffic engineer. Highway departments in, say, St. Louis, whose relatively clear roads would be the envy of many a traffic manager, ask for widening. So do those in smalltown Sauk Centre, Minnesota, the tree-shaded model for Sinclair Lewis's *Main Street*. "It doesn't seem to penetrate," says an official in Atlanta, whose "Spaghetti Junction," the largest interchange in America, jams the district of House leader Newt Gingrich. The "spaghetti" proliferates, and so do the nicknames for the junctions of the expressways nationwide. "Long Island Distressway" is the one used by New Yorkers. Orlando's Interstate 4, already six lanes choked to a standstill, will need twenty-two more lanes by the millennium, regional planners insist. New Jersey's ex-Governor James Florio says, "our highway 287 is a parking lot." Everywhere roads expand, and so does traffic.

So, of course, have cars and the miles they travel. In the two decades after 1970, vehicle miles increased 90 percent and the registrations of those who drove them by more than 70 percent. In that time, wrote Downs, "The number of cars and trucks in use increased nearly 50 percent, twice as fast as the number of households in absolute terms and one-third faster in relative terms, faster, too, than the number of licensed drivers." The momentum has yet to subside.

At Home as We Range

So it is that we spend our lives behind the wheel. With almost two motor vehicles for every household, the car has become the ship of the highway desert. A multipurpose vessel, the automobile is outfitted to allay our hours sequestered there, a home away from home. The motor vehicle is a private chamber to telephone a buddy or boss with one hand and little concentration, a powder room to put on makeup, a cafeteria for lunching—at times simultaneously. We play *Moby Dick* or Stephen King on tape, and run a cellular phone or fax. Otherwise tidy human beings smoke and toss their cigarettes; otherwise decorous ones floss their teeth. Self-professed safe drivers take notes, talk to their clients, fight with their mates, or, incredibly, read or watch TV. Our backseats and trunks have become the attics of America.

In artist Anthony Natsoulas's sculpture a ceramic man is tucked into a real car seat. He is shoeless, his cigar in one hand, his phone attached to his ear in the exhibition *Los Angeles Drives Me Wild*. The artist has stationed a pizza in the figure's lap, a book between his legs, and a crumpled soda can on the floor. Life imitates art. "Going for a ride just isn't what it used to be," another sculptor in the exhibition labeled his piece. His "urban assault mobile" brandished a pistol and a ball and chain above a collection of license plates. It isn't all imagination. "You look up and see brake lights in your face, and you just have to jam on the brakes," a real-life driver described an accident in Washington, D.C. Down falls the computer, if not the driver. These are the hazards of trying to make up for lost time. But there are worse ones, like the Virginia commuter who crashed and died as he was consuming his lunch with fork in hand on a dog day in August traffic.

Automobile advertising goes to great lengths to befog these unnerving events. In the vast, untenanted scenarios delivered by Madison Avenue, the red racer swirls across an empty landscape. The great escape machine, built into the American dream of the getaway, beckons. No mountain or prairie, no desert or glacier is beyond four-wheel drive. In endless hours of television, the nation's quest for mobility is dramatized by such views. Commercials sell our shared imagery of the ninety-mile-an-hour roads less traveled. American corporations spend $40 billion a year to promote the car, $1 billion from GM alone.

With the ring of the cash register, advertisers concede the animosity and virtual warfare bred by the frantic search. "WLDNCRZY" (wild and crazy), said a Subaru commercial; "Presenting A Car Well Prepared To Take On Your Fellow Driver." A photo of license plates bore still other words: "NASTY1," "EAT DUST," "NUTS 2U," and "IG02XS." It's a jungle out there. As gridlock frays nerves and distances increase, driving accelerates aggression. "Look at it this way. Since the next guy is capable of almost anything, shouldn't the same be true of your next car," the advertisement concludes.

The stalled traffic has also given us a new breed of entrepreneur. On the Cross Bronx Expressway, highway peddlers cruise from lane to lane hustling mobile phones to the immobilized vehicles. In Boston vendors sell coffee by the tollbooth at jam-packed Callahan Tunnel during rush hour. Hawkers of newspapers at exits and stoplights share space with pushers for charities, bogus or real; street merchants sell cellophane-wrapped day-old roses. Entrepreneurship also lives on the road in the perceived menace of window washers wielding squeegees. Some drivers find intimidation in the strong-arm aggression. Others have sympathy for the pathos of "Will Work for Food" signs as the homeless stake out exit ramps in Manhattan, Los Angeles, or West Palm Beach.

In the desolate world of the parking lot, criminality grows. Stores distribute antitheft pamphlets in supermarket lots. Thefts, vehicle snatchings, and other hostile acts of our violent society swell on the highway. Actor Michael Douglas, the iconic angry white man in the movie *Falling Down,* was driven to rampage by L.A. traffic. Sexual symbol, getaway vehicle, or status object, the car has also become the weapon of choice, say some behaviorists and police. "The ideal vehicle for 'type A' personalities," a Mitsubishi ad crowed. "Aggressive on the outside. Uncompromising on the inside." Given the anonymity of tinted glass windows, isolated highways, and sidewalks emptied by a driving population, the car culture sets the stage for antisocial behavior.

The Los Angeles freeways looked like a shooting range as fierce motorists took potshots in the early 1990s, about the time "drive-by shooting" entered the lexicon. By 1992 "carjacking" was another new phrase added to the dictionary of automobile crime. Don't look the other driver in the eye, the cautious advised as tempers rose. "Aggression Gets Wheels" was the headline used by one article describing a deadly incident that resulted from a "mistake." "The 'mistake' in Brighton (Massachusetts) was not accelerating fast enough for a green light," the *Boston Globe* began its compilation of car-bred Christmas violence. "In Brockton last Friday, the mistake was tailgating. In Peabody, Monday night, it was passing in a no-passing zone." In Miami rent-a-car companies installed "panic buttons" to be used to call for help. The device came from Avis for a $5 a day charge, "a safety and security issue," said the company. Sales of cellular phones record both busy, car-bound lives and the nighttime fears of drivers on the lonely roads of an asphalt nation.

Dancing with Cars

Along with these dirges, we hear and read odes to the automobile. The romance of the road pervades our fantasies. "Americans love their cars" echoes with numbing regularity. Who has not heard or ut-tered a tale of the rite of passage that begins with the first license or the first set of wheels? Who has not expressed the inclination to go "on the road," in a swoon to the automotive dalliance of Jack Ker-ouac. The flexibility of car travel, the instant gratification, the indis-pensability of an automobile in a world designed for driving—all resound. And the one-million-plus cars sold every month attest to their imperative.

So bound are we to the sentiments—and the sentimentality—so dependent are we on this singular style of movement, that we must sometimes strain to hear or acknowledge the alternative view: that our culture's submission to a car-dependent way of life will only get worse. Listen to Madison Avenue and you hear the inconveniences amid the lore: "The 19th unwritten law of driving: the shortest dis-tance between two points is always under construction," says an Isuzu Trooper advertisement.

"You're an hour from work. You can't change your job. You can change your space," a Lexus commercial goes on. Personal space, the advertisers mean, as the camera closes in on the driver's cornucopia of interior fittings, from cup holder to stereo. Yes, this is an entice-ment for a pleasure vehicle. But it is also an acknowledgment that fancy fittings are the best we can do to ease the commute.

Gridlocked Lives

When sales reps concede the car's inconvenience, something is askew. The nation is in gridlock. And not just on the road. The nation is in "lifelock" to the automobile as the dominant means of transporta-tion. It is in its grip so securely that we can barely perceive how both the quality of mobility and the quality of life have diminished. For the startling fact is that it is not just the journey to work, not only the dashboard-pounding commuter, who creates the bulk of traffic and logs in the lost time, but all of us. In fact, the commute itself con-sumes less than one-quarter of our trips, a smaller percentage than two decades ago. Specifically, work-bound travel devours only 22.5 percent of the pie graphed by the *Nationwide Personal Transporta-tion Study* of the Federal Highway Administration.

Statistically, most of our expanding hours behind the wheel, nearly eight of every ten vehicle miles we travel, have nothing to do with work. Neither are these miles vacation trips or long-distance travel, the reasons Americans give for buying the first—or second or third—automobile. Such holiday trips consume fewer miles than might be expected, a scant 8 percent of our total mileage.

What sets the odometer reeling is something else. It is something less critical than life, liberty, or the pursuit of happiness. And that is errands. According to the highway administration study one-third of the miles we travel go to consumption and family chores. A bottle of milk, a tube of toothpaste, a Little League game, taking grandma to the hospital or junior for eye glasses spin the miles. The ministuff of life clogs the nation's roads. Another third falls under the "social and recreational" category. These are the hours of amusement and friendship reached by wheel: a workout, a movie, a dinner. Total these lifestyle choices and tally the chores to consume, survive, and fraternize and we have covered two-thirds of our driving miles, more than half of the ten to twelve thousand miles of travel per car per year.

"Trip chaining" is the traffic engineers' word for these serial pickup trips. They come to six round-trips a day per household to cover the so-called family and personal category of our car-dependent lives. This eternal need for a ton of steel creates the shop and drop cycle that runs us ragged. To-ing and fro-ing, we spend our time and our horsepower on an endless round of errands. And we don't much like it. "I live in car country," a man from Rapid City, Iowa, said to me. "I need to use my car to buy a bar of soap," he complained.

Where has this rush of travel come from? Why are we so subservient to it? Some of it is demographics. Census figures tell us that we have shrunk the size of households, multiplied the number of them, and added cars for working women. Some of it is car-fed sprawl. We have sent drivers outward to settle their homes and two-car garages ever further into the hinterlands. We have deserted the compact cities and inner suburbs that offer varied housing, walkability, and public transportation. Housed at the periphery, half of all Americans own more than one car, one-third purchase a second car, and one-fifth own yet a third. Twin movements in housing and highways support and encourage movement to the outskirts in single-family dwellings.

We still build this free-standing Ozzie and Harriet house on the lone lot at the end of the road. Despite the fact that families with children under eighteen constitute only 26 percent of the population, we build for bygone demographics. In the years since *Leave it to Beaver,* the nuclear family of working dad and stay-at-home mom has halved in numbers, while the number of working women has risen to 46 percent of the workforce and hit the road. Thus the count on licensed drivers is 20 percent higher, and the women accounting for that increase have doubled the miles they drive.

In the great diaspora after World War II, Washington paid for the American dream and it was fulfilled. With the federal government financing 90 percent of the interstate system, the nation took to the highways, and the moving vans headed to the hills. The population of the suburbs tripled; the number of dense, walkable, transit-based cities shrank. "I want," Erma Bombeck, the bard of the lawn culture, wrote as she bought the second family car, "to go to the store, join a bowling league, have lunch downtown with the girls, volunteer, go to the dentist, take long drives in the country." She recorded her weekly ethos in the seventies. "I want to whirl dizzily in a cloud of exhaust, rotate my tires with the rest of the girls. Don't you understand? I want to *honk* if I love Jesus!"

Today everybody is honking at once. Distance and spatial segregation—here housing, there stores, elsewhere work—make every trip a separate car trip to a separate place. And inconvenience, mileage, and traffic multiply. On Cape Cod summer shoppers have to hit the stores before 7 A.M. or after 9 P.M. to do their errands. Crossing Cape Cod's main artery, Route 28, on foot in July can take ten minutes. "This morning at a shopping mall, I spent 20 minutes looking for a sweater and half an hour looking for my car," writer Ralph Schoenstein described parking panic in New Jersey. "Looking for my car is even better exercise than looking for my glasses, because the average parking lot is bigger than my house—or my neighborhood."

The trying lifestyle that has evolved from the automobile is the truth of fact and the subject of fiction. Mary Cahill's novel *Carpool* described one woman's life on wheels. "5:30—Take Phil to swim practice. . . . 7:00—Hurry home to make breakfast and get everyone up. . . . 7:15—Push Phil out door into school bus. . . . 8:00—Pick up Crista Galli. . . . 8:10—Drop Crista Galli and . . ." "Mental, physical and spiritual cruelty," Cahill called it. Forget car pooling. With the mileage of the lone commuter up 35 percent in the past two decades, driving togetherness fell an almost equal amount. Some 91 percent of all households own a car.

Mom at the Wheel

The single-occupancy vehicle is a staple. And the driver of its miles remains disproportionately a she. "So where is Mom? Didn't she help Dad turn the American wilderness into a cement desert bright with golden arches?" Gore Vidal has asked. She is putting more hours behind the wheel than Russian women spend in food lines. Women not only chauffeur the bulk of America's children but also care for the nation's dependent elderly, stock the shelves of America's kitchens, and have jobs.

In a society that still apportions family chores to women, today's carburb mom, if she is lucky, is dropping the kids at the day care center, putting in a full day's work, caring for grandma and grandpa, and running errands. So, of course, is dad, but not by as many multiples, since women drivers are putting in twice as many miles as the norm. In less than ten years after 1983, women's travel quadrupled. And, by dint of those numbers, their lives became frantic. "It is women who do the driving," says Sandra Rosenbloom, of the Drachman Institute Land and Regional Development Studies at the University of Arizona, who has studied gender differences and what the traffic engineers call "transportation demand management," how to travel back and forth to a job in an orderly fashion. How to manage the unmanageable may be a woman's issue, but the transportation, the demand, and the management in this new field also apply to men, says Rosenbloom.

Rosenbloom's study of why working women drive alone and the implications for travel reduction programs underscored their household chores. Women do not take the direct route; their path is littered with errands and drop-offs because of the fact that "working mothers are much more dependent on driving alone than comparable male parents." How to solve the problem? Do environmental measures and travel reduction programs hurt working women? Rosenbloom's study asked. Her conclusion was yes. Penalties on automobiles penalize the female driver far more than the male.

Isn't that depressing? I ask her. It is dismal that positive programs to help the environment and reduce travel hurt female drivers. More than that, how shortsighted to make women and the environment adversaries. How grim that the report, funded by the U.S. Department of Labor's Women's Bureau, concludes that the environment, the economy, and even the personal life of women have to suffer to ease the way for this vehicular bondage.

"You wouldn't believe how owning their first car frees women," is Rosenbloom's response.

Ah, Freedom, mobility, Ah, the open road. I mull over her words. How familiar . . . how romantic . . . how like a—man.

A woman in Hillsborough, Missouri, near St. Louis, discussing day care on a National Public Radio series, described her agonizing decision to quit work and stay at home with her young child. She recalled the hassles, the chaotic life, the clock without stop in her earlier life as a working mother. Then she described the pièce de résistance that sent her out of the job market and home: the forty-five-minute drive to and from her day care pickup. The Child Care Action campaign newsletter phrased it concisely: "Time famine a national issue." Sociologist Arlie Hochschild of the University of California has put it another way: working mothers "talked about sleep the way a hungry person talks about food." But the cartoon character Sylvia tells it better in words in *From the Journal of the Woman Who Never Wastes a Moment of Her Day:*

> This morning, while stopped at a traffic light, did some embroidery using the pre-threaded needle I keep on the passenger seat, dashed off a note to a shut-in on the stationery I keep above the visor, and partially filled out some medical insurance claim forms. . . . Later, caught in rush-hour traffic, I rolled down my window and screamed at the man next to me, "Your wife is cheating on you with a flight attendant," which always relieves any tension I'm carrying in my neck.

"Liberation" is the word commonly used to describe how the automobile has released women from social control and geographical confinement. *Taking the Wheel,* one recent history, assessed the freedom that arrived with the internal combustion machine in the early twentieth century. Mobile? Maybe. Yet, it is a false form of consciousness that fails to assess women's enslavement to the motor vehicle in the auto-dependent households and society it has helped install.

Most Americans lack stay-at-home options. The single-parent head of one-third of our households with children under eighteen, the less affluent, the households "daylighting" and moonlighting to survive cannot afford to do so. With two wage earners now joined by three-job couples working fifty hours a week, life behind the wheel becomes ever more relentless.

Parenting comes in both sexes, and at 5 A.M. on a brisk fall morning a Maryland widower backs one of his three cars out of the driveway of his modern Colonial and heads to his job in Washington, D.C. Harried on departure, he leaves work early to return equally distraught to complete the life of the after-hours chauffeur: one son to basketball, another to home, a daughter to music. It is typical of the Beltway, where the average home houses three cars, one for mom, one for dad, and one for junior of driving age. It is typical of suburban America too.

In *Ties That Stress,* David Elkind, a professor of child development, describes the modern home as a "railroad station" for Mr. and Ms. America's comings and goings. More likely it's a cabstand. Time-starved parents chauffeur immobilized children to sports and chores, and genuine sociability goes. The dining room table is more a revolving platform than a nuclear family idyll as one parent arrives home late while the other finishes the rounds of pickups at piano lessons and Scouts. In her book *The Overworked American,* Juliet Schor allotted a seventy- and eighty-hour workweek for the adults serving as the economic mainstay of the American household. She did not separate the automobile component, but considered the car factor in her categories for "care of the sick and elderly," "acquisition of goods and services," social and recreation time, and churchgoing hours. Go beyond these time drains to include the specific "transportation of people." Add "car maintenance and repair," from the normal oil change or inspection to registration. Then ponder the hours for the random accidents of a broken window, run-down battery, snowstorm, or overheated engine. The breadwinner-cum-buyer behind the wheel has lost not just leisure but life.

The Automotive Playpen

When autonomy depends on the automobile, all suffer. And those served—the children in the backseat—are as deprived as those who serve. Transported every which way from childhood through adolescence, young people lose their independence. They fail to expand their horizons, to see new surroundings, or to acquire independence and liberty on their own. The outside world dominated by the road bores, and television or computer games beckon. A study comparing ten-year-olds in a small, walkable Vermont town and youngsters in a new Orange County suburb showed a marked difference. The Vermont children had three times the mobility, i.e., the distance and places they could get to on their own, while those in Orange County watched four times as much television. To paraphrase the architectural verity, we shape the land and the land shapes us.

Given our far-flung, single-family, single-use suburban environment that purges pedestrians, given our urban environment drained of life by flight, given landscapes lacking sidewalks and multilane roads that terrorize parents and children alike, impaired mobility is more than inevitable. It is a social tragedy. "I am writing this while seated on the stoop of my house in one of Boston's inner suburbs," historian Clay McShane observes in his *Down the Asphalt Path*. "I am watching a parent two houses up the street teach his eighteen-month-old toddler, who is not yet toilet trained, how to walk. Every time she steps off the curb, he swats her. . . . In motor age America, children require street discipline at an early age. They have since the coming of traffic," he writes. Children are "probably the biggest losers."

Our auto-dependent mobility denies the child's. Across America children and young people are the victims of declining transit services, suffering not only from the debasement of walking and bicycling by the car but also from its depletion of public transportation. This deprivation extends throughout adolescence. In all but a dozen or so cities, the streetcar or bus taking the teenager to a lively urban core beyond the limits of the everyday has atrophied or disappeared. Walkers or even bicyclists who traveled freely to school, sports, or friends in times past can no longer make their way without peril. Sidewalks are few, cars many; even the mall is asphalt wrapped. We fear for children of all ages. From the toddler wobbling off the curb at his or her peril to the teenager on a bicycle forced to vie for space with the speeding internal combustion machine, our children's road-warped lives fill us with dread.

Teenagers drive while parents shudder. The media records the death and mutilation of the gun culture, but the car culture is statistically more threatening. According to figures from the Federal Highway Administration and the Justice Department, an adolescent suburban male is more likely to be killed by an automobile than his urban peer by a gun. Teenagers, of course, relish the rite of passage to freedom. Our communal memories hold the anxiety, then the pleasure of securing a license, the first glide alone and out the driveway on one's own. We seem to forget that the "freedom" is reduced by the servitude of a car-bound society that denies movement any other way. Forced to own an automobile to see friends or get around, teenagers are hostage to paying for it by working at low-wage jobs, forsaking studies and even socializing to flip burgers in a mall—in order to move around in the suburbs—to the mall.

A reporter from the *Pilot* in Norfolk, Virginia, doesn't accept my negative view. He has called to discuss the positive side of life in the sanctuary of the driver's seat. "People have told me it's their only time to themselves," he said, describing an article he was writing on its joys. Yes, I said. Yes, I understand the lure of the road, the stillness of this chamber of isolation. I acknowledge—I remember—the world of mom happy to finally find a few moments to catch up with her small passengers or dad, at last able to exchange a word or two en route to soccer practice. Isn't it life on the road that busies their days, that deprives them of healthier moments of peace and privacy, prohibits neighborly interaction and denies eye-to-eye contact, though?

Trashed Mass Transit

The alternate, of course, is not so easy. A few summers ago, in a rash moment of research frenzy, I decided to make my way a hundred or so miles from Massachusetts to Maine: first to Portland, then to a Casco Bay island by public transportation. If I had been taking a *Trip to Bountiful* on *A Streetcar Named Desire,* my friends couldn't have clucked more. The trip involved a bus, a ferry, and a van, in sequence. All of these worked well enough, but even the director of Maine's Campaign for Sensible Transportation gave me the feeling that I wasn't altogether—well—sensible.

Returning to her native New England from Europe, writer Alice Furlaud shared my experience as a nondriver. A trip from Boston to Cape Cod took as long as the trip across the Atlantic, she reported. "On the telephone, the Plymouth and Brockton bus company had given us three different versions of their schedule. All official, none correct. We waited, standing up, for an hour in the Peter Pan bus terminal. . . . It was cold." The same sense of rural America as a place where people without cars have a shadowy, shamefaced existence pervaded her arrival. "In that Cape Cod village, where the bus finally let us off, the post office is three-eighths of a mile from the house where we were staying." Laden with a shopping bag, doused by the rain, she made her way on foot, ignored on the packed highway.

Driving into Old Age

Autonomy depends on the automobile. And in an aging population, this dependence is no small matter. "I do not like to drive past pretty houses in the lovely New England countryside," writes Paula Boyer Rougny in Maine's *TrainRider,* "with the knowledge that within the walls sits an elderly person of wit and compassion who, due to slight physical frailty, is denied a driver's license. I approve the state's denying her a license; I deplore the national tragedy of drive-fly-or-rot that turns vital human beings into prisoners with no one to talk to and nowhere to go." In rural America, where nearly half the elderly are in poor health and 60 percent are not licensed to drive, there are many such prisoners. At least half the rural elderly live in areas with no public transportation, but the urban and suburban elderly, for all the better facilities, have problems too.

The average American now age sixty-five will live to be eighty-two, five more years than the predicted life span two decades ago, and the number is rising. More Americans will live into their eighties; the number of ninety-year-olds will increase. Throughout the country the very elderly comprise the fastest growing portion, with some 3.3 million people over age eighty-five, and their number will rise seven-fold in the next quarter century, according to the Bureau of the Census. Of course, these citizens are healthier, livelier. But putting more miles on their cars will produce more accidents. Nondrivers will proliferate. So will difficulties for them.

"Neck stiff from arthritis?" asked one article. "Use your mirrors more carefully to check traffic," it quoted an instructor of the senior set. "Deteriorating vision? Avoid driving at night," the instructor recommended. That word "avoid" again. Nevertheless, accidents happen. One spring such accidents seemed to collide with one another. There was the seventy-four-year-old motorist who skidded into Washington Square Park in New York City, slaying five people; soon after, in the same city an eighty-seven-year-old man hit seven people, leaving one dead. It was a bad month but not unique.

The Driving Skills Timeline of the American Automobile Association is enough to make a pedestrian take cover. A sixteen-year-old male leads their chart of risk versus experience in his tendency to take chances beyond knowledge. On the other end of the lose-lose situation, drivers over age sixty imperil themselves and others when they overestimate their physical abilities. Visual acuity drops from the age of thirty, and drivers grow sensitive to glare, it reports. Night vision begins to decline at age forty. From age fifty-five, more than half of all people need glasses. The majority of those over age seventy cannot focus thirty-one inches from their eyes. And, by that point, the AAA chart says dourly, "night vision almost vanishes."

In response, traffic safety officials want to set age limits, requiring tests and relicensing. But such solutions penalize as much as one-third of the driving population. Autonomy demands mobility and mobility demands a car. Even before America got grayer, we can all recall the personal incidents of older Americans killed by chance or incompetence on the road. The memory of my mother-in-law's elderly friend, fatally wounded by the guardrail that pierced her car on the Merritt Parkway and killed her two grandchildren as well, clings to my mind twenty-five years later when I ride that route. Middle-aged sons and daughters shake their heads at parents who keep their cars garaged even as old age incapacitates them. Drive or not, they cling to their automobiles and pay the insurance, excise taxes, and parking fees, since selling them symbolizes captivity and social death.

"I know my vision is impaired but I still have good reflexes," says a World War II vet, not yet seventy, who forfeited driving to take the train. "Also," he goes on, a bit defensive about this vanishing symbol of manhood, "three hours driving with my knee collecting fluid. . . ." Still, he confesses, apologizing for his machismo, "I didn't want *not* to do it." Why should he apologize? It is a society whose driving policy is cruelly calculated to deny alternatives that should apologize.

The Gray Panthers, the venerable activists for the rights of senior citizens, have attacked the federal government for creating "severe accessibility disadvantage" in highway-dependent development. By funding freeway growth that stimulated sprawl and diminished public transit, Washington discriminated against millions of Americans, the Panthers declared in 1992. Nonmotorists must get equal treatment. Those concerned with the "graying of America" plan only for life on the road. "Fifty-Five Alive" and "Mature Drivers" courses grow. Suggestions evolve. Create larger signage. Change colors and directions, advocates suggest. Road strips have widened from four inches to six. These are palliatives, however. The prescriptions never include looking at the source of the problems: the single-minded way of mobility—the private car.

Why not instead prescribe the creation of housing within a walk of the old corner store? Or ensure public transit by bus or van to downtown? Rarely do the prescriptions call for a public expedient like installing elevators or making escalators work in impoverished public transit stations. Seldom do we hear anyone suggest easing pedestrian street crossings or incorporating services within a walk or public transit ride—not any of the approaches that defined movement humanely in the youths of many of those now elderly.

Aberration and Excess

Discrimination and immobility hit others than the gray-haired set, of course. We are all "temporarily abled," as the advocates for the disabled note. We are all temporary drivers. Our access to the world is fragile. A broken ankle, a sprained wrist, poor hearing or vision can render any one of us immobilized.

"Should People with Dementia Drive?" The question leaped off the publicity release from the annual meeting of the Transportation Research Board. "To catch the eye of the press," said the communications director. Caught I was. The answer was clear, of course. A person with dementia should not drive. Or was it? In fact, a society that handicaps walkers or denies public transit's survival inevitably drives the mentally inept and the physically impaired to take the wheel. Physical disease and mental disorders may, after all, be on- and off-again affairs. Medication stabilizes many people. The disabled can function and produce. When producing without a car becomes impossible, a productive life becomes equally so.

Drunk drivers menace themselves and society. Such organizations as Mothers Against Drunk Driving (MADD) have made their restraint a priority and the "designated driver" a social convention. Intoxicated driving is an indefensible act, of course. The authors of *The Ecology of the Automobile* argue that the penalty for lack of sobriety—or Dionysian excess of any sort—is far too extreme. It is the need to drive that makes a night of drinking deadly, they assert.

Contemplate the success of the new tools to punish deadbeat dads. By revoking licenses, officials force recalcitrant fathers to pay their debts quickly. The fact that fathers are more closely bonded to their automobiles than to their families is a measure of our submission to the automobile—the only common passport to citizenship and shopping. The problem, of course, is a society that provides no other option to the partygoer, or the intractable parent or, sadder still, a society that denies movement to any of the suffering or ill disposed.

"I am impatient," the abovementioned *TrainRider* article went on, "for the day when trains, light rail vehicles, and vans will serve kids too young to drive, senior citizens too old to drive, the handicapped, and unadulterated aficionados of read-while-you-ride. I want to see school buses (with an exception for genuine rural areas) struck from the national budget as children ride public transportation along with the rest of us." In Rougny's view, "Not only will we save billions but the few little monkeys who make school buses into animal houses will be influenced by 'unseen social controls' to behave in a civil fashion, even give up their seats for some of us. It will be good for us and good for them." "Unseen social controls" is a phrase plucked from the 1970s, from a more caring, more urban time. It is a long way from the notion of author-planner Jane Jacobs, whose "eyes on the street" spoke of civil neighborhoods, to today's talk of roughneck bus riders, teen crime, and car wars in the empty wastelands of America's parking lots.

The Reduction of the Public Realm

It is our asphalt nation that has eradicated the public realm and the public space to provide those eyes. Denied the right or place of assembly in a car-filled landscape, shunted from car-dominated privatized spaces, citizens allow political life to wither. The call to community formed by an intimacy with one's surroundings and neighbors dwindles, and civic values fade.

Such lack of social space, social controls, and mobility narrows us in infinite ways. Merging the privacy and isolation of the automobile, gated communities, the fastest growing residential segment in the nation, hold 4 million Americans in aloof citadels, "secluded from the world at large, yet close to all the finer things in life," as Downs of Hillcrest near Dallas advertises. Here, the civic scout—the doorbell ringer, the political signature gatherer—has no access. Bolts, security devices, car codes, and guards keep out the uninvited. Delivery trucks, guests, and even residents have trouble gaining entry. Four private watchmen stand guard at one such development, Bear Creek in Seattle. Private streets and private sewers, private lives remote from the communal needs of civic caretaking, isolate Americans.

"Why don't the Amish use cars?" asked a tourist brochure from western Pennsylvania. "The Amish believe that cars pull people apart, and that a car distorts its owner's sense of self-importance in a world where humility is a necessary virtue." Besides, *The Guide to the Amish Country* went on, "they haven't adopted the belief that faster is automatically better." One doesn't have to adopt a Luddite mentality or the "voluntary simplicity" code of environmental purists to admire this mind-set—and to wonder what accounts for America's belief scheme based on hypermobility, on an odyssey to nowhere.

"The Amish don't believe that the internal combustion engine is inherently evil," the guide observed. "Their primary aversion to cars is their belief that cars pull families apart." That same summer, five Amish children died when hit by an unlicensed teenaged driver in a crash in Wooster, Ohio. Ten others were seriously injured. More than horse-and-buggy solutions are needed to curb our cars, but the evidence accumulates that the unruly vehicle exacts more than it rewards.

"Houston is the modern world par excellence," architect Daniel Solomon has put it. "The young man who drove me to the airport says he lives thirty miles from school, a one-hour drive each way," he observed. "His 2½-year-old truck has 78,000 miles on it and he hasn't been anywhere. Fifty times the Odyssey, eight times the travels of Marco Polo, how many hundreds of times the walks of Leopold Bloom? And with what density of experience, what learned in his 78,000 mile journey?" Triple the route of Phileas Fogg, double that of astronaut Neil Armstrong too.

For what deprived sensibility? For what homogeneous experience?

The conformity of the highway and its speed-first purpose has defined the conformity of its artifacts and by-products. Standardization begins on the roadway with the depersonalized pit stop eatery, Roy Rogers's "free-fixings," or Pizza Hut's "personal pan pizza." It permeates the fast-food companies' concentration on snacks you can eat with one hand. According to the Worldwatch Institute, food for one-armed eaters (the other hand presumably on the wheel), eaten in the nine hours a week they spend driving, accounts for forty-six cents of every food dollar spent on meals and snacks out of the house. It may sound ludicrous to blame the car for fewer oven-baked potatoes and more fatty french fries, less grandma's chicken soup, and more franchised chicken nuggets, but the junk food diet—and the environmental toll from its trash (almost as much energy as comes through the

Alaskan oil pipeline)—also stems from the wrappings of the highway-based franchise. The car, a longtime generator of the drive-in, drive-out fast-food restaurant, is scarcely the sole villain in the growth of Kentucky Fried Chicken (now KFC) and Taco Bell, but it is an accomplice.

And yet, the heartbeat response to the love affair with the automobile thumps on. Environmentalists active in the crusade to eradicate the highway, pedestrian advocates mad for sidewalks, bicyclists congenitally fearful of the motor vehicles on their routes, and activists in T-shirts bearing "Obstruct Traffic" logos still speak of the courtship, the freedom, the romance of the road. Route 66 has passed from adventure to nostalgia, and still freedom lies along the "blue highways," to use the title of the early 1990s best-seller.

Why can't we step back and see the servant become master? Why have we failed to see the consequences of the car's mischief, its downright malice to community life and autonomy for many? Media theorist Mark Crispin Miller, in analyzing television, that other so-called technological servant, has speculated that the medium is so integral to the ambient culture that we can no longer isolate ourselves to gain a perspective on our place within its landscape. There is just no surveillance point from which to stand aloof and view the impact of television's toll. The analogy with the automobile holds. The world through the windshield and the world through the television window alike isolate us from our surroundings.

The automobile has usurped even more of our point of view, however, by infiltrating our private and public space. We can always switch television on and off; thus it cannot entirely eradicate our vantage point. So engrained is our acceptance of the automobile's dominance, however, that we cannot back off and see the disservice of this "servant," the flaws that are intrinsic to automobility.

Be still our restless hearts. Look past the romance of the road and we will see that mobility has vanished completely for the third of the nation that cannot legally drive—those 80 million Americans who do not operate automobiles because they are too old, too young, or too poor.

Step back and observe, and the minority becomes an oppressed constituency, while even the majority appears harassed by the vehicle from which it supposedly benefits. Read ahead to see the degradation of the landscape and cityscape, the debasement of our environment and health, and the erosion of our personal and national economy by the car culture. *Access for All* was the title of a pioneer plea for human mobility two decades ago. Today's sequel should be called *Access for Whom?*

OPPOSITE: The refuse of the car culture—cast-off tires, leaky batteries, junked automobiles—afflicts impoverished communities. Neighborhoods like Chicago's Lawndale are blighted by both the car's debris and the auto-oriented policies that empty cities. (Photo: Camilo José Vergara)

The Geography of Inequity

"As soon as people become tributaries of transportation . . . the contradictions between social justice and motorized power, between effective movement and higher speed, between personal freedom and engineered routing, become poignantly clear."
—Ivan Illich, *Energy and Equity*

"I went to join the revolution, but I couldn't find a parking place."
—song on National Public Radio, April Fool's Day 1993

YOU SEE THEM standing by the bus stops of the nation: the working poor, the carless forced to the margins of society. Unshaded in the relentless heat of summer, unsheltered in winter, they queue by the roadsides and wait. The long commute in an automobile finds its parallel in the time consumed by those who wait for public transportation. "You already know who these people are. You see them every day. They fit the 'Profile of Public Transit Passengers' perfectly," as former Surgeon General Joycelyn Elders described the fringes of motorized America. They are women, people of color, the elderly, the disabled, the poor. Public transit systems "serve the 'have-nots' in our system."

The statistical profile bears Elders out. In larger cities 60 percent of mass transit riders are women, and 48 percent are African-American or Hispanic, more than twice their number in the population. While many "haves" get good service, 38 percent of transit riders are "have-nots," surviving at just about the poverty level, with family incomes of less than $15,000, according to a study by the American Public Transit Association. The 9 percent of households that own no car comprise one-quarter of the population, with the lowest economic strata and the most oppressed minorities among them—those who, in Jesse Jackson's words, "take the early bus"—most penalized. Dependent on transit trips to get to work, to health care—to life— they face a system decimated by automobile subsidies.

The car culture has thus become an engine of inequity, raising high the barriers of race and class. Transportation that is difficult at best, nonexistent at worst, darkens their lives in myriad ways and adds to the financial and social inequity they suffer.

You see or share the ride with these people everywhere: at a bleak bus stop along a hauntingly empty Dallas street one spring Saturday; on a bus ride jammed with low-wage workers lumbering into downtown Pittsburgh one fall afternoon; on yet another bus creeping slowly, slowly, at ten miles an hour into downtown Los Angeles. Worse, you see them waiting for the buses that *don't* come: in blustery Minneapolis, where riders huddle against a windswept wall; on a sunbaked bench on the outskirts of Las Vegas, where a would-be passenger wilts in the heat; in affluent suburbs and corporate gold coasts, where the gold of that realm doesn't sift into the pockets of employees who lack decent transportation to get to work. The tales, often horror stories, multiply, high among them a blind colleague's harrowing trip when the bus he was riding in Phoenix broke down, depositing him by the highway to take the long walk home. "My fourteen-year-old son sees the bus go by and he calls it the 'loser cruiser,'" says planner Anton C. ("Tony") Nelessen. But those in "loser cruisers" are the lucky ones. In Vail, Colorado, downtown merchants rejected buses altogether, voting down a sales tax for transportation to carry their resort workers home.

Being physically relegated to the back of the bus ended with the civil rights struggle. But those symbolically relegated to the back of the bus become second-class citizens in a mobile society. Hank Dittmar, director of the Surface Transportation Policy Project, put it in historical perspective: "Some 40 years ago, Rosa Parks sparked the greatest social change of my lifetime by refusing to sit at the back of an Alabama bus. Today Rosa Parks might find bus service nonexistent in her community. Or she might find that people of color were the only passengers on the bus."

Even low-income neighborhoods fortunate enough to have trains or streetcars tell tales of service run amiss—of broken escalators for hospital-bound Harlem riders, of a Chicago elevated train so broken down that the transit authorities attached an empty car at one end to buffer bumps. Peruse fact and fiction and a paint-by-numbers portrait emerges. Paul Auster draws this view in his novel *Leviathan*. "Dozens of cars drove past the house, but the only pedestrians were the very old or the very young, little children with their mothers, an ancient black man inching along with a cane, a white-haired Asian woman with an aluminum walker." A racist and inequitable society heightens poverty. A car-dependent one underscores and enhances the divide with a lack of mobility.

The Stuck Society

The problem is not just that the poor are carless. Some of the most affluent Americans own no automobile. It is that a society that shorts public transportation in favor of the private vehicle deprives the poor of any other way to move. It is not merely that the down-and-out lack automobiles but that our highway-oriented public policy has financed the outward-bound corporation; it has funded the house at the end of the road and separated the poor from jobs that can be reached only by car. We have done so for so long that those most abused by the chronic injustice of a car culture can no longer pinpoint its pains.

Ricardo Byrd, director of transportation programs for the National Association of Neighborhoods, sees the consequences of car-dependency for the poor. "If you ask people is there a transportation problem in the hood, they'll say no," he muses from his Washington office one summer day. "If you ask them, 'Are you interested in talking about transportation?' they'll say no," he goes on. Then he pauses. "If you ask them, 'What are your problems?' they'll say, 'Well, man, I can't get to the hospital.' If you ask them, can they get to their jobs or housing, they'll say, 'Oh yeah.' "

Last Exit Isolation

Red Hook, the storied South Brooklyn longshoremen's enclave of *A View from the Bridge, On the Waterfront,* and *Last Exit to Brooklyn,* is a case study of the isolation and inequity of the car culture. Now devoid of its former shipping, the racially mixed neighborhood (49 percent African-American, 41 percent Hispanic, 8 percent white) is the quintessential stockade of the auto age. Cut off by three highways—the Gowanus Expressway, the Brooklyn-Battery Tunnel, and the Brooklyn-Queens Expressway—and punctuated by a 1939 public housing project, it is an impoverished peninsula.

Red Hook overlooks Manhattan, yet it could be the longest trip in New York for some 13,000 inhabitants, says Philip Kasinitz, a sociologist at the City University of New York who documented the problem. "You can see Manhattan but you can't get there," he says. "People find it hard to take jobs," says Kasinitz, charting the problems of public housing residents. "They have to sprint across a three-lane highway which goes under an underpass and walk three blocks through a hostile Italian community to get to the subway." That's just to get in or out of the center of the neighborhood, says Kasinitz. To get from the farthest part of the project or beyond demands an extra two bus stops. Unsafe without a car, public housing residents may stay out until six or seven in the morning to avoid the trip home in the dark.

Red Hook's isolation has given it a perverse "end-of-Western-civilization" chic to the artists and activists attracted to its warehouses. Nonetheless, working life for the old residents is an oppressive circle. The highways that destroyed the neighborhood caused its emptying. The emptying produced low density, which undercut public transportation and kept income down. The low-income inhabitants lack money to buy a car and hence find work, and, thus, the neighborhood deteriorates further. It is a cycle. A few years ago, Kasinitz conducted a survey at the South Brooklyn Local Development Corporation, an employment agency interviewing out-of-work community members applying for jobs. Three hundred people came looking for work, but only 9 percent of the adults had driver's licenses. "Here's a place that hires a lot of truck drivers and this agency couldn't place them."

Most urban areas don't have that hiring capacity. For forty years two out of every three new jobs have been exported to the suburbs. Funds have gone to roads, not bus or rail; to private homes, not walkable city apartments; to corporations in the distant suburbs, not inner-city industry. Carless city dwellers get handcuffed to home and hence cut out of the workforce. While the world perceives poverty as a result of carlessness, it is dependency on the car that is the culprit.

With suburban jobs now outweighing urban ones by large multiples, the center city poor lack, as the Ford Foundation summed it up, "Access to Opportunity." The inequity begins in the very first search for a job and extends to daily life. "You speak of job opportunity, [but] they don't have a clean shirt, much less physical transportation or literacy skills," observes Michael T. Savage, deputy director of HUD's Economic Development. "You have jobs over here. You have the community over there. Transportation is one of the overlooked arts in economic development."

"I was standing on a rail platform," Ricardo Byrd went on describing his experience on another day. A man offered a job tip to a woman friend as they stood waiting. The job seeker responded with just one question: "How close is it to the bus?" "That was her *first* question," said Byrd. "Her second question was 'How much do they pay?' " Even Byrd was surprised at transportation's place at the top of the woman's list.

Byrd also recalled the case of a factory looking to relocate near the U.S.-Mexican border to take advantage of the North American Free Trade Agreement (NAFTA). When the would-be builder looked at a site in a Latino community, he saw a highway. A wonderful highway it was, he told Byrd, the ultimate in accessibility. But he shook his head. "These are minimum wage jobs," said the employer. "How can my riders get to work?" For another Southern plant—a spanking new factory not one-quarter mile from low-income housing—it was still no-go. "It's one of the high crime areas," he said. No one would stand at the bus stop on the street outside the project. No one would provide a transportation feeder to circle into its threatening maze. Fear of the streets, bad weather, distance, and sporadic service made the bus a bad trip.

Organizers of the model recruitment program of the Church Community Jobs Commission have also explored the problem. Seeking to link their African-American church in Oakland with AT&T job hunters, they watched the applicants dwindle when would-be employees learned that they would need a car to get to work twenty miles away. The most burdened bear the double burden of inaccessibility. In the end, poor transport does not issue from poverty, but lies at its very roots and sustains and perpetuates it.

"The transportation costs associated with all this mobility are regressive" in the view of Alan Hughes, author of "The New Metropolitan Reality." In the modern city work, shopping, schooling demand travel. "And what for most people is a low-density lifestyle becomes for the poor and low income a set of costly barriers." Everyone suffers from the automotive sources of pollution, congestion, and other such exactions, of course. The less fortunate can neither flee nor adjust to them with flexible work hours, telecommuting jobs, or the extended arm of the cellular phone. A "concentration of poverty and de-concentration of opportunity," as Hughes phrases it.

Lately, advocates have sued to right inequities in the mass transportation system itself. They claim that while the well-to-do have secured more commuter rail service, the impoverished have faced cutbacks. In 1994, a twenty-five-cent fare raise and the end to a bus pass in poorer neighborhoods, coupled with the allocation of a few hundred million dollars to a suburban rail project, roused the Los Angeles Labor/Community Strategy Center to secure the services of the NAACP Legal Defense and Education Fund. Together, they sued the transit authority for class bias, discrimination against people of color, and malfeasance. They argued that, since the bus riders made less than $15,000, had no car, and were nonwhite, the malapportion-ment of funds reflected bias.

A year later New Yorkers addressed the transportation equity issue by protesting steeper bus and subway fare hikes for urban versus suburban commuter rides. The Urban League and Straphangers' Campaign filed an antidiscrimination suit charging "class warfare." They based their argument on the same principles of bias, that the price increase violated the 1964 Civil Rights Act by misserving African-Americans, Hispanics, and Asian-Americans—the majority of city transit riders.

Sometimes subtle, sometimes blatantly biased location policies pit budgets for sleek transit lines like Metro in Washington, D.C., or the Green Line in Los Angeles against buses. For years racist policies have compounded the issue of poor public transportation; from the Red Line in Boston to the MTA Central Light Rail Line in Baltimore to L.A.'s new subway, officials have shifted transit lines to separate the impoverished minorities from the wealthy.

Advocates from other cities have rallied to correct the problem of the racial injustice involved. Yet for all the validity of their search for equity, pitting the affluent commuter against the inner city bus rider ignores the fact that each is subject to the inequities of the automo-bile age. In a world bereft of decent public transportation, the rich and poor grapple for fragments when they should be allies against automobile dominance.

Captive Lives

"Captive rider, captive labor," was the conclusion of Sandra Rosen-bloom's study of the spatial constraints on women's employment, based on low-skilled women in Tucson and Phoenix. "Spatial entrapment" was the term with which another study described the impact of distant jobs, costly cars, and feeble public transportation on the mobility of African-American women. Maps from the Bureau of the Census show an overlap—"spatial coincidence" in the jargon—of households in poverty, female-headed households, and households without an automobile.

The welfare plan drafted by Bill Clinton early in his presidency acknowledged the cost of dependence on the car. By upping the value of the automobile to allow welfare mothers from $1,500 to $4,500, Clinton tacitly acknowledged the high entry fee needed to find work. In fact, his welfare "favor" reflected the punishment of a world unworkable with less than two hundred horsepower—and a $4,500 entry fee—a world where upkeep on a car may cost as much as raising a child, where physical distance and poor transportation keep the marginal from finding child care, jobs, or needed services at all hours. Such distressed systems are not merely ill served or underserved. With the weekend curtailments of mass transit, they're scarcely served at all.

The pursuit of services, shopping, movies, or health as well as wealth is onerous. A Boston City Hospital report recording dropouts from a prenatal care program cited transportation as the patients' single largest complaint. Richard J. Jackson, director of the Center for Environmental Health at the Centers for Disease Control and Prevention, remembered his stint watching sick African-American children one afternoon in an emergency ward. "The mother was there," he recalled one incident. "She didn't call a cab. She didn't drive to the hospital. She took one or two buses there." And the next day "if she didn't work, her co-workers might think it was unrelated to the transportation issue," he said.

Not only jobs but also services, health high among them, are out of reach of those without transportation. With 9 percent of households lacking cars altogether and still others running clunkers, access to doctors, hospitals, and clinics is arduous. Dealing with an unsound transportation system affects choice, health, welfare, and livelihood to further paralyze the poor.

Not only do these low-income lunchpailers use twice as much mass transit as upper-income people, their bus trips take twice as long in traffic on surface arteries clogged with cars and interrupted by stops to mount and discharge. Fully two-thirds of the 8.5 billion transit boardings in the mid-nineties were on such poky trips.

For all the swifter service of a dozen streetcar cities, the divide between the carless and the car laden has accelerated with the velocity of a Grand Prix racer. In Southern California, homes with two or more cars rose from 7 to 70 percent of households in the past four decades. Those served by public transit trod water at 4 percent, the study *Efficiency and Fairness on the Road: Strategies for Unsnarling Traffic* points out. As a result, one car serves every three poor people in Los Angeles, compared to the national average of one for every single man, woman, and child.

Elsewhere, the situation is comparable. Those with the most money travel the most. Those with less travel less. In New York City moderate- and low-income households drive one-fifth the miles of those who earn incomes over $40,000. This great mobility divide widens the gap between the haves and have-nots throughout the nation.

Home away from Help

The outmigration spurred by federal funds for highways and homes since the 1920s, when suburban car owners split off from urban public transportation riders, has enhanced divisions of race and class. Subsidized, car-based segregation by race and microsegregation by economics has heightened plantation politics, perpetuating urban poverty. Such walls of poverty, structured by the car culture, constrain black well-being beyond the public abuse of racism or any personal shortcomings.

The misappropriation of moneys to the car culture plays out in rural America too. Poverty-stricken West Virginia, for example, shows how the car culture afflicts the rural landscape. A new four-lane highway, so-called Corridor H, threatens the region's country amenities and comeliness. Promoted by the powerful Senator Robert Byrd, claiming to aid the most disadvantaged, this pork barrel project would gnaw the graceful hills, degrade farmland for useless roads, and encourage strip malls at the expense of small stores. Like the coal mining that cut raw and ugly gashes in West Virginia's hills, the road would debase those least able to sustain a living. Nonetheless, roadmongers persuade the disinherited to opt for a quick financial fix that will destroy their heritage and livelihood.

Since World War II auto-centric policies have eroded the nation's public transportation agencies, now receiving one government dollar for every seven handed to the car. Transportation and home ownership subsidies for the motor suburbs and deprivation for the city centers contributed to the 37 million Americans in poverty entering this decade, the highest percentage in more than a quarter century. And, as the decade continues, basic transit services shrink and fares increase, draining mobility for low-income and minority Americans. In the end our transportation triage undermines the poorest cohort of the country; it helps create the underclass that impoverishes, erodes, and segregates the larger nation.

Split Riders, Split Society

Following a bus stop shoot-out by teenagers in the parking lot of the Trumbull Shopping Park, the mall owners prohibited the inner-city buses that deposited them there. Other carless visitors to the two-hundred-store mall were also excluded. "Security," said mall operators. "Racism," residents protested. "A subtle apartheid that is really going to hurt the handicapped and elderly the most," one transit board district member insisted.

"When they cut down on the buses, I'm going to have to stop shopping here," said one passenger. "The problem is the people in Trumbull don't want blacks and Puerto Ricans coming to their mall. Who else uses these buses?" she asked. Despite the insistence by the lawyer for the transit district that stopping bus service would violate the constitutional rights of assembly and equal protection under the law, service was cut. Two months earlier, the Seven Corners Shopping Center in Falls Church, Virginia, had also tried to halt bus service from Washington, D.C., because of construction plans. In this case Washington's Metro said no. The forty-year-old bus stop mall that officials would shut was the nexus of sixteen transit routes where some two thousand riders transferred, many of them immigrants.

Not only the cost of a car but the insult of the road it travels on hits low-income Americans hardest. "White men's highways through black men's bedrooms" went the saying as road builders bulldozed fragile communities for the interstate system. The swaths cut by roads and expressways through the cheapest tracts of land displace and isolate the down-and-out and even their moderate-income neighbors. "In the '40s and '50's, it was the tracks which reinforced racial and income segregation and displacement," a 1990 study on marginal communities by the National Economic Development and Law Center noted, "but in the 1960's, '70's and '80's, it has been the freeways, highways, and their accompanying borderline office-commercial development which displaces, segregates, and divides communities."

The roads not only belt threadbare communities, putting them on the "wrong side of the tracks," but they create the ghetto itself. The blight and traffic they cause, the ceaseless noise and fumes, sack the weak. The visual detritus of the motorized world is dropped on their doorsteps. Their mean streets hold the repair shops and car washes, the spray paint services and tire marts, the muffler stores, auto parts dealers, and glass vendors. Body shops, used car lots, and parking lots are their neighbors. It is these precincts of poverty that endure the abandoned gas stations, old garages, and vacant lots. It is the poor and communities of color who are bombarded by toxic "hot spots" loading residents with pollutants. Car and bus emissions—carbon monoxide, particulate matter, lead deposits—sit on their stoops.

The phrase used by the environmental justice movement is "disproportionate siting." While it is the auto age that creates such poisonous debris, it is disproportionate siting that puts six of Manhattan's seven diesel bus depots, all carcinogenic, in Harlem. Already a partial valley bounded by highways, northern Manhattan serves as a basin where asthma, frequently caused and intensified by such conditions, is the most common diagnosis in the emergency room at Harlem Hospital Center. A concentration of some 80 percent of asthma deaths occurs mostly in such vulnerable neighborhoods in New York City, California's Fresno County, Cook County in Illinois, and Maricopa County in Arizona. The 1994 study "Not Just Prosperity: Achieving Sustainability with Environmental Justice" showed that zip codes and jobs correlate with nearness to waste sites, In other words, exposure to such waste and environmental toxins matched race and income. This is the classic case of rich people polluting onto poor, spurred by the auto age's pollutants and spatial segregation.

While the poorest levels of society suffer from roads, highways erode the living standards of those less far down the ladder. As frail neighborhoods crumble in the shadow of the highway, they lose their property value and tax benefits. The crumbling exit ramps, the colossal columns, and the gloomy underbellies accentuate the shabbiness of some dwelling places and undermine the labor to improve others. The area surrounding the Cross Bronx Expressway, which slices through several neighborhoods, is typical. "You gotta do something about mess," the *Bronx News* headlined one article as the borough filed suit to force the city to clean and maintain the community. The "mess" was discarded tires, refuse, litter, wild plant overgrowth and corrugated cardboard boxes that spilled across a community ravaged by the highway at its edge and the arteries jutting everywhere. The weedy parking lots and barren spaces, the trash, graffiti, and pot-holed streets that the highways breed maim the homes, parks, and shops of older urban neighborhoods.

Anti-highway crusaders have taken up the cause to stop such highways. When the Loma Pieta Earthquake damaged the structure of Oakland's Cypress Freeway in 1993, the Church of the Living God Tabernacle and the Clean Air Alternative Coalition filed suit to cancel its rebuilding. "The areas near the proposed route were 92 per cent people of color," *No Sweat News,* the organization's newspaper, reported. "Freeways have caused high cancer rates in the communities alongside them and high incidences of lead in the brains of our children living in these communities," said the group's dynamic leader, Chappell Hayes. In fact, the soil in parts of West Oakland's target zone crisscrossed by highways qualified as an EPA Superfund site for its lead contamination. The coalition's suit claimed that the proposed freeway violated Title VI of the Civil Rights Act of 1964, which prohibits discrimination in any federally financed project. Since 90 percent of the interstate was to be paid by the U.S. government, highway infrastructure more than qualified, attorneys argued.

"The brunt of the proposed project's negative social, human health and environmental impacts—including those associated with noise and air pollution, the dislocation of persons, the condemnation of homes and businesses, the chilling of economic development, as well as the disruption of the life of the community—will be borne by minority residents of West Oakland, including plaintiffs."

Little more than a year later, Hayes, the galvanizing plaintiff, died of cancer. The road, with a very few concessions to the community, was on its way. Caltrans, the state highway agency, offered token recompense. The coalition's question remained unanswered: "Why is it worthwhile spending $750 million on the 1.5 mile Cypress Freeway, so that wealthy drivers can save a couple of minutes getting from Castro Valley to downtown San Francisco, but not worthwhile to spend $1 million to improve AC Transit to allow low-income better access to jobs and education?"

War of the Dinosaur

In southeastern Washington, D.C., on streets shaded by trees and bordered by the blue green boundary of the Anacostia River, highway officials have tried to cut through yet another minority community, this time to build Barney Circle, a traffic rotary. Images of dinosaurs decorate the trim brick houses and "Stop Barney" bumper stickers appear on cars. Before "environmental racism" entered the national consciousness, before the Beltway was built, before Washington was a self-ruled district, this African-American neighborhood near Capitol Hill lived in an embattled state fighting against an inner belt that would have destroyed it. In one of the nation's major freeway fights, the activists mostly won.

Again in the mid-1990s, however, a fateful document came out of the drawer and onto Federal Highway Administration and public works drawing boards. The $20 million East Leg project, a mile-long, six-lane highway and bridge, revived old emotions. "The last of the 1960s fights, the first of the 1990s," Christopher Herman, an EPA planner who spends his days dealing with international issues, calls the group fighting the déjà vu battle at his doorstep the "Citizens Committee to Stop It Again." In the spring of 1995, the Federal

Highway Administration set forth its environmental assessment on the Barney Circle interstate, which was slated to chisel off parts of Anacostia Park. "While D.C. is severely short of funds, and Metro is raising prices and slashing service, the [Mayor Marion] Barry Administration still supports this road"—a road for suburban commuters and Beltway bypassers, said the District of Columbia's *Auto-Free News.*

A month after the Sierra Club and the Washington legal firm of Covington & Burling had filed suit, Herman pointed to the narrow strip of pasture at the water's edge, near the city's first African-American boathouse, threatened by the linkage to Interstate I-295. Though the area is supposedly protected, this road, allowing some 86,000 cars to pass the open space each day, has progressed. This time, however, fearful city highway engineers tried a public relations ploy. "This is a project for the community," the engineers said. "We want to take traffic off the streets." They made it a point of pride to absolutely prohibit condemning residential structures, says Herman. Instead, they took the neighborhood's green space. Hiring their own researchers, the activists made still one more discovery: they found that the road would not only hurt the district streets, but cause still more traffic, the study found, congesting the city by throwing extra vehicles onto Independence and Pennsylvania avenues and bringing still more cars to the neighborhood it would supposedly protect. Herman took me along the "senseless" route. "A scam," he says.

Such routes are not senseless to those who use them, of course, only to those whose vulnerable neighborhoods they traverse. In Atlanta the most powerless neighborhoods were forced to see and smell two thousand chugging diesel buses carrying 1996 Olympicgoers, but they had to beseech MARTA, the city's transit agency, to serve their own West End. In impoverished West Dallas an eight-lane highway threatened an equally needy neighborhood.

There Goes the Pocketbook

Adding financial injustice to vehicular inequity, neighborhoods afflicted by highways make car ownership pricier there. Higher insurance rates stem in part from theft, blight, and accidents in such road-impacted neighborhoods, in part from insurers' racist and class biases, which adopt a policy with benefits for "preferred" drivers. In turn, higher prices make finding a paying job more arduous and add to such blight. Racist redlining is compounded by the proximity to freeways, the scourge of abandonment, and highway and housing policies that nurture suburban lifestyles. No matter that the poor are particularly ill served by car-oriented policies, they pay automotive taxes along with those well served. In New York City, for instance, low-income households drive one-fifth as many miles as wealthy ones. The gas, excise, and other taxes they pay, much of which go to the car, are the same percentage, however. Calculating expenditures on gasoline as a percent of income, the lowest 10 percent of households pay four times what the top 20 percent pay. It is typical that the poor pay sales taxes, gas taxes, and other subsidies for highways while they drive the least.

"I live across from a housing project," says Michael Vandeman, a California physicist and wildlife advocate who gave up his car and speaks heatedly, lacerating highways as the killing fields of animals. But he is equally humanistic as he sees one car per household in his neighborhood, and "many times, these cars are up on blocks," awaiting service. Deprived of regular, reliable service, burned with more fallible, less safe, older vehicles, the owners are too poor to give proper care or buy insurance. "Ghettomobiles" is the nickname for these junkers with shattered taillights, rusted doors, and other signs of ill maintenance. If, as officials claim, 10 percent of old cars exhale 50 percent of our pollution, those with less money for repairs send more such toxins into their own environs.

Snuffing out Cities

A population immobilized by the car culture hurts the urban poor the most where they live—in the inner city. With almost a third of Americans recorded in central cities at the last census, the fate of the destitute and the prosperous nation that enfolds them are enmeshed. Some 35 percent of the needy inhabit the nation's thirteen largest cities, and the car-sacked landscape encircling them has reinforced their segregation today as it has for the three decades since historian

Robert Fogelson explored the taproots of the Los Angeles Watts riots in *Fragmented Metropolis*.

It was not wealth per se that bothered us in the Reagan-Bush era of mushrooming millionaires but the fact that "the wealthiest 20 or 30 percent of Americans are 'seceding,' " as Labor Secretary Robert Reich has observed. They are withdrawing into separate, often self-sufficient suburbs, where they rarely even meet "members of non-wealthy classes, except in the latter's role as receptionists or repairmen." What really bothers Americans, Mickey Kaus argues in *The End of Equality,* is class segregation. For if the car is that "perfect executive decompression chamber," as the Lexus ad people put it, what does life in this ultimate isolation booth on sequestered highways leading to insular communities do to political life?

"There are no rallies. There are no neighborhood walks. There are no encounters with the public," a reporter described the 1994 electoral campaign. Removed from "the other," abandoning the personal—the public—side of politics, we absorb mostly television messages—the lines paid for by special interest groups or wealthy backers. Quarantined by the car culture, we barely notice that the privacy of the automobile leading to the detached suburb at the end of the highway has created the malaise of the good-hearted. Ours is an automobile-driven isolation so pervasive that its implications seldom surface. Social inequality, Kaus writes, "is at the core of liberal discontent." Yet, it is "subliminal."

The private sphere is where the principles of the marketplace, i.e., rich beats poor, dominate. Public space is where the principles of equality of citizenship rule. But public space, the stage of social life, is destroyed by our auto-oriented design that nullifies walking and intermingling. Sequestered by income, deprived of parks, bankrupting Main Street for malls, we no longer rub shoulders with our neighbors, rich or poor, deprived or thriving, that tousled mix of age, race, and experience. All of the same breeds fear of the other, and the everyday intercourse of public life, the plural, multicultural world of a civil society, vanishes.

Once it was otherwise. "With a nickel I'd get to Queens, twist and zoom to Coney Island, twist again towards the George Washington Bridge—beyond which was darkness," novelist Leonard Michaels once recalled. "I wanted proximity to darkness, strangeness. Who doesn't, indeed? The poor in spirit, the ignorant and frightened." Who doesn't? All of those rendered unfeeling by the car's banishment of the diversity, the street life of urban America. Crime reigns when such streets are empty. Incivility stems from lack of public space. Neglect comes when money heads outward, following the drift of drivers in their private cars to their vacuum-sealed surroundings.

Isolating the Other

A "homeless vet" waves a sign beside the exit ramp as we pass him in Los Angeles. A pathetic figure, he attracts my gaze. Not so my companion's. The vet's dog, caked with dust, is a "good prop," says my otherwise humane friend behind the wheel. Compassion fails in the antiseptic ambience of the automobile environment. No sweat. No sight of the poor.

Does this privatism, this death of shared space, breed the death of common concern regardless of race and class? Does it account for the death of public life? Certainly the car and the single-use suburbs it serves breed the solitary pattern that makes us lose what yet another critic of the social order, Ron Powers, has called the "last great place." The pubs, the coffee shops, the communal collage vanish. Cordoning us from community life, the car accentuates an environment of exclusion. The mall café is our vacuous symbol. Its umbrellas lack breeze or sun; its security guards manning the escalators to handcuff spirited teens; its architectural island walled by the automobile, offers access only to the licensed shopper. No public realm here.

I remember a sign I saw next to a shopping center. "Areas in this mall used by the public are not public ways, but are for the use of the tenants and the public transacting business with them," said the large print. "Permission to use said areas may be revoked at any time."

"Revoked at any time"?

Places that "revoke" their publicness revoke our citizenship. No city can be revoked. No true community can be a private way. Written or unwritten, these Keep Out notices are the virtual charter of the car's kingdom, of a fortressed America that breeds spatial inequity. The mall is that kingdom's moated castle. In New York a woman was arrested for breast-feeding in a mall and then released. "Breast-Feeding: A Civil Right," said an editorial. Not according to the mall owner. "This week Governor Mario Cuomo signed a bill that protects a woman's right to breast-feed her babies in public and private in New York State. Why on earth, one might wonder, does any state need such a law." Why indeed? But it wasn't the first time, the editorial went on, describing a second nursing mother arrested, reflecting the editorial writer's protest against "the prejudice against women."

The writer hadn't heard or seen the Keep Out signs that lace America. No stray "loiterers," thank you. Entry is at the disposal of the private owner and patrolled. Keep out Salvation Army Christmas kettle bearers. Keep out picketers at malls across America. Keep out those who don't look quite right. The rules are written for owner and occupier alike. Even store owners and workers suffer from the exclusivity built into their turf through the restrictions on their own time and style. Tysons Corner, the vast upscale shopping arena in northern Virginia, insists that shopkeepers not put For Lease or For Sale signs in their windows lest they suggest less than a sunshine spirit of prosperity.

Compounding our flight from the poor, the gated community off the road insulates access and shrinks public space still further. The tyranny of its own majority reinforces homogeneity. Heritage Hills, a condominium development in Westchester County, north of New York City, barred the school bus from traveling through the complex. Roped off into segregated segments by the spirit of exit ramp America, even those who share income, class, and color lose access to the diversity of age and activity as they succumb to the look-alike ethos of the car culture. Can it be less than meaningful, then, that, as auto sales boomed in the 1970s and 1980s, Woodstock Nation evolved into Cocoon Country? At one extreme, we have urban centers as depositories for the needy with their urgencies for food and shelter—their hands outstretched as they stumble into the path of the prosperous. At the other, we have affluent auto-bound America sequestered by color, income, and age.

Somehow, the agony of this traumatic split in mobility is ignored. "We are seeing the final democratization of travel" jumped out at me from a report one day as I compiled the numbers and the faces left behind by our asphalt nation. This rhapsody for the late auto age stopped me in my tracks. It was written by a data consultant waving the flag of personal freedom as the frontispiece of the *Nationwide Personal Transportation Survey*. "We are seeing the final democratization of travel as young and old, low income populations, and women make immense strides in personal transportation," the consultant, Alan Pisarski, wrote. Democratization? Doesn't the reality of an immobility register on his screen? Strides? Look at the social consequences for the vast population. Ask the poor, ask the carless, ask the old and the young (with an estimated 80 million Americans in just these two last categories). Ask the Americans denied mobility and access to the system altogether. Ask the 9 percent of households who have no car. Ask yourself, your friends, your family. Do they see strides in these decades of rampant motorization?

The saying goes that a good society takes care of its people at the three most critical times in the human cycle: in the dawn of life, in the darkness of life, and in the twilight of life. A car-based society cripples all three—those in the dawn of life, the young; those in the darkness of life, the poor and disabled; and those in the twilight of life, the elderly. We are all young once and will all grow old. At one time or another in our lives, we are majority and minority alike. We suffer ourselves and, in the circle of caring, suffer yet again when those we care about are hurt by a car-dependent society.

OPPOSITE: This splendid interior of the former Michigan Theater in Detroit, now a parking garage, is a graphic though not unique example of the damage wrought to architecture. (Photo: Camilo José Vergara)

The Landscape of the Exit Ramp

"Premium sound system. Leather furnishings. Sophisticated climate control. It's enough to make your house jealous of your garage."

—advertisement for Nissan

"American consciousness has been saturated by two verbs, the Ur-words of daily life, to drive and to park."

—Richard Ingersoll, "Death of the Street," in *Roadside America,* Jan Jennings, editor

ALWAYS BUILD ON the brow, Frank Lloyd Wright would tell his disciples. "No house should ever be *on* a hill, or *on* anything. It should be *of* the hill. Belonging to it." And so he built his winter colony below Arizona's Camelback hill in deference to the rise. Taliesin, "shining brow," he called it.

The master architect was scarcely noted for his modesty. Wright did not defer to nature from reticence but from a sense of the natural order of the landscape. In this way he began to shape the winter encampment of Taliesin West outside Phoenix in 1937 and, year after year, unfolded his home and studio along its horizon. It was an architecture honoring climate and place, as considerate of its surroundings as the breezeway built to capture the gusts of summer on the desert, as heedful of the elements as the overhanging roof that shaded the summer sun. Wright called his architecture organic. "A desert building should be nobly simple in outline as the region itself is sculptured," he wrote.

View from the Brow

It is midday and we are standing by Taliesin's "brow," at the Scottsdale, Arizona, site. The Southwest's cold season is warming to spring, and the desert blooms make the most of the coming cycle, with color hued to sunnier days. The late winter brittle bush is flecked with yellow, and the dangling tamarisk with its red tags of flowers looks dashing against the sandy landscape. The feathery paloverdi, the saguaro, and the teddy bear cactus pose as if awaiting the camera crews coming to shoot the site for Wright's latest canonization. The stone and wood and glass of his home and studio are of this place.

When we scan the surrounding settlement that has evolved since the late 1930s, though, we see a vastly altered view. Beyond the "shining brow" staked out by Wright and his apprentices, the sense of desert has vanished except as a pejorative—the asphalt desert, barren and lifeless. The flatland once stark against the rolling hills, the sunny desert purpling into oblivion in Wright's day, is now the outskirts of one more sprawl city. Here, a new kind of suburban desert emerges thrusting Taco Bells and Super-pump gas stations onto the landscape.

"If you turn around and look at the view, it speaks for itself," our guide, a lanky Taliesin apprentice, observes. "You can see where our property ends," he points to the strip hard by the power lines where nothing is "of" nature at all. "It's what we call 'Taco deco,' " he says with a rueful smile. "This is what's left of the desert," he goes on, turning towards Wright's oasis. "It's carefree, it's dirt resistant," he describes the desert ecology in the language of vinyl floor ads. Alone on this broad mesa, Wright's low building and cactus-studded habitat have fended off the highway landscape.

Below Taliesin on the nearby road, ironically named Frank Lloyd Wright Boulevard, we pass Scottsdale's cookie-cutter clutter—Montana Rancho condominiums, pseudopueblo walls, scattered shopping strips, and malls. The corridor of road taking us back to Phoenix is congested, the buildings to either side helter-skelter and charmless. A one-story antique mall sits across the Tarmac from a child care stop, next to a Wallpaper Joe, split from a storefront chiropractor. All are disconnected and unreachable on foot. Behind them the endless cul-de-sac subdivisions and copycat houses proliferate, oblivious to place.

Wright himself loved fast cars and single-family homes. He plotted what he called his Broadacre City Plan of 1935 for the suburban dream, a scant five hundred houses per square mile. "Every Broadacre citizen has his own car. Multiple lane highways make travel safe and enjoyable," the architect imagined. The private home on the endless road. Nirvana. "No railroad, no streetcar . . . No headlights, no light fixture . . . No Glaring Cement roads or works . . . No Slum. No Scum," the architect wrote. No encroachments, no menace. Wright's vision of the highway shaping the city seemed benign.

How, then, would the master have dealt with the consequences of his plan in today's servitude to the four-wheeled vehicle? Though Wright's scheme of living was a departure from the tight-meshed city, it had order and grace. His was a bucolic Eden, the "scum" extinct. What, then, would the architect have said of the new kind of scum, the scum of sprawl, his harmonious living gerrymandered by the quest for life behind the wheel. This desert of strip islands is, in fact, post-Wright—but wrought by him. It is what critic Richard Ingersoll has called "the Darwinian adaptation of motorized humanity."

Photographer Pedro Guerrero, who was hired by the architect, knew and shot the area half a century ago when Phoenix was a thirtieth of its current size. Guerrero, who captured Taliesin's desert solitude in *Picturing Wright,* reflects sadly on the "sea of development." The architect picked the place to get away from "civilization," Guerrero recalled one day, "and now it's barking at its heels." The photographer remembers his first visit, when "Scottsdale Road was a gravel road. You took a right by a landmark and into a gravel road. It was rutted. There were dry creeks, arroyos and such. There was just nothing at all. Just barren desert."

The suburb sliding into Phoenix is something now, something all too familiar. This former outpost is the mirror of the last quarter century where, as historian Richard Sennett has described it, "one ceases to believe one's surroundings have any meaning save as a means towards the end of one's own motion." Here is where the car lives, says the architecture. Designed for the moving vehicle along the space-grabbing, free-for-all highway, defining land use by its voracious needs, Phoenix is a city at an end point. Grown from 17 to 420 square miles in forty years, it has ten times the acreage of Manhattan's grid. Thirty miles at its widest side, Phoenix is about the length of the nation's most populous city and more than two-thirds its width. Its vast agglomeration of a million residents is less than Manhattan's million and a half, and its vast acreage could swallow Gotham with miles to go. The numbers tell a simple story, a tale of the road-wrapped sprawl that has defined architecture for a generation. Here, the rush to inhabit the land off the exit ramp after World War II hoisted the population of this Sunbelt city from 120,000 to 1 million by the mid-1990s, depleting land and settling newcomers in promiscuous disarray. The ratio of human beings to asphalt environs explains the formless spread of motorized America, removed from the urban and suburban design of the past.

The Name of the Game

Phoenix represents the new architecture of the car-bred generation, Arizona planner Marc Fink has written, looking for acceptance. "The street as the conveyor of vehicular traffic is the central focus of the Sunbelt city. It defines neighborhood and unifies the city," he observes approvingly. "Towards a Sunbelt Urban Design Manifesto" he calls his thesis, as if installing a concrete channel for cars could create urban design, any more than depositing the *Apollo* on the moon could create a lunar city. Boasting only a few concentrations of building or spots to walk, Phoenix is the antithesis of Frank Lloyd Wright's "place." Far more than wasted Detroit, it is the embodiment of Anyplace, U.S.A. Its contrived language of place contradicts any search for manifesto or identity. Central Avenue, at thirteen miles, is the opposite of "central," while the so-called Downtown District Development, a whopping ninety blocks, is so long that it negates any definition of "downtown" and "district."

Phoenix's bleached landscape epitomizes the exurbia that author Joel Garreau described in *Edge City*. Expanses of metropolitan areas like Atlanta or Princeton, New Jersey, regions in Texas, in Southern California or outside Washington, D.C., are our new "hearths of civilization," in Garreau's semantics. Chockablock with more parking spaces than people, Phoenix is a fit icon of America's architecture of the exit ramp.

From afar I had read of the city's architectural achievement and hoped for an exemplar. During a snowy winter in the East, one lecturer came to describe Phoenix as "the next Champs-Élysées of the West, like Christmas for capital improvement projects," the centerpiece of a new era of public works, a showcase of how to make the highway scenic and the infrastructure elegant. "Our city goes with the automobile," Deborah Abele, the city's historic preservation officer, told me. "We don't vilify the automobile out here," she offered, with a slightly embarrassed laugh. "We have some of the prettiest highways," she said. "One of the things that distinguishes us is our freeway." Her preservation efforts go to save the emblems of Phoenix's birth and history—here a diner, there a sign ("you know, those big, flashy fifties ones," the icons of the Populuxe era).

And so, I take her instructions and head out to see the park decked above the highway and some walls decorated by artists in the public art program, where the "highway and landscape have begun to enter into a new civic partnership," as I was told. Instead, I found—its absence. The vaunted artist-designed highways—a fleet of highway walls scored into patterns, dappled with murals, softened with plant-ings, and even buried and surmounted with a pleasant park—are fragments. The boasted infrastructure, a small park praised for soft-ening the space above the roadway, is minimal; the walls along the highway, scored in different patterns, are little more than incised lines against the unredeeming asphalt. Elsewhere, the colorful clay pots shown in photographs shrink into picturesque miniatures when placed in this gray wasteland. Like the linear bikeway built by the riverbed, they seem slim compensation, a doily adorning an over-stuffed sofa, more antimacassar than architecture. How could such fragments work in a municipality so scattered that even sensible plans to alleviate the ugliness or create a center seem puzzling.

On another afternoon I visited Roger Brevoort, a preservation planner. Housed aloft in the new City Hall with its adorned plaza, he narrated the origins and recent growth of Phoenix. The city had barely begun building a downtown when the 1920s sped motorists out to the periphery, he said, leaving in its wake a few downtown art deco buildings and a nearby neighborhood of cozy bungalows. We visited both, first the core, a few streets, more block than center; sec-ond, a grid of streets of some charm and substance, with their sloped tile roofs and groomed front yards. The sidewalks that predated the car's dominance were lined with upstretched palms. The snug, lolling blocks created a haven. Alas they made barely a dot on the map as I weaved in and out in search of the monuments of road and infra-structure.

From the "center" of the city, I joined Michael Cynecki, a traffic engineer, to visit the periphery. Dedicated to quieting the local streets, this advocate for more walkable neighborhoods drove me along the arterial. We rode by Phoenix's far-flung neighborhoods. Ten, fifteen, twenty minutes away from the downtown, the sprawling homes con-trasted with the pre-1920s sidewalked space at the old core. The looping cul-de-sacs had become so heavily impacted by the traffic created by their layout and distance from commerce, their tranquility and safety so assaulted, that even this laissez-faire community voted to limit access by cars. To block off traffic, the city stationed orange-colored buckets and peeling wooden horses to narrow streets at in-tersections. The measure has worked for safety, Cynecki said. Less so for transportation as a whole or for the surroundings, where the road-taming artifacts add their own litter. Someday funds may alter the contours permanently and gracefully, Cynecki hopes. For now the barriers are a reminder of the atomized urban design of this Southwest city. They are more a testament to its ill-planned growth than a positive solution.

"The Valley's addiction to cars and trucks is growing even faster than its population," an article in the *Arizona Republic* has acknowledged, predicting a population increase of 100 percent but with vehicle miles traveled up 122 percent in the next two decades. "Isn't this coming traffic a replica of the trend that snagged that other sunny dreamland, Los Angeles?" I asked the preservationist Abele. Can growth last?

"Well," she admitted slowly "I say one hundred years from now we're going to look back at it like the cowboy days—it's freedom. It's not without its cost," she went on. "Still," she conceded, "I think of this as the last day of the cowboys, the frontier. It's like the last remnants of an era."

The Semantics of the New Space

So what is this land spawned by the car? An "edge"? a "city"? Both at once? How can something be a city (a core) and an edge (a fringe). The phrase is self-contradictory, even silly. And, if not edge city, then what? What does one call the architecture bred by the automobile?

The word mavens have been hard at work to find an appellation. A whole lexicon of phrases has arisen, many floundering with the impossible. From "urban villages" (Christopher Leinberger and Charles Lockwood) to "technoburbs" (Robert Fishman), the geographic expressions try to supplant the old "exurbia," which for long described the ring beyond "suburbia." "An . . . agglomeration within the metropolitan region," one planner offers the tongue-twisting mouthful. And others who study the built environment expand the terms. The Southern California Institute of Architects calls its journal *Offramp*.

Some are downright pejorative—"exopolis," "silicon city," "Galactic City," "a radical deconstruction," and, yes, "pepperoni pizza." Some more neutral—"postsuburbia," "metroplex," "satellite city." The name game falters and fails. And the very lack of consensus confirms the inadequacy of image or identity. The mind fails to conceive what the eye cannot see.

A generation ago, planner Kevin Lynch's classic definition in his *The Image of the City* posited a place where visual form reinforced memory and served as symbol. Now, for the first time in history, design capitulating to the car has killed off such images, along with aspirations for place making. The uncentered, formless cities, the multinucleated Phoenixes and Atlantas, Houstons and Albuquerques, seem only source material for what James Kunstler called the "geography of nowhere." The "agglomeration" of parts that make up this geography bears no kinship to Lynch's "imageability," to his visible world.

How can you mold, shape, make habitable the buckshot disarray of all those malls, minimalls, strip malls, corporate malls, housing malls? How can there be any urban design manifesto when motion dominates and development is promiscuous. When architecture is designed for automotive movement, for the whir of the road, for isolation not community, spread not core, the road undermines the built environment.

The Urban Intruder

As an architecture critic, I came to this view slowly. Life in a walking city cushions the slights of the auto age. Slowly, though, and over time, the lesions to my hometown of Boston penetrated my consciousness. As the 1960s wreaked havoc on my city, cherished neighborhoods, brick bastions of grace and community, tumbled. Towers, adrift in plazas, rose, while historic structures fell. And, as the landscape of the 1970s and the 1980s occupied my writings, I came to realize that the designs I saw often literally housed more cars than human occupants: that building to building, place to place, office complex to complex, dwelling to dwelling, every institution and every structure did obeisance to the automobile.

To be sure, Boston's pedestrians are notable—or notorious—for their assertive stance against the automobile. Indeed, the word "jaywalker" was invented here. On foot, Bostonians bully the car. They slap the hoods of idling automobiles as if they were nasty children. Even in this walking hub, however, the 1980s boom years saw the motor vehicle create a subcity of garages and parking lots, gnaw the sidewalk, and slick the city's surfaces with oil. Garage doors and black hole entrances lacerated the street. Walking by the city's newer buildings, the pedestrian is now as likely to be ambushed by a car sliding from some underground garage as visually assaulted by gap-toothed parking lots and eerie garage facades.

"Plan for People, Not Just Autos," I wrote of this new architecture genuflecting to the highway, severed from the old. Copley Place, the city's first in-town mall, disowned its Copley Square neighbors, the magisterial Trinity Church and Boston Public Library. A maze inside defined by the dimensions of its parking garage, an aloof consumer fortress outside, it was subservient to the road. Tourists and shoppers could barely cross its circling arterial. Cars whipped by, freeway style. A sidewalk entrance was rare. A few blocks away, the state's new Transportation Building was similar. Paying no heed to the foot-based transportation used by 48 percent of those who moved through downtown Boston on foot, it was effectively moated off from the city by an interstate-scaled street.

Although the city has salvaged the human quality of its old streetscape, other new downtown designs, however contextual or pseudohistorical in profile, serve the automobile: the maw of an 850-car garage, the gash of a roundabout hotel drop-off, or loading docks fronted by drooling dumpsters mar the sidewalk. Pedestrian passage has become a walk on the wild side.

I have watched this deference to the automobile in worse ways across the continent. Time after time, I have witnessed environments become asphalt encrusted as the urge to hold the cars of shoppers or homeowners has taken primacy. Despite better intentions, it has become apparent that an almost mathematical inevitability lies behind such design, a formula based on the fact that each and every motor vehicle is a consumer of some seven spaces.

The numbers are comprehensible. At rest, the automobile needs three parking spaces in its daily rounds—one at home, one at work, and one in the shopping center. In motion, going through the ritual of to-ing and fro-ing, driving along the street, circling through the garage to reach that parking space, it needs more. The space for the car's entering, the radius for its turning, and the dimensions for its sitting idle mean that asphalt competes for space with architecture and wins.

Put more mathematically, in an office building handing out one parking spot for every employee's automobile—that's 150 to 200 square feet per car, plus aisles and access lanes—adds 300 square feet per driving employee to the actual structure. In a shopping center the five spaces for every thousand square feet of store means fifteen hundred square feet of parking. Zoning and building codes insist on ever more space for ever more cars at home. Those one-, two-, and three-car garages define the design.

As economist Donald Shoup summed it up, "Form no longer follows function, fashion or even finance. Instead, form follows parking requirements." In the end the car's horizontal needs at rest and in motion mean that architecture is car bound.

On the larger scale, city by city, suburb by suburb, we have a hard-topped nation. From 30 to 50 percent of urban America is given over to the car, two-thirds in Los Angeles. In Houston the figure for the amount of asphalt is 30 car spaces per resident. The more distant suburbs are tougher to assess but worse. On the outskirts, mall lots, defined by the needs at the most jam-packed periods of shopping at Thanksgiving or Christmas, stand empty much of the year. Ironically, this means that peak time requirements hurt rather than help the surroundings and make real estate pricier.

When pavement dominates, other axioms flow as inexorably as concrete. When flattening for parking is more profitable than restoration for renting, every building, however historic or attractive, becomes a lure for developers to demolish for its "highest and best" use. Too often, that means its potential as a parking lot.

If "the car should be a servant to the city," as one transportation official put it, its uncapped appetite has made the city dweller a slave. In the suburbs it is worse. There, a clutch of cars occupies the first floor of an apartment building, raising the residential quarters on stilts above a ghostly cave of cars. Angled parking before the front of a minimall ruptures the sidewalk for pedestrians. Everywhere, free-for-all spaces slice the forecourt of motel or supermarket. Sidewalk and street tree vanish for driveway; walkability gives way to drive-ability.

Design à la Motorized Mode

What does this mean in terms of new architecture?

Just after my return from Phoenix, I was asked to moderate a panel on the new design modes of the day. "Megaprojects: the Cutting Edge Form of the Mid-'90s" was the title. One of the mega-architectural forms was the much heralded Mall of America in Bloomington, Minnesota, the other Cleveland's Gateway development, a large sports complex. A former mayor of Minneapolis and a Cleveland developer were to discuss the evolution of these latest, and arguably largest, gestures of modern architecture. "What Is 'The New Public Realm'?" was the program's title and question. The Mall of America outside Minneapolis suggested defining it by size. As big as seventy-seven football fields, this "Vatican of Consumption" is the epitome of gigantism, so big inside that managers had started giving identification bracelets to young children so that they wouldn't get lost, so large outside that parents needed the same help to find their cars. The second giant, the Gateway baseball stadium and arena multiplex, was a twenty-eight–acre structure, well designed for walkers, I was told, in downtown Cleveland and paying attention to its streetscape. Yet, an overview showed highways funneling into the "new form," and a press release informed me that its two and a half acres of underground truck docks were designed to assist in receiving and removal. To do so "discreetly in an urban environment," the release went on, provoking new definitions of "discretion" and "urban."

Whatever their purpose, these megaprojects embody a public architecture more suggestive of the freeway and the exit ramp than the human being. They formed a series of bigger-than-ever boxes bound by asphalt. Stripped-down blocks on the outside, over-wrought cake and circuses within, they were twin offspring of the auto age. Whether the Mall of America, with its theme park designed to appeal to the mentality of shopping till you drop, or Cleveland's happily more urban site still orchestrated to "take me out to the ball game," the car dominated the entry and parking dictated the design.

The most mean-spirited and common highway megaproject was not on our agenda, however. The so-called big box, the superstore retail warehouse of discount goods, is proliferating without benefit of professional recognition. The Wal-Mart or Home Depot could not survive without the roads that wind through the countryside and the asphalt encasement to hold the customers' cars. This architecture without architects stems from a car-dependent culture where the difficulty of multiple trips and the undermining of small, walkable shops have turned the home into a warehouse to store goods in bulk. The form, the moonscape of the superstore parking lot, reflects its function grimly. This windowless packing crate, barely camouflaged, displays the spatial appetite of the automobile, just as surely as its upscale kin.

Once again, the names of these architectural forms reflect our late auto age: "complex," "megaplex," "mall," "cineplex" are on the ascendance. Cafeteria, pub, row house, two-family, three-decker, apartment—building forms of variety and humanity—are often threatened and seldom reproduced. "Within the last decade or so, whole categories have become endangered species, including such once-basic staples as variety stores and movie houses. The landscape of Main Street might as well have been the victim of a pogrom in terms of mid-20th century storefronts," writes critic Richard Longstreth.

One cannot blame the highway alone for the conformity and vapidity along its edge. The conglomerization and franchising of the nation have played a role. Yet, it is the interstate and arterial that nullify the natural topography and draw buildings from their Main Street identity. "No surprises," boasts the Holiday Inn slogan. Definition disappears in the design of the nation's staple motels, its burgeoning Wal-Marts, its corporate office parks and complexes. Whether an old mill made over into mixed-income housing or a new condominium cluster, design for the motorized mass frustrates individuality. When cities become car warehouses, architectural civility shrinks. Like edge city, car-based design is an oxymoron.

"Supposing things changed, and the landscape and towns, especially new towns, were completely overrun with pipes. Huge aqueducts, sewers, and storm drains all over the place, twisted, knotted gaggles of them pushing everything else out of the way—so many pipes that you could hardly find anything else," writes architect Daniel Solomon in *ReBuilding*. "For us, it is not pipes that are the problem, it is cars."

For us it is some 200 million moving vehicles traveling 2 trillion-plus miles a year on roads and ramps, along with parking lots for resting. As the speed and the search for parking became the Holy Grail, the urban axiom has evolved: easy to park, hard to live; easy to live, hard to park. Lewis Mumford, the urban prophet, predicted no less: "The right to have access to every building in the city by private motorcar in an age when everyone possesses such a vehicle is actually the right to destroy the city."

The Pedestrian Attack

If bad architecture is the shadow of the motor vehicle, good design is the footprint of a walker. Anton Nelessen calls planning for the pedestrian the "DNA of design." A pedestrian requires 5 square feet when standing and 10 on the hoof. A car and its access, as noted above, demand 300 square feet when standing, 3000 when moving at 30 miles an hour. In commercial terms each shopper takes 70 times his or her floor space to drive and park the car.

On the public as well as the private level, we plan for the latter. Federal policy reinforces the desolation downtown. It orders the central post office to the outskirts, drawing customers from Main Street grocery stores and shops. Local policy in the form of zoning or codes insists on superscale parking, undermining walkability still more. In the end the auto age has spawned a world where the pedestrian is scorned and public space has dissolved, eradicating stable surroundings where people congregate. Sculpted public space becomes secondary to space shaped for motion.

Displacing the walker with the architecture of the exit ramp has destroyed what planner Peter Calthorpe defines as an aesthetic of place. Calthorpe, arguing for "pedestrian pockets" as the core of design, casts this aesthetic in four dimensions: scale, pace, pattern, and bounds. An auto-centric environment is the antithesis of all four. The

scale swells to the overblown size of the highway, standardized, isolated, and lacking texture. The pace is that of a seventy-mile-an-hour
driver viewing only land-blurring backdrops and featureless boxes.
The pattern is the unleashed, randomly moving vehicle, not the defined and ordered sidewalks, entrances, and facades of traditional
pedestrian streets. And the bounds of the road are, in fact, boundless
and amorphous. Given free rein to trample any place, sacred or profane, the highway defined as a straight line between two points
negates the human dimension.

While architects theoretically do deference to the classical goals of
"firmness, commodity and delight," uttered by the ancient Roman
Vitruvius, the Hippocrates of architecture, highway architecture
eradicates the creed. It replaces notions of firmness (stability) with
mobility, commodity (functionalism) with access by the car, and delight with utility. "Autodysformia," architect Richard Register labels
the malfunction that banished the ancient mission.

Pulling the Welcome Mat

On a mission of my own, I set out on mass transit and foot to explore housing for my elderly mother. I got directions to reach a new
assisted-living home in a compact older neighborhood with nearby
shops, mass transit, and apartments. "Walk up a hill, take a left and
a right, but make sure you don't come in the front door," the woman
from marketing instructed. "You'll see what *looks* like the front
door," she went on, "but you can't go in it." The parking lot was the
entry. The entry as the architecture's welcome mat, the grand door or
arch, has diminished. Public buildings parallel the homeowners' entrance through a garage, where foot-friendly means putting the pedal
to the metal.

Later I visited Las Vegas to see another Sunbelt city dealing with
an architecture of the auto that ignores the walker. In the last generation *Learning from Las Vegas*, a tract by architects Venturi, Scott-
Brown and Izenour, admonished architects to accept the glitz of
drive-by design on the strip. It became a seminal text on buildings as
billboards.

It is not only on the gambling strip. The same windshield vision has abetted design as a bold, undifferentiated logo or billboard, and design as logo has bred trophy architecture, an oversimplified, bulbous, and overscale building. Drawn at the driver's scale, the one-liner image, works at sixty miles an hour. The billboard on the strip and the billboard of a simpleminded high-rise facade or broad box both stem from the homogeneity of the view from the road. "Architecture for speed reading," historian Chester H. Liebs described the view through the picture windshield that accompanied the view from the picture window as the post–World War II auto boom began. The drive-by style still monopolizes. Blame an age without the craft to soften bigness with detail, if you will. Nonetheless, whether a postmodern ornament or the sliced, diced, and slivered forms of deconstruction that seem to mimic our splintered and segmented arterials, new modes say more of our vehicles than ourselves.

More than style is lost in planning that puts the automobile first. Urban movement on foot and a lively streetscape are at hazard. On a Las Vegas corner, as the cars condense into a moving mass of steel beneath the foul air, you can see the less flashy effects of building for the automobile. There may be more foot traffic here than at most American intersections, but crossing the street is an ordeal. Traffic makes walking between the Roman orgy of Caesar's Palace and the less trendy gambling halls a menace.

The tourists, hardy souls, wanted to cross. They pressed the stoplight as we waited one summer night, and I began to count the seconds for the pedestrian light to change. The restless crowds edged out into the shiny stream of cars. It seemed interminable. We waited and waited. A minute or two more and the traffic sign's walk light flashed. Then the race was on. "God, they're going to kill us," said a woman in a pink sweat suit as she scuttled onto the island between the two roads. Trapped together, midpoint, on this concrete island, we watched the cars collect. "You want me to go back and press the button?" asked the woman's male companion. I began to count. We waited again. The woman, too, rolled her eyes to heaven, or to the god of the gaming tables.

Las Vegas's planners are not indifferent to the pedestrians marooned by this still from *American Graffiti* downtown. There is a pedestrian bridge for those unwilling to take the shorter route described above. Designers have revived the older downtown too, with a pedestrian mall complete with laser show faux sky. Other plans have emerged to accommodate the nation's largest influx of people, five thousand newcomers a month. From 1990 to 1994 the city grew by 150,000, and as the residents moved in each month, the land of blackjack dealers and croupiers became a touchstone of rapid growth and development.

The Garage Called Home

Summerlin, an ideal community as described by the Las Vegas Regional Transit Commission, is a place where settlement is growing. Created by Summa Corporation, Howard Hughes's real estate firm, the community encompasses twenty-six thousand acres in the vast sweep of desert heading west from Nevada toward Los Angeles. The Country Club Hills's so-called estates, a two-story Shangri-la of the opulent, sits among a potpourri of walled miniranches and mini-malls. Even in this hub of affluence, the ponderous houses selling for half a million dollars form an arc, cheek by jowl, around a golf course. At their front doors the two-car garages and driveways supplant the front lots of the grandly titled Vintage, Bel-Air, Augusta, and Canterbury houses, denying visual privacy or walkability for all the nouveau castle's heft.

The architecture of the single-family home thus suffers the car culture's assault. In the suburbs and exurbs, the cold serviceway of carport or Tarmac replaces the front door and hall as the dominant design feature. The porch is long gone, the tree is hostage to the driveway. Architecture heads to the rear, both physically and metaphysically.

The construction of this "carchitecture" begins benignly. "Curb-cut" is an innocuous word used to describe the slice the builder takes in the sidewalk to make the driveway that shoots the automobile toward the house and nibbles away the pedestrian zone in new town or old. A snip and a swath of asphalt wounds a vintage community like Queens's Sunnyside, with its neighborly housing fronted by tidy lawns and sidewalks, as parked cars chew the front yards. In the Bronx, along a new development of clapboard row houses, automobiles at right angles to the curb clutter the street. At a Los Angeles apartment the motorist plunges into a subterranean garage, exits into its dank space, then weaves through dismal corridors to reach the unit door.

Again, Calthorpe defines the automotive origins: "To walk or take transit is a public act which makes the street a safer component of community. To drive is a private act which turns the street into a utility." The process is cyclical. The pedestrian daunted by the hostile streetscape takes to the car. Deprived of life, the street is widened and demeaned. The walker additionally assaulted by cars, curbcuts, treeless sidewalks, unwalkable patches of turf, cracked pavement, and faceless buildings retreats still further. The ills accelerate. The street becomes more perforated, killing variety and demanding security in the form of bolts, chain-link fences, and facades fortified against belligerents. The community moves inside; children play behind closed doors. It is not that people give up on the street. The street gives up on them. Empty streets and scary spaces emerge in the hollow landscape of a car-bound world. The gated communities, fortress facades, windowless environments of an asphalt nation ensue.

The walled, or gated, community is the most blatant isolationist expression of motor-minded America. Concentrated in America's new Southwestern and Western suburbs, some 30,000 such luxury encampments secure Americans, bolting the nation's chariots and their drivers in a house-fortress wrapped by walls and manned by guards. And so need for security becomes a self-fulfilling prophecy. Locked and barricaded by devices that range from moats in Boca Raton, Florida, to a hydraulic device that shoots metal cylinders into the tires of invading cars in Santa Clarita, California, this defensive architecture is penetrable only by car. Parking characterizes its innards, walking to that car its chief human movement. The design symbolizes the fear of otherness and the end of tolerance at its extreme, adding to the perceived menace by emptying human life outside the complex.

Civic Form

The street is the community's living room, public space our stage to live our lives as neighbors. Buildings enframe these settings. In the neighborhood their design elements—the doorways, stoops, and sidewalks, the curbstones, fences, and gates—are the artifacts of interaction. These elements of the walker's world of design frame and shelter us as friends, conduct us as pilgrims on a journey, and intercept or stall interlopers by subtle means. The porch, the gate, benches, lampposts, curbings, all scaled to the walker, invigorate our steps in urban and suburban life. All these amenities, all these elements, said, "Walk, stop, sit awhile" before the motorcar shifted the world toward asphalt. The sidewalks of the time were richly textured by the buildings that encircled and enlivened the encounters of street life. Ornament reigned. Crossed by grand streets and sacred boulevards, by profane alleys or humble paths, the neighborhood was enriched by the embellishment.

Once, the porch was the apron of the house. It was the public-private realm par excellence. Partaking of the intimacy of the interior and the sociability of the exterior, the porch spoke to the neighbors: "Come in, visit awhile." Here, householders could shuck peas and share the cordiality of conversation; teenagers could rock as the dimming hours of sunset turned to the dark of night. It was a middle-distance design, a public-private space that integrated the singular with the communal. So it remains in neighborhoods where the flow of traffic or daily life allows.

The stoop of row house life shared this sociability. It was the stone ladder for games of ball, the right-angled throne for doll playing and chatting, the launching pad for feisty politics, the backdrop for the weekend tag sale. To this day the stoop remains all of these. Somewhere between public and private, the porch, the stoop, the front stairs created an outdoor living room—off the street, yet of it, the staple of urban life.

When the automobile intruded on human intercourse, older forms of architectural discourse declined. As the rush of traffic grew louder and the lure of television and air-conditioning drew Americans inside, the front yard was usurped by the automobile; the back yard, a refuge from its noise, became the living quarters for the private life of lounge chair and barbecue. The garage and driveway consumed more sidewalk. Transition places vanished, along with the street as public space. Wide streets, treacherous intersections, and fast cars blurred our view and corrupted our built environment. Details vanished.

The very illumination of the evening, the way we perceived light vanished.

Urban light, once the artful form-giver illuminating evening, flooding majestic buildings, or dappling narrow streets, succumbed to lighting shaped for speed. Rarely do we set incandescent orbs on ornate poles at the sidewalk's height or shower a public entry with focused lights. Instead, the traffic engineers' goosenecked forms and elevated poles create a tunnel down the road to nowhere. Light, the fabled definer of architecture, the agent of comfort, security, and sense of place, was altered. Raised high above the sidewalk to benefit the parking lot, not the pedestrian, distant, mechanical light stalks shoot toward the skyline, not the street. Across the continent the highways' omnipresent wattage does one more thing: it deprives us of our view of the stars.

Such civic form makers, the scaffold upon which we hang an architecture of the public realm, recede even faster in the suburban sprawl world of back-office business parks, superstore malls, and planned residential developments. As designer Gregory Tung has observed, "The types of streets and urban fabric have mutated and multiplied; yet most are being illuminated by widely spaced, look-alike cobrahead and shoebox streetlights." Gone is the anthropomorphic fixture whose glow signified human warmth.

Urban Mauling

Distressed by the trashing of America, we try to replicate the architecture of memory. City Walk, built by Universal Studios, is the latest evocation of walkable design in Los Angeles. A mall in the form of an urban environment, it tries to capture city streets down to the chewing gum embedded in its surfaces. Shop by shop, it replaces Los Angeles's icons with mock-ups—here a copy of a familiar health club stands next to a copy of a delicatessen. For all its walkability, this fabricated city is entered by motor vehicle through a garage, isolated from the street, private and homogeneous as a mall.

There is no city here, rather a tokenism of the city's loss in its hate-love affair with the highway. Missing the real animation of urban life, City Walk and theme parks like it create a tepid memento of architecture before its enslavement to the car. "People don't want to have to choose between antiseptic and antisocial," Fred Siegel, a design professor at Cooper Union, has criticized the complex. And yet, even the vestige of urban life and urban density encourages crowds to jam into the faux streets of Disney World. Instead of ameliorating the rough life of the city created by a rubber world, suburban environments bloat their forms and invite mall walkers to march in lockstep.

Ultimately, the phrases "urban planning" and "urban design" become a charade as city builders follow the dotted line defined by the width of the road. "In the United States, the phrase 'urban planning' is an indefensible euphemism," the authors of *An Elephant in the Bedroom* insist. "Urban planners do not plan. They follow along behind the parade of those who do—the land developers. The role of professional planners is to sweep up and organize the dung." Strong stuff. But is it too stern to describe the subdivisions, the robotic malls, the instant Edens and theme parks where genuine public space succumbs to an uncivil substitute? In its place the giganticism of the interstate reigns. "Big modernism, roaring freeways, icy highrises on windy plinths, intimidating concrete canyons, storage-like housing, relentless paving everywhere, the assassination of nature—all intimate the end of the polite role of architecture," critic Richard Ingersoll observed. Speed replaces civility in the auto age.

A Taj Mahal for the Motorcar

So much for landscape architecture as well, I think, as I take my last voyage in search of the real thing, heading to what one writer has called the "corporate palace par excellence." Located in suburban Beaverton, Oregon, the greenopolis outside Portland, the Nike headquarters here is the epitome of try-hardest architecture, the quintessential environmentally correct environment. It is the only place in America where "going outside for a puff" means having a run, not a cigarette, and architects and landscape architects have worked to plant the message of good health and good design.

Nike's banner-lined eighty-foot walkways straddled by lagoons greet visitors like a shrine. They form a processional to the classical palace on the corporate "campus." The monument to grandiose design is also a memorial to corporate fitness, with a mile-and-a-half running track circling the complex. On the 174-acre corporate estate, the sneaker company has secured a $65 million Taj Mahal to business-cum-recreation. Architecturally, modern and postmodern merge as architects Thompson, Vaivoda & Associates deploy domed roofs and a gabled entry atop the high-tech cubist entrance, while landscape architect Linda L. Royer pulls out all the stops on the grounds.

Around the edge of the campus, an earth berm shields Nike's fifteen hundred employees from noise and serves as a jogging trail. The trail rolls up and above the campus, descends by a road, and passes a nature preserve. At the front of the complex, a tunnel through a raised mound creates a walkable "gateway" for those without benefit of car. Dollar chits for "running, biking or skating" encourage walkers to shed the internal combustion machine. The Portland Metro light-rail will arrive. Even the parking lot is naturalized with enough leafy matter to constitute a do-it-yourself salad. Manicured, connected, embellished, the Nike complex offers an array of green spaces.

Somehow, however, the imperial path seems window dressing. For what is this processional anyhow, the supposed walkway and entry to this Shangri-la of sneakers? The true gateway, like that of City Walk, is auto based. Its twelve-hundred-car parking lot is the actual front door of this one-use, drive-to world of containerized campus architecture. There is no orientation around the walkable transit line to come. More staged than experienced, the formal pomp-and-circumstance route to the posed palace begins to appear as artificial as a theme park.

If auto-centric architecture holds sway even in this do-good design, is it predestined to happen everywhere as spaces become "hardscaped"? At the Haverford Arboretum in Pennsylvania, landscape architect Bruce Kelly, known for his careful refurbishing of New York's Central Park, approached me one spring day shaking his head as he tried to describe redesigning a New Orleans park. "All they talked about was where to put the cars," he said sadly: it was landscape as "parkingscape." What to plant, how to shape an appealing place, was secondary, he sighed. The parking's asphalt gash defined the planting program; notions of tending the greenery or design were an afterthought.

Years ago, driving on a highway with my daughters, I evolved one more axiom: "The more exit signs, the less city; the less city, the less architecture." Count the exits, I instructed them as we drove across New Mexico. One, two, three, four exits, they duly noted. Five, six— the numbers mounted. We counted more than eight, as I recall, while driving in the outskirts of Albuquerque, that sprawling noncity. The higher the number of exits to a place, the less likely a true place would be there. It wasn't accidental. The high ratio of highway and ramps to a center inevitably made for centerless sprawl.

An Arterial Aesthetic

Whose fault is it, I have wondered, watching the planners in my own town try to design the visible element of their late auto age highway and tunnel. Some doors down from my Boston office, the earlier elevated highway that blighted the city is about to be buried and the connections and surface that lid it adorned. It is the last link in the interstate, I'm told, and sinking the so-called Central Artery in Boston will do two things. It will ease through drivers, skipping under the city, as they travel from the North Shore to the South Shore or back. And it will relieve the mammoth "Green Monster," the artery separating the city's waterfront from its downtown. The cost of the five-mile "Big Dig" is $10 billion, and growing. The completion date is 2010 and lengthening. In tandem, its tunnel to sweep commuters under and through the city and its surface—bridges, sidewalks, ramps—is up for beautification and connection. Can an eight- to ten-lane roadway be beautiful? Will it be? Can there be a true aesthetic of vehicular space?

Architect Hubert Murray was optimistic as he proceeded to show us the ultimate in highway-based design one night. "Coast to coast without a traffic light," the architect enthused. How to give "clarity, safety and orientation to the driver" and "accommodation, meaning and sense of place" to the neighborhood was his aim and theme. Murray titled his speech "The Mother Lode," to show how the architecture of the new road would better Boston. Slides of fifteen-foot-high models and their origin addressed the way he approached its design. Would the retaining walls be patterned or plain? The metal panels for shafts stretching skyward as vents be peaked or flat? The entrances be stepped or straight?

Then there were the views of piers and viaducts: would they be columned or severe? And the tiled walls of the tunnel to the airport: bedecked with planes or abstract patterns? "We started out with bold ideas," Murray declared. Not to be. Only a red stripe one way, a blue stripe the other, scored the walls to mitigate the millions of white tiles in the tunnel. As for the vent shafts to shoot the car emissions above the city, they would be little "telltale iconic caps."

When Murray displayed the model of the twin four-lane roads—a total of eight lanes downtown above the buried tunnel, lanes that would still send motorists dashing through the central city between the waterfront and historic Quincy Market—pedestrian advocates were not pleased. The view of spreading, spiraling exit ramps and the landscape "amenity" of a grid of giant red-leafed trees marching like British grenadiers down the middle of an asphalt wasteland didn't win any fans either. "The trees are straight, the concrete is serpentine," a British landscape historian seated by me said archly. She was dismayed that the curve of nature would be ruled into the Euclidean geometry of the road.

Murray spoke of it all with enthusiasm. Yet, when I called for more information on the day after his talk, the architect seemed uncertain of his enthusiasm. Was his seven-year stint worth it? I asked. "It's the last stop in a generation of stuff," he described this dinosaur of the auto age. "I'm antipathetic to cars," Murray insisted as we talked, "but it became clear to me that this project was going to happen and so I took it on as a challenge. Since these things were happening," he accepted the premise, "what can I do to mitigate them? That was the political paradigm," he continued. Do you participate or stay on the sidelines? "I have to say, 'Was it the right decision?' "

The answer seemed clear to me and others in these parts. Years of squabbling to make a highway bridge across the Charles River still produced a monster design; agitation to ease the ramps as they exited into the city, to subdue the harsh structure plunging through the artists' community at Fort Point Channel or the corners of Chinatown, the North End, and East Boston, did little to soften this relic from the age of the interstate. What difference could the texture, the daub of color, the height, the shape, the material make when the form is highway derived and the function is to feed the highway culture? Even Murray had his doubts about its civility that day. "After eighty-hour weeks for four years, I'm not sure it was the right thing," said the architect.

Planning for such sixty-mile-an-hour speeds, designing for wastelands of parking, for corridors of concrete, the architect's work has inevitably become carchitecture. Denying the three-mile-an-hour pace of the walker, the world seen from the porch, the surroundings in all their tender detail at an easy pace, once close-scaled places have spread into a blur with all the individuality and identity of the freeway.

OPPOSITE: This tenacious tree notwithstanding, it is the automobile that has the last laugh. The highway's conquest of habitat depletes resources, destroys plant and animal populations, and assaults the environment. (Photo: Allan Dietrich)

The Road to Environmental Ruin

*"Today a magnificent instrument has ruptured the human envi-
ronment in the name of progress. Its terror has been accepted as
a fact of modern war—almost as if it were a sacrifice of war."*
        —Kenneth R. Schneider, *Autokind vs. Mankind*

*"One errant Old World primate species is now changing the
global environment more than that environment has changed at
any previous time since the end of the Mesozoic Era sixty-five
million years ago."*
        —E. O. Wilson, "Biodiversity, Prosperity and Values"

"STAGE ONE SMOG alert predicted for tomorrow. Air quality unhealthy. Please Rideshare," said the sign posted by the Los Angeles Rapid Transit District. To an out-of-towner the notice in the lobby of the nation's most notorious polluters seemed quite casual, but it was telling. We have reckoned with the sight and smell of air befouled by the automobile for years, if not in such an offhanded way. Every time a jocular radio announcer declares a "no-breathe" day, every time we read of "nonattainment" regions—regions that have not attained air the EPA deems fit to breathe—we have testimony. It is a truism that the internal combustion engine which powers our automobiles releases more carbon monoxide, reactive hydrocarbons, and nitrogen oxides in the atmosphere than any other urban or industrial source. The automobile is not just a moving vehicle but also a "mobile source of pollution." And the evidence accrues.

"One one-thousand," environmentalist David Burwell counted, clocking an instant in the polluting life of the automobile. In that single second America's cars and trucks traveled another 60,000 miles, used up 3,000 gallons of petroleum products, and added 60,000 pounds of carbon dioxide to the atmosphere. If the canon of the environmental movement is to "tread lightly on the land," nothing treads more heavily than the licentious motor vehicle. Traffic is what the eye can see; a car-packed lifestyle and landscape oppress our existence. The motor vehicle and its by-products sully the earth at every turn. "A car," to quote another truism, "is a machine that produces pollution." Multiply the single engine of contaminants by 200 million motor vehicles and you have our major environmental villain.

As the decade began, a degree of alarm not heard in years issued from the nation's earth stewards. True, America had doubled its fuel economy and cut per-car emissions. Yet, by doubling the miles driven in the previous two decades, drivers had totally outstripped such advances. In 1991 the Union of Concerned Scientists moved from focusing on nuclear energy to censuring the internal combustion machine. The Natural Resources Defense Council concurred a year later that the car was "the worst environmental health threat in many U.S. cities." The most rapidly growing source of U.S. emissions, Worldwatch concluded the following year.

Despite new environmental controls, reductions were down a scant 1 or 2 percent, and the car's list of pollutants was filling the graphs. Even the EPA, which boasted that each of our cars produced 60 to 80 percent less pollution than thirty years earlier, was admitting that, all in all, "most types of air pollution from mobile sources have not improved significantly." The environmental watchdogs were holding motor vehicles to blame for up to half of all smog-forming volatile organic compounds and nitrogen oxides, more than 50 percent of hazardous air pollutants, and 90 percent of the carbon monoxide found in urban air.

"What went wrong?" the EPA asked.

America's urge for mobility taken to the extreme was the answer. Dirty trucks, dirty diesels, dirty cars—and, of course, their drivers, whose new muscle cars and vans were slurping more gas and accumulating more mileage en route to an estimated 3 trillion miles a year by the end of the millennium.

And there was, of course one more thing: global warming. In the mid-1990s, computer modeling, while not definitive, suggested what had looked ever more likely—an overheated planet. With more burning of fossil fuels, more destruction of tropical rain forests, and pollution of the ocean killing algae, temperatures were rising. Science was confirming the car culture as a culprit. Our fossil fuel vehicles were not only consuming more than one-third of all U.S. energy but also exhaling two-thirds of its carbon dioxide emissions, one-quarter of its chlorofluorocarbons (CFCs), more than 50 percent of its methane, and 40 percent of its nitrogen oxides, plus most of the carbon monoxide.

Taken together, such gases trap heat on the planet. Sealing the warmth of the day, this lid of greenhouse gases raises the temperature of the earth. As reports emerge, fears of melting ice caps, coastal flooding, and potentially devastating climatic change grow. With every roll of the rubber wheel, with every spit from the nation's tailpipes, the thermostat spins. The earth's climate is endangered, and the aberrant weather persists to warn us of the threat.

A Whole Earth Assessment

Such emissions are the most conspicuous and potentially cataclysmic piece of the toxic pie. They are widely known and frequently reported. Agencies offer wedge charts for ozone precursors—the chemicals that rise from the earth, mingle with the sun, and create smog. Yet neither the numbers nor the presentiment of megachange has penetrated the consciousness of those who help create the predicament. "I come from a carbon monoxide city," said Transportation Secretary Federico Pena, former mayor of Denver. Incredibly, he joked about "the brown cloud" that shrouded his city in a speech lending weight to yet one more road to compound America's pervasive environmental intruder. The project, Boston's Central Artery, would encourage more driving, hence vent more bad air, and accelerate the cycle.

If we fail to absorb these larger damages from the car, we have barely bothered to compile the smaller ones that may be cumulatively as damaging. With our eyes sky bound to the gray wash over the blue horizon, we neglect a holistic appraisal of the impact of the motor vehicle. It is a tripartite pollutant. From the start of its production, through its traveling on the road, to the final disposal of its fluids and parts and its related path along the highway—not to mention the highway itself—our automobiles take an enormous toll. The energy to make them, the smelters that pour out their toxins, the trucks that dump the wastes of their heavy metals—our mining, refining, and framing of the automobile and its infrastructure—alter the earth.

In a way our lack of computation is understandable. So widespread is this artifact that it seems impossible to break down and calculate all its bells and whistles: the oil filters, mufflers, and catalytic converters, the hoses and belts, not to forget the oils in road building or the coolants from air conditioners that, for all the restrictions, still destroy the ozone. Auto paint shop or auto factory, oil refinery leak or asphalt runoff, the automobile's abuse overruns our capacity to record it.

Sit in your car and brake for a traffic light. From the CFCs in the foam seat that cushions you to the asbestos in the brake pads beneath your foot, you are driving a pollution machine. To rephrase an environmental slogan, if you got caught driving a car across state lines, you'd go to jail for transporting toxic waste. Despite calculations and legislative efforts to curb pollutants, we have yet to make a total "environmental impact statement" of the car's depletion and dispersal of nonrenewable resources, its destruction of habitat and health.

What explains this shortsighted attitude, I wonder, as I leaf through a magazine and find the Nature Conservancy endorsing General Motors? The auto company's advertisement depicts the organization's president, John Sawhill, atop a GM truck tracking bison in the wild. "People and nature can live in harmony, according to John Sawhill," says the script. "That's a goal General Motors shares."

For their "sharing," the environmental organization received $5 million handed out over five years. The Nature Conservancy's project manager tells me why. "They [GM] respected the Nature Conservancy and our nonconfrontational approach to doing business and they like doing business with us," she says. One may well wonder whether being nonconfrontational is the right approach when environmentalists deal with the biggest mobile source of pollution. But the bigger question is, What blinds this organization to the fact that it is consorting with a major annihilator of its land conservation? Nor is the Nature Conservancy alone. The practice of accepting car advertisements is widespread. Bicycling or environmental magazines that would not dream of running cigarette commercials sprinkle their magazines with glossy motor vehicles poised in the natural wonders they abuse.

Paving the Planet

"A car that makes you wish the whole world was paved with concrete," a Chevy Camaro advertisement declares. No need for wishing. It already is, and perhaps that accounts for its invisibility. Wrapping the nation in 38.4 million acres of roads and parking lots, our hard topping has as much if not more impact than the car itself. In built-up areas we devote more land to our cars than to our homes. In the wilderness we lay 370,000 miles of road on just the Forest Service's 300,000 square miles, more than a mile of road per square mile of wooded wilderness.

We have "planted" a vast asphalt monoculture since World War II, a blanket of concrete as big as Rwanda. Almost any aerial view shows massive freeways, ramps, and interchanges swaddling acres of land. The antithesis of a healthy environment, this slathering of concrete assaults. From the road slashed through a hill or gully to the coiling ribbon that rolls from sprawling house to house, the highway disrupts habitats and abets erosion. The polluting vehicle that travels its route channels a lethal runoff of antifreeze and oil of refrigerants from coolants and brake linings, plus the fallout of particulate matter, nitrogen, and the salt and dirt that slide off the impervious road into the earth.

"I saw the stuff running off the parking lot, and it made my face turn green," said one manager at Raytheon, the huge defense contractor. This manager, charged with cleaning the most toxic wastes of all—the military contaminants formerly released into waterways at some sixty defense plants across the country—was nonetheless astounded by the excretions of the automobile. Tackling the poisonous residue of the military age was nothing, the manager told an attorney from the Conservation Law Foundation. "The real challenge lies ahead in the parking lot runoff."

Driving with Blinders

Many of the environment's keenest advocates have failed to perceive this challenge. "NUCLES"—nukeless—said the license plate of one activist driving to a Tufts University environmental conference I attended. I did not see the mileage on the car's odometer, but the Maine license plate suggested that it had traveled some 100 miles from out of state to promote the very environmental causes its vehicle assaulted. Well and good the "nukeless," but what hysteria would ensue if the owners of such nuclear power plants produced a minuscule fraction of the documented toxins spewed by these cars?

The same failure to see the sabotage of the car culture emerges in the rush to create a "clean" car or a "green" car. Environmental advocates have offered the electric automobile as a safe way out. "Clean fuel" conferences, solar vehicle races, and hybrid cars hyped at green conferences abound. In the White House love fests with automakers, chief executives, and bureaucrats endorse this supposed solution. Forgetful of battles against nuclear energy's so-called clean fuel, they strive for a mythic "zero emissions" vehicle, barely heeding the counterwarning that emissions elsewhere are inevitable.

Similarly, an industry of computerized Intelligent Vehicle High-way Systems (IVHS), so-called smart cars with techno-fix electronics and dashboard devices, have poured off the drawing boards. The name for these concepts has changed to Intelligent Transportation Systems and the federal funding grown, but the motor vehicle orientation stays. Deeper environmental questions rarely sound: How could some new fuel, some tinkering with miniparts of an unbalanced transportation system, really leash this voracious consumer of land? How could they reduce its waste products? Halt its bad habits?

"It is hard to imagine or define the full scope of the automobile's impact on the American landscape or on the global environment in the 20th century," a cover article on the electric car in *Audubon* stated. "Each possibility has both environmental costs and environmental benefits," it went on neutrally. "At the heart of questions about the cars of the future is the matter of motive power, of what kind of engine will propel them: Will they be petroleum powered, as they are today? Coal fired? Hydrogen fueled? Biomass burning? Electricity driven?"

Alas, this "heart" is but one of the organs that pump poison into the system. The assessment was dead wrong. Not once did the article pause to consider the broader consequences of "personal transportation devices." It did not examine the fact that the alternate source of power for these cure-all cars—coal, in most cases—is itself a menace. It ignored the fact that, with clean or dirty fuel, the car's parts and path remain destructive. The law of the environmental age that there is no free lunch never made it to their plates.

Perhaps the myopia persists, I begin to think, because the warning signs of the damage of the auto age do not flash across the environment like the Los Angeles billboards advising motorists to blow the whistle by calling smog alerts. Or, perhaps here too the ubiquitous nature of the automobile explains its invisibility. "The sky was a crimson battlefield of spring, but London was not afraid," E. M. Forster wrote. Like the industrialized England of *Howard's End* in the early 1900s, "Her smoke mitigated the splendour, and the clouds down Oxford Street were a delicately painted ceiling, which adorned while it did not distract. She has never known the clear-cut armies of the purer air." Are we, too, the children of the auto age, so removed from nature—from "the purer air"—that we are blind?

"It's totally gray here," my niece told me on the phone from Los Angeles one afternoon during the fires from the South Central riots in 1992.

"Is it the fire or smog?" I ask.

"Who knows," she replied.

Who does know? "Who hears the fishes when they cry?" Thoreau asked more than a century ago. The mind does not absorb what the eye cannot see, the pioneer ecologist Aldo Leopold has observed. What, then, would make the issue visible? Statistics are impressive, but not sufficient. Could there be environmental emblems of the auto age to help the eye see how our planetary health and well-being are being affected? To find them, I decide to seek tangible, material instances.

Looking for Billboards

Remarkably, two of these images fall quickly in place. Bookends of our car culture, they stand at either end of the continent. The view to the east I already know. The salt heap in Portsmouth, New Hampshire, has long dominated the city's shore. Piled by the picturesque shoreline, the fifty-foot-high mound of salt for winter roads is an old landmark, a comfortable "enemy." It is so routine that one preservationist speaks with admiration about its rainbow colors, its historic vitality as "a sign of the old working waterfront." From this "historic" heap comes the 176,000 pounds of corrosive, polluting road salt spread across the Granite State's highways each year. Sprinkled on roads from the Atlantic shore up through the White Mountains, past mill and mall, to keep snowbound traffic moving, the salt siphoned off from the mound is low on the list of threats from the auto age. Still, its invasiveness may be a microcosm of even the most "benign" intrusions on the ecology.

A UPI photo introduces me to the other bookend image across the continent. Its view of the Royster facility in Tracy, California, the world's largest tire dump, shows a veritable moonscape of tire rejects. The mountain range of discarded tires dwarfs the workers tending them. While the seemingly innocuous salt symbolizes the insidious taint to the earth at ground level, the striking scenario of tire rejects is a reminder of how the supposedly harmless rolling stock of the car lords it over the heights.

The Tracy Odyssey

First, then, I head out to the Golden State to visit Tracy's lunar landscape. Driving an hour or so across the rural flatlands toward the middle of the state, I pass the dry brown hills parched save for the occasional scrub oak and eucalyptus. The bare roads brightened by yellow oleander hug the highway median. Finally, the highway verges toward my destination. On the road's barren surface, the remains of a snake consumed by a vulture look no more lifeless than the arid world around.

With 28 million junked tires, 10 percent of the nation's holdings at some 140 sites, California leads the nation. But the real Tracy, the kingdom of tiredom that greets us, seems more prosaic than the surreal phantasm that drew me here. The hillside of tires, some shredded, some simply stacked, climbs the slope ring by ring over a wide range. It is their number rather than their starkness that astounds me—and that impacts the environment.

Heaved at the rate of roughly one per vehicle each year, or 250 million tires nationwide, and predicted to reach a billion by the year 2000, such tires do damage before they even climb the mount. Spinning through the countryside, each one loses a pound of rubber every year before it gets to this final resting place. And, as the small grains rise into the sky, they filter down into our lungs and waterways.

The sites themselves also cause trouble. Sometimes the volatile mix of air and rubber kindles spontaneously; sometimes the sites attract vandals who ignite the fires, sending dark clouds of acrid black smoke to darken the sky like lava-spewing volcanoes. Tires are as inflammable as the oil from which they are made, and the worst of the 176 fires in the last two decades incinerated some 7 million tires, according to a congressional report, fouling the air of four states and polluting millions of gallons of water with zinc and heavy metals.

The height of the dump I visit has earned this site the name

"Mount Royster" for developer Chuck Royster, who envisioned turning the rubber to profit by recovering its oil. His was a common dream, and still is, despite the fact that recovering the two and a half gallons of oil locked inside each tire has so often proved impractical. The baled tires, stacked tires, slashed tires creep up the hill this day, their rusty rims and occasional crops of grass reflecting the three thousand per week—week after week—scattered or stacked after shredding and moving nowhere fast.

Would-be recyclers share the Mount Royster dream. Now a trendy recycling item, some tires have reinvented themselves, making their way into local stores as pocketbooks, briefcases, and even as a tire vest. Others have even appeared on the pages of the L. L. Bean catalog bearing such conspicuously green labels as "Deja Shoes." ("Sturdy heel counter is built from polystyrene cups, tire rubber and other recovered materials. Very little is new except the shoe—and is recyclable by the manufacturer," the catalog notes.) Jungle gyms. barrier reefs, and trash pails use them, as do hoses, exercise mats, and even feeding pens. Highway agencies have tried to coax communities to make them an additive to paving materials to give longer lives to roads. When the new highway bill, ISTEA, ruled that builders must use tire rubber to fortify roads, the mandate set off a firestorm of protest. As for the less usable elements of the tire, the lead, cadmium, and zinc remain in the sites, dormant and meaner than a junkyard dog.

For all its potential, a raveled tire is a hostile neighbor and hard to recycle. No chamber of commerce sends out engraved invitations to burn the oil-packed objects next door, since, even without igniting, they produce such known carcinogens as benzene. Settled into wetlands, they make tidy homes for mosquitoes and rodents. Packed in sealed containers from Japan, they imported the Asian tiger mosquito, an agent of disease, in what one U.S. environmentalist called "a splendid mobile pram." Typically, the tires from Tracy's Ripleyesque dump were no black gold but helped bankrupt CMS, the company that attempted to turn them into useful energy. "You can't bury 'em. You can't put 'em in the water. No one will steal them. They're just there," says Tom Sheldon, who worked at CMS, Mount Royster's neighboring tire dump.

The "Airport Incident"

"It burns like lava," Santa Rosa district attorney Jeffrey Holtzman, a few hours north of Tracy, describes the tires that caused the so-called airport incident in his town. "You have the simmering cauldron of fires. You can minimize but not eliminate the fire danger," says the attorney, who heads the environmental and consumer fraud division of his county. Holtzman makes his assessment from the damage done by an infinitely smaller number of tires than Mount Royster's. In 1993, 20,000 of them caught fire and, in a thirty-hour blaze, left a heap of black pollutants and a mountain of unresolved legal procedures in Holtzman's office.

Located near the city's airport in Sonoma County, the illegal pile caught fire, clouding the air with a smelly black cloud. Health warnings alerted the community, sending the elderly inside and children home from school. The Red Cross set up emergency shelters in a veterans' hall for refugees from a nearby trailer park. And, as the fire persisted, threatening to ignite a mound of half a million more tires on the same seventeen-acre site, firefighters shot foam and hydrocarbons to stop the flames—the same materials used to extinguish a tanker or oil refinery blaze. Other crews worked bulldozers, constructed catch basins on the edge of the property, and built ditches to catch the runoff. Most of the chemicals used to control the blaze flushed into a nearby creek, while the 15,000-foot black plume of burning hydrocarbons and other hazardous chemicals rose. "An alphabet soup of chemicals," said the chief of the Northern Sonoma County Air Pollution Control District as the greasy black rain settled on the homes and fields of what the billboards labeled "Sonoma County: America's Agricultural Heritage."

Days later, as the fallout continued, a dozen tank trucks siphoned off contaminated water laced with zinc and oil from the tributary of the Russian River that provides drinking water for Marin's and Sonoma's citizens and for their famous wineries, then trucked the toxic runoff away for disposal. The direct cost of the cleanup of the fire's debris, plus disposal of the ash and water used to fight it, neared a million dollars. It generated criminal charges against Round To It Recycle, the storage company that, nomenclature notwithstanding, never did get around to tidying up their dump. The punishment was ninety days in jail and a two-thousand-dollar fine for the million-dollar blaze that, their lawyers insisted, left the town "unscathed."

"Unscathed" is of course a relative word. For the same potential exists in dozens of sites around the state from the 28 million tires in legal sites identified by officials and from more in illegal ones. Earlier in the year of my visit renegade fires figured in the scare following the discovery of gasoline contamination of sewer lines and a blaze in a tire dump in San Luis Obispo; another official suggested that the continuing threat in Oakland would be "an inferno worse than the Oakland Hills fire." Mere weeks after the Round To It Recycle blaze, a Phoenix grass fire ignited a hundred thousand tires. Later a Philadelphia highway was aflame from tires. And all this from what had seemed the least menacing of the automobile's kit of parts.

Salt of the Earth

The other bookend in this environmental quest for the benign is more subject to "seeping" than "scathing." Still, the salt is flying high, wide, and prickly from the piles of Portsmouth's mountain when I return to the East Coast, and Mary Power's household is absorbing its effects. The executive secretary of the state's Coastal Zone Management can look out of her fourth-floor window at the gritty mound high above the city's historic district. "Winter mornings, there are trucks lined up for half a mile," she says. They spit their own pollutants. From her windows Power has a clear view of the salt. Heaped like snow behind a cyclone fence, it blows in the wind, chipping paint and pollutants off cars and into the environment and gusting toward her home. Power has wiped down the white dust that slips through her windows and taken a cloth to their fine grain on her furniture. She has repainted her clapboard house regularly. "We have to buy a new car every two years," she says.

The shortened life of her Snowbelt automobile (one-third the life span of vehicles in Sunbelt climates) is shared by other Granite Staters who suffer from the salt distributed from the site. The salt not only corrodes cars but also rusts out bridges and other infrastructure in the state. The megasprinkling from Portsmouth's heap, plus the bagfuls doled out by the corner store, attack not only houses and artifacts but also natural habitats. The salt runs into wells and wetlands by the road, salinizing groundwater. Its blight on trees in the Northeast and Midwest is familiar.

The sugar maple, native to New England and source of maple syrup, is the most noted casualty. But trees and native forests throughout the region have felt the impact, especially along highways. Acting in concert with acid rain, largely from coal-burning electric generators in the West, the salt used on the ice and snow causes roadside canopies of trees and vegetation to wither. Botanist Peter Del Tredici, the director of living collections at Harvard University's Arnold Arboretum, calls road salt a major factor in the destruction of trees. Attacking the fungi that nourish their roots, the salt weakens the trees. Slowly, they languish and die. "Starting in the twenties, the trees which were traditionally used have gone into decline," he says. You can see it along the Arborway built a hundred years ago, in what Del Tredici calls horse-and-buggy planting. The old varieties are now dying, and whenever botanists try to plant oaks, they have to do so three times. For all the growth in the number of America's forests, their variety has shrunk. Tree planters and landscape architects shift to salt-resistant trees like the Norway maple and the sycamore. Meanwhile, rural vegetation bears the brunt of the rain of salt, and urban street trees suffer too.

"It's not benign at all," Del Tredici demurs. "It describes a certain kind of plant community. Salt is the primary selecting force that determines what lives and what dies," he continues. Salt sterilizes the soil and makes it hospitable to weeds. "Ragweed prospers under the reign of salt," the arborist points out. In rural areas weeds displace native plants, intensifying poison ivy on highway edges and explaining the recent increase in allergies and itches in the environs of roads.

Back at the Portsmouth site, with the wind whipping off the Piscataqua River in Portsmouth's working harbor, the spilled salt that crunches underfoot spreads as I grind by the base of its minimountain. Ironically, this six-story peak of salt stands adjacent to a heap of rusted cars stacked in a junkyard. "New Hampshire's largest import and largest export," goes the local joke.

New Hampshire's highway officials, the most auto-minded in the region, call the deicing powder the foundation and salvation of the northern New England road system. Yet, concern grows about its trace amounts of zinc, cadmium, and other metal toxins, its erosion of monuments in cities, its pouring of toxic metals into the groundwater and wetlands and soil. And the cumulative ecological impact and economic injury cause disquiet.

To what purpose? some ask. And not even the Salt Institute in Virginia has found data on whether salt does lessen traffic fatalities. One study found that "the probability that the pedestrian is killed is greatest when the road surface is dry, and least when it is ice covered; when the visibility is clear, pedestrian fatality risk in a crash is twice what it is when it is snowing." In short, if reducing driving reduces fatalities, encouraging or increasing mobility by spreading salt in bad weather elevates them.

And so, as my cross-continental journey ends, my curiosity expands. If these are the little-noted side effects of the least-feared substances, what does that say of the litany of agents at the top of the heap? "A side effect," biologist Garrett Hardin has written, "is a surprise result the existence of which you will deny for as long as possible." How many such side effects—and massive ones—can we continue to deny?

A Full Pollution Package

While Americans are in denial, we have Germany to thank for a more thoughtful accounting. In the mid-1990s, researchers at the Environment and Forecasting Institute in Heidelberg pieced together a fuller portrait of car pollution and energy consumption. To do so, they divided the automobile's life into three stages: first, its manufacture; second, its use on the road; and third, its disposal. Probing each period, the scientists diagrammed the car's typical ten-year life. Taking a German middle-class car (roughly the size of an American Ford Escort), and tracing 85,000 miles of traveling, they calculated the making, operating, and discarding to do their assessment.

Step one in the Heidelberg study charted the manufacture of the automobile: what was consumed in its creation? The environmental toll in extracting and carrying raw materials to the factory and transforming them to make the motor vehicle was astonishing to those who had reckoned only the life after birth. Before the motor vehicle had even left the plant, the car-to-be had produced 29 tons of waste and 1,207 million cubic yards of polluted air, the researchers reported. In fact, virtually all of the waste of the one-ton vehicle had occurred. Nearly half of its lifetime emission of dirty air had fouled the atmosphere, and the vehicle had not yet traveled a single mile.

During step two, on the road, researchers reported that the automobile pumped another 1,330 million cubic yards of polluted air into the atmosphere and scattered 40 pounds of worn bits of road surface, tire, and brake debris on the highway. Now the dream car was ready for the automobile graveyard.

In the third and final step, when the car's useful life was over, there was still more air polluted in dumping it. At 133 million cubic yards, plus the PCBs and hydrocarbons that accompanied the burial, the car produced another package of 66 tons of carbon dioxide and 2.7 billion cubic yards of polluted air.

The scientists in Heidelberg have compiled the fullest sense yet of the life cycle damage done from the factory to the garage to the waste heap. Their calculation of the expenditure of energy and destruction of nonrenewable resources disproves the conventional figures. Especially surprising, the researchers set the environmental cost in making a new car at more than 33 percent of that expended during its driving life—the shocking equivalent of driving 35,000 miles. The environmental toll of driving the car was 60 percent of the total burden. The disposal constituted the remaining fraction, some 7 percent.

Separating the carbon dioxide produced by the car, the researchers assessed 15 tons for step one (manufacture), 45 tons for step two (driving), and 6 tons for step three (disposing), a total of 66 tons over the vehicle's lifetime to help heat up the climate and cause global warming.

Consider also that the Heidelberg study is based upon conditions in Germany, where recycling, smaller cars, and conservation reduce the numbers, compared to throwaway America. The 20 million U.S. cars discarded each year, largely without recycling, are larger, more intrusive, more toxic and often left to rot. Significantly, and destructively, in this country we ignore the environmental consequences of production. As the Germans reckon it, driving an aged automobile is salutary compared to creating a new one. Our public policy endorses replacing cars that have a lot of life left—hence encouraging the purchase of more new cars, which pollute far more in the making. By encouraging the trashing of old cars, Americans abet the auto industry more than the environment. By allowing polluters like Exxon to buy and junk timeworn cars to reduce the penalties for their oil spill, we compound the misdeed.

A Leaky Vessel

It was in 1989 that the *Exxon Valdez* slammed into a reef in Prince William Sound and burst open in Alaska's pristine waters, the most infamous discharge of oil since the spill in Santa Barbara, California, that had prompted the first Earth Day in 1970. Every season, it seems, the scene is repeated: oil barges hit sounds and marshlands, filling newspapers with the disasters done. In the notorious Alaska spill, havoc mounted and penalties for Exxon's misdeed were amassed daily. While juries have penalized the oil industry, and rightly, it is not just our freighters that do the devastation. The on-road consumption of fuel accounts for half of all petroleum consumption nationally. With two-thirds of America's petroleum going to transportation (almost four-fifths of this to motor vehicles), it is our driving. As Greenpeace advertised at the time of the trial of the *Exxon Valdez* tanker captain, "It wasn't his driving that caused the Alaskan oil spill. It was yours."

In the name of safety standards, regulators force the U.S. oil industry to buy equipment, to install simulators, and to train operators to clean the slicks. The Massachusetts Maritime Academy in Buzzards Bay houses a 2.5-million-gallon oil spill simulator to teach experts how to respond by playing out various scenarios so that they are prepared for the real thing. Crews go through their paces double time. To what avail? "If we had all the equipment in the world at *Exxon Valdez*, we might not have made more than a 10 to 20 percent difference in the amount of oil we picked up," John Gallagher, the academy's director, described the failure of containment. What can be done? a reporter asked the cleanup instructor. "Identify the location of all the churches so we can pray." Less driving would do too.

Not only our tankers fail; the whole system is a leaky vessel. The spills that hit the headlines comprise only one-fourth of the pollution, according to the National Academy of Sciences. Production itself takes another toll. The construction of the rig and the drilling process produce massive discharges of toxic, radioactive, and other pollutants. Petroleum refineries, one of the largest sources of toxic air pollutants, are twelfth on the list of 174 categories of polluters as defined by the Clean Air Act. Gas station tanks each year may leak the amount of fifty such spills.

"Certainly *Exxon Valdez* has an important implication," says Judith McDowell, an oceanographer in physical marine science at the Woods Hole Oceanographic Institute, "but in terms of petroleum hydrocarbons entering the water, surface and chronic spills are more important." Car owners dump 100 million gallons of used motor oil a year into the ground, storm sewers, or waterways; home mechanics pour 2.5 million gallons into drains and sewers each year. Seeping into the groundwater, one gallon of petroleum can contaminate a million gallons of drinking water virtually forever. Altogether, some 240 million gallons of oil are released into the environment annually from the 10.8 billion barrels a year used in U.S. transportation.

Oil digging, oil changes, oil product manufacturing, oozings from pipelines, the leaky underground oil tank where you gas up—all these everyday comings and goings of the petroleum-fueled motor vehicle pollute 40 percent of the nation's waterways. More petroleum hits the oceans from road runoff, more from the routine flushing of tankers and other oil industry practices, than from tanker spills.

The ripple effect of road wash impacts streams and ponds, lakes and rivers; it poisons the organisms of wetlands, fishes, insects, and plants, and afflicts amphibians, the frogs and salamanders in a worldwide decline. The car's nitrogen oxide contributes to the acid rain that hits the ground, washes into the threatened Chesapeake Bay, and acts as a fertilizer. The fertilizer spurs the growth of algae that not only block sunlight from bottom grasses where fish breed but rob oxygen from the water. The fish and other aquatic creatures deprived of oxygen drown. Whether the 20 million cars junked a

year or the 200 million moving ones spilling toxins into the groundwater, whether a highway gouge funneling mud into a river or the
road runoff carrying myriad suburban and urban toxins, the automobile afflicts America's already troubled waters.

Road Kill Recipe

The road is a potent invader as well as a lethal corridor. It decreases
environmental diversity. Already damaged lakes and ponds die; living
creatures and plants weaken and diminish; aquifers for drinking
water are destroyed. "Road kill" describes the uncountable animals
slain by drivers on the road. Still more animals become endangered
and extinct by road corridors when habitats are split, highways excavated, and settlement runs amuck. The Florida panther dwindles in
the state's Big Cypress Swamp as a result of Interstate 75, which cuts
through it, while "sportsmen" in off-road vehicles plead for more
parking from which to launch their brutal odyssey and wreck more
habitat. The principal cause of the death of southern Florida's endangered American crocodile is the car. *A Field Guide to Flattened Animals* even charts the multitude for macabre tourists. The California
gnatcatcher, unfortunate enough to live in the critical habitat of Laguna Greenbelt, the last undeveloped coastline in Orange County, is
menaced by planned roads.

The state of California's policies have given the tripling population
access to some 5 million acres of wildlife habitat since 1945. No
wildlife or wilderness protection can ameliorate the roads widened or
the parking lots excavated for the car. According to the Environmental Defense Fund, the greatest destruction of species occurs from this
habitat damage. "The most devastating environmental crisis of the
turn of the millennium, second only to global warming, is the destruction of wild and rural habitat—and the automobile is the main
culprit in that rout," writes Jim Armstrong, in *Orion*.

The chemical agents of highway upkeep itself add extra poisons to
their diet, and ours. The New Jersey Turnpike Authority violated its
Clean Water Act permit 4,937 times in the five years before 1991. In
Springdale, Washington, a boy scout on his way to school was
sprayed with weed insecticides used on the edges of the road. *Trans-*

portation Research News, the research bible of the Transportation Research Board, recently pondered on the proper way to keep down weeds. Lauding the power of chemicals to tidy up road edges, it mourned the threat of environmental concerns. "The outlook for highway maintenance departments is not good." Environmental considerations were interfering, wrote A. Ray Tarrer. The chemical engineering professor bemoaned the "hefty" costs caused by federal environmental regulations restraining everyday toxins. The herbicides, deicing chemicals, and underground storage tanks, all restricted for safety reasons, were causing problems in right-of-way programs to keep roads clipped, the bureaucrat fretted.

To manicure the offending roadway, three approaches were offered, he noted. There was the inexpensive way: douse the roadside vegetation with hazardous chemicals to retard and control weeds and rambling growth. Then the more expensive—cultivating, trimming, and mowing. And the still more costly—biological restraints. "Improper weed control could endanger the traveling public and the mowers themselves," he worried. Increasing the number of mowings per year, however, would drastically increase costs.

What to do? "Educate the public and promote positive opinion regarding herbicides." *Positive opinion regarding herbicides?* Did we hear that right? Talk about the killing fields.

Even without benefit of poisoners, the highway itself kills, replacing green fields and forests, consuming wetland and desert, farmland and prairie. Fast-adapting forms become bioinvaders, breeding the foreign and often malignant ecology of "weediness." An asphalt nation suffocates regional ecologies. The suburban lawn culture that follows in the highway's wake brings those "fertilizers, growth promoters, hormones, insecticides and fungicides," of Fay Weldon's *Heart of the Country,* to create so-called green deserts. The car kingdom's suburban and exurban empires are replete with other internal combustion engines to groom this turf. All those snowblowers, garden tillers, lawn mowers, and weed trimmers mutate the land into a monoculture. They also account for 10 percent of the nation's dirty air—5 percent from the lawn mower alone, the EPA reported.

"Antifreeze may save your car but it can kill the environment," a helpful hint column in the auto section addressed the homeowner.

Pets are drawn to the sweet smell and taste of antifreeze, the newspaper warned. "If dumped on the ground or into a storm sewer, the highly toxic substance can pollute water and kill plants and wildlife." Not to worry, though, the article concluded. "For most people, antifreeze can be safely disposed of by pouring it down a toilet or sink." The chain from hand to habitat has yet to penetrate.

Undermining the Global Model

Our car addiction not only hurts America, it sabotages global environmentalism. The hypocrisy of America preaching from behind the wheel cripples efforts to curtail consumption worldwide. That we, who own half the cars, produce half the automobile's carbon dioxide emissions in the world, and manufacture one-quarter the vehicles, would try to keep global populations from following our behavior is a mockery. The American dream of the freedom of the road stokes the world's fantasy, fueling the urge to add to the planet's fleet of 400-plus million motor vehicles.

"In the beginning, all the world was America," John Locke wrote in the seventeenth century. If this were literally true today, dealers in every Chinese and Indian village, in every Latin American barrio or African township, would be selling a million cars a month for every 260 million people. And well they might. A billion cars was one prediction. Add that to today's congested Third World cities dense with pollution already and the results are staggering. "Don't Go Down the U.S. Road," one activist advised delegates meeting for the first Earth Summit in Rio de Janeiro in 1992. Some chance. "Dear Friends, especially from fellow deforesting nations," the plea of Jan Lundberg, head of the Fossil Fuels Policy Action Institute, began. His invocation might have better read, "Dear carbon club members," or, more ominously, "Dear friends and fellow gamblers on the fate of the earth."

The motto for the first Earth Day in 1970 by another activist, Charles Komanoff, still applies: "The Earth Is a Closed Garage." We all live in this finite space. The tires, the salt may be the least of it; the global warming could be the most of it. In between, the pollutants accumulate. Awareness of the noxious by-products of the auto age, their downslope and downwind consequences, seep into public awareness. Pollutants may have only tiny amounts of toxicity, but cumulatively they are chilling. In *The Short History of Progress,* mathematician Norbert Wiener uttered a profound warning. "It is very well for the classical economist to assure us suavely that these changes are purely changes in degree, and that changes in degree do not vitiate historic parallels," he observed. "The difference between a medicinal dose of strychnine and a fatal one is also only one of degree."

Let's go beyond the NUCLES and put that ecoslogan on our licenses. Recall the "obvious," the air pollution; the "innocuous," the tires burned and the salt spewed. Chart the notorious, the oil slicks, and the pervasive, the road-wrapped forest and wilderness, desert and swamp. Tally myriad yet more ruinous offshoots of the car culture, chemical by chemical. One needn't be apocalyptic to think that the car more than any other human artifact or intrusion could, indeed, be the "fatal" difference.

OPPOSITE: Feel safe? For all the crash tests and safety devices lauded by automobile manufacturers, some 120 Americans die in fatal accidents every day. As the number of drivers rises and speed limits increase, the number of victims mounts. (Photo: Peter Yates. *New York Times* Pictures)

Harm to Health
and Breath

"You wouldn't buy a cheap parachute.
You wouldn't buy a cheap pacemaker.
You wouldn't buy a cheap crash helmet.
Let's discuss cars."

—advertisement for Mercedes-Benz

"When I die, I hope I go like my grandfather did, peacefully
and in his sleep. Not screaming, like the passengers in his car."

—sick joke

THE SUBJECTS IN the photo would have looked at home in an *Aliens IV* advertisement: dummy heads, corkscrew necks, android bodies. These life-sized dolls were not simulating aliens, though, but crash victims. If the subjects looked like science fiction, the script was more so. Written by General Motors along with Ford and the U.S. Department of Transportation, the test scenario called for a mock accident to jar, shatter, and maim the dummies serving as the driver and passenger stand-ins who would, one day, be impervious to such blows.

"Dummies Get Smarter for Car-Crash Tests," said the headline describing the sophisticated level of testing. Below the headline the ghoulish picture showed a pregnant dummy. The caption duly noted that the tests showed the rising safety levels of motor vehicles. Technicians who had formerly studied how much force it took to break a rib and how much "deceleration a body could stand before internal organs were torn loose" had advanced. They could now study such questions as fetal impact or "how far a foot can bend in a crushed car before the ankle snaps or the ligaments tear." The writer was positive, however: "Now that better protection of the head and torso means that more people are surviving crashes, the protection of their legs and feet has suddenly become more important." And so, the industry testers explained, their latest research agenda was to study moms-to-be.

This research is typical of the showboating that substitutes for real solutions. The dummies don't, in fact, reproduce what happens to a passenger. Dummies have no physiology, according to John H. Siegel, surgeon and trauma researcher at the New Jersey Medical School in Newark. They don't misbehave or wriggle if they're children or hold a cellular phone if they're adults. In fact, such doll-like figures have little relevance.

This is how the car manufacturers dabble on the fringes of the carnage that ranges from the roughly 2 million "merely" disabling motor vehicle injuries to the 43,000 fatalities each year. Yet, somehow our theology of life and mortality by driving seems resigned to such statistics. For all the numbers, manufacturers speak of safer cars. Safety officials talk of improvements in deaths per mile and deaths per 100,000 population. Even as driving has increased, the casualty numbers stay the same, the experts say enthusiastically. Alas, the "experts" either don't absorb or fail to record the obvious: while the percentage of maiming to miles has gone down, the actual carnage has not.

And where else do we accept some 120 deaths a day so offhandedly? Imagine a major plane crash each afternoon. Recall the sirens, the news reports, the detail, the alarm, the investigation. As I write these words, a call comes and, eerily, a friend's daughter has died in a car crash in Indianapolis. Who doesn't have such memories? I need both hands to count the accidents to friends and family: the grandfather I never got to see, killed while crossing a street; the son of a childhood companion burned to death near a turnpike tollbooth; a pedestrian advocate and friend hit by a car. Personal accidents, familial accidents, the incidents and near incidents of those near me, and always—always—the fear for those on the road. All our lives are littered with such anguish.

John D. Graham of the Injury Control Center at the Harvard School of Public Health put it dramatically in the *Annual Review of Public Health*: "At current mortality rates, a baby born today has roughly one chance in seventy of ultimately dying in a traffic crash." An engineer recorded it in military terms: during the same forty days of the Persian Gulf War in which 146 men and women were lost fighting to keep the world safe for petroleum, 4,900 people died with equal violence on our country's highways.

The car remains the single greatest killer of young people. In fact, the car deaths of adolescent males in the suburbs equal the gunshot deaths in the city. Together they make the sixteen-to-twenty-four-year-old age group the only cohort whose life expectancy hasn't increased since the turn of the century.

Stagnant Morbidity

After endless stonewalling and loss of life and limb, automakers finally responded to safety concerns. Antilock brakes, seat belts, and air bags were installed. Yet, researchers suggest that such safeguards are offset by greater driver risks—and with children, the last had lethal consequences. Thus for all the success in getting manufacturers to install such safety devices and drivers to buckle up, the 43,000 yearly death rate has stayed the same and the number of crashes scarcely dwindled.

To this day traffic accidents are the largest cause of crippling injuries to the brain and spinal cord. The trauma, the pain and suffering amount to ten to forty injuries of more or less severity per 100,000 people. And these are only the accidents that reach police reports. Two-thirds of all accidents "resulted in no reportable injury to occupants," Graham writes. Reflect on an unrecorded rear-ender with its barely noticeable bumps and nudges at the time. We walk away and declare ourselves relieved by our "escape." The operative word is "reportable." For who cannot remember the injury that surfaced two days afterward, the whiplashed neck after a chain collision, the wrenched shoulder after a crash, or the cranky back that worsened, ice packs and warm soaks notwithstanding. The hidden injuries, those soft tissue impairments not visible until six to eighteen months or more, produce an often undiagnosed chronic pain and suffering by their victims, according to those who treat them.

Not only drivers get smashed, of course. One-fifth of those 43,000 people killed each year are pedestrians and bicyclists. And the damage is done not only by private cars. When a truck driver falls asleep behind the wheel and crashes, he can take four or five people with him. The number of trucking accidents alone has reached 4,500 per year in the 1990s, killing 5,200 people, nine out of ten in cars or on foot. Crashes caused by blind spots on trucks are numerous. The fatigue of underregulated, overworked truckers was the subject of a *Washington Monthly* report. The magazine called the traumas "Road Kill." Clearly, an autopsy is in order.

Police do an autopsy of sorts. "Vehicle autopsy" is the way police assess the damage when something goes awry but they can't find the precise cause. Some vehicles, like the increasing number of light trucks and sport-utility vehicles, remain exempt from safety requirements. One-quarter of the driving fleet now consists of these more dangerous vans, minivans, pickup trucks, and four-wheel-drive vehicles, in which the center of gravity is higher and the effectiveness of earlier safety hardware unknown. Experts try to keep up with these safety issues. The Center for Auto Safety looks for the mechanical causes of accidents. Ralph Nader's Public Citizen crusades against delinquent automobiles. The media pay attention. Cars are recalled, and back they go to the manufacturers. Still, the accidents never cease, speed limits are raised, and as the number of vehicles on the road grows year by year, so do the accidents. Iron out every kink in every car, kick every tire, and road kill would continue with ever more cars.

Personalizing the Problem

Instead of flaying the car, or the excessive amount of travel forced on us by an auto-dependent society, we do a behavioral autopsy: we criticize the way we drive. "Cars don't cause accidents," as the saying goes; "drivers do." Bad driving or bad drivers should take the rap, to be sure. Yet, the conditions that spark bad driving may he partially car induced. The Union of Concerned Scientists cautions that high carbon monoxide concentrations on crowded roads can restrict oxygen flow to the brains of drivers sitting in traffic, potentially impairing their performance. Exposure to congestion incites behavioral and physiological reactions.

Exiting from the grim arterial, devoid of nature and demanding alertness to fast motion or no motion alike, the unhinged driver lands at the public port of call—the parking space. There, beside the meter, the parking brawl replaces the street fight or playground battle of the past. On many streets screaming drivers stage a weekly drama. The swearing, car-slapping, fist-waving uproar over parking shatters the air. And where else does one see such rage? On the road, of course, where the common hand signals for left and right turns have been supplanted by the gesture for "up yours." The competition to get away from the stoplight first, to get there sooner, to ease the headache of the horn mounts; the frustration of traffic thrombosis, gridlock, the annoyance of stop-and-go driving heads from home to office, office to home.

If brawls and tantrums don't make it to the research labs, at least the largest contributor to the nation's noise level should. When I ask a spokesman for the National Safety Council about the automobile's noise disturbances, he launches into a discussion of the pros and cons of cushioning the sound. It soon becomes apparent that he is not talking about shielding the neighborhood from the automobile, but about soundproofing the car's interior to benefit the driver within. This response would be incredible if it were not typical of the invisibility of human damage from our car-centered society.

At the least, however, the sound of the automobile—from horns to screeching brakes to just plain traffic—has earned the term "noise pollution." In animals, such noise pollution alters the pattern of activities, raises the production of stress hormones, and, in some species, depresses reproduction rates. In humans, the "din of inquiety," as 1930s planners put it, and freeway gridlock join a host of effects that are the corollary of stress: blood vessels constrict, blood pressure rises, pulse and breathing rates mount, extra fats siphon off into the bloodstream, and the blood's magnesium level falls. Raymond Novaco of the School of Social Ecology at the University of California, Irvine, among others, has reported that freeway gridlock can increase blood pressure and intensify negative feelings, anxiety, and irritability. It can lead to more sick days, lower productivity, and increased employee turnover.

"Speed kills." Safety experts have made the phrase a byword. But in 1995 the U.S. Congress, flushed with the victory of less-government slogans, raised the speed limit, increasing the risk for more accidents. As the foot-down frenzy continues, we lose more lives and increase pollution from more fuel burned per mile. According to National Safety Council statistics, rural drivers on open roads are already involved in two and a half times the fatal accidents of slower start-and-stop city drivers. Bumper stickers tell us to "drive defensively." In an individualistic society, it's up to us. "Behavior may be up to a thousandfold more risk-determining than the car itself, and only about a twentieth of crashes do not involve driver factors," energy expert Amory Lovins concurs. Easily said, but a society that offers no other form of mobility must share the blame.

And where else but behind the wheel is inattention so fatal? What other momentary distraction becomes a crime with such lethal consequences? A bad day at work, a bad night at home, the slights and sufferings of existence—or the reverse, their joys—preoccupy the brain. Be it ecstasy or hardship, such reactions to daily life are dangerous behind the wheel. Trapped in traffic, or bored by the vacant highway, we jiggle cellular phones or flip through tapes in our mobile nests. The children squabble. A companion annoys or engages us. We turn around. We look or talk. And why not?

Why not? Because inattention ranks eleventh on the National Highway Traffic Safety Administration's list of causes for fatal accidents. For the truly "defensive" driver, the car is no agent of freedom then, but a constricting test of concentration. On the road we forfeit the otherwise forgivable right to muse, to fantasize, to fight—to live.

The car culture romanticizes recklessness and risk, and the car's heft and speed allow it. The highway exists as raceway in car advertising, pop music, fiction, film. In the fifties, it was Jack Kerouac's *On the Road*; in the seventies, *American Graffiti*; and in the nineties, Michael Douglas's *Falling Down*. The romanticizing media make safety last. Add the machismo of driving and the tedium of the road, and you have a brew as deadly as alcohol. Add real alcohol, and you have the estimated 18,000 people killed by drunk drivers each year. For all the success of Mothers Against Drunk Driving in making "designated driver" a byword, the menace worsens.

The car is a weapon for homicides and suicides. "Suicide alley" was coined not just for dangerous corners; it also indicates the deliberate act of the driver, absorbing the message of motorized power and the highway. Psychologists assign a proportion of car crashes to the category of suicides. Statisticians can't define the reason for the crash in which a car hits a pole or tumbles into a gully. We have anecdotal evidence and intuition, however. Even that icon of stability, Barbara Bush, shocked Americans when she wrote of her temptation to fly off the road or smash another car during a period of depression.

A Sedentary Station

Forget these catastrophes; lives spent behind the wheel diminish our physical well-being. The poor posture framed by the shape of the car seat and the time spent behind the wheel undermine fitness and sound bodies. Workstation ergonomics has become a field for worry—and for workers' compensation. In the standards of the Occupational and Safety Health Administration, job-related afflictions from driving are listed as a factor under repetitive motion injuries. Those who make their living selling or trucking or commuting on ten-to-twelve-hour-a-week drives can attest to that. Truck drivers, for one, get compensation for such driving-related injuries. While cases of carpal tunnel syndrome have made the computer the villain in repetitive motion injuries, the car becomes equally taxing over time. Try sitting with hands outstretched, legs shooting outward, back vibrating, body sinking into seats with misplaced wedges and one-size-fits-all headrests. Not only does the mishap of banging into a pothole cause injury to passengers, but the ordinary ride takes its toll. The constant, "unperceived" low-level vibration causes muscular and skeletal damage. Out of synch with the natural vibration of the human body, the resonance of the car and its occupants leads to pain and eventual damage.

Consider the seat's safety tilt to protect the neck by thrusting the head forward. Thus consigned, the long-term driver or rider has assumed a posture that can cause injuries as painful over the long run as a crash in the short term. The angle of the bucket seat in a sporty vehicle has replaced the upright bench recommended by orthopedists, adding to the distress. To secure a racy look, car makers wedge the driver into an even more stretched posture, extending the hips and legs to reach the gas pedal. But even perfect alignment in the long and static pose represented by ten to twelve thousand miles a year behind the wheel results in mechanical loading that in time yields pain and physical impairment. With muscles tense, posture sedentary, head angled, wheel clenched, driving exacerbates the chronic conditions of slipped discs, hips out of joint, and hand and shoulder problems. "Motorists' spine" and "drivers' thigh" entered the vocabulary two decades ago. The mileage grows and with it the maladies.

As we drive more, we walk less. And our highway-oriented public policy reinforces this sedentary lifestyle. Streets for cars are shoveled. Sidewalks for walkers are unplowed, forcing pedestrians to slip on icy surfaces or share the plowed road with motor vehicles. Streets are wide, and pedestrian lights too short to allow crossing easily and safely. Shopping malls, the quintessential icon of the auto age, are so disconnected that walking from home is impossible. The end of the ambulatory age makes us car potatoes. To compensate, we buy treadmills. We seek out health club bicycles to work off the fat we accumulate sitting in our cars and offices; we pace off miles on our StairMasters or treadmills to avoid the unpleasantness of competing with cars for road space outside. With one-third of all Americans carrying extra pounds, according to the Institute of Medicine, our total girth has risen 8 percent in less than a generation. It is scarcely coincidence that the most car-bound, most sedentary populace on the planet is also the pudgiest.

Driving every which way is not the singular cause of out-of-shape America. Nonetheless, the danger has become obvious to health professionals, many of whom credit obesity, increased incidences of cardiovascular disease, diabetes, hypertension, stroke, and some forms of cancer to forfeiting a trip on foot for the wheel. A Brown University study estimated that we could reduce the $50 billion spent each year on heart disease if every sedentary American walked an hour a day.

Collisions producing chronic back pain are only one penalty on human health and breath. The environmental ills spelled out previously are obviously human ills as well. The ground level ozone that harms the environment is a hazard to human beings. The water polluted by road runoff threatens man and woman as well as beast and tree. "The Plain Truth About Car Covers—and Why You Should Use Them," advertises one catalog. "You don't have to own a 300SL Gullwing to use a car cover," it goes on. "Park any car outside and the effects of dust, pollen, bird droppings, acid-rain, snow, pollutants and relentless sun will eventually damage paint and chrome." Never mind paint and chrome. How about flesh and breath?

Unfit Air

"Chronically health-conscious, the upwardly mobile residents of West LA eat their high-fiber breakfasts and pound the center strip of San Vicente Boulevard with their Nikes," a tourist guidebook notes, and "then, with little sense of irony, shower and head for work on the 405 Freeway, an artery hopelessly clogged with the metal platelets of automotive congestion." When University of California scientists did postmortems on 100 seemingly healthy young accident victims in the region, they found that 80 percent had "serious lung abnormalities" and 27 percent "severe lesions on their lungs."

"Don't underrate the improvement in air quality," Mary White of the Centers for Disease Control and Prevention insists, "given the level of development we enjoy. . . ." Don't ignore the reduction in carbon monoxide given the vehicle miles traveled. Appreciate the "mere" 43,000 accident fatalities, given our extra driving, I have heard otherwise humane human beings utter elsewhere. The givens are less than unacceptable. The apologia does not lessen the health risk. Consistently, the studies show that cars have improved, and consistently, despite improvement, studies show that one-third to one-half of us are still breathing air the federal government labels unfit.

As we jog, walk, bike, or drive we still inhale smog-formed chemicals. On sunny days the chemicals from our tailpipes and industrial plants raise ground level ozone concentrations beyond safe limits. On smoggy or even "normal" days, jogger advisories alternate with cautions to the elderly and young not to breathe deeply. Restaurants in Los Angeles ban smoking at dinner, then send their patrons home in traffic to breathe the worst air in America. While the cigarette wrapper bears a warning, the cars that speed us to illness and mortality are unadorned. The Environmental Exchange, a Washington, D.C., coalition, expressed it this way: "Air pollution doesn't produce dramatic pictures of oil-soaked ducks and dead fish, but it actually causes a thousand times more harm to humans and to nature than the largest oil spill." How do the auto companies differ from the tobacco industry? For "smoking" substitute "driving," and you could apply the surgeon general's sticker—"Driving Causes Lung Cancer, Heart Disease, Emphysema, and May Complicate Pregnancy"—on the windshield.

Scientific studies continue to link the ongoing failure to meet federal ozone standards to visits to hospital emergency rooms for asthma and other respiratory problems. Wheezing, coughing, and panting, healthy adults and exercising children show signs of lung damage from tailpipe emissions. Some 54 million Americans live in counties that do not meet at least one national air quality standard. As the number of people with asthma has grown, the American Lung

Association has declared that 100 million Americans live in areas where ground level ozone concentrations regularly exceed federal guidelines. And, living in places with unhealthy levels of smog, some 30,000 people a year die from respiratory illnesses stemming from the car's airborne toxins, which are also implicated in some 120,000 premature deaths.

Simply put, "cars have bad breath," as one environmental biologist observed. The airborne emissions are deadly, Charles Levy of Boston University goes on to say. "The agencies looking at studies of toxins, many on animals, cite acute toxicities—lungs, respiratory, eyes, nasal passages." Such chronic poisons ingested through the lungs and penetrating into the body through the respiratory system, or even through the skin, hit the stomach and bloodstream. Together, they interact, increasing the probability of disease years down the road—cancer, lung diseases like asthma and bronchitis, possibly cardiovascular conditions. "Certainly when there's a smog dome over L.A. and the air is dangerous, people with heart conditions, older people, people doing heavy work show symptoms. Over the long term there's a chronic toxicity," Levy says.

The evidence is omnipresent, from the brown haze of wintertime Denver to the gray of New England summers. As the 1990s have progressed, evidence has accumulated that the EPA standards are too low. "Even in cities whose air quality meets federal standards, air pollution may contribute to death rates from lung cancer and cardiopulmonary disease," the *New England Journal of Medicine* has declared. "Health effects of smog: Worse than thought." Beyond that, even the less visible particles are far more lethal than supposed. Particulates of less than ten microns (PM10) rank side by side with the more studied larger particles in new EPA labors.

Even as our reluctance to curb pollution rises and "live-free-or-die" drivers press for the freedom to pollute, heavier cars contribute to the damage. By buying more muscle cars, vans, and recreational vehicles, by adding more mileage through highway-based sprawl, by spewing diesel fuel from the trucks to serve these widespread communities, we exacerbate the blitz on human health. And as the auto age advances into a new millennium, the phrase "healthy limits" becomes even more beyond our means.

Life and Breath Besieged

"Gasp!" said an advertisement in *Earth Journal*. "What can you do when high pollution days interfere with your fitness schedule?" The magazine had the answer. "Breathe easier with Greenscreen, a carbon-filtered sports mask you can wear to filter out lead, carbon monoxide, sulfur monoxide, dust, pollen and other nasty elements." You could even look chic, it seems; the model in the ad peered out from under a Greenscreen mask available in three styles.

Levy, the bearded textbook writer who abandoned his proverbial professor's pipe to clear his personal air, compares tailpipe discharges to those of smoking. "Still up there," he describes the rates. Alike, says Levy, "the free radicals from cigarette smoke and car engines, those attackers of the immune system, are ready to detonate." One more dose and they can interact in synergistic ways, activating a potentially deadly disease in susceptible individuals. All these pollutants are mutagenic, causing changes in DNA, the cells' blueprint, passed on to the next generation.

Polluted air on the street isn't all, of course. The thinning of the ozone layer of the upper atmosphere caused by CFCs has caused scientists to sound the alarm and industry to reduce their use. It has propelled the government to send "UV (ultraviolet) alerts" to clear beaches and drugstore counters to stock up on number 30 sunscreen lotion. Scientists have labeled the rays of ultraviolet light responsible for a multitude of ecological impacts and health effects, including skin cancer and cataracts in humans. "An epidemic of skin cancer," Peyton E. Weary, a dermatologist and past president of the National Association of Physicians for the Environment, calls the 1 million new cases reported in the United States each year. A national emergency undeclared, he says. Within a decade, our car air conditioners will still account for the majority of CFCs in this country, according to the EPA. One current substitute, HCFCs, is not sufficiently studied and might even add to the problem.

It is a common predicament. As additives and new products emerge to make the automobile a good environmental citizen, so do by-product problems. "New and improved" is not what it used to be. Yearly, it seems, "advanced" products enter the market and in short order are enrolled on the list of toxic suspects. No sooner had manufacturers signed on to oxygenated gas when complaints of nausea in passengers popped up in Alaska and elsewhere. The additive methyl tert-butyl ether (MTBE) was the villain. Scientists suspected that it caused the dizziness and stomach distress, but the jury is still out. As for the dangers in other unknown pollutants, their time may come.

Fuel itself has become more polluting, the EPA admits. As lead was being phased out, the formulas that compensated for the octane loss made gasoline more likely to release smog-forming volatile organic compounds (VOC) into the air. "If you just solve the problem by technical means or by fuel, you're sometimes not going to solve the problem," says Dan Greenbaum, head of Health Effects. The director of the National Center for Environmental Health, Richard J. Jackson, also worries about the synergistic effects of one chemical on another, of quantities unleashed. "There is no such thing as a safe auto fuel," he concludes. "It's assessing the least risk."

Present in large doses, mixed with unexamined chemicals, even the seemingly benign can become the malign, as we have seen. Multiply the new chemicals and combinations by their vast application in 200 million motor vehicles and who knows? What better way to experiment with spreading a pollutant than to run it through our tailpipes and drive every which way, Jackson observes sardonically. When every solution is a 200-million-vehicle solution, a 2-trillion-mile solution, the health impact becomes formidable. In the end a safe drive, like a clean car, is not only an oxymoron but a dangerous one.

In the seamless web of nature, the harm to habitat is the harm to human health. Fouling the earth and fouling its inhabitants are inseparable. Here at the so-called top of the food chain, the water we drink, the food we eat, the air we breathe, the entire way we live are corrupted by a toxic artifact. The car, its pollutants, its highways, its trips from shop to shop have a subtle but compound effect. We cannot define the threshold of human health. We play at the margin of safety for our persons—our planet. And where, what, and how much we drive heightens these personal and global perils.

OPPOSITE: Roads like the Century Freeway near Los Angeles don't come cheap. Construction and maintenance, as well as the personal and public toll of driving, make the car a pricey necessity in an automobile-dependent society. (Photo: Eric D. Raper. Associated Press)

The Cost of the Car Culture

"Those most married to the freedom of four wheels might be surprised to know just how big a chunk of income they are sinking into that hunk of metal."
—chairman of the Los Angeles County
Metropolitan Transit Authority

"We buy our cars to go to work and then we work to buy our cars."
—Elliott Sclar

WHAT DOES IT cost to turn the key? What does it cost when Americans step on the pedal of the one, two, or three cars in their driveways? How do you tally the price of revving up our 200 million motor vehicles?

The spring sky minted a bright blue shone through the picture windows of the Kennedy Library as Douglas Foy turned to an assembly on "Shaping the Accessible Region" and asked the city and transportation planners the critical question: "Who knows what it cost you to get here?"

The director of the Conservation Law Foundation, who bikes twenty miles to and from work each day, Foy faced his audience of local seers and hastened to answer it himself. "I would defy anyone in this room to tell me what it costs to drive to this spot. Or take the train to this spot. Or fly here and drive to this spot—or however you got here."

The "here," a trip to the conference overlooking South Boston's waters, offered two possibilities to the traveler. On the one hand, those listening to Foy's speech, "The Green Alternative," might have driven down the notoriously congested Southeast Expressway out of the city, pivoted down and around a confusing boulevard, taken a left and then a right, woven to the site, parked by the asphalt-wrapped library building, and walked the last twenty-five yards or so. On the other hand, they might have taken public transit and arrived by a series of transfers—light-rail to heavy-rail to bus. Either route was anything but easy or "accessible."

So what is the dollar expenditure for this tortuous trip? "It is impossible to determine the true price or cost of that accessibility," Foy answered.

"This," the environmental lawyer declared, waving a dollar bill as the television cameras recorded the event, "is 'the green alternative.' If we don't get the price right and if we don't start charging people the right cost for our transportation, we will never solve the environmental problem."

In Boston, a transit-linked, walking city, the car's costs are as prohibitive as elsewhere. The Conservation Law Foundation's economic study *Road Kill*, prepared by Apogee Associates, assessed an average cost of eighty-seven cents a mile for driving in the city's rush hour. Insurance fees alone came to a dollar per gallon of gas. Three billion dollars went to park commuters' 200,000 vehicles. Automobile fees and taxes covered less than half of the government's costs, and the rest was hidden. Elsewhere, the rate ranges from $1.15 to $2 a mile.

"But we don't want to know that when we pull in to the pump. We don't want to make the equation," Foy said. In terms of equity, he went on, "a poor Roxbury mother taking mass transit at rush hour pays for 80 percent of her costs a few miles in the inner city. A stockbroker driving his BMW to the suburbs at that peak congestion period pays only 20 percent."

"Who's subsidizing whom?" he asked.

That's "tacit car welfare," Foy concluded.

The Highway Bill

About the time that Foy was questioning the costs, Los Angeles, the mecca of the motorcar, was opening the most expensive freeway in the history of the United States. At $2.2 billion, the seventeen-mile Century Freeway was the costliest ever, a high in any Guinness book of roadway records. Even Angelenos wired to the region's wraparound highways found its scale awesome. The freeway's five stacked levels of highway, seven miles of ramps, two miles of tunnels, and eleven bridges span acres east and west from the airport. One of the freeway's interchanges loops so high that it achieves a roller-coaster high of seven stories.

The Century Freeway, ironically heralded for the Green rail line down its center, racked up steep costs in both mitigation fees to neighbors and construction costs. It took Caltrans, the state's department of transportation, thirty-five years in planning and almost $130 million a mile in building costs to polish off the road and its high-tech fixes: from the car pool lanes and rail to the electronic bells and whistles used to control the flow of an expected quarter of a million vehicles a day, plus compensation to the 25,000 residents uprooted from its path. A once-in-a-century event. Or so officials said.

If the Century Freeway was state of the art, it did seem a lost and dying one. With a scant 114 miles left to finish the nation's 42,500-mile interstate system, the freeway was the century's last, officials said, a summit in the high-priced history of Southern California's highway construction. That construction had cost $1 million a mile in the 1940s, had reached $30 to $40 million a mile in the 1960s, and, by the time the Century opened, had peaked at $130 million. A "dinosaur," said critics.

Or was it? Whatever you call this pricey sweep of Tarmac, the graph of costs per mile is still rising. That same year, 1994, the road work touted by the secretary of transportation for a National Highway System program cited 156,000 miles of "improvements." Tinkering with the existing system, widening and extending roads, carried a price tag of $6.6 billion. Add that to $93 billion in overall federal, state, and local spending during the year. At the least, one thing was sure: we have hardly ceased running up a bill to hard top the nation. To traffic engineers this means happy motoring. To the cost conscious it means bloated Caltrans-style budgets.

"And my father when he died gave me a highway system that was fully paid for. He did not give me debt," I had heard Senator Bob Kerrey of Nebraska intone on the campaign trail. "No debt?" Senator Kerrey's math was faulty in the extreme, but his failure to calculate the price tag of the car culture was typical. Roads cost as much as the mortgage on a house, more than our groceries. Was that the wisest gift from father to son? Maybe he should have given him a transit system.

Like the pork barrel road projects that legislators cart home—and budget cutters ignore—the financial freedom of the road is as mythic as the freedom of a driver stuck in traffic. While critics tar "subsidized" rail and paste the prefix "money losing" on mass transit, we rarely consider the deficit-breeding, subsidized automobile. Kerrey's words, like the nation's mind-set, reflect our unawareness of even the most conspicuous public obligations to uphold the automobile's sway. The "*free*way" is as much an oxymoron as the "*express*way" at rush hour.

The Sound of Money

The cash register is ringing ever louder across the country. From the $1 billion Corridor H in rural West Virginia, at $10 million a mile, to the $10 billion Central Artery in dense Boston, at $2 billion a mile, with lesser sums of a million or two here and there for reconstruction and widening, the road gong sounds at $30 million a mile for new roads. Highway department shelves bulge with plans to build them, filling in the linkages from the faded highway maps of times past. With the interstate system almost finished, the federal government is ushering in twenty-one new "high-priority corridors" and seven beltways. "Old think," says the Surface Transportation Policy Project. New think, too, unfortunately.

Beyond this new construction, we're also looking at reconstruction. The burden goes beyond laying new asphalt; it extends to maintaining the old, at $200,000 to $400,000 a mile simply to repave. Even as Federal Highway Administrator Rodney Slater spoke of the need "to finish up the last bits and pieces" of the interstate system, as if trying to win a clean plate contest, the nation's old road system was unraveling. Our infrastructure is failing faster than our capacity to restore it. The need to reconstruct our 576,000 highway bridges, resurface our aging interstates, and maintain some 4 million miles of roads across the continent is rising. Meanwhile, skimping on maintenance takes a toll. Every year we fall $17 billion short in needed road repairs, and the wear and tear from this neglect will mean more in delayed maintenance. As we build new roads and slight older ones, the gap grows. And with it the debt to future generations to maintain these roads and support the traffic they breed.

The futility of easing congestion is scientific truth as well as popular truism. Anthony Downs's studies of convergence and the mathematics of Braess's paradox have proved that expanding highway capacity slows traffic. Yet, we are funding this cycle. Generated traffic, the congestion generated by widening roads, adds not only to our personal discomfort but increases the financial load of lost productivity. As we build, we pay—and push the debt down the road still higher.

Joe Vranich, former head of the High-Speed Rail Association, put it this way: "We 'invest' in airports. We 'invest' in highways. But we 'subsidize' trains." Motor vehicles and trucks get a free road. Airports are underwritten by the government. Barges glide through waterways built by the Corps of Engineers. Rail mostly pays its way and begs for the rest. Subsidies and biases have created a lopsided economic policy. Elmer Johnson, a former General Motors vice president who left the corporate driver's seat, cites figures parallel to Foy's in a report for the Urban Transportation Project. "The suburban commuter pays only 25 percent of the costs of travel to the central district by car." Private industry's trucks, which do twenty times as much damage to roads as cars, pay only 40 percent of their way.

Sticker Shock

What, then, is the burden on the sticker price of driving? What does it cost per vehicle for the user and society?

The charge is twofold, internal costs and external ones. Simply put, economists figure an average of $6,000 in internal, or user, costs and another $3,000 to $5,000 for the external, or social, costs per car per year borne by the public.

The first is what we pay out of our own pocketbooks. Every year, we hand out $6,000 to own and operate a two-year-old vehicle, to pay for its gas, parking, tires, depreciation, maintenance, and insurance, plus tolls for the administering, building, repairing, and operating of roads. Direct costs are visible. We open our wallets and pull out more for our car dealers, mechanics, and gas stations than for our grocers. According to the U.S. Bureau of Labor Statistics, the average American household allots almost a fifth of its budget for the car and its related costs. With 1.77 cars per household, we're spending 6 percent more on the car than on income tax, making the car second only to the home in the family budget and close behind our mortgage fees. That's only the visible half.

The second, the external costs, could be more. This second sum, $3,000–5,000 (but as much as $9,400 by some estimates), reflects the indirect costs of market and nonmarket expenditures. Things we rarely consider bear a dollar sign: from parking facilities to police protection, from land consumed in sprawl to registry operations, environmental damage to uncompensated accidents. These intangibles weigh us down as we pay for the car's share of municipal and state taxes and traffic congestion. According to one estimate, exactions from U.S. cars and trucks carry three-quarters of a trillion dollars in hidden costs each year. Nationally, that's thirty-five cents a mile, in dense urban zones up to a dollar and a half.

Who pays for this? Such costs come not just from our own purses. For all the heated arguments about the gas tax (at its lowest in seventy-five years), it covers only 60 percent of our road costs. Other sources go unweighed. Though we dispense over $16-plus billion a year to the Federal Highway Trust Fund from our gas taxes and other user fees, it isn't enough. Not nearly enough. The rest comes from general taxes, with money from property, sales and sometimes gas taxes used to fund local roads. By hiding roadway costs in general taxes, property taxes, and sales taxes, our transportation accounting cloaks the price and promotes demand.

The whole economy suffers from the automobile's disproportionate and unseen costs. The Automobile Club of Southern California assesses the cost of driving a relatively new car fifteen thousand miles a year in Los Angeles at the national high of $7,127. Examined closely, however, that is only a fraction of the total expense. Parking given to downtown employees, for one example, is an eleven-cents-a-mile subsidy to the driver, sixteen times more than the federal gasoline tax he or she pays for the commute. In the four decades prior to 1990, installment debt multiplied by twelve times—40 percent of which goes to finance the automobile. No wonder General Motors Acceptance Corporation (GMAC) is the largest consumer finance institution in the world. And we haven't touched such pricey corollaries as cellular phones to save time spent behind the wheel.

In the Tick of Time

Save time? We actually lose it. The costs of our 8 billion hours a year stuck in traffic range from $43 billion, according to the Federal Highway Administration, to $168 billion in lost productivity estimated by other economists. According to Chicago's Metropolitan Planning Council, $2 billion a year of this comes from Chicago alone. By the turn of the century, one estimate cites the national total at $400 billion a year.

Sitting stuck in traffic actually accounts for less than one-quarter of the time spent in tending the vehicle that serves us. "The typical

American male devotes more than 1600 hours a year to his car," Ivan Illich wrote in *Energy and Equity* two decades ago, when Americans put in less mileage. "He sits in it while it goes and while it is idling. He parks it and searches for it. He earns the money to put down on it and to meet the monthly installments. He works to pay for petrol, tolls, insurance, taxes, and traffic tickets. He spends four out of his sixteen waking hours on the road or gathering his resources for it.

"And this figure," Illich went on, "does not take into account the time consumed by other activities dictated by transport; time spent in hospitals, traffic courts, and garages: time spent watching automobile commercials or attending consumer meetings to improve the quality of the next buy. The model American puts in 16,000 hours to get 7500 miles; less than 5 miles per hour."

Today those hours have risen and so has the car's price. The average car buyer must spend half a year's salary for an automobile. Auto industry figures tell us that the purchaser making a median $36,000 a year spends half a year to pay for a car. Over the long haul a "twenty-something" entering the workforce will spend four years of his or her life behind the wheel driving to the office. Like it or not, every family is in the transportation business, expending $9,000 to $11,000 in internal and external costs a year to drive each of their one, two, or three cars an average of ten to twelve thousand miles apiece.

Discussing our predicament, one transportation historian put it more positively. "We have built a transportation system, a great one, you know," he observed in 1992, "only the entry fee is $10,000." That fee has now almost doubled. And even this "entry fee," the money handed to the "gatekeeper," the car dealer, provides mere access to the "great system." Whether one pays a gate fee of a whopping $18,000 to $20,000 for a car hot off the assembly line or a more modest sum for a secondhand vehicle, the car's purchase just lets the buyer join the fray. For the automobile's price tag would be a ticket to nowhere without that wide array of fees, the vast, sometimes hidden schedule of personal, governmental, architectural, and environmental exactions already discussed.

It is assumed that the two million-plus motor vehicles bought each month attest to their value or necessity. Conventional economic wisdom tells us that they profit their makers, pay their workers, and help their users, or else the numbers sold would shrink. The two industries that form the bedrock of our transportation system also form the bedrock of our—and the world's—primary industries: automobiles and oil. Six of America's ten largest industrial corporations are either oil or auto companies. According to the American Automobile Manufacturers Association, a fifth of the U.S. gross domestic product (GDP) is dependent on the auto industry, while the Big Three—General Motors, Chrysler, and Ford—employ 2.3 million Americans in more than four thousand manufacturing facilities and eighteen thousand dealerships. One out of every six U.S. workers makes a living in an auto-related industry, producing cars, oil, or highways, repairing cars, parking cars, making parts, selling parts. "Our economies are literally driven to work," writes David Morris of the Institute for Local Self-Reliance. More than 60 percent of the oil, 50 percent of the rubber, 67 percent of the iron, 20 percent of all electronics and aluminum, and 20 percent of all carpeting—the rugs beneath our gas pedals—go to the car.

If the car is at the top of the pyramid of the American economy, it may be sinking that economy. The skyrocketing figures ignore the fact that one-half of the oil and one-third the automobiles sold in the United States are imported. They ignore the social and environmental costs. They put the insurance costs that add to our debt on the positive side of the ledger and list production as a plus without citing depletion of resources and spewing of chemicals as a minus. Despite the automobile's place at the centerpiece of the American economy, despite giant highway projects that feed local economies, the carmakers devour more than they deliver.

Other Balance Sheets

Economists and environmentalists outside the industry have other calculations. Beyond the obvious costs of upkeep for our restless chariots, they try to assess the complicated indirect, or social, costs. In *The Price of Mobility: Uncovering the Hidden Costs of Transportation,* the Natural Resources Defense Council figures these costs at $1.2 to $1.6 trillion annually for passenger ground transportation, of which the bulk goes to the car. In the council's reckoning that's "greater than our total national expenditure on either education or health," more than anything but our homes. Singling out the environmental and health downsides discussed earlier, the American Lung Association computes the health effects of air pollution at $50 billion annually, and the National Safety Council reckons $176.5 billion due to motor vehicle fatalities.

When we consider what the driver doesn't pay directly, it becomes clear that municipal authorities—and thus taxpayers—are holding a very large bag. Nationally, some 70 percent of all state and local law enforcement activities are expended on traffic management issues—a giant 20 percent of state budgets going to the car. In New Jersey, typical of the suburbanized nation, motorists pay $733 million a year less in user fees like gas taxes and tolls than the state spends in building and maintaining its roads. The rest is a taxpayer subsidy extracted through nonautomobile fees like the property tax. New Jersey spends $3.2 billion on roads, while drivers pay $2.5 billion. In New York the total doesn't include estimates for the damages from traffic accidents, congestion, pollution, and noise, which are put at $23 billion a year.

We can barely quantify, much less comprehend, such abstractions. Even when we assess the total risks versus the benefits, damages versus gains, the costs seldom reflect the true expense, for economists set low numbers on such factors as ethical, cultural, or aesthetic worth. It is hard to value the full price of oil wars and crop pollution, accidents and hours in traffic, noise and land consumed; equally difficult to calculate the worth of quiet or clean water, the financial penalty of the highway's proximity, its noise, its theft of farmland. Yet, there are starting points, and ecological economists have begun to devise more holistic accountings. From mainstream number crunchers to environmental advocates, they are searching out the numbers.

Staging the Cost

On a brisk October day that made the sensibly shod visitors to the Annual Pedestrian Conference in Boulder, Colorado, long to head off to the city's walking and bike paths, I joined an assembly of alternative transportation advocates to hear a presentation on the "True Cost of the Automobile."

Jammed together in a conference room, the audience listened closely as speakers cited subsidies to auto owners and the need to recover costs. Shoulder to shoulder, they took zealous notes on the price of auto dependency as the author of the study, researcher Michael Voorhees of Boulder's transportation department, rose to break down the cost of our hypermobility. One by one, Voorhees punched out the numbers: some $158 billion spent by motorists for new and used cars; $89 billion for gas; $34 billion in tires and other parts; $20 billion in insurance; $6 billion in auto registration fees. Eyes began to glaze as his statistics showed a whopping $68 billion spent in storage and parking and "minor" millions here and there.

"Factor in the cost of the Persian Gulf War . . . our addiction to Persian Gulf oil, with all the attendant national security risks," Voorhees's voice trailed off in describing the way we defended the barrels of oil imported from the Middle East. The cost of "chaperoning our oil freighters was seven times that of [paying for] the oil itself," he was reminding us when a flash came through the window.

Unobserved, a car had crashed and caught fire just outside our window, and a police car had responded. In minutes the sound of a siren pierced the street, and a second light from a second vehicle, a fire engine, blinked. Through the curtains we watched firefighters wash down the fuming car. Steam issued from under its hood. The whoosh of hose and water sounded through the room. And, as Voorhees rattled off more numbers, another set of lights sent a red glare through the gauzy curtains.

The light flicked through Voorhees's list of the price of municipal services for the car. The damage. The exactions. Distracted, the audience shifted its glance outward as another noise resounded through the street. Minutes later, an ambulance arrived. A tow truck with three city workers pulled up in midsentence as Voorhees tallied the cost of maintaining the highway as a public utility. "The County Hospital Emergency room costs, the car wrecks—"

Finally, the spectacle outside was over. The lights stopped. The tow truck doors slammed shut. The ambulance driver and his aide pulled off. The municipal workers left. The last city employees headed back

to their cars. The police started their motors. With one last blast of
the siren, the fire engine left. The silence was stark.

"Did you stage that?" asked a spectator.

The message of men, money, and mayhem enacted through the window was both pointed and comical. The emergency had ended. But,
as someone reminded me later, it was less dire than it might have
been since the emergency was resolved without the added consequences of significant traffic congestion. In Los Angeles, it would
have taken far longer for the ambulance to arrive at rush hour and
half an hour just to get patients through traffic to an emergency
room, wasting half of what trauma surgeons call the "golden hour,"
the first essential moments for life and death after an accident.

The stage play of municipal services was only the most dramatic il-
lustration of the costs that afternoon and a fragment of America's
total. When engineer Stanley Hart broke down the costs for
Pasadena, California, for example, he found that for every dollar the
motorist provides, the city spends $8. The money goes to fixing
streets, policing them, sweeping them, installing traffic signals, and
the like. Cars alone take 40 percent of the city's police calls, 15 percent of its fire department runs, and 16 percent of its paramedic services. The same numbers, more or less, apply to the Denver and San
Francisco city budgets. In New York, "Subsidies for Traffic" breaks
down the figures similarly, with the fire department answering more
than 14,000 calls for car accidents and 8,700 for car fires—some 15
percent of all fires—which consume 5 percent of its total budget.

Counting the Real Beans

Bean by bean counter, economists have begun to try to include such
consequences in a holistic rendering. Laboring to green the GDP,
economists acknowledge that consumption carries dollar burdens in,
say, pollution as well as profits in production, that for every material
gain there is a material loss. There is, as Richard Norgaard phrased it
in a report on sustainability for the World Bank, an "intergenera-

tional equity" issue in development, a question of fairness. In the case of the automobile the inequity is that one generation makes the gains and pollutes, leaving the next to pay the debt. Spend money on manufacturing a polluting engine or a waste-generating product and the U.S. Department of Commerce registers a plus, since however money changes hands is irrelevant to its definition of material well-being. Walk instead of ride—a healthier route and a cheaper one, common sense would argue—and you deduct from the GDP.

The sense that growth's claim on natural resources bears a price tag has begun to hit the federal government as well as the environmental and anticar constituencies. "Every time a tree falls in a forest—especially if someone cuts it down—an economist somewhere should feel a twinge," *Newsweek* put it. A tree is part of our national wealth. Its loss should not go into the profit column.

In *A Wealth of Nature,* William Worster rejects the Holy Grail of technological progress, asserting that "there is such a thing as too much productivity, too much chasing after wealth." The ethical anti-consumerism of the "voluntary simplicity" movement insists that progress unleashed is an attack upon the earth, that economic development is a bombardment of resources. At the least, explorers of such belief systems ask our motorized society to record its depletions of the planet in red ink. The air-conditioning that cools us employs chlorofluorocarbons that destroy the ozone. The roads that provide mobility destroy biological corridors. From the tailpipe toxins wafting into the sky to the bits of rubber tire flaked onto the earth, all bear a negative impact. They tally a bill for health and welfare for our and future generations.

Consider the cost of the car's contribution to lung cancer, emphysema, and other respiratory and pulmonary problems and its effects on plant and animal life and ecosystems. We should at least put a price tag on the extinction of bird and beast, the befouling of drinking water, and the disruptions of dwelling places caused by the ever reaching road. In "Valuing the Health Benefits of Clean Air," the Environmental Defense Fund sets $3.7 billion as the cost of deteriorating health linked to the car's smog and particulate pollution in Southern California. The Foundation on Economic Trends records crop yield losses from car emissions at $1.9 to $4.5 billion for wheat, corn, soybeans, and peanuts. And speaking of downed trees, remember those assaults on their roots and trunks by salt and the bumps from cars parking on city streets.

Who could or would set a figure on the price of the greenhouse gas emissions of our fossil fuels? Since the carbon dioxide from the fossil fuels used in the world's cars causes 50 percent of global warming, and America's automobiles cause half of that, the question is unavoidable if agonizing: is it worth a planet to buy that bar of soap? In truth, the errands that put half the mileage on our odometers become even more appalling. Do such comparisons seem excessive or apocalyptic? In this geophysical experiment with our piece of the universe, it is at least arguable that we are making Mephistophelian deals with extinction. Can we safely deny that our actions—our driving—could have disastrous consequences?

The Foreign Model

"Do something outrageous: Drive a car today" was how the *Manchester Guardian* reacted to the Heidelberg study of the full cycle of costs in making, driving, and discarding a car: "The private car is an environmental, fiscal and social disaster which would not pass any value-for-money test." The researchers charting the car's cradle-to-grave impact summarized it monetarily as well as environmentally. "This," they wrote, "is a State subsidy equivalent to giving each car user a free pass for the whole year for all public transport, a new bike every five years and 15,000 kilometers of first-class rail travel." If this is how the Germans with their balanced transportation view it, what does that say of America? The researchers who did the study are certainly wiser about using public transportation, bike, and rail. With their better, more comfortable, safer, easier, and cleaner mass transit, their smaller cars, and superior recycling practices, both of goods and cities, the environmental consequences of their cars are far less exorbitant than our own.

"Are bicycles making Japan more competitive?" yet another international observer, Walter Hook of the Institute for Transportation and Development, asked. Yes was his response. While the Japanese walk, bike, and pay three times our gas tax, we pull mere pennies from our pockets at the pump and then subsidize the car. The Japanese pay 9 percent of their gross national product for transport; the United States pays 15 to 18 percent. Europe does better, too. By paying a truthful $5 a gallon, plus three to five times what the United States pays in visible car-based fees, the Japanese and Europeans have an awareness of costs. That consciousness makes them decrease their driving and curbs cars in cities. It encourages a more compact land use policy and hence promotes four to eight times as much public transport. The reverse obviously holds: Americans pay less for gas and little for tolls and user fees—and this freewheeling policy encourages them to use almost five times as much gas per capita as residents of European cities and ten times as much as those in typical Asian ones; to drive infinitely more, undercut mass transit, build more roads, buy more costly cars, pay more in personal and social fees, and spend more for maintenance.

In the end, America's highway-oriented system saddles the nation. In the view of economist David Aschauer of Bates College, spending on public transportation has twice the capacity to improve productivity as does highway spending. A nickel spent on mass transit carries at least twice the impact of a nickel spent on roads. A billion dollars invested in mass transit produces seven thousand more U.S. jobs than does the same amount spent on road construction. A ten-year $100 billion increase in such transit investment would enhance worker output five times as much as if made in roads. "Public transportation spending carries more potential to stimulate long-run economic growth than does highway spending," Aschauer concluded.

The pro-automobile policy that undermines public transportation also undercuts our place in the global market. "Feeble," financier Felix Rohatyn has called American infrastructure efforts. Global or local, businesses depend on the public's investment in an efficient transportation system as much as on the spending of its own private capital. Yet, the White House has still to act, focusing instead on a partnership with the Big Three to create a clean car rather than delving into shaping new ways to move people.

Furthermore, by focusing on the jobs the automobile industry contributes, we ignore those that measure its exactions. Transportation consumes one-third of all U.S. energy used annually and two-thirds of its oil, half of which is imported. Oil alone is 60 percent of the U.S. trade deficit, and automobiles and auto parts account for two-thirds of our trade deficit with Japan. Meanwhile, the cost of extracting petroleum rises as we labor to clean, find, or dig for oil reserves predicted to dwindle and become pricier on their way to exhaustion. We also must defend oil. The Cato Institute calculates the military allotment to defend Middle East oil reserves at $50 billion a year. As we add further to the national debt by importing oil, which uses 18 percent of our GDP—twice that of Japan's bikers and walkers—our driving deep-sixes the American economy.

In terms of personal use, as well as GDP, the American family spends around 20 percent of its annual income on transportation, plus hidden costs. The Japanese spend only 9 percent, despite having more expensive cars, while Europeans spend a scant 7 percent. While Americans take only 5 percent of their trips on foot, Europeans and Japanese take 20 to 50 percent of their trips on foot and garage their pricey cars. In land costs our highways often steal almost half the space in our cities, Japanese roads one-quarter. In the fifteen most congested U.S. cities alone, our car-bound transportation system adds about $7.6 billion to the price of goods. In the suburbs the motor vehicle brings the cost of sprawl.

Sprawling Calculations

The land bulldozed into asphalt is a so-called opportunity cost—a minus in the lost opportunity to use the land otherwise. To be sure, the farmland paved and the open space or city split by an arterial, sprouting a hard-topped four-leaf clover, benefit a segment of buyers and sellers. The industry supporting our million-plus housing starts a year depends on it. Yet, adding a value to the losses—from loss of community to loss of present or future use—changes the equation. This sprawling "gasphalt" nation gift of land to cars, trucks, roads, and parking lots is a disaster. Compile the highway's giant gulp of 3 million miles of road covering sixty thousand square miles, and we see the land loss we suffer. Consider the car's many small swipes of seven spaces apiece to move and park, and we see how such subsidies drain the economy. Parking, 95 percent seemingly free to the driver, is, in fact, a drain, adding more than $600 to a home and $1,200 to an apartment. For the 85 million employees given apparently free parking spaces worth $1,000 apiece, it amounts to an $85 billion lure. "It's your second home. Invest wisely," a billboard depicting an automobile advertised. Invest, we have. No other country carries our loss in property taxes from such "investments."

The 1.5 million acres of arable land lost each year to roads and sprawl also carry costs in loss of freshness, open space, and scenic values. We pay for the portage of our fruits and vegetables, trucked in from far away as fertile farm soil closer to home is despoiled by development. Grown on massive fields, more mechanized and oil-consuming than the farms once near populated marketplaces, the typical bite of food in America must travel 1,300 miles to the dinner plate. It does so on long hauls on heavy trucks, on trucks that damage the pavement at ten times the rate of cars.

Tabulating Sprawl

How, then, do we figure in the cost of sprawl? Does anyone even ask? is a better question. Rolf Schmitt, head of the Department of Transportation's data collection for the Bureau of Statistics, has done so. "I usually see panic in their eyes when I say, 'Why don't we do that old "Cost of Sprawl" study again?' " he says. This Department of Housing and Urban Development study, published in 1974, calculated compact development at 40 percent of the cost of low-density sprawl. Denser living meant less air pollution, less energy consumption, less water use, less soil erosion, and maintenance of farmland. Why figure? The 1974 equation still holds today. Sprawl costs even more twenty years later, more in pollution, more to send Americans outward, to desert the central cities and create rambling suburbs than close neighborhoods. And the reasons are clear. While the population of a city like Chicago has stayed almost static, the metropolitan area has grown 55 percent, meaning that the city must provide services for a developed area that has grown by half. Not only do developers pay less of the cost for land and facilities, but, by the simplest geometry, spanning ever greater distances means spending more money on more infrastructure—longer wires and pipes for water and sewage, drainage, and electricity—and more leapfrog development that shreds an acre for every built one.

Twenty years after the 1974 study of sprawl, an American Farmland Trust report for Loudon County, Virginia, reinforced the fact that new homes on virgin soil produce a net public cost of $700 to $2,200 a dwelling even when they are built at five units to the acre. In dollar terms, according to the Cornell Cooperative Extension of Dutchess County, New York, homeowners demand $1.12 to $1.36 for every tax dollar they give, farmers only twenty-one to forty-eight cents. Every time a company moves to the outskirts off an exit ramp, it drains settled areas, burdens new communities with buildings and transportation, and costs abandoned older cities and towns in unemployment. In their new digs employees drive twelve times as much. The cycle gets us nowhere except more time behind the wheel, more sprawl, and more costs from the lower density.

After two decades of decentralization, taxpayers pay more, far more, to scatter than to settle in tightly knit urban areas, more to heighten auto dependency through sprawl than to lessen it through close-knit settlement and infill. The meandering, outbound land patterns that replaced Main Street with mall, old housing with new, downtown office with corporate estate, ongoing institutions with fledgling ones benefit their builders. Yet, they cost their new users and drain their old ones of historic downtowns, small towns, and inner suburbs of shops and services, concentrating poverty and deconcentrating opportunity.

Forcing the Market

"Market forces at work," auto-dependent Americans shrug, and developers insist. "Is it a purely free market force," Gordon Linton of the Federal Transit Administration responds, "when a suburban jurisdiction offers a factory owner a multiyear tax abatement to build a new facility there while the U.S. government tax structure encourages him to abandon an old one?

"Is it a purely free market force when state and federal tax codes make the construction of new facilities more attractive than the rehabilitation of old ones?

"Is it a purely free market force when the very same federal government that reshapes the entire landscape with an interstate highway system dismisses urban mass transit as a matter best dealt with at the local level?" he goes on.

Is it, to add to Linton's questions, a free market when motorists escape charges for their pollution, their accidents, and other tolls on street and planet? Is it a free market when free parking, one of the major costs of driving, is handed out to employees and other privileged nonpedestrians?

Is it free choice when well-fed political action committees (PACs) and highway lobbies keep the pork barrel full and deprive the poor, the old, and carless Americans of their mobility? Or, finally, is it free choice when federal or local growth launchers favor a selected minority of landed interests and developers, burdening taxpayers? The land bears the price of their sprawl, and so do we. Sprawl is space. Space eats dollars and megadollars to shift our nation from the city to the countryside, creating buckshot suburbs and mammoth coils of arterials to connect them.

Given free turf, complimentary right-of-way, and other subsidies for the better part of the century, the road gang has expanded the highway from four lanes to eight or ten or twelve across the country. Is it a free market, or road welfare, when the government hands out ninety cents for every dollar of these extensions, these loops, these widenings? Is it a free market, or even a fair market, to make the whole nation pay, willy-nilly, to build, say, the 1970s interchange that financed Union Carbide's departure from New York City to Danbury, Connecticut, draining the city for an exurbia that, in turn, paid the price when the company went bankrupt? It is one thing for Oregon to lure computer companies to its so-called Silicon Forest with an enterprise zone, another when federal taxes from the other forty-nine states pay for the accompanying highway infrastructure. The Federal Reserve of Minneapolis has asked for the war among the states to end. By subsidizing new roads, along with infrastructure and other benefits, the coin of the nation fortifies one town's capacity to poach jobs at the expense of another, a giveaway of resources. Subsidies rip off urban Peter to pay suburban Paul, old town for new, Frostbelt for Sunbelt, and create the classic zero-sum game. That's more than "spatial inequity," that's highway robbery.

The way of collecting these subsidies further creates a false perception—the illusion of a free road. While that 90 percent funding to build highways comes from Washington, the money to lay tracks, buy streetcars, or maintain buses issues largely from local sources. When the public has to vote and pay for mass transit visibly from their property taxes, but invisibly from the hidden cost of their cars and the federal angel, the playing field tilts. In short, when the roads seem free, the choice is scarcely so.

The Spatial Shuffle

"We buy the best parts in the world," a Toyota Camry advertisement boasts in trying to show its U.S. loyalty, "no matter which state they're from." The advertisement diagrams the car's parts, extending the line from its bumper, seats, headlights, windshield to their place of birth. From headlamps secured in Illinois to weather stripping in New Hampshire, it is a long route to get 174 parts from over thirty-nine U.S. suppliers headed to the $2 billion Georgetown, Kentucky, plant. We know who benefits, but what does it cost to get these steering columns from Vermont, these catalytic converters from California, and these carpets from North Carolina? In pollution, in time, in oil subsidized by the Pentagon.

This spatial mismatching and subsidizing hits cities hardest. Our most central economic and intellectual centers get the most abuse. The income transfer from city to suburb has harmed the thirty-four hubs around which the lives of more than half of all Americans revolve. It has drained the cities that power our intellectual and financial lives, lessening these proven efficient and generating cores for ideas that have reigned throughout history. Casual exchange, easy proximity, are crucial to generating ideas. Eliminating that, we diminish the spread and enhancement of individual knowledge. If we allow cities to decline further, to transfer their functions to exurbia, we pay for the further decline of the American intellect and empire.

In-house sprawlbuster Constance E. Beaumont has described the downslide for the National Trust for Historic Preservation. With the road as colonizer, "exurbanization" launches the momentum to destruction and disinvestment, she began. As home owners, businesses, and institutions move away from traditional urban centers, they set the stage for underuse and eventual downfall. Homes, schools, churches, courthouses, city halls, hotels, libraries, and other historic buildings vanish, for neither the public nor private bodies can tend to underused architecture. Down come walkable small stores. Up go warehouses, superstores, and megamalls. Disinvestment in the former, overdevelopment of the latter constitute an income redistribution that betters few. According to economist Kenneth E. Stone, within five years of a Wal-Mart's opening, small towns within a twenty-mile radius find that net sales are down 19 percent. Towns farther away, but within a short drive, slide 10 percent, and as big box stores approach the larger cities, downtowns experience the same effects.

What does it cost when cities are dismantled, when the ladders of upward movement they offer for the poor, the elderly, the young are destroyed? What is the price when we limit and disown access for the most needy, when we ghettoize many of our poorer workers, force our suburban ones to drive ten to twelve hours a week, and hence further impoverish the nation? Few economists venture to put the inequity and inhumanity of our mobility "divide" in dollars. But it is there, along with the economic value of the architecture, community, or amenities lost by the so-called free ride.

Money-Losing Bungle

Distance is dollars. Congestion is cost. And, as the Europeans and Japanese know, walking, biking, and public transit lower costs. The urban axiom holds that the more public transit riders, the less the cost, and the more drivers, the higher. Talk about losing money. Public transportation gets rapped for low profits at best; automobile subsidies are ignored. A one-mile trip for a carload of rail passengers equals six to ten miles avoided by car. Over any given distance, the automobile expends more in terms of energy, amount of lane capacity, and capital. And that's not calculating the environmental or land use exactions. The fact that rail transit is fixed means that it stabilizes the land, gives some permanence to place, defines how to locate buildings and services, and creates compact, less costly living. Its stability is at least as much a plus as the automobile's vaunted flexibility.

The great raid and the great drain on mass transit—the tracks annihilated or gone to weeds, the bus routes languishing, the streetcars and subways underfunded—wound us all. Money drafted to fix potholes and widen roads comes from property and sales taxes, regressive and resented ways of levying fees. A black hole for taxpayers, maintenance extracts endless fees. Such tariffs hurt local government and public services. Policing for automobile infractions shortchanges other public needs. The shortfall of dollars for car-based services runs high. There is indeed no free lunch—no free ride.

And yet, I see too many signs ignoring these realities. I see construction notices and highway crews from coast to coast. I see new rail construction stall and service get slashed and hear of new and expanded roads everywhere. It is sobering to pass road crews cropping a red cliff for a highway widening in the spectacular scenery of Sedona, Arizona, or to see the struggle to maintain Sinclair Lewis's historic Main Street without cutting into its tree-shaded lawns. It is more than sobering to consider the excavation of scenic Ministerial Road in Rhode Island, to watch a road-widening into Florida's coral reefs or witness overpacked Cape Cod stuck in traffic with nothing more creative than another traffic-inducing bridge. "Your highway dollars at work" is an epithet of the late auto age.

"Each improvement stimulated traffic . . . and demanded more improvements, which brought more traffic, and so on, down to the present and seemingly on to an indefinite date in the future." These words recorded the tale of the Lincoln Highway, America's first transcontinental road, launched more than eighty years ago. The predictions held. "Each improvement stimulated traffic . . . and demanded more improvements. . . ." The more improvements, the more boosters gloated. More improvements and more traffic. By 1956 the largest road project in the history of the globe was the answer: the Interstate Highway and Defense Act of that year was passed. And the increments went on. Today, the bulk of that interstate system has been completed. Yet, there are plans for so-called lesser roads to cover the continent. A road cut here, a highway there, a widening elsewhere—all bear that archaic word "improvement."

"Our street-system capillaries, now too narrow and inelastic to permit the larger flow of persons and goods, are backing up the circulation," still another article declared in 1932. "Instead of the great convenience which it is, the automobile is rapidly becoming the Frankenstein of the economics of city building." The condition *Survey* magazine observed two generations ago is embedded in the landscape and in new sages who remind us that "on urban commuter expressways, peak-hour traffic congestion rises to meet maximum capacity."

Yet, we fail to hear. Like the smokestack industries of the nineteenth century that promised a blooming economy even as they deflowered "England's green and pleasant land," these mobile smokestacks of the twentieth century promise to deliver, but they destroy.

It is time to have it otherwise. Just as we learned that we must examine the environmental consequences of unleashed consumption, so too we must learn to let the car stop driving the economy. It is time to look back on our history, to see the origins of today's predicament. We know that the automobile has impacted our lives and landscape. We have seen how it has rolled ruthlessly across our environment and hurt the national health. We know the financial penalties.

It is time to see how the voracious icon of the twentieth century's hypermobility was unleashed. Perhaps if we can see how the motor vehicle was transformed from a symbol of galloping reform into deadly horsepower, we can learn from our past. We must trace the car tracks on the landscape of the past to proceed to the future.

OPPOSITE: In New York, McKim, Mead and White's magnificent
Pennsylvania Station was erected to celebrate the glory days of rail travel.
(Collection of the New York Historical Society)

PART II

Car Tracks
The Machine That Made the Land

"Automobiles have come and almost all outward things are
going to be different because of what they bring."
—Booth Tarkington, *The Magnificent Ambersons*

OPPOSITE: A victorious suitor mocks his competitor's automobile in 1914. In short order, Henry Ford's Model T, the machine for the masses, would replace the horse and buggy with other flights of fancy. (The Library of Congress)

Model T, Model City

"Only by motor car can you climb such heights and halt where you will and as long as you will, then flit away as fast as you will over a land as immeasurable in terms of human feet as America."

—Motor Life

"The automobilist is killing or maiming many victims and kicking his dust and smoke in the face of the other fellow [but he] is the only one who can today get back and forth with ease over the great district of greater Chicago."

—George Hooker, in Paul J. Barrett,
The Automobile in Urban Transport

THE ERA THAT saw the motorcar emerge as a machine for the masses was lit with grand expectations. "There is a promise in the sky of a new day," crusader Charles Mulford Robinson declared. The spirit of the Progressive movement in politics, buttressed by progress in technology, was changing the nation's outlook. The "White City" built for the World's Columbian Exposition in Chicago in 1893 had stimulated the "City Beautiful" movement. Idealists for parks and civic spaces, slum reform, and city building were trumpeting a new Providence. Urban planners and reformers viewed the landscape of America with optimism. "Whatever was dingy, coarse, and ugly is either transformed or hidden in shadow. The streets, bathed in the fresh morning light, fairly sparkle, their pavements from upper windows appearing smooth and clean. There seems to be a new city for the work of the new day," wrote Robinson. "Cities grow in splendour."

Many reformers, watching the horseless carriage puffing along country roads, believed that the automobile would be an agent of that renewal. The motor vehicle would decant the teeming city into the countryside and connect the countryside to the city. It would serve mobility and opportunity at once. Despite its gawky, almost comical appearance, the motorcar would be a savior. "The general adoption of the automobile was the most important reform of the pre–World War I era," historian James J. Flink has observed. Consciousness I, he calls this era, when the auto's infancy coincided with the Progressive zeal to remedy the ills of the social and physical landscape.

The arrival of Henry Ford's Model T in 1908 marked the coming of the auto age. Rolling off the assembly line every three minutes by 1913 ("just like one pin is like another pin when it comes from a pin factory"), the Model T was a miracle of mass production. Rising higher above the rutted roads and given a more powerful engine than its predecessors, the Model T was easier to fix and grew cheaper by the year. In the century's first decade, automobile registrations rose from 8,000 to 469,000.

Ford's machine for the masses paralleled the expanding infrastructure and the inventions of the early twentieth century: the streetcar tracks laid, the electric wire installed, and the sanitation introduced.

Together, it was thought, these technologies would relieve America's overflowing cities. No less a nineteenth-century aesthete than Henry Adams believed the new-fangled would aid the antique: "My idea of paradise is a perfect automobile going thirty miles an hour on a smooth road to a 12th century cathedral."

Looking back through the perspective of an asphalt nation, the development of the horseless carriage now appears more ominous. Sepia photographs and film give witness to how "outward things" did, indeed, change with the birth of the automobile. Juxtapose Main Street, Houston, in 1900 and interstate-girdled Houston in 1990. Contrast postcard Los Angeles laced with streetcars and stucco bungalows under a baby blue sky, with L.A.'s pollution-mired skies and stalled drivers in the late auto age. We see how the spirited towns and leafed-over suburbs vanished. We see the verdant hills and blue velvet valleys now smoggy with roadsters' fumes, their bridges rusting beneath apocalyptic air.

The Agent of Advancement

If the years after 1908 seem a marking point in the dismantling of America, the story is more complex than our myths of the "Machine in the Garden," however. For the irony of the automobile's coming-of-age remains just this: the machine that made and unmade the continent rolled into a nation that was hell-bent on beautifying its surroundings and bettering itself. With a vigor born of the ills of their time, Progressives sought to ameliorate mean streets and relieve crowded tenements, to purge disease and poor sanitation. And the motorcar, an attractive reform by one measure, because it required individual but not collective action, would be a potent tool in this arsenal of betterment.

From the dawn of the auto age to 1920, when 9 million motor vehicles tooled around the country, the nation was urbanizing, overcrowding its cores. Henry Ford was one of many farmers unyoked from the countryside to the city by the industrial revolution. From 1900, European immigrants landed at the rate of a million and a half a year. Their jammed quarters and squalid streets dismayed reformers. New York's wretched Lower East Side had parallels in the teeming misery of other of the nation's cities. In her Chicago settlement house, Jane Addams dreamed of relocating slum dwellers in rural America. "The noisy ugliness of towns" appalled planner Charles Eliot. The brutality of the industrial city would prompt his peers to seek the automotive solution: disgorge them by car to the countryside.

Urban Beautification

Advocates for aesthetic improvement allied with those who would bring fresh air to the tenement dwellers within the city itself. Along the ravines of Pittsburgh, the plains of Chicago, and the soil charred by San Francisco's great fire, planners labored to create splendid settings. At Addams's Hull House, Dwight Heald Perkins, architect for Chicago's school system, and park maker Jens Jensen contrived a comprehensive city park system. The motto "To make our city loved, it must be lovely" was etched on the plan for Minneapolis.

The city must also be motorized. "Motor colonies" would save money, according to crusader Herbert Ladd Towle. They would stop the cancer of corruption, Lincoln Steffens wrote in his classic muckracking work *The Shame of the Cities* (1904). The motorcar would end the scandal of St. Louis's suburban railways and Philadelphia's streetcar franchises. It would reform the likes of Chicago—"first in violence, deepest in dirt," as Steffens had it—emptying the den of crowded immigrants and lessening the control of the scurrilous machine politicians downtown.

In 1893, the year of the World's Columbian Exposition, historian Frederick Jackson Turner declared the frontier closed. Americans now needed to reach out to new "frontiers," to shape new land close to home. In the nineteenth century electric rail had performed that job, extending from cities into "streetcar suburbs." Philadelphia, New York, Chicago, Boston, and smaller cities had annexed countryside, villages, and suburbs along the lengthening rail lines. In the twentieth century the car would complement this search for space.

Civic movements to adorn the expansion excited the country. In Washington, D.C., the City Beautiful designers, Daniel Burnham, Charles McKim, and Frederick Law Olmsted, Jr., drafted great avenues and malls, parks and parkways on their maps. Inspired by the White City of the Chicago exposition, their 1902 Senate Park Commission plan stamped harmony on the nation's capital. Its vision awoke the national consciousness. Arguably the nation's first comprehensive planning document, Washington's map for noble vistas became a model.

In 1908, the same year as the debut of the Model T, some 2,500 improvement societies were striving to uplift their surroundings. Municipal art societies addressed urban issues. "If we take every element of ugliness one by one, and try to root it out, the task will not be difficult," wrote one Chicago art historian. A dozen or more other cities had similar plans. Gopher Prairie in Sinclair Lewis's *Main Street* was not the only place where a newcomer could fantasize "that a small American town might be lovely."

No more would putrid, bloated cities spew rickrack buildings around their peripheries. The tangle of freight yards, gasworks, and blighting industry would dissolve. Majestic terminals, grand streets, and plazas would replace ramshackle train stations, ugly tenements, and homely public buildings. Burnham and Edward H. Bennett drew monumental axes to make their Windy City livable and workable. In the 1909 Chicago plan, Burnham's maxim prevailed: "Make no little plans; they have no magic to stir man's blood." Reordering the cityscape to upgrade streets, ease traffic, elevate urban arterials, and create regional highways studded with classical edifices, the planners worked to ease the advancing auto age. They installed imperial European parks and vistas and, perhaps unwittingly, the motorways of tomorrow.

A Ford in Our Future

Such optimistic notions of a model city lit the Progressive landscape as Ford, the farm boy from Michigan, took money won from racing to assemble his first roadsters. Transforming a handmade artifact for the elite into a mass-produced helpmate for the many, he launched the vehicular revolution. Ford's motorcar "for the multitude" became a catalyst. Light but powerful, to take country roads in its stride, the Model T made driving ever more popular. A twist of the crank, a touch to the pedal, and off went the twenty-horsepower beast with its five thousand parts. General Motors, founded the same year, couldn't compete. The low $850 price of Ford's vehicles rolling off the initially stationary assembly line in 1908 was halved by the time he scored his next advance, the first moving line, built at Highland Park, Michigan, in 1913. A year later, sales passed the first million mark, more than all competitors combined. Next the master manufacturer began work on his vast new River Rouge plant in Detroit, the colossus of the day.

Ford's "tin lizzie," or "flivver," was a favorite. Its inventor was a hero who would make workers and drivers one, raising their wages while lowering the cost of their cars. The unemployed attracted to the Highland Park plant by Ford's $5-a-day wage came to Detroit with disease and settled in slums. Indoor plumbing was rare in the boardinghouses where they were jammed for lack of housing, and disease was rampant. The environs Ford built altered that. "North of the business section are miles of cottages, the last word of modernity, each surrounded by lawn and shrubbery and having—perhaps one in five—a neat garage in the rear," wrote reformer Towle. "Shade trees line the streets; at frequent corners stand white sanitary drinking fountains, and everywhere are automobiles. Hardly one vehicle in twenty is horse-drawn. Naturally the streets of Detroit are clean. And the motor vehicles! They are radiating, imposing structures, all steel and glass," he wrote exultingly. "No dingy loop-holes for windows, no haphazard ventilation here! The mark of the efficiency expert is seen even in the buildings, and we shall find it everywhere in the work itself."

Crusaders endorsed Ford's "lever to move the world." It would serve everything from recreation to sanitation. The motorcar would toll the death knell for the 14 million horses befouling the nation, would end the disease caused by disposing of tons of manure and carcasses. In the city it would release traffic, relieve crowded trains, and decongest the tenements. In the country it would get the farmer "out of the mud," emancipate farm women, and knit the family together. And, as Detroit grew from 300,000 people to nearly half a million, with twenty-seven factories assembling more than $200 million worth of parts, the scenario seemed likely. Not until another generation and another consciousness would Americans note the parallels between Ford's assembly line workers and the living cogs in Charlie Chaplin's machine age *Modern Times*.

The Railed World

For the majority of early twentieth century travelers, mobility still meant rail. The Americans who had replaced the horsecar with Frank Sprague's streetcars a generation earlier had shaped a remarkable web of tracks, far-flung and permanent. The electric streetcar and railroad expanded the city, connecting neatly lined streets of houses and transfiguring country bumpkin crossroads into villages and towns. Human mobility along a fixed track defined the landscape. From hub to spoke, the city was elongated. Traction magnates stretched their landscape horizontally, while buildings at the center soared vertically. Lofty towers shaped a dense downtown. Municipalities grew into modern metropolises.

The so-called networked city depended on pipes for water and sewage to improve their sanitation. Electricity powered their downtowns with lights bright enough to dull the stars, elevators to carry them up steel frame skyscrapers, and street railways to transport the multitudes. Technology was altering urban America. Bound by rail to the walking city, the passengers of the steel rail epoch tripled in the decade before World War I. The motorcar would abet all this, many thought.

Rural Progressives especially favored the automobile. The motorcar was to rural America "what skyscrapers were to the urban south: an undeniable sign of economic vitality," wrote one historian. Reformers endorsed the gas buggy as the agent of change. It would carry the postman with Rural Free Delivery and the doctor with his black bag; it would get the farmer's goods to market and stop the exodus of country children, discontented with the loneliness of farm life. Good roads would also constrain the power of the railroad's "devil wagons." These so-called good roads progressives, led by the Grange and the Department of Agriculture, fought for the automobile in the opening hours of the auto age.

The Restless Wheels

In time city observers began to be less sanguine. As more motorcars swarmed through their congested thoroughfares and the urge for speed followed, the city street, the public turf where neighbors socialized, pushcarts jostled, and children played, became cluttered. "Only agile pedestrians can survive," noted the *New York Times*. Accidents prompted safety measures—rotaries, stop lines, and one-way streets—but they didn't slow the course. The automobile was altering the "meeting-places and playgrounds and making the street a menace," historian and reformer Charles Beard cautioned in 1912. Cars, introduced into the old carriage routes in parks, changed their pace. "A new era of speeds had arrived," said Flavel Shurtleff. No city of 100,000 in the United States should fail to widen streets or lay new ones, he suggested. Like many landscape architects, he planned for a shifting America. Tame the picturesque curve. Fix the right angle to let motorcars merge. Deploy traffic schemes to ease congestion.

As the automobile gained prominence, it even went indoors. Architect Ernest Flagg built an arched entrance and garage inside his city home. *Architectural Record* called it "A New Type of City House." Frank Lloyd Wright, like other architects, designed a built-in garage for an Oak Park home. In Queens, where lack of space for cars hurt home sales, builders staked out wider lots to allow automobiles. Development spread. "The automobile has caused the word 'suburb' to carry miles further than it used to until now it has come to signify to the motorist almost any place where gasoline may be readily obtained," one woman driver observed.

Those who designed the land noted the change, but not always happily. "The automobile people tell me that it will be impossible for me to secure a car with a short enough wheel-base to make the turn," a client wrote John C. Olmsted, suggesting that the landscape architect alter the radius of the driveway to assist his motor vehicle. "Of course it can be done by backing but you are doubtless familiar with the noises that occur when the gears are changed and the engine reversed and know how distracting it is," the owner fretted. The landscape architect was not charmed by the car's precedence in his plan. "We cannot think it a very bad thing that you may have to back your car in turning," Olmsted wrote back testily. But the client, and the car, would win.

The architects' search for harmony didn't stem the automobile's intrusion. The home of Mayor Hazen S. Pingree, who shaped his reform policies to make Detroit the "City Beautiful," was sold to be converted into a garage. "Garages to the right of it, garages to the left of it, our new art center," a cartoon in *Detroit Saturday Night* depicted the motorcar's displacement of the surroundings. "Honk," said the script below the drawing.

The "honks" began to echo as the parking problem grew. In 1910, Detroit's Cadillac Square was downed for a parking lot. Cars were left standing dead center in broad streets and congregated in open spaces. They were wedged onto sidewalks and blocked minor side streets. The "promiscuous rapidity of traffic movement" bothered residential streets. Local officials deplored "scorchers" and mounted antispeeding campaigns. In 1916, *Automobile Age* noted the situation with alarm. Plans for street widenings and sidewalk narrowing to relieve congestion filled engineering and traffic manuals, though "the result has appeared to be exactly the opposite," the *Municipal Journal and Engineer* noted—not for the last time.

When bottlenecks came, planners looked to more roads. In the 1911 plans for Seattle's growth, arterial highways mattered more than civic centers and trains. "Boston 1915" was equally highway-oriented. Chicago voters balloted for bonds to widen Twelfth Street and Michigan Avenue at the same time that they built new railroad stations. "The city's growth will be retarded with a tendency to develop congested, undesirable and unhealthful districts unless rapid transit facilities are provided," some planners warned. Yet, while European transit builders, who had formerly lagged behind the United States, expanded rail lines and quadrupled ridership, Americans began to let their cars overrun downtowns. Did the Continental planners have more respect for their heritage or less deference to the new technology than their American cousins? Either way, sixty separate legislative bills reflected a "widespread demand" for Congressional action on traffic, and the motorcar was the means.

A new vehicle also joined the rolling stock across the country. The truck now became a tool for agriculture. Out came the rear seat of the farmer's Model T, in went produce, and a new era of transport was born. The age of trucking began to replace the era of railroad freight in dispersing goods to outlying areas where more motor vehicles began to travel on pleasure drives or for settlement.

Americans exulted in their widening range. "You and I—all of us—used to choose our homes for their nearness to train or trolley," Towle enthused. "A mile from the station, half a mile from the trolley, was our immutable limit. The gates of Paradise would not have tempted us further." By bridging the gap between rail travel and the horse, the motorcar added threefold or more to the habitable areas outside cities. The low-cost automobile was working its alchemy. Landscape architect Warren H. Manning expressed the same wonder at the lengthening radius of travel. "Auto vehicles . . . can come to a city, in a day, from sixty miles away, more easily and as quickly as can a horse-drawn vehicle, with less than half the load, from twenty miles away."

Paving the Road

From the first, carmakers joined the ranks of the enthusiasts. Local auto clubs merged to form the American Automobile Association (AAA) in 1902. Three years later, the Society of Automobile Engineers was organized. Manufacturers lobbied locally and promoted nationally to push their highway agendas. States took on the job of replacing private toll roads and turnpikes with public roads, seeking ways to raise taxes for these roads and "scientific" means to construct them. By 1914 the American Association of State Highway Officials, the coming oligarchs of the highway, had set highway standards. The federal Office of Road Inquiry, an offshoot of the bicyclists' influential League of American Wheelmen, broadened into the Bureau of Public Roads. Its mission was to build highways, train engineers, and coach speakers to convey the joy of smooth-riding roads.

The powerhouse among road makers was Carl Fisher. A founder of the Indianapolis Speedway, this promoter par excellence cooperated with the Packard and Goodyear companies to push for what was called a "Coast-to-Coast Rock Highway." In 1913, Fisher changed the proposed name to the "Lincoln Highway" to capitalize on the patriotism associated with the Civil War president. The next year, work on the first transcontinental highway began. Planting "seedling" miles as samplers of roads to come and organizing supporters, the association advanced the slogan "Let's build it before we're too old to enjoy it."

The need for roads was obvious. Of the dirt paths that passed as roads, only 7 percent were paved at the first census of roads. A mere handful boasted gravel surfaces. The rutted, bumpy country roads, washed out during the muddy season and known as "wiggle worm" roads, were a menace.

For all of the Ford's mechanical ingenuity and improvements, the nascent car remained erratic. Breakdowns marked its trip at speeds of less than twenty miles an hour. A popular song of the period, "He'd Have to Get Under—Get Out and Get Under . . . to fix up his automobile," described one suitor's mishaps. Though eager to woo his passenger, the driver was forced to "get out and get under" at critical moments as his car failed him.

The goggled motorist in his duster was still compelled to drive in an open-air vehicle. The rains doused riders and the unpadded seats jolted them. Even with the Model T's relative ease, starting the car remained an ordeal. Not until 1912 did electric starters end the arm-wrenching chore of cranking. The fancy Pierce-Arrow and Packard belonged only to those rich enough to hire chauffeurs to fix them. The lingering social inequity prompted the then college president Woodrow Wilson to suggest a ban on the motorcar so as not to further split the rich and poor. Though the call of the wild beckoned the wealthy motorist with a gypsy spirit, early motoring made demands on pocketbook and patience. Compared to the mature streetcar, the motorcar was a toddler. The nickel trolley ride remained the mainstay.

Moving the Multitudes

These were the years of the trolleying sentimentalized in the movie *Meet Me in St. Louis*. As World War I neared, everyday Americans moved by rail. Streetcars located near homes connected their surroundings to a downtown center, then sent passengers home by discharging them at nodes where shops and stores and neighborhoods evolved. Complex and comprehensive, the rail network consisted of streetcars plus two other forms of movement on tracks. The interurban, the electric streetcar, and the long-distance passenger train formed a splendid tripartite system of mobility.

The largest of these track systems, the 250,000 miles of railroad lines that defined the continent's architecture of settlement beginning from the mid–nineteenth century, was the envy of the world. The second, the sturdy interurban, meshed city and city, city and countryside over many miles. The lightest, the electric streetcar, the city's artery, connected downtown and neighborhoods, the dwelling and working places of America. The efficiency of this triad of railed movement set the outlines that produced the finest streetscapes and architecture in America.

The interurban, the least known today, was a favorite. A bruiser of a vehicle compared to the trolley, it rolled through city streets, loping from state to state and taking the longest stretch—215 miles from Toledo to Cincinnati—in a breeze. Cheaper to run, the interurban took more trips, if slower ones, than conventional trains, allowing farm families easier access to towns. Half-train, half-trolley, the rugged electric interurban had its heyday from 1904 to 1918, when it opened more than five hundred miles of lines a year. By World War I, the system had reached its peak, at 72,911 cars.

An opening of a new interurban line was a time of celebration. Theodore Roosevelt called the parade of the Pacific Electric "marvelous." Its heralded Big Red Car packed the Los Angeles Festival of Flowers with 100,000 people. Moving through the Southern California orange groves or downtown, the Pacific Electric linked more than a thousand miles in fifty-plus communities to define the region. Los Angeles had the longest routes in the busy nation, but even the interurbans of Massachusetts and Ohio laced nearly three thousand miles.

The trolley, the most omnipresent of this trio, scooted through a more diverse and populous world. The streetcars gliding down elm-shaded Orange, New Jersey, or slicing between Colorado Springs's brick buildings toward Pikes Peak, united the nation's cores. From the "wilderness" line of Portland, Oregon, to settled Massachusetts, whose system tied the eastern tip of Cape Cod to the western corner of the state, the streetcar wed the neighborhoods.

Not only did streetcar lines help commuters, they restored week-end travelers, too. The "lightning cars" that transported commuters downtown on weekdays carried them to amusement parks and picnic groves on weekends. The pleasure gardens, casinos, and resorts that streetcar owners sponsored at the ends of the lines helped fill the fare box on off-work days. Beachgoers and boaters of all incomes shuttled out of town on wicker seats in open-air trolleys to Coney Island in New York and Riverside in Chicago. Weekenders traveled to amusement parks at Norumbega in Newton and White City in Worcester, two of Massachusetts's thirty-one pleasure grounds. Willow Grove in Philadelphia, Balboa Park in San Diego, and Brighton Beach racetrack in New York drew thousands of picnickers and pleasure seekers on mass transit. One hundred million fares a year came from these "electric parks."

The open-air trolley was a favorite. It gave "mental exhilaration," said one passenger. The cure for insomnia, according to a doctor. "Marriages based on streetcar courtships seemed to stick," wrote one reporter. Trolleys for fire engines, trolleys for mail, trolleys for parades and Christmas shows downtown—even a trolley for women only—filled the streets. A white hearse trolley took Americans to their final destination. At the time of their pre–World War I peak, some 60,000 streetcars rolled on 26,000 lines.

"With clanging streetcars, shaded residential streets and Sunday excursions, everything appeared to be at peace and in balance," said the authors of *Access for All* as they looked back in awe. If service was sometimes sparse and accidents common, the thirty years before 1920 marked a peak of ridership. From 1890 to 1920, ridership would soar from 2 to 15.5 million passengers a year as the golden age of streetcars succeeded the golden age of rail.

The transit builders dealt positively with the longtime rush hour stampede heightened by the competing motorcars. Railmen won some support from planners and municipal officials. Planner Edward M. Bassett insisted that "rapid transit is the only thing that will bring low rent and sunny homes to working people in great cities." Cities began to add new rail lines and also worked to build undergrounds. When Boston opened the nation's first underground in 1897, ridership accelerated. New York followed in 1904 with its first subway, the Interborough Rapid Transit (IRT), which connected Brooklyn with the Bronx through Manhattan and created a building boom in shops and apartments along Broadway and the West Side. Philadelphia finished its elevated and subway system in 1909. Officials proposed the same for Chicago, Los Angeles, and Detroit, as ridership tripled between 1904 and 1913.

New York's grandiose expansion defined its place at the peak of the world of rail. The city, on its way to becoming America's rail showplace, completed the first stage of construction with a celebration. Top-hatted Mayor McClellan told crowds at its opening in 1904 that the IRT was "the greatest underground railroad in the world." By the end of the first year, some 400,000 passengers a day rode the line. Undaunted by Manhattan's rocky undergirding, its rivers and swampy marsh, the subway plunged, then climbed, in a Promethean infrastructure. For all the jamming and jostling, for all the laments of mingling the washed and the "great unwashed," such systems worked magnificently.

A new transit infrastructure also shaped the city's portals. The monumental Brooklyn Bridge, gem of its century, was reinforced in 1907. Bridges filled to capacity prompted alternate routes for crossing Manhattan's rivers. In 1908 crews scooped twin tunnels for the railroad through the Hudson and East rivers, from Pennsylvania Station. The world's largest steel-arched bridge for trains, the Hell Gate Bridge, emerged, and the Queensboro Bridge spanned the East River in 1909, followed by the Manhattan Bridge at the end of the decade. And, as building proceeded, outer boroughs hitched themselves to the lengthening rail lines to stitch together America's greatest metropolis. Handsome stations matched the audacious enterprise. Ornament enhanced subway entrances; tiles and terra-cotta embellished their interiors. Festive terminals gave ferries a waterside entrance gate.

Civic Space

Rail builders adorned the nation's public space most splendidly. In New York terminals of heroic grandeur arose at the Pennsylvania and Grand Central stations. Lofty structures in their own right, the stations served as superb connectors and city strengtheners. With an air of majesty, the 1911 Pennsylvania Station was poised along Seventh and Eighth avenues and their cross streets. Its columns and eagles carved in granite stirred passersby; its interior steeped in the glory of the Baths of Caracalla greeted passengers "with the immense and distant sound of time," in Thomas Wolfe's ode:

> Great, slant beams of moted light fell ponderously athwart the station's floor and the calm voice of time hovered along the walls and ceiling of that mighty room. For here, as nowhere else on earth, men were brought together for a moment at the beginning or end of their innumerable journeys, here one saw their greetings and farewells, here, in a single instant, one got the entire picture of human destiny.

Beneath a colossal steel and glass concourse, Pennsylvania Station's multilevel structure was linked smoothly to street traffic. Its passageways were married to the city, blending place making and people moving artfully. In an expanded civic gesture, the station's architects, the firm of McKim, Mead and White, designed the post office across the street as a matching "bookend."

Crosstown, Grand Central Terminal, a decade in the building, stood grandly above its network of rails. Improving the grim yards to the north, the terminal also served as a catalyst for altering Midtown New York. This imperial station, by Warren and Wetmore, linked luxury hotels, corporate offices, and residences above once wasted blocks. Under its twelve-story ceiling, the Beaux-Arts building set three princely windows divided by columns of equal magnificence above the spacious lobby. On the wall its communal clock ticked away the hours of arrival and departure.

Across the country, too, Union Stations aspiring to glory were built as rail competitors united. In Washington, Chicago, and St. Louis, builders strove to achieve City Beautiful munificence. With lengthening rails, new terminals, and well-groomed surroundings, they enhanced the once grimy outskirts of cities like San Francisco and Kansas City, where Woodrow Wilson opened Union Station as the gateway to the West.

To be sure, riders and reformers often found the gold of the golden age of rail tarnished. Rail barons and trolley franchise owners were, after all, speculators. They used patronage and payoffs to achieve their ends, building their routes not only to accommodate passengers but to profit from the real estate they owned along the way. The quality of the rides was mixed and sometimes dangerous. Ladies in Edwardian dress stepped gingerly aboard trolley cars, while boys in knickers rode outside and clung for life to the railings in the midst of the horrendous traffic. The streetcars were packed so close on city streets that a person could walk from one car's rooftop to the next, critics complained. And, as brazen motorists added to the glut of wagons, trucks, and pedestrians, traffic grew.

A Transportation Frame

Progressives nonetheless labored to secure legislation to improve maintenance and to ease jam-packed rides, while America still centered itself around rail. In this last period before the automobile gained dominance, trains, trolleys, and interurban lines tied the walking nation along a nucleus of stations and structures. At every stop along Main Street, bars, stores, and so-called taxpayer strips opened; the intersections, squares, and triangles where they appeared formed neighborhood hubs. Historian Chester Liebs calls them "zones of transition," serving rider and driver, walker and biker. Whether an early A&P or a movie palace, the shops beneath their broad awnings framed communities. Rail transportation created zones of life as well as corridors of movement, reinforcing the art of collective living.

Joined to these rail monoliths, downtowns continued to intensify and grow. Chicago's elevated Loop, an iron skeleton against the sky, brought 750,000 commuters into a city pulsating with civic improvements. Around the Loop and its destinations, a parade of streetcars, wagons, bikes, and motor vehicles circled the emerging institutions of art, finance, and education. Similarly linked by the longest rail lines in the nation, the population of Los Angeles swelled to 600,000, while Detroit reached almost a million people in the century's first two decades.

Vulnerable though these cores would prove, the mobility and urbanity framed by the streetcar and train were extraordinary. Travelers could cross the downtowns of America as fast as they ever would. Foot, bike, horse, carriage, rail—the modes of movement were myriad and harmonious to city making, and designers still did their best to buttress them. In Detroit, the nation's fourth largest city at the time, landscape architect Frederick Law Olmsted, Jr., sketched a balanced transportation-based vision for the waterfront. Designing a quay and promenade along the Detroit River and improvements in Belle Isle Park and Cadillac Square, he worked comprehensively. His boulevards, though wide enough to readily accommodate the automobile, linked the city to a handsome rail hub; his workers' housing was accessible to tomorrow's transportation. "There is no haste about the realization of this dream," the landscape architect noted. "Detroit has all the ages before it." His words, so poignant now, bespoke the brimming optimism of the day.

Not every city reknit its worn and tattered fabric as part of a public transportation plan. Yet, mayors called upon to reduce "congestion" looked for broader enhancements. The New York mayor's Congestion Committee integrated housing, taxation, factory distribution, zones, and height restrictions with transportation, integrating stability and mobility needs. The committee proposed banning cars below Houston Street and conceived of certain streets as playgrounds. In 1910, Pittsburgh Mayor William Magee, worried about the travails of "looping, of through-routing, of transfers, of compensation," formed the Pittsburgh Civic Commission to summon yet another fulsome Olmsted plan.

Cities from Hartford to St. Louis repeated the mayors' calls to ease traffic through integrated planning. "Creating an organic plan" would solve congestion, Herbert Croly wrote in *Architectural Record*. In 1909 the first National Conference on City Planning was summoned to do so. Sharing the "desire to abandon the wildcat individualism which is sure to transform every city block into a heterogeneous monstrosity," the conference saw the answer in setting height ceilings. The way to stop another Woolworth tower from soaring sixty stories and blocking its neighbors' light was to adopt limits on height. The way to stop noxious industries from blighting dwellings was to restrict work to special spaces. Such spatial segregation became known as zoning.

Zones and Corridors

Devised in Germany to order land use, zoning divided the city into its functions. According to the dictates of zoning, buildings must be classified; the city must be laid out with different functions for different parts of town. By forbidding bakeries to sit beside homes, or unsanitary industry to loom over backyards, zoning would upgrade neighborhoods. No more would gasworks or smokestacks, mill or glue factory send toxic fumes and noise through communities. The city could now tell builders where and how their property should appear—its height, its type, its use; realtors could insure permanence and, not incidentally, protect their property. Less happily, few suspected that zoning would segregate life and mandate still more travel down the road.

Slowly, city making evolved into formal city planning. Before, said John Nolen, landscape architect and planner, there had been "no knowledge of, no interest in city planning. We are standing on the edge of a great change in living conditions in America." By 1913, twenty-two cities had land use controls. In the decade before World War I, more than one hundred towns and half the fifty largest cities had undertaken comprehensive planning. What mattered was not simply architecture; corridors of motion were considered in these plans as well. "The most important consideration of the city plan, and one to which everything practically leads in the end, is the street system," to improve "traffic stagnation and pedestrian congestion," Edward Bennett told the Fifth National Conference on City Planning in 1913.

And yet, for all the priorities to "pedestrian congestion," the largest part of all the new street corridors lacked plans for more public transit. As New York began to experience traffic jams twice a day and parked cars narrowed its thoroughfares, new streets were designed with the motorcar in mind. By World War I, every city would display that automotive mindset.

If the car could not be curbed, it could be appeased, landscape architects believed. They could adjust to the motor vehicle. They could design hidden driveways, streets of varied size, curving roads, and tasteful garages for suburban homes. They had the "moral obligation" to create elegant designs that would embrace the motorcar. Whether it was South Pasadena's Women's Improvement Society sponsoring a watering trough to green a traffic island, New York's Municipal Art Society installing street lights in Manhattan, or the Olmsted brothers firm planning trees to arch over roads in Palos Verde and St. Francis Wood in San Francisco, subdivisions were adorned for the motorcar.

A Railed Garden

In Queens, hard by the site of a coming commuter line, there was an exception to the auto-oriented design in the motor suburbs. Here, one new community based its plan on balanced transportation—coordinating foot, rail, and rubber wheel. At Forest Hills Gardens, Margaret Sage of the Russell Sage Foundation sought to create a total neighborhood for the middle class, to turn the subdivision into a rail-linked design. The philanthropist chose Frederick Law Olmsted, Jr., and architect Grosvenor Atterbury to do the job. The 1912 community they planned still shows civility and intelligence.

Meander through this railroad community's sun-dappled streets today. Descend the steps from the commuter rail station and stand by the picturesque stone wall and embankment. Envision the homeward-bound worker stepping down this rocky crest, crossing the street to the grassy island, and surveying the red-tiled, picturesque Forest Hills Inn at Station Square. Imagine the passenger strolling for a late-day visit to its arcaded shops or heading home to the housekeeping apartments nestled above its English tearoom architecture. Then, move on. Walk under a canopy of trees dense in their late spring foliage to reach the next ring of semidetached row houses, an easy walk from Station Square. Finally, approach the outer ring, where the compact dwellings give way to single-family homes.

This development, almost eighty years old, stands as a sample of land use planning, a model of transit-oriented design. Forest Hills Gardens's gracious amenities have concealed the fact that its design follows rigorous principles of movement. The classic formula was, and is, almost mathematical. Its aim, to place passengers within a five- to fifteen-minute walk from public transportation, was methodical. First, tuck the majority nearest to the rails in close-packed housing and services. Next, shape a slightly looser, more distant ring of row houses a walk away. Last, settle a few residents in single-family dwellings at the fringes. The wisdom of this principle endures, as does the desirability of the community. Though pulled by the outward thrust of commerce and commuting in the auto age, Forest Hills Gardens's sylvan and architectural appeal and its financial value continue. Its sense of community, sensibility as a plan, and worthiness as a social ideal are immediately recognizable.

Elsewhere, preauto America's transit-oriented design also achieved the art of place making by shaping dense communities near rail with minimal space for cars. Gathering dwellings within a short walk from public transportation, architects and planners reinforced mobility and congeniality alike in these neighborhoods. While some Americans opted for single-family homes, the denser clusters of cozy craftsmen's cottages or multifamily buildings supported rail, enlarged housing options, and gave a sense of community. In Illinois, Lake Forest's Market Square, with its two turrets, Linden Court in St. Martins, Pennsylvania, and other residences grouped compactly elsewhere shaped the dense places to support rail. Alike they blended amenities and ease of motion.

The array of housing alternatives in such walkable neighborhoods was prolific. The nineteenth-century city's residue of brick and brownstone row houses, its three-deckers in Boston, palm-studded courtyard apartments in Southern California, and Chicago three-flats mixed density with charm. Whether single-room rentals in a city, suburban boardinghouses, or spacious bay-windowed New York apartments, these dwellings had a comeliness, cogency, and mobility. They provided varied menus for urban living far beyond the single-plate mode of the lone house on the lone lot that came with the car.

"City-embedded" suburbs still hooked by rail to downtown

showed in the work of enlightened realtors like developer Jesse C. Nichols. Along with other so-called community builders, Nichols found well-designed walkable colonies to be marketable. He planned his ten-acre Country Club District in Kansas City with walks and paths to coordinate automobile and rail travel.

Roland Park in Baltimore was another example of a subdivision linked by rail and available by motorcar. The Olmsted firm executed the splendid subdivision on a 550-acre craggy landscape. Pedestrian-scaled and transit-linked, the community offered fresh air and water and a thirty-minute streetcar ride down Roland Avenue to downtown. The "remote" suburban life it encouraged was so novel to city dwellers that one local magazine instructed them on how to care for their grounds. Here, too, the scheme relied on a good transportation model: duplex dwellings gave density to support transit, as did a shopping center with stores below and community space above. Paths cut through the backyards and common steps leading from plateau to plateau made walking easy and kept cars at bay.

Parkway and Speedway

So it was that transportation remained "thoroughly harmonized," as *Railroad Gazette* had described it in 1904. Automobile roads even showed grace in the infancy of the motorcar. The open space of the Rock Creek and Potomac Parkway in Washington, D.C., begun in 1913, orchestrated rural and sylvan scenery as passages for play. For decades its well-tended footpaths, bridges, statuary, and bike paths set a precedent for expansion. Scenic roadways created an "outlook" on nature's wonders in America's most picturesque places. Engineer Samuel C. Lancaster raised his skills to an art, taking advantage of spectacular views in designing the Columbia River Scenic Highway, built from 1912 to 1915. The first and perhaps most beautiful of such roads, the gorge's highway was adorned with handsome bridges, viaducts, and tunnels leading to a spectacular resort.

Elsewhere, everyday roads bowed to the topography. Ambling down New England country lanes or taking in the coastal highways in sun-kissed Southern California, motorists were offered joys and adventures, mechanical mishaps notwithstanding. In Alta Vista, in

Louisville, Kentucky, John Olmsted spaced roads "to orchestrate the scenery blending into the park and connecting to the park's bridges with curves which were manageable for the growing automobile traffic."

The Arroyo Seco Parkway, which would eventually become Los Angeles's first freeway, set standards for graceful motorways. Speed was second even in the City of Angels, where some fifteen thousand automobiles, one for every eight residents, were tucked easily into city streets and downtown buildings stood in close ranks, a match for the urban East.

Nonetheless, the motorcar's needs for speed, distance, and efficiency were taking precedence. To some, the magnificent promenades, from the Grand Concourse in the Bronx to Fairmount Parkway in Philadelphia, foretold the coming highway age. Like their Parisian source, Baron Haussmann's Champs-Élysées, America's long radial avenues were "in greater or less degree out of scale with our poor legs and with our desires, which are rather for comfort and ease than for theatric splendor," one contemporary complained. Others praised their speed and grandeur.

Burnham's "make no little plans" for Chicago forecast the scope of car-based arterials to come. Seated beside Henry Ford at a dinner party, the architect absorbed the industrialist's vision of the people's automobile. Himself the owner of three cars, Burnham would survey San Francisco from his driver's seat—the original windshield appraisal. Other promobility architects, "motor boys," in the words of historian Clay McShane, were also beginning to refashion urban America for the motorcar. The ceremonial boulevard, though greened and graceful, replaced the narrower streets used for play and congregation, enhancing the vehicular route for the leisured classes.

Even before the Tin Lizzie, two arterials of major moment had paved the way for the future in 1906. The first highway dedicated to the motor vehicle was, in fact, a raceway for wealthy car collectors, the privately owned Vanderbilt Motor Parkway on Long Island. This toll road, carved for fifty miles in an uninterrupted flow of overpasses and tunnels, was the nation's first limited-access highway. A "Motorist's Paradise," noted *House Beautiful*. "Upon this modern Appian Way . . . one may speed to his or her heart's content, unmo-

lested by police, with the element of danger reduced to a minimum—
no children to dodge, no horses and buggies, no trolley cars and railroads to worry about."

This road was some distance from the word "parkway," coined by
Frederick Law Olmsted, Sr., for his nineteenth-century carriageways.
Olmsted's designs were for pleasure drives, "for rest, recreation, re-
freshment and social intercourse." The cars replacing carriages reflected the urge for speed and the hunger for space. And it had access
everywhere. In 1912, the same year Ford registered seven thousand
dealerships, San Francisco's Golden Gate Park became the last city
park opened to cars. Suggestions for double-decker roadways and
other haste-making devices began to appear. "The modern development of beautiful two-level highways should afford the thrill one has
in driving through Fifth Avenue without the delays caused by crosstown traffic," one planner said.

A second parkway, the four-lane Bronx River Parkway in Westchester County, had nobler aspirations environmentally and aestheti-
cally. Echoing the conservationist anthem of President Theodore
Roosevelt, it aimed to clean up the polluted Bronx River and sweep
away the shantytowns on its edge. Almost two decades in the making, the sinuous Parkway's sixteen-mile green corridor, by landscape
architect Gilmore D. Clarke and engineer Jay Downer, set standards
for design. Like the streetcar shaping new suburbs, the parkway enhanced towns along its route and encouraged elite commuters to
move outwards by motorcar.

The Advancing Auto Age

In fact, everyone seemed to drive such motorcars as the 1920s
neared. A Woodward Avenue homeowner mourned the automobile's
noisy trespass on his street. "The old-time charm of Detroit as a resident city has almost completely fled," he said. Traffic to Ford's Highland Park plant drove residents to outlying Grosse Pointe.
Congestion and pastoral dreams sent Americans to bucolic fields.
Even in the motor suburbs, the automobile brought more problems
now. Some home buyers avoided Jesse Nichols's car-filled boulevards, paying more for houses on narrower, calmer streets. Zoning,

much overrated as a goal, would falter when applied to the car-oriented suburbs. Its codes would indeed quiet neighborhoods. Alas, they would also widen the distance between work and home, rich and poor, black and white.

In town it was worse. The artifacts of the auto age began to loom large in many neighborhoods. During the "tower era," a policeman stood raised high above the street in a glass box, controlling traffic with a white light. Gas, once sold inconspicuously at the corner store or garage, moved to the curbside pump. The first gas station in 1905, the Automobile Gasoline Company of St. Louis, became the first "drive-in" four years later, to be supplanted by the lookalikes of chains as oil producers sold their wares along America's crossways. The parking lot appeared, and other "firsts" were logged: the first licenses and registrations, the first automotive mail deliveries, and the first traffic signals lined the streets.

From the first garage in Brooklyn in 1898 to the first concrete highway, a one-mile section near Detroit in 1909, a network of regulation and ritual had been installed. To this day, Manhattan's anti-auto activists still commemorate the first automobile traffic fatality, in 1899. The glow of red kerosene lanterns once warning of ruts were replaced with sophisticated lighting. The first red and green traffic light stood on a corner in Cleveland in 1914, and the first yellow light in Detroit three years later. The first gas tax, a penny a gallon in Oregon in 1919, took hold to pay for highway growth.

Laws for safety, tests for licenses, speed limits for roads, rules for headlights, and mandates against drunk driving were instituted to tame the unruly vehicle, though the new automobile laws busied the "entire force" of the Illinois secretary of state in collecting fees. "Thus far," wrote Herbert Ladd Towle, "the saving and expense about balance. Whether they do so in practice will depend largely on the outlays for commutation, extra fuel, and servants' wages."

Government outlays to serve automobiles increased. In Washington, President Woodrow Wilson signed the Federal-Aid Highway Act of 1916. The act called for the establishment of a highway department in every state. It supplied $75 million for five years and demanded that localities create highway departments to match these funds. A year later, every state had done so. Designed for rural America and the 3,617,917 motor vehicles still "stuck in the mud," the bill was supported by farm groups and suburban realtors and promoted by the American Automobile Association and the American Association of State Highway Officials, two groups whose power would become absolute in a generation. The government had declared its obligation for a federal transportation system.

The growing lobbies of manufacturers and car clubs pushed for more and better roads, and the Office of Public Roads groomed more "object-lesson" miles to show the beauty of smooth travel. Highway boosters now tagged the word "memorial" on the roads across the country: Ocean to Ocean, Dixie Meridian, Southern National, and Yellowstone Memorial highways publicized their routes. Promoters ranging from the American Road Builders Association to the Association for Standardizing Paving Specifications worked to move the motorcar.

Eschewing the Crowd

The lure of the road, taking them back to nature, mesmerized ever more Americans. Earlier in the century "See America First" had meant by rail. Now it was "Thoreau at 29 cents a gallon." Another writer addressed "M'lord autocamper's castle," declaring that "the auto contains everything wanted—bed, board and shelter." "Time and space are at your beck and call: your freedom is complete. . . . If one doesn't like a neighborhood, a day's run will change the state and scenery."

American Motorist magazine noted that "gregarious transportation has, of course, made wonderful strides but the individual has had to sacrifice much of his liberty of action to take advantage of it. He must go with the crowd at the time that the crowd wants to go and by the route the crowd takes." Buy a car and you were on your own, shunning "gregarious transportation" for your private frontier. Technology and modernity behind the wheel appealed to Progressives. Enchanted by professional expertise, they endorsed "experts as apolitical automatons." They deferred to the sway of the traffic engineers who now found the streetcar rigid. With congestion mounting, the trolley was blamed for lessening efficiency and for inflexibility. Assaults on its operators grew.

Public Transportation Slights

The financing and policy of public transportation also helped to nurture road builders over rail. Simply put, a road to a motor suburb paid for by the government cost developers nothing to build or maintain; a trolley line there taxed the owners for both. The developer of a motorcar subdivision could secure a road and city services free from the public. Street railway owners had to finance the tracks plus paving, snow shoveling, and other city fees. Crowding, "gouging," and poor maintenance were inevitable, and stirred still more protest.

Other economics favored rubber over rail. After 1906 the cheap oil from the new fields of Spindletop, Texas; the invention of the gas hose; and the declining price for artificial asphalt speeded growth. So did political preferences. Unlike the British government, which in 1909 appropriated the gas tax for all uses, American officials dedicated gas revenues exclusively for car and road maintenance. In the end the 10 million private car owners driving into the 1920s were bankrolled, while public transit riders were shortchanged. In the four years after the beginning of World War I, 137 electric railways covering some nine hundred miles of track went bankrupt. The irony and inequity would endure.

And yet, for the time being, the balance did not tip. Harmony seemed at hand. The streetcar held its own: straphangers doubled their number, tripled their speed, and quadrupled their mileage in the first two decades of the century. Big city traction systems competed to benefit from "the riding habit." Workers walked to trolley lines or journeyed to their jobs on foot. Two miles was nothing for a walk to work. The horseless carriage was still second to the dray and horse; the slowly emerging bus and truck seemed helpmates. The car lobby and enthusiasts did not override the power of the railroad or streetcar owners. The scant 310,000 car commuters made only a ripple in the sea of the 14.5 million who rode the rails and the millions more on foot. For all the invasion of the motorcar and the seedy aspects of urban life, planners remained optimistic. Reformist impulses could be fulfilled, and the motor vehicle could serve as a social agent, as Herbert Ladd Towle concluded in his missionary tract:

> Has not the automobile proved its mission? Greater liberty, greater fruitfulness of time and effort, brighter glimpses of the wide and beautiful world, more health and happiness—these are the lasting benefits of the modern motor-car. Its extravagance is passing with the novelty of speed; the rational balance of service and expense will ere long be struck, and cars built in conformity thereto. And then we shall thank God that we live in the Motor-Car Era!

So it remains that, on the horizon of American history, the Model T and the model city stood silhouetted against a promising vista as the twenties neared. Whatever the view from our late auto age, not even the most vociferous Luddite would have guessed that the first— the private car—would eventually erode the latter—America's public conveyances, its civic conscience, and its aesthetic concerns. Americans embraced the motor vehicle. Helpmate to the train, relief from horse and wagon, counterpart to the trolley, many felt it could only aid the urban core. The rubber wheel city, our sprawling outerlands and car-crossed downtowns, were down the road.

OPPOSITE: As the twenties embraced the motorcar, traffic on New York's 42nd Street and other big city streets caused motorists to clamor for more driving space. The streetcar gave way to the private vehicle, and public transportation began to falter. (Corbis-Bettman)

From Front Porch
to Front Seat

"You can today judge a civilization by the condition of its roads."
    —S. S. McClure, founder and editor, *McClure's Magazine*

"When you advance the throttle and glide through 'SOCONY TOURS' you will be agreeably surprised to find a service station 'just where you needed one.' "
    —Standard Oil New England Tour Guide, 1925

"The problem of transit and transportation alone is quite enough to demand the reconstruction of the modern city!"
    —Frederick Etchells, introduction to Le Corbusier,
        The City of To-morrow, and Its Planning

THE DOUGHBOYS CAME marching home from World War I to a nation en route to automobility. The twenties roared, and the automobile raced across a self-confident country. "Fordismus," the Germans called the optimistic era. In this booming decade the motorcar would carry America toward postwar recovery—and the full-fledged auto age.

At the beginning of the decade, the stock characters of American literature shared the passions of the 2 million car buyers a year. Sinclair Lewis's quintessential real estate agent in *Babbitt* was tooling to work in his beloved automobile, while F. Scott Fitzgerald's protagonist in *The Great Gatsby* was buying an opulent yellow Rolls-Royce. Babbitt and Gatsby were opposites in glamour, yet kin as they basked in the car's reflected glow.

The mass-produced motorcar fired the engine of prosperity. During the bull market of the 1920s car registrations tripled to more than 26 million. More than half of all American families owned a car, and by the decade's end one-fifth possessed two. The car that consumed 90 percent of America's petroleum, 8 percent of its rubber, and one-quarter of its machine tools and repair and service facilities fed the boom. By the mid-1920s, car wares ranked first in value of production. No wonder songs like "You Can't Afford to Marry Me If You Can't Afford a Ford" and "Take Me on a Buick Honeymoon" were hits. From Presidents Warren G. Harding's complacent era of "normalcy" and Calvin Coolidge's laissez-faire prosperity to Herbert Hoover's paralysis in the Depression, the automobile stood stage center, symbolizing the prosperous period. Not until the Depression would Americans note the downside of that bounty, that too many of the economic powerhouses were bought on the installment plan.

Anything-goes America was on wheels, not only Flaming Mame "wearing leopard-skin coats, driving expensive roadsters, and generally raising hell" or Clara Bow picking a red Kissel to match her hair. Every man was Midas in autoland—the clerical worker with a $2,300 income who went for the $700 Chevrolet, and the $1,300-a-year factory employee with his $400 Model T bought on time. One engineer called the disease that afflicted the young speedsters of the working classes "gasoline rabies." Even migrant workers crossed the country in battered cars, earning the label "auto-tramps."

Whether for a mass buyer or a millionaire, the horse-and-buggy style of Ford's Model T began to seem pedestrian. "Why is the Model T like a bathtub?" went the joke. "Because nobody wants to be seen in one." Shunning the attitude of the "deacon" of driving's assembly line and low-budget look-alikes, a reorganized General Motors with a new chief, Alfred J. Sloan, outjazzed the competition. To make the automobile a status purchase, Sloan hired the natty style maker Harley Earl from Hollywood, where he had customized the stars' cars, and let him run the company's Art and Color Section. The Duco brand colors available by 1924 would give the beautyless black vehicle a longer, lower, brighter, and, by now, affordable competitor. With Earl at the design helm, GM introduced the concept of the annual model in 1927, changing details of the design every year and enhancing the car's appeal to the fashionable. Chrysler also grew to comprise one of the Big Three, and the trio drove the era of excess and consumerism.

The spirit of the age showed smartly in these auto designs. The word "styling" applied to the Chrysler with its balloon tires and low-slung look, to the spoke-wheeled Kissel speedster, and the customized Cadillac. Styling made the car; the car made the man; rising mileage made the age. Frank Lloyd Wright, with his flowing neckties and smocks, matched his motorcar to his dress and his deportment. Driving his custom-equipped automobiles over the speed limit, and flouting social mores by consorting with married women passengers in the open-air seats, he symbolized the racy freedom of the auto age. The freedom displayed more somber moments too, when Isadora Duncan's fringed shawl caught in the rear wheel of a Bugatti racing car in which she was riding and broke her neck.

The *Harvard Alumni Bulletin* fretted that the automobile was undermining family values: "The motor car induces idleness and is a distracting and unsettling influence." Prohibition's roadside speakeasies symbolized the tawdry lawlessness of the motor age. The shifting mores of the age of joyriding were sending couples "to where the eye of the most sharp-sighted chaperone could not follow, and in the darkened rooms or parked cars to engage in the unspeakable practice of petting and necking," noted Fitzgerald in *This Side of Paradise*. An Atlanta judge was horrified: "It is not too much to ask the parents to throw in the clutch and put on the brakes or our entire civilization will take one last joy ride to destruction."

Motorcar manufacturers emphasized frivolity and sobriety alike in full-page magazine spreads. The extravagance of their advertising copy helped advance the age of annual models and hucksterism in the first consumer era.

It wasn't just the imagery that grabbed Americans, however; it was the trip, both long and short—the mobility. Blessed with more time for leisure, Americans with a back-to-nature urge fed by the motorcar could head to camping grounds. As the car increased its penetration of the wilderness, visits to areas of the National Park System swelled tenfold. By 1922 two-thirds of all visitors to Yellowstone arrived by car, only a third by rail. Family-filled cars pulled into motor parks or roadside stands and stayed overnight, off the highway. An architecture of rustic cabin courts and motels spilled along the roads—and into the landscape to serve them. National Forest Service employee and pioneer ecologist Aldo Leopold brooded about their impact. Wilderness must be "kept devoid of roads, artificial trails, cottages, or other works of man," he wrote. Tourists felt otherwise.

The Automotive Exodus

Motorists made an even more sweeping and prophetic exodus. They accelerated their move from city to suburb and from farm to downtown, equipping their new homes with a range of new goods. The motorcar that carried the consumer items of the Jazz Age outward smothered the Progressive vision for the car as agent of reform. Plodding George Babbitt felt that his "motor car was poetry and tragedy, love and heroism," but the heroism was no longer in the service of humanity. Material "progress"—refrigerators, washers, radios, telephones, toasters, and vacuum cleaners—excited the national passions more than Progressive politics. The children of the full-fledged auto age disowned betterment for speed, philanthropy for prosperity, and craftsmanship for technology.

Historian James Flink's definition of the first auto age as a period of Consciousness I describes the initial urge to reconcile efficiency with humanity, individualism with Progressive impulses. In those times the motorcar coexisted with aesthetic and community concerns. Not so in the 1920s. This was the time of Consciousness II; in Flink's diagram it was the era when the automobile became icon. Commanding the streets, gutting the city for traffic and parking, the motorcar was an avaricious idol. In the heyday of freewheeling capitalism, Americans worshiped the internal combustion machine and what *Fortune* magazine later ironically called the genius of "technology with its dream of engineer saviors."

Function Follows

Whether or not they were saviors, twenties engineers were certainly better mechanics. Cars were more comfortable. Electric horns, starters, and lights spread. Roofs were sealed. By the decade's end buyers would purchase four times as many automobiles with closed roofs as with open ones, speeding off in any weather, any season, any place. Forget the need to "get out and get under." No need to plug leaks with chewing gum. No more flats before the first hundred miles. Brakes held, spark plugs functioned. The typical mileage rose from 4,500 to 7,500 a year. The 5.5 million cars owned by the time of the Depression fortified automakers and parts manufacturers. Equally significant, they bolstered a vital sibling—the petroleum industry.

In an earlier era the nation had sought petroleum to fuel its lamps. With the birth of electric lights, oil had become nearly obsolete and drilling ceased. The search for black gold took off once more, driven by the automobile's growing market for gasoline. Wildcat drillers found new wells in the 1920s, and soon oil derricks lined Los Angeles's roads, filling the gas tanks of America and, in turn, bringing new residents to the balmy city. Ocean traffic also grew as entrepreneurs headed to foreign shores to thicken the flow. The cheap gas of the oil rush fueled the auto boom. The oil companies staking out new fields in Texas, Oklahoma, and California pushed for larger sales and more filling stations to expand their territories.

The gas station came to Main Street. The earlier grocer or general storekeeper dispensing gas became a serviceman in a filling station that displayed familiar artifacts and company colors. "The tall red iron gasoline-pump, the hollow-tile and terra-cotta garage, the window full of the most agreeable accessories—shiny casings, spark-plugs with immaculate porcelain jackets, tire-chains of gold and silver"—all fortified Babbitt. Brandishing company signs that beckoned buyers, the oil industry altered the nation's landscape. While the oil tycoons' wells spurred dispersed settlement by automobile, their clout and contrivances changed political mores. The Teapot Dome Scandal in 1922, involving oilmen's bribes, sullied the Harding administration, inaugurating petroleum politics as we know them. Henceforth, the need for oil to power America's automobiles would sway war and peace, foreign affairs and local ones. Interwoven demands—the thirst for mobility and the thirst for oil—had coincided in a landmark moment. The petroleum age had begun.

The petroleum-fed automobile combined with a Goliath, the truck. World War I, the first motorized war, had taught the government to value the internal combustion machine. An amazed world watched the French move troops to the Marne in Parisian taxicabs and supply besieged Verdun by truck. Allied tank superiority powered the successful drive against oil-poor, motor-poor Germany in 1918. The motorcar was victor. At home, too, the war had demonstrated the power of motorization. With hard-pressed trains drafted for war duty, trucks carried food and household goods, the staples of domestic life. As the 1920s began, 1 million trucks were registered. By the end of the decade, that number had tripled, attracting the nation's goods away from rail.

The modern motor bus, another rubber-wheeled vehicle, vied more seriously with train, trolley, and interurban as the 1920s evolved and the trolley's finances declined. Sold by General Motors salesmen whose maneuvers would earn opprobrium, the motor bus spelled trouble for mass transit. In turn, the replacement of streetcars by buses and the need for more transfers made suburbanites buy more cars. In concert the truck, the bus, the multiplying motorcar, and cheap gas powered the auto age and undermined the monopoly of the rails.

Good Roads Heroes

If mobility was to be the new norm, however, it needed one more ally—reliable roads. The rutted dirt roads that flattened the tires of the turn-of-the-century cars still pockmarked the country. At the beginning of the decade, only a third of the nation's roads were reckoned to be drivable. Boosters of the motorcar preached road building with missionary zeal. Bad roads slowed the mails, they argued. They also impeded auto sales. The gospel of speed powered the gospel of good roads. In 1920 the lobbyists secured a powerful advocate in Washington when Thomas MacDonald, a young man from Iowa who became known as "Mr. Highways" and "The Chief," joined the Bureau of Public Roads. At its helm he would one day command an empire of asphalt.

A young army captain opted to help with the job of motorizing America. Bored with military life, West Point graduate Dwight D. Eisenhower agreed to conduct a motor convoy. In one of many stunts calling attention to the sorry conditions of highways, Eisenhower's convoy dedicated "Zero Milestone" near the White House lawn and chugged forth at less than six miles an hour. His caravan of forty-two trucks, motorcars, motorcycles, and mobile field kitchens and repair shops crawled through "darkest America," as the future president recalled. Eisenhower felt dismay at the roads, which ranged from "average to non-existent . . . not quite so good as even the slowest troop train." As president a generation later, he would sign the Interstate Highway and Defense Act of 1956, putting Washington dead center as the engine of highway making.

Government policies—land laws, grants, subsidies, and bureaucracies—had always moved the nation. From turnpikes to canals to railroads, the nation of "individualists" had depended on federal support. The government intervention augured by the first Federal-Aid Highway Act of 1916, to "get the farmer out of the mud," began to expand. In 1921 a new Federal-Aid Highway Act put the government bureaucracy in the road-building business to "close the gaps" on primary rural roads. To launch a national highway system, Washington would split the cost evenly with the states. Localities followed suit. By mid-decade highway building costs exceeded a billion dollars a year. Street and highway building comprised the decade's second largest government expense, the backbone of the auto boom.

Thus allied with the government, the growing auto industry, its lobbyists and profiteers, local allies and national agencies, automakers and gas station servicers, carried out the Lincoln Highway's motto to "build it" before they were indeed "too old to enjoy it." Crews paved the Lincoln Highway to send the glossy all-weather motor vehicles on their way and other roadsters followed suit.

Some designers still favored fitting the highway into an older route in the tradition of Olmsted's scenic parkways. Edsel Ford, Henry's son, hired landscape architect Jens Jensen to design attractive segments as prototypes. An advocate for native plants and "prairie rivers," Jensen based his "ideal section" in Indiana on the aesthetics of its natural context, planted with wildflowers, hawthorn, or crab apple and lined with hiking trails. Curving the road through a grove of trees or placing a footpath by campgrounds, he tried to make a prairie highway that meshed with its environment. It was, said a press release of the time, a "harmonious plan which with modifications can be adapted along Lincoln Highway and other main roads anywhere between Omaha and New York City."

Not everyone in the go-fast automotive era agreed. The landscape architect himself worried about the avarice of the period's "pavement-minded" outlook. He dreaded that highway engineers would find the expense of his model road "unwarranted," and he was right. By and large, Jensen's would be the road not taken. When avid motorists and road builders surged ahead, the urge for asphalt overtook serving nature.

Pelting Public Transit

As car ownership grew ever larger, train and trolley suffered. Even as streetcar ridership peaked at 15 billion, motor traffic was gaining on it. A generation of drivers joined Babbitt in "the game of beating trolley cars to the corner." The motoring nation claimed dominance on the crowded streets. The rail that carried the suburban commuter to the walking city would fall from its early 1920s peak of 47 billion passenger-miles per year.

To some extent streetcar franchise owners and railroad men shared the blame for their fate. Owners often feared and disdained the government. More real estate promoters than people movers, they acted in shortsighted and mercenary ways, raising prices, bribing officials, and abusing or ignoring patrons. Auto manufacturers, on the other hand, cozied up to politicians and bureaucrats.

The temper of the times and the rules of the road also continued to favor highway men, economically, bureaucratically, and politically. Economically, the motorcar was grabbing a free right-of-way, while the privately owned electric streetcar or interurban had to pay for its route, maintenance, and other fees. Bureaucratically, the motor truck was unhampered in carrying the nation's goods, while the trains faced the Interstate Commerce Commission's "iron hand" of reform and their own sometimes conflicting interest in trucks. Politically, widening a road was expedient, quickly showing its worth, while a rail extension took years to build. Perversely, too, the cars that clogged the city streets were deemed "democratic" and hence were subsidized. The rail that moved the masses was called "corporate business" and was penalized.

Such beliefs dictated the downslide of rail. When rail was failing, straphangers did not fight for public funds to improve service but rather fought against the owners. When motorcars faltered, drivers and the auto industry fought for more aid for the automobile. This blindness would prove tragic to public transit—and, in the end, to public space, public land, and public life. Thus constricted, the three forms of railed transit—streetcars, interurbans, and railroads—saw their profits shrink still further. "Colonial Americans had little choice but to walk to their jobs in the city," streetcar historian Mark S. Foster has observed. "Their heirs had almost no alternative but to drive."

In the early 1920s no one could have prophesied such a future. In 1919 a discouraged Henry Ford had thought of quitting the automobile industry for the trolley business. As the decade advanced, however, drivers went on a spending spree in the nation's forty-three-thousand automobile dealerships, and set America behind the wheel. Route 66 became a symbol of the times. Founded by another booster, highway commissioner Cyrus Avery, it was the nation's ribbon of commerce, stretching twenty-two-hundred miles from Chicago to

Los Angeles. "The Mother Road" and "Main Street of America" for Edgar Lee Masters, Sinclair Lewis, and Thornton Wilder, it became synonymous "with garden scarecrows, porch swings, watermelon feasts, lemonade stands, and children sticking their stocking feet out the back window of the family car as Dad made time on the road." Or so one fan wrote years later, when sentimental America was singing "Get Your Kicks on Route 66."

Architecture of the Road

The kicks, or at least the services, spread to the strips built for the motorist's needs. Owners ordered highway-minded signs and buildings to fit the new form of movement, one-liner images to grab the attention of the motorist traveling at thirty-five miles an hour. Diners with dog faces, buildings shaped like milk bottles, or the famous Brown Derby restaurant speckled the streetscape. One hundred tile-roofed pagodas rose near Milwaukee; multiple steel tepees dotted Lawrence, Kansas. The Colonial motel court, the Art Deco diner, the Renaissance filling station, and countless service stops catered to the motorist's eating, sleeping, and drinking needs. The new "roadside boards," today's billboards, designed to catch the driver's eye in eighteen seconds, peppered the highways.

Slowly, commerce for the moving vehicle, not the shop window for the pedestrian, began to shape America's highway architecture. To "Make Them Remember the Place" was the way Shell Oil explained its shell-shaped gas stations. Though their whimsical symbols appeal to us now, the dreary little roadhouses and gas pumps and sheds were lackluster and worse. As auto age advertisements and strip developments cluttered the landscape, reformers feared the banishment of nature. They attacked "the sordid ugliness of cheap commerce." Developer Jesse Nichols scored "glaring billboards, unsightly rubbish dumps, hideous rears, unkempt alleys, dirty loading docks." The filling stations and ramshackle structures scattered beneath stark power lines bothered Benton MacKaye, the foresighted naturalist with "his heart in the crumbling country towns." This Yankee conservationist grieved over the auto age. "The motor slum in the open country is today as massive a piece of defilement as the worst of the old-fashioned urban industrial slums," he wrote.

Bridge and tunnel makers began to gouge channels, dig through rocky passes, and clamber over "impediments" to create more roads like Route 66 and other scenic highways for the moving vehicle. Workers burrowed under the Hudson River, inserting two massive tubes and covering them with 4 million tiles for the first tunnel exclusively for cars. On opening day in 1927, some 51,694 curious motorists paid fifty cents a trip to drive through the Holland Tunnel. That same year the West Side Highway, America's first elevated, opened. The infrastructure for the automobile grew apace: a few miles from the Holland Tunnel, the George Washington Bridge was planned to go to New Jersey; Pittsburgh's "high-speed road" to follow the Monongahela. By the mid-1920s, hardly a city street lacked pavement, while roads of passable quality had multiplied on the periphery. By the time the 25 millionth car came off the assembly line in 1925, the first traffic engineering textbook had been published.

Americans willingly dug into their pockets to pay for road expansion. In 1919, ten years after the first gas tax, every state possessed the power to charge three to four cents a gallon. Never before or again have so many Americans so enthusiastically said yes to taxation.

The institutionalization of the automobile advanced. Traffic fatalities accelerated, along with the devices to control them. Signs became more uniform from state to state, and surveys counted traffic. Parking regulations were put in place. Traffic lights gave less time to walkers and E. P. Goodrich suggested overpasses to get rid of them altogether. "The pedestrian was a most serious hindrance," said one traffic engineer. In 1923, less than a decade after Boston had invented the word "jaywalking," Los Angeles won the dubious achievement of banning it. Two years later, more commuters came downtown by car than public transit. By the decade's end, the city's Wilshire-Western intersection, "the busiest street in the world," would be crossed by 7 million cars a year.

Outward the Course

And where were they going with all this speed and muscle, all this moving of soil and transforming of space? Away from the crowded city, joyriding to a new frontier. "Every multi-lane ribbon of concrete was like the touch of Midas, transforming old pastures into precious property," historian Kenneth Jackson describes the twenties poetically in *Crabgrass Frontier*. Pushing outward, the automobile was creating a real estate boom beyond the center city—and, here too, the price was still right. Where the developer of the streetcar suburb had paid his own way, the motor colonist had yet another free ride. Not only would the municipality pay for the road, but it would also string a wire or lay a gas pipe, build schools, finance services, and charge the taxpayer for their upkeep, supporting, yet again, the car-bred exodus of the American dream. The own-your-own-home movement to Eden was on.

The inducements to diffuse settlement were even more tempting and interwoven: they were geographical. While the trolley lines radiating from a hub had left empty lots between their fixed rails, the flexible motorcar let developers fill the leftover space between the spokes, leapfrogging outward to the green fields and farms in the angles between streetcar routes. The persuasions were also economic. With easier mortgages from bankers, bedroom suburbs, like suburb-bound cars, would boom on the installment plan. Whether simple frame houses or gracious residences, the single-family dwellings lured urbanites to flee the city in a broadening arc.

The spatial transformation changed not only the look of the land but its domestic architecture. As the front seat gained parity with the front porch, neighborhoods altered. The place where folks congregated in the waning hours of a summer day now faced a noisy intruder. A car trip, not a hammock, beckoned. The sidewalk began to yield to the motorcar. "The automobile has made a big difference," Jesse Nichols told realtors in 1921. A trip behind the wheel shortened "the distance between points so greatly that the use of sidewalks, for instance, has fallen off immensely." In some cases only one side of the street had a sidewalk. "We are not using sidewalks the way we used to," he continued. The house set back from the street and the deeper lawn made a more beautiful street because you did not have the "two harsh lines of sidewalk." Or so he termed the walker's territory of an older socializing space.

The front door shifted too, as the motor entrance gained prominence. So did the garage. With a careful developer, the resting place for the automobile might resemble a garden pergola; with a careless builder, any old box would do. Either way, the garage began to supersede the front door. "Why not keep your automobile in the house?" one writer asked. The home itself began to change to store the automobile. The walk-in entryway of times past had greeted the visitor with a grandiose roof and expansive front door. The 1920s motor-minded family began to enter the home through the dank garage.

Though the schism between foot traffic and motor traffic deepened, ideals of neighborhood and walkability did persist in the emerging auto age. John Nolen continued his task "to produce local Happiness" in his "National Exemplar," Mariemont, Ohio, and in more than four hundred commissions of carefully wrought plans that he fashioned through the mid-1930s. Harland Bartholomew, Arthur Shurcliffe, and some two dozen architecture firms drew community plans with contoured streets, handsome dwellings, and public and semipublic spaces that kept the car in its place.

Community-conscious realtors like Nichols and Edward Bouton continued to develop thoughtful projects. Aiming to improve on the auto strip, in 1923 Nichols placed America's first shopping center at his earlier Country Club Plaza. There, he shaped a compact Mediterranean ensemble, with alluring turrets, tiled roofs, and other Seville-bred motifs. By tucking general parking behind the building and putting angled parking before it, Nichols's plaza respected sidewalk life and served shoppers escaping the snarls of downtown. Nichols also managed to integrate lawn beautification and bird conservation while installing a motorcar agency and a White Rose filling station as a "fashionable part of the design." Though conceived with cars in mind, his urbane plans worked as a village settlement that made a thriving contrast to nearby neighborhoods laid out by more speculative builders.

On narrow, tree-lined streets, aspirations of the late Progressive period still lingered into the 1920s. Planners like the Olmsted Brothers' firm, Henry V. Hubbard, and Stephen Child continued to stamp their mark on the onrushing auto suburb. Zoning—"keeping the furnace out of the living room"—was ruled constitutional by the Supreme Court in *Euclid* v. *Ambler* in Cleveland in 1926, and some planners even moved beyond zoning's narrow exclusions to opt for wider regional plans. If landscape architects skipped the city center for decentralized subdivisions, their designs treated the new lands tenderly. Siting and street making were fused. Updating places like Palos Verdes in California or Roland Park in Maryland, the Olmsted firm tailored movement to topography. In their work at the Highlands in Seattle, the roads were plotted at an easy grade with automobiles in mind so as to create ever changing passages of scenery, with a majestic vista of Puget Sound and the Olympic Mountains.

Nonetheless, the motor vehicle and the road gained primacy. The city felt the outflow. The growth of even thriving urban areas was slight compared to the 59 percent rise in the suburban population. In the seven years before the Depression, new homes built moved close to the million mark per year. The car led the way to the suburban boom. Grosse Pointe pulled people from Detroit, Elmwood Park from Chicago. As the automobile made the suburbs accessible and mass transit's growth stagnated, "settling" people became "sending" them. And congestion grew. "Their [the cars] very numbers begin to distill the poison that blights the paradise they seek," was the way Frederick Law Olmsted, Jr., voiced the hopeless paradox.

Retooling for Traffic

Some urban policy makers went so far as to suggest kicking the automobile out of the core. Chicago merchants, still in a building boom through the 1920s, acquiesced to the notion of banning parking in the Loop. Less successfully, Los Angeles attempted to remove parked cars from downtown. Downtown retailers mostly wrapped their city stores with parking. In Chicago the Jewelers Building tucked a garage inside to house as many as 550 cars. Most retail stores began to send branches to follow their customers to the periphery. In 1925, Sears, Roebuck decided to open only suburban shops. Here, the style suited the motorist. Storefronts like those in Cleveland's Shaker Square were set back from the street to serve angle parking in front or wrapped with asphalt all around.

Worried as their downtown trade fell from 75 to 25 percent, Bullocks-Wilshire designed for the auto age, opening a branch department store with bold windows to lure the passing motorist, not the pedestrian. In 1927 the retail store took to the Miracle Mile. It placed its main portal, a grand entrance, to the rear through the parking lot. Thus, the auto age's parking-dominated architecture was installed. Soon other shops flanked what critic Reyner Banham calls "the first linear Downtown," creating a blend of walking and driving pleasure by hemming the street with fashionable store windows and tucking cars to the rear. The City of Angels, where all but 6 percent of the families now lived in single-family homes, was, in Banham's words, "the first real monument of the Motor Age."

Planners shifted their scale of design to road scale and their orientation from sidewalk to street. Designers of chains like A&P or Piggly Wiggly, now self-service stores, paralleled the elongated highway in extended aisles. Owners enlarged Main Street stores from the walker's window-by-window pace to become three doorways wide with an adjacent parking lot. Gas stations shot across pedestrian space. Sidewalks shrank. In Kansas City, Missouri, a filling station opened every two or three blocks. Merchants, motivated by the perpetual problem of car storage, built "car parks" for customers. The architecture of the auto age impinged on residences. "This home to be wrecked—splendid locations for filling stations, garages, hot dog stands, laundries, etc.—Greed and Grab, Agents," went the script of a tabloid cartoon prophesying the fate of Wilshire Boulevard.

The need for traffic flow in the city caused more butchery to old buildings and landscapes. In 1921, Manhattan officials eliminated half of the mall of Park Avenue to let traffic flow. In 1924, Andrew Mellon, secretary of the Treasury, told *Collier's* magazine that he would like to move the Washington Monument for more parking. The heirs to the obelisk in Buffalo's Niagara Square proposed still more City Beautiful buildings to fill in public space, yet the city took a hatchet to its elms to widen Delaware Avenue to sixty feet. "A platoon of the city's oldest residents went under the executioner's ax. They were in the way," declared the *Buffalo Courier*. So was the City Beautiful movement, and as business migrated outward, the city itself seemed merely a pit stop in the flight.

Flight to the Sun

The drivers who fled the rooted cities were joined by those who mo-
tored to warmer climes. America's manifest destiny seemed to be to
drive South for play and settlement. "Motor-busses roared down
Flagler Street, carrying 'prospects' on free trips to watch the dredgers
and steam-shovels converting the mangrove swamps and the sand-
bars of the Bay of Biscayne into gorgeous Venetian cities for the
American home-makers and pleasure-seekers of the Future," was the
way historian Frederick Lewis Allen portrayed the colorful Miami
scene in *Only Yesterday.* In the speculative boom of the 1920s, developers filled the Miami Beach swamps with $100 million worth of
construction in just three years. From 1920 to 1925, the city grew
from 30,000 to 75,000 people.

The Dixie Highway, the Route 66 of the South, running from
northern Michigan to Miami, was clogged at all hours. One traveler
caught in traffic recorded license plates from eighteen states among
the sedans and flivvers in line. The developers of the Sunshine State
of Florida and the city of Los Angeles in the "boost—don't knock"
decade seemed miracle workers brought by car from every part of the
country. South Beach in Miami began to blossom into a colorful
streetscape. In California, Santa Barbara, recovering from a 1925
fire, shaped a beguiling Mediterranean downtown that drew hundreds to its temperate climate. Architect Addison Mizener, outfitted
in flashy Hawaiian shirts, brought a Spanish flair with arcaded shops
and splendid homes for the wintering millionaires in Palm Beach,
Florida. In Boca Raton, he constructed a pink stucco resort replete
with a gold-domed town hall, modest worker homes, pastel bungalows, and a shaded, walkable Main Street. The flamboyant architect
offered total mobility for walkers, with gondolas plying the cobalt
fingers of sea and lake to ferry visitors from the railroad station to his
watery fantasy.

Los Angeles, possessing one motor vehicle for every two of the arrivals and doubling its population each decade, still boasted urbane
designs. Mediterranean facades decorated apartments and defined
side-by-side bungalows. Courtyard housing edged sidewalks, their
landscaped common spaces allowing for both public and private use.

Southern California's architects turned revival forms into sophisticated apartment buildings for the Eastern-bred acting elite who came to Hollywood. Whether the buildings were drafted by architects or hammered together by everyday builders, terraced in the hills or snug by the street, they shaped walkable environs while accommodating the car. From Santa Monica to Beverly Hills, picturesque multifamily dwellings, their entries overhung by rippling tile roofs, supplemented the staple single-family house.

Art Deco Downtown

Most downtown hubs still flourished amid automotive dispersion. In their encyclopedic survey *Our Cities To-day and To-morrow,* Theodora Kimball Hubbard and Henry Vincent Hubbard noted that "all the great cities have thriven and increased": Philadelphia, Chicago, and St. Louis incrementally, Dallas by doubling in size, Los Angeles and Detroit by leaps and bounds. The ten largest cities tripled their office space. An exuberant design mode of the machine age arose to decorate this last whirlwind of creative urban architecture. While "Bull Market Georgian" spread into the suburbs, the Art Deco style—vertical, hard edged, bold—began to embellish city facades. Born in Paris's 1925 Exposition Internationale des Arts Décoratifs et Industriels Modernes, these European-bred zigzag shapes, framed by brick and bronze, enhanced modern apartment buildings. Images of lightning bolts and exotic plants decorated interiors. Egyptian, pre-Columbian, or Jugendstil motifs adorned skyscrapers. Vivid terra-cotta and glass tiles enhanced their designs. In Manhattan the Art Deco skyscrapers soared, their height transforming them into urban mountains. Their stepped-back shapes, dictated by Manhattan's ordinance of 1919 to let in light, created a new skyline and streetscape that bestirred civic pride.

Designs for the Empire State Building and other lofty structures emerged in the final hours before the Depression. Detroit bedecked its environs with the work of the gifted factory architect Albert Kahn, who built the motor manufacturers' colossal plants, while George Post shaped the city's splendid downtown department stores. Chicago architects lit up urban design around the Loop. With buoyant reliefs and notched bases, the elegant towers of the Wrigley, Telephone, and Standard Oil buildings stood stark against the sky. The era's picture palaces, "an acre of seats in a garden of dreams," lent opulence and verve to urban centers everywhere, even if parking caused complaints. From Automats to telephone companies to Woolworth's five-and-dime, such Art Moderne partook of the car culture yet brightened the city face of Jazz Age America as the decade closed.

To compete with the spreading suburbs, city builders displayed high style and innovative interiors in housing, too. Tudor City, in mid-Manhattan, coaxed the middle class into a suburb that seemed to be a city within a city. The picturesque mid-rise Deco Gothic eased domestic life for its inhabitants with kitchenless suites and shared food service for singles, hardware shops and other stores and services, and an enticing park. Other, older inner suburbs sported apartments with "modern Gothic" shapes outside and department stores and stylish restaurants within. Walkable and transit-based, they made old cores ambulatory as they tried to accommodate the automobile.

City traffic departments still paid attention to the old "municipal arts," adorning iron street signs with silhouettes of stagecoaches. The design conscious pondered what to do with gas pumps sprouting along sidewalks. "Curbing the Curb Pump," *American City* magazine put it, picturing "service stations as an asset to the city" disguised as Tudor cottages, becolumned bungalows, and Spanish missions. Deco ornament might also garnish an automated skyscraper garage northwest of Columbus Circle or a handsome pier building waterside; patterned brick enlivened many a subway entrance's facade.

The Twilight of Rail

American architecture rallied in the spirited hours before the Depression, with some of its crowning achievements pegged to rail. Daniel Burnham and Edward Bennett's still pertinent Chicago Plan emerged in Union Station in 1925. On opening day Cleveland's "Union Station on the Square" proclaimed itself the "heart of the city and hub of urban transportation." "Gateway of continental travel," its boosters declared. They believed that the placement of the new fifty-two-story terminal tower at the heart of the fan-shaped route through Cleveland's geography destined it to be "the center of a metropolitan system of rapid transit, now in the making." Before the Depression the city's Van Sweringen brothers, "the wonder-boys of railroading," had acquired seven railroads. They looked out from their observation post and saw "the fringe of homes moving farther and farther out . . . evidences of the abundant opportunities with which the city beckons" and built rails to their real estate projects. The shaded lawns and homes of Cleveland's Shaker Heights marked the final flourish of the streetcar suburb in the early hours of automobile ascendancy.

"Cures" for Congestion

Twilight it was. For, as traffic grew, cars continued to squeeze trolleys and congestion stultified the city. "An echo of hell," one New Yorker described the travelers' frayed nerves, the scrambles for parking and the jammed, impoverished transit ride. Gathering six hundred New Yorkers to reform the situation, the Russell Sage Foundation financed a study of the city's population, traffic, government and neighborhoods. Thus, the "monumental" ten-year, ten-volume New York Regional Plan was born. Opting for planned dispersal from the bursting city, the document's drafters envisioned a titanic network of physical forms to maintain productivity and cope with the congestion that had quintupled cars to 600,000 in the decade before 1927.

A myriad of corridors—radial and circumferential, bypassing and connecting, elevating walkers and tucking cars below—characterized their 1929 plan. These would send Manhattanites outward, ending "the unsightly congestion and turmoil of the present. Pedestrians will move about through the arcaded streets, out of danger from traffick [and] protected from the snows of winter and the glare of the summer sun." Drawings that seemed science fiction visions with futuristic highways in the sky replaced the old, down-to-earth sketches based on a faith in urban progress. Alas, the planners' orderly, if highway-oriented, scheme would underestimate the power of the automobile to override their designs.

The street corner tide of traffic and the exodus of city dwellers and merchants prompted other city plans. Angelenos, too, stewed about the cars colliding with the crowds of walkers, carriages, and trolleys. Chicagoans feared for the future. "Unless remedial measures are taken, no one can say what this waste will be in the future, if the daily use of the automobile is not superseded by elevated arterial transportation but continues to increase at its present astounding rate," said one observer.

What were these remedial measures? Widen roads, said Hartford, Cleveland, and Indianapolis. New street plans, said Wichita. Extensions in Chattanooga, bridges in Johnstown, Pennsylvania. Planners and engineers labored to give the automobile more space—and roads a new form. In 1928, New Jersey's Woodbridge Cloverleaf, based on a Parisian design, begat the first of what Lewis Mumford called America's "national flower."

Unleash the auto. Make traffic flow, said officials. Double-decking streets, eliminating grade crossings, fixing signals, inserting new roads were "improvements" advanced to relieve the traffic crisis. "There is practically no limit to the rapidity of service with automobile traffic. It is only a matter of providing road space to accommodate the incredible number of vehicles," said the manager of the Chicago Motor Club in 1924. In the thirty years before 1929, Chicago spent a fruitless $400 million to do so by widening streets. Accidents merely multiplied.

Stitching Whole Lives

One assembly of young planning reformers sought other means to stem the crush. "Loath to live fractured lives in either city or country," they formed the Regional Planning Association of America in 1923. "The first organization in America to critically assess the new order created by modern industry and mass transportation," the association concerned itself with leaving open land and creating closed communities. Architects and dreamers Clarence Stein and Henry Wright, along with naturalist and planner Benton MacKaye, would work to promote the designs. Unlike New York's similarly named Regional Plan Association, which they attacked, these design colleagues had no truck with realtors. Given voice by the poetic and moral suasion of Lewis Mumford, its members worried about the "dinosaur cities." They equally scorned the suburban castle in the land and the farm communities "swallowed up sooner or later by the swelling tide of city congestion." They deplored the alternatives offered by the modern landscape.

Writing together, Mumford and MacKaye lamented the highway landscape: "There is the vast, spreading metropolitan slum of multiple gas stations and hot-dog stands; and on the through highways there is the conflict between speed, safety, and pleasure." They grounded their plans in the ecology of the valley and the region, based on English planner Ebenezer Howard's satellite cities surrounded by greenbelts to contain growth, keep work close to home, and end congestion downtown.

In 1924, on an empty site in Queens, New York, the RPAA members launched their first offering—Sunnyside Gardens. Instead of "semi-detached houses whose surrounding open spaces are covered by a multitude of auto drives and garages," as Mumford wrote, they transformed their greened fifty-five-acre-tract into close neighborhoods. Walkways and pedestrian alleys connected Sunnyside to other vigorous neighborhoods and all of Queens. The gridded blocks, broad interior lawns, and shared courtyards, all without a single garage and a fifteen-minute subway ride from Times Square, reached heights of urbanity and intimacy that endure to this day. "Its gardens and courts kept that friendly air as, year by year, the newcomers improved in the art of gardening," as Mumford recalled in *Green Memories*.

The Motor Age Aftermath

Alas, their next project showed that the reformers had absorbed the car culture of the time. The community's label, "The Town for the Motor Age," made it evident. Not yet viewing the car as the arch villain, the Regional Planning Association of America sought to harness the automobile as an adjunct to rail and to keep the surroundings safe from the street. In Radburn, New Jersey, motor vehicles and power lines would sanction "Garden Cities," green oases designed to insulate the so-called neighborhood unit. The architecture by Stein and Wright, with landscape architecture by Marjorie Sewell Cautley, aimed to isolate motorcars, with their noise and smell and dangers, by splitting foot traffic from car traffic with cul-de-sacs and underpasses. Living rooms surveyed interior lawns laced with pedestrian paths where youngsters could walk to school or play without seeing a single car.

Unfortunately, the "Radburn idea," with its fight-through-flight mentality and its auto-centric design, had a less ideal future down the road. Unhinged from Mumford's regional planning message, the New Jersey site now suffers from the traffic near its door. The reformers' dreams of a Garden City blend of life and nearby work have vanished. Radburn's immediate heirs—the towns Stein and Wright planned for Chatham Village in Pittsburgh in the dire days of the Depression and those of Stein at Baldwin Hills Village in Los Angeles a decade later—however congenial—lacked the transit links and city-embedded appeal of Sunnyside. Their work would fill the textbooks, but in practice the developments now look more like single-use auto-dependent subdivisions than reform.

Late Pleasure Drives

For now, the early aspirations of landscape architects endured. The scenic ideals of the parkway movement blended ease and beauty of motion in New York's Hutchinson River Parkway in 1928, the Saw Mill River Parkway in 1929, and the Cross County Parkway three years later. Parks commissioner Robert Moses's Henry Hudson Parkway, swinging by the West Side, eased life in its neighborhood and had peers from Jersey City to Chicago, Boston to Philadelphia. Powered by a regard for "scientific" planning and artistic passion, other parks and parkways designed from 1919 to 1932 witnessed the "birth of an energy-intensive society" that their creators felt could channel the car's speed. Designs by landscape architects like Warren Manning showed curbs on park roads, splendid stairways, and ornaments for tarrying, not racing. Pleasure driving constituted half of all California's travel, Frederick Olmsted wrote.

Though the efficiencies of the Long Island Parkway stirred Robert

Moses, autocrat of the auto age, the parks commissioner had not yet attained his full authority. Moses continued the Westchester and Long Island road extensions as scenic parkways, not thoroughfares, sending motorists from the city to the seashore, much as the railway builders had sent them to other pleasure grounds. His Jones Beach, dedicated the year of the Great Crash, was a splendid sunshine retreat for city dwellers. Overflowing with ornament and architectural elements, it was a symbol of civic delight. Yet, the signs were clear. Moses's low bridges that deliberately restricted bus passage for the poor foreshadowed the future when the park man's dreams became the city's nightmares. As agent of the motorized movement, Moses had an outlook that would mark America.

A Thousand Cuts

Park advocates were not sanguine in the encroaching auto age. "The service of motor-traffic, recreational in only a minor degree so far as the park system is concerned, has become the main consideration for the park administration," Sylvester Baxter wrote in the *Boston Evening Transcript*. "Hence the chief stress is laid upon the development, maintenance and policing of the boulevards and parkways." A survey by Theodora and Henry Hubbard expressed similar apprehension that "greater width and wider curves and the necessity for avoiding all blind corners make the automobile road, in its appearance and its use, destructive of natural beauty." And Arthur Shurcliffe feared the threats from the "new mode of conveyance" that attacked the green space's curvaceous angles, turning radiuses, entrances, grade crossings, and upkeep.

The menace grew in blueprints for cities: St. Louis's riverfront scheme boasted "a great area for parking" and "automobile storage." When Dallas removed the tracks from Pacific Avenue, it was called an "improvement." The urban assaults multiplied in places to park cars: ramped garages to link theaters, offices, and banks, and separate garages to serve department store shoppers. The number of traffic timers, parking meters, signs to hurry, and signs to slow increased. And so, of course, did motor vehicles. As streams of trolleys and weaving cars competed for city space, the cars won out. Two decades after the City Beautiful movement, congestion drove planners to endorse emptying, not beautifying, the urban core.

The Great Divide

To be sure, more than half the nation continued to live in urban America. Yet city growth had reached a watershed. The great divide that separates post-1920s cities from their ancestors is the divide between a human-oriented world and a car-oriented one. No more did a fan-ribbed pattern of settlement center around the vertical downtown or village cluster where the train or trolley stopped. Motorizing America limned the car-based sprawl to come. Not one city of "splendour" would surface after the 1920s launched America's "autohegemony."

In the neon city of downtown, streetcars still clanged. Despite the changing "riding habit," only 3 out of 120 cities lacked rail. Streetcars got more comfortable, their colors brightened. Transporting baseball fans to Louisville's stadium or scenery seekers to Lookout Mountain in Chattanooga, the rail lines lengthened. At mid-decade Detroit bought seven hundred new streetcars and boasted the longest trolley car in the nation. On the eve of the Depression, plans for subways in the center, elevateds in outlying areas, and buses in thinly populated places were on urban America's list. Even in fragmented Los Angeles, the Pacific Electric interurban built a short subway, while, to the north, San Francisco planners dreamed of regional rail despite the move to automobile hegemony.

"Harmonious" viaducts for steam railroads protected pedestrians in St. Louis, and trolley tunnels headed through the hills of Providence, Rhode Island. An eight-block subway for its surface-car line was under construction in Milwaukee, and others awaited authorization. Rochester, trying to relieve downtown traffic, placed a streetcar and interurban in the old Erie Canal. Planners from Washington, D.C., to Ponca City, Oklahoma, scored new lines on their maps.

Street railway men were fighting for survival, however. Advertisements suggested their predicament. The traction operators' concern with "Making Transportation Pay" in a 1926 issue of a trade magazine became a more tremulous "Popularizing Public Transportation" and then the blatant "Selling Transportation." The chairman of De-

troit's Rapid Transit complained, "We pay through delays and reduced efficiency. We pay through nervous wear and tear, through loss
of property in blighted areas, and lessened values." Even Clarence
Stein blamed streetcars for the chaos downtown. Subways, a long
time in the making, won few new fans. And, as public transit showed
its troubles and profits shrank, the railways sputtered along in red
ink. "Bandits," the riders called the traction magnates, while the
public asked, Why stand in line, why face the hurry-burly of
strangers when the car promises comfort, privacy, and personal mobility? Demoralized, mass transit was caving. The steady parade of
streetcars traveled on to extinction.

The mandate for wider roads and multilevel highways, spiralling
to span some vast space with air-bound structures, revealed the ex-
pectation that the motor vehicle could control urban and technological reform to fashion a better world. Improved lighting, contouring,
and flattening, along with safety features, would help traffic flow,
said William Phelps Eno, a traffic expert who proposed making
plazas into parking with a quick chop to interfering street trees. The
32,500 car-related deaths a year at the end of the decade would decrease. Technological innovations could curb the carnage. Hugh Ferris's 1929 "Metropolis of Tomorrow," with its piled roads and
futuristic interchanges, was a dramatic and popular image. Reformers believed that inventions like the "freeway" were promising and
would reduce the ever-growing menace to health from fumes.

"Destroy the street," said Le Corbusier. In fact, the fountainhead
of modern architecture predicted the future that modernism would
introduce in 1929. The architect's "Radiant City" showed urban
towers set in parks and wrapped by roads. Roads freed from walkers
filled the drawings of his classic *The City of To-morrow*. It was the
American joyride, and no one paused to consider future loss as the
thrill of a new machine gave wheels to their whims. In Consciousness
II, in this takeover by the car culture, reform was not an issue. Stability and urbanity were secondary, if not negative, aspirations. Speed
and automobility mattered most. From the Bureau of Public Roads
redrawing state plans "to improve alignments and eliminate curves,"
to Le Corbusier exulting in the new geometry of power, all would
agree on the shortest distance between two points.

To motoring America, "fill 'er up" was indeed the national "have a nice day" by the decade's end. In 1928 consumerism seemed endless. Poverty looked as out of date as the horse and carriage, and America, as Herbert Hoover put it, was "bright with hope." Yet, the bargain was struck: automobility would replace all other forms of movement. In October 1929, Hoover's brightness dimmed, the feverish bull market went black, and hope crashed. Unbeknownst to those building for an unceasing tomorrow, the lights of the star city were flickering with that hope. The automobile had and would eclipse the past. "Changed. So changed," as *The Magnificent Ambersons* would conclude.

OPPOSITE: Even during the Depression, Americans took to their automobiles. Public support for the car culture prevailed as the Roosevelt administration funded road construction to provide new jobs and new highways carrying still more cars. (Farm Security Administration. Photo: Dorothea Lange. The Library of Congress.)

Driving Through the Depression

"Oppose with all your strength and power all proposals to penetrate your wilderness regions with motorways and other symbols of modern mechanization. Keep large sections of primitive country free from the influence of destructive civilization."
—Horace M. Albright, director, National Park Service, 1933

"Speed is the cry of our era, and greater speed one of the goals of tomorrow."
—Norman Bel Geddes, *The Machine Age*

THE NATION DROVE from the great boom into the Great Depression, literally and figuratively. America's 26 million automobiles, more than one for every household, carried them. A teetering Europe, a depressed countryside, high production with low wages, and stock market speculation precipitated the fall. But the car culture paved the road to "Black Tuesday." Buying on time, the wage earner had handed out as much to the car dealer as to the mortgage banker. Driving would not cease.

Americans were not only paying for their "easy-credit" loans. Their municipalities were paying for expenses swollen by the car and the costs of its sprawling settlement. In 1933 the President's Research Committee on Social Trends confirmed the car's exactions: "This taking to wheels of an entire population had a profound effect on the aggregate burden of taxation." In the city the automobile created the burden of motorized police, traffic cops, and traffic congestion. In the motor suburbs its sprawl caused steep fees for new schools, facilities, and support systems, from traffic lights to garbage trucks and snowplows. "Imperceptibly, car ownership has created an 'automobile psychology,' " the committee noted. "The automobile has become a dominant influence in the life of the individual and he, in a real sense, has become dependent upon it."

In the aftermath of the Crash of 1929 the mood of desperation was palpable. Thirteen million jobless Americans stood in breadlines. The number of New Yorkers selling apples for a nickel reached six thousand. The auto industry felt the decline fiercely. By 1932 half the auto plants in Michigan had closed. The saturation of the car market combined with the Depression shut down one out of three dealers. Within a year after the stock market crash, the number of auto workers had shrunk by 100,000, reflecting and accelerating the dwindling car sales. Wage seekers lined the streets of Detroit from late night to morning waiting for employment offices to open. The statement by former GM president Will Durant, now bankrupt, that his losses would make a pile a hundred thousand miles high didn't inspire confidence.

Consciousness I, the embryonic age of the automobile, had been succeeded by Consciousness II during the veneration of the 1920s. The Depression delivered a crushing blow to all that, it seemed. Was a new consciousness, a sense of the culpability of the automobile, at hand? Would a sense of its liabilities shift the nation's attitude?

No second thoughts beset Henry Ford. "We believe that the automobile is in itself, both directly and indirectly, an important wealth-producing instrument," he observed in 1930. On the heels of hard times, Ford was still mouthing the enthusiasm of good ones. The next year, production stopped at his Model A plant; the following year, unemployed workers demonstrated at the formidable River Rouge facility, seeking the number-one capitalist in his lair. Four men were killed in the ensuing violence.

On the Road to Nowhere

Nonetheless, the fantasy of automobility endured alongside the Depression's realities. Shows for custom coachwork remained popular, and Cadillac's "veritable cathedral of a car" was issued in the midst of economic paralysis. "Standard of the world," the company boasted. "We're a two-car family," Plymouth advertised, suggesting that its low price allowed the family to have two automobiles. No wonder the gas lines paralleled the soup lines, as Americans traveled some 200 million miles a year. In the eight years after the Crash, the number of cars grew by 3 million. More than half of America's car owners, a quarter of the nation, kept paying on the installment plan. How else could they keep on the move?

Decrepit Model Ts, chockablock with their families and their furniture—their future—helped tenant farmers become transients in the aftermath of the Dust Bowl. The hoboes who hit the road on foot or lived in boxcar poverty on the rails joined the army of despair. Impoverished Americans dragged car seats from auto graveyards, transformed shells of old automobiles into sheds, or became squatters building "Hoovervilles" from scraps.

Yet, confidence in the motorcar's technology was pumped up by the Century of Progress Exposition in Chicago in 1933–34, with its slogan "Science Finds, Industry Applies, Man Conforms." Man conformed, indeed. "Who Serves Progress Serves America," a sign offered in an exhibition at the General Motors tower, where "we're-in-the-money" optimism reigned. Here, a visitor could pick the materials to fit out a car, watch the streamlined shape assembled, and drive the new motor vehicle out the door. "America was the only nation in the world that ever went to the poor house in an automobile" was Will Rogers's famous crack.

Americans drove to work, even relief work, taking their cars to collect the food dole. When a local transit company offered free rides to a WPA site, people refused. However poor, *Mass Transportation* reported, workers found money to buy gas and oil for their automobiles. They had to, for the car had stretched the arc of their search for work by spreading jobs outward.

While workers idled, President Herbert Hoover, an engineer by profession, fumbled his way through the economic down cycle, still funding highway handouts. The president had entered office promising "two cars in every garage." Imbued with the "ideology of expertise," he viewed the traffic engineer as hero. The passion endured. When the Depression hit, the laissez-faire president spent $175 million on roads to ease unemployment. Pushing a few projects like the Hoover and Grand Coulee dams for the jobless, however, didn't compensate for his insistence on a balanced budget and his "whistle-while-you-work" attitude that "prosperity was just around the corner" and that "self-reliance" would find it. In the 1932 election Hoover faced the popular governor of New York, Franklin Delano Roosevelt. Roosevelt was elected, and the New Deal began.

New Deals and Ideals

Equipped with new ideals based on the old Progressive ones, the president summoned a renowned "brain trust" to ordain a "new deal for the American people," and "the Roosevelt Revolution" was launched. The celebrated first 100 days concentrated on jobs as the primary mission. A bill to "employ the largest possible number" in "useful public works" was passed. In 1933 the Federal Emergency Relief Administration sent $500 million to state and local governments and $3 billion to Roosevelt's emergency Public Works Administration (PWA).

Since the "perfect" civic works were quick-fix, pick-and-shovel jobs, such as highways to carry city dwellers to make-work projects, the "revolution" was manifested as a familiar turn of mind and habit: the bulk of New Deal programs that nurtured the jobless would be engineered in concrete. Almost half the 2 million workers paid would build street or highway projects. From the first pump priming on, Roosevelt ratified the romance of technology and the road.

Like Hoover, Roosevelt had no compunction about throwing coins into the highway money pot. The Civic Works Administration (CWA) boasted 500,000 miles of road building. "Three loud cheers for CWA! . . . It is actually getting out some of that Public Works money," a reporter noted "The CWA gangs, some 20 men, were putting shoulders along an old and rather narrow paved road. It was a nasty morning. Cold. And sleet. But they looked cheerful. Thirty-hour week. 40 cents an hour—CASH," he wrote.

The labor paid for by the PWA and its successor, the Works Progress Administration (WPA), had long-term implications. Across the alphabet of agencies, from the massive Tennessee Valley Authority (TVA), with its Norris Freeway in 1938, to many miniprojects, 80 percent of the New Deal's expenditures went to roads and construction. The Roosevelt administration thus advanced the motor vehicle, providing the nation's chief industrial product with the arteries to carry it across the nation and, eventually, to downtowns. From 1930 to 1940, surfaced road mileage would double to 1,367,000 miles.

In affirming highway building, Roosevelt emulated his predecessors. Though a sentimentalist about trains, he sped the motorization of America. In 1932 and 1933, for the first time, the federal government allowed roads to go through urban as well as rural America. Still more significantly, in 1934 it admitted these routes into the federal highway program. Though the son of a railroad man and a campaigner for integrating road and rail, Roosevelt was a product of his times. The car was "king of the roads"; the streetcars were paupers. Mass transit secured only one-tenth the WPA funds spent for road improvements. Only one city, Chicago, received subway money from Washington, for a small line under State Street. Funds for roads were free for cars, trucks, and buses; funds for trains were loans. The WPA's funding ratio of road to rail was twenty to one.

New Deal housing notions also abetted the flow away from the

central cities and to the motor suburbs. The sick housing industry
held an army of the unemployed, and as each day saw more than a
thousand homes foreclosed, Roosevelt acted. The single-family home
remained lodged within the heart of the gentleman farmer from
Dutchess County. In 1933, New Dealers initiated the Home Owners
Loan Corporation to refinance 250,000 foreclosed mortgages. A year
later, it provided guarantees for mortgages through the Housing Act
of 1934, lowering down payments and insurance and stoking the
construction industry and suburban home sales. The act also established a fateful housing policy. Since insured loans went through
bankers, the mortgage program ranked the residences with the least
risk as the most valuable. The most risky sites, urban neighborhoods
or African-American communities, had the least value. Hence, they
bore bad marks in the color-coded maps of the mortgage officers.
"Redlining," as it would be known, had begun.

Planners dreamed of more housing enclaves, too. The so-called
Hoovervilles would yield to greenbelt communities. "Tugwell-
towns," named for planner Rexford Tugwell, aimed to bring sunshine and order. To aid 600,000 bankrupt farm families, the
Resettlement Administration planned fifty subsistence rural communities. These developments would reduce land costs and decongest
slums as the poor spilled out of crisis-ridden cities and into "rurban"
places. And so, burning the lights late at night, architects felt that
"they were planning a new world."

The New Deal planners fulfilled the pastoral dream of New Towns
in three decentralized greenbelt towns, the first nationally sponsored
home building since World War I. Greenhills near Cincinnati, Green-
dale near Milwaukee, and Greenbelt, Maryland, near Washington,
D.C., opened in the late 1930s. Based on Mumford's Garden Cities
concept, they were buffered by open space and endowed with close
housing and walkable shopping centers. Their architects reiterated
the Sunnyside and Radburn visions of community life, unsullied by
traffic or urban grime, and created developments open to moderate-
and low-income families. Here, children could play in green fields
and their parents could move on wide, straight streets. "The town
was a jewel set in a green forest" was the way one resident recalled
the white-painted houses and nature trails of the "Emerald City" of

his youth. Such places generated fond memories for the more than four thousand families housed in them but held little use as a model. Work and home remained split. Their ideal, "A Garden Home You Can Call Your Own," simply helped transform rural nostalgia into a flight to the road's end.

As for the urban housing built by the New Deal, it was slight and inadequate. The city suffered severely in the Depression. In mid-decade the Federal Housing Authority (FHA) reported sixty-seven urban areas in which one in ten homes had no indoor sanitation facilities, and one in four no bath or shower. The scant twenty-five thousand new units erected in five years were barrackslike, underfinanced, and segregated. The Housing Act of 1937 decentralized housing out of the city and did little to help slum dwellers. Housing advocate Harold Ickes's fondness for "the face of nature" to relieve the cities' "pockets of shame" was not an urban housing solution.

Cities remained the center of Depression malaise and neglect. Their expansion ceased or declined compared to suburbs. Twenty-five percent of Detroit's growth was on its periphery, only 3 percent within the city. Likewise, Chicago's suburbs swelled 11 percent, the downtown less than 1 percent. Vast acreage in the central business districts fell for parking spaces. The old star city had become a "constellation," said the Hoover Commission. The National Resources Committee, the nation's planning board, used the word "conurbanized" to describe the sprawling East Coast, the "megalopolis" to come.

In the last analysis, then, Roosevelt's crusade to relieve "one-third of a nation ill-housed, ill-clad, ill-nourished" failed on the first count, the housing front. The notion to scatter housing to greener lands and the 1934 act's mortgage insurance merely spurred the horizontal flow, facilitating the motorist. With highways and housing, Roosevelt helped stamp the automotive tomorrow. "The American people could not have done worse in 1932 had they deliberately set out to elect a president who was ignorant of the implications of the automobile revolution," Flink and others have concluded.

———

Mobile "Park Squares"

Obviously, the New Deal molded more than an asphalt job-making agenda. As the government ventured into the helping business, the armed forces of the Depression aimed to domesticate and define the landscape. Programs allied employment with artistry, reclaimed dirt-poor land through soil reclamation, and supplied relief from dust storms and floods. Post office murals, landscaped parks, and highway picnic spots left a legacy.

The Civilian Conservation Corps (CCC) dressed young recruits in forest green garb to plant millions of trees, clear beaches, build dams, and construct bridges, fire towers, and phone lines. Depression leaders created work and promoted play in new or rehabilitated parks from Philadelphia to Kansas, Dallas to San Francisco. "Franklin Delano Roosevelt Parks" would dot U.S. maps, and zoos, aquariums, botanical gardens, and playgrounds would blossom.

Child of the Hudson River Valley and cousin to Theodore Roosevelt, the president believed in the redemptive power of nature. Listing himself in *Who's Who* as a "tree farmer," he absorbed the conservation legacy and integrated natural resources into his social policy. His New Deal parkways would be to the East what national parks were to the West: "park squares" for the people, a place for manicured recreation and union with the outdoors. On worn tracts and scenic routes, CCC crews planted trees and scooped out roads to connect open space to serve nearby towns. While their roads usurped some greenery, the young workers built rocky pools and log lodges to ornament the landscape. They constructed rock-studded shelters by the roadside, log lodges in bucolic settings, river walks and aquatic parks in urban America, and vast forests across the continent.

Although the ghost of the freeway yet to come hovered over its design, the Mount Vernon Memorial Highway, begun the year of the stock market crash, was a "masterpiece of the cubical treatment." With well-planted vistas and congenial, rustic bridges, it stretched from the capital to George Washington's home. Its landscape architect, Gilmore Clarke, based his work on Westchester's Bronx River Parkway, harmonizing the roadway with the natural setting of the terrain. Another scenic road, Skyline Drive and Blue Ridge Parkway in Virginia, sought to reinvigorate depleted land and uplift the poor communities in its environs. Curving leisurely across the mountain landscape, with plantings to mend the worn land and outlooks on "the native American countryside," the majestic parkway rolled almost five hundred miles along the spine of the Shenandoah and Smoky Mountains. Yet it, too, would help suburbanize northern Virginia

The heralded Appalachian Trail, conceived by Benton MacKaye to preserve a swath of wilderness through the east as a footpath and retreat, took hold. Founded on the conservationist's invocation "to speak softly and carry a map," this levee against a landscape debased by unplanned human erosion evolved admirably. By 1937 the walking trail extended 2,050 miles from Mount Katahdin in Maine to Georgia. New Deal workers adorned other travel routes, from the Natchez Trace Parkway through Mississippi and Tennessee, the splendid Merritt Parkway through Connecticut, and the grand Columbia River Parkway and Gorge in the Northwest to modest Rhode Island roads and picnic groves.

These New Deal artifacts of motion linger on the landscape to delight and memorialize their labors—and the road not taken in design. "Utilitarian monuments," said New Deal planner Charles Eliot, "mute reminders" of a federal presence. They are mementos of a time when even the most mundane jobs were precious, wrote the Depression landscape historian Phoebe Cutler. "The Depression outhouse, school building, or picnic shelter testify to humankind's pluck, its grit for survival. The stone furniture, rock pylons, and shake roofs in their dignity and charm illuminate the small scrappy creative core in us all."

Yet, these monuments and the economic relief they represented do not negate the fact that the ambitious size and impromptu planning of New Deal public works would have sorrier consequences. "Motor roads and other improvements are coming in them [the parks] so fast that they are gradually beginning to lose some of their attraction," complained George Horace Lorimer, publisher of *The Saturday Evening Post* and wilderness advocate. Films of New Deal youth corps members felling giant Sequoias or a glimpse of Jens Jensen's Columbus Park in Chicago, where work crews hard cropped his signature design, show the less pleasant face of the pick-and-shovel jobs approach.

The work-first bent, allied with the devotion to the motorcar, overwhelmed respect for the landscape. The Tennessee Valley Authority, which harnessed regional planning to topography, secured more for electric power than rational planning. Vast projects like the Bonneville Dam on the Columbia River or the waterworks of the Central Valley Project in California, designed to put nature in the service of "progress," had a downside. Such superscale projects would grab the water, alter the environment, and enable road-based development. The very parks that stood as peaks of achievement—some 7.1 million acres of national park expansion that included the Everglades National Park in Florida and the Death Valley and Joshua Tree national monuments in California—would suffer when opened to the highways.

Even at the time, the New Deal's mandate for action disturbed conservationists. Trampling the vanishing wilderness appalled Aldo Leopold, the environmental seer: "We stand guard over works of art, but species representing the work of eons are stolen from under our noses." In *The People's Forest,* Robert Marshall of the Forest Service bewailed the loss and sought a "green retreat." Together, Leopold, Marshall, MacKaye, and others formed the Wilderness Society in 1936 to protect the shrinking natural world.

In built-up cities and suburbs, the roads took their toll, too. As governor of New York, Roosevelt had endorsed the parkways that Robert Moses thrust through the wealthy estates of Long Island. Though Roosevelt bristled at the bullying builder, he shared his principles. New Deal relief funds were funneled through Mayor Fiorello La Guardia to this "Caesar among park directors," and the city became an exemplar of road building. At the helm of more and more agencies, Moses used federal funds to build swimming pools; he repaired Rockaway Beach, and dragged sand from forty miles away to create Orchard Beach, advancing road-building aspirations all the while. With money secured in 1934, Moses pushed his West Side highway project along the waterfront. With another $42 million in PWA money, he launched his long-stalled Triborough Bridge from Harlem to Long Island.

Steeped in the flow of New Deal money, Moses's projects simultaneously made things "grayer" and greener, his biographer Robert Caro wrote in *The Power Broker*. It was typical of the times. The park commissioner's fine extension of the Bronx Parkway to the Taconic alternated with dismal acres of parking. Intrusive roads gnawed at fine greenways and beaches. Democracy was tedious, Moses would say. As the former parks man battled road "obstructionists," his green roots in the parkway movement shriveled. From his colossal power base, Moses would badger communities, destroy parks, and assault riversides, making his name an epithet and New York a mock-up of the highway age to come.

In the broke 1930s, as in the go-for-broke 1920s, the auto industry's clout also grew. In the early days of the Depression, states shifted gas tax funds from supporting roads to paying for broader needs. Alarmed, General Motors banded two thousand groups into the National Highway Users Conference to lobby against the practice. When GM howled, Washington yielded. The gas tax went back to the highway-firsters. The fledgling automobile organization had showed its muscle. The infamous "Road Gang" of automakers would roll their roads across the continent.

The nation was waiting. "Our street-system capillaries, now too narrow and inelastic to permit the larger flow of persons and goods, are backing up the circulation," warned an article in *The Survey* in 1932. The car was becoming an impediment instead of a guardian angel. Its agents in Washington, and elsewhere, altered that. A slew of toll roads would ease its route.

The Merritt Parkway led the way. Commodious in design and decorated with Art Deco bridges, the Connecticut parkway still demonstrated how to motorize gracefully. Begun in 1934 to ease congestion on the Boston Post Road, it managed to combine grace and speed. The builders even made a jog to save a tree on its route. ("It's a rather nice tree," Connecticut's governor replied to critics.) Financed by the PWA and local funds to connect the Wilbur Cross Parkway and create a through route across Connecticut, the road manifested a trend: though designed to cut traffic, it compounded it. Though built to ease congestion and stop road building, it facilitated the opening of more suburban land in Fairfield

County, Connecticut, hence generating more cars. Like the George Washington Bridge's failure to relieve traffic through the Lincoln Tunnel, this newest highway followed the axiom "If you pave it, they will come."

And come they did. "Improvements" and more improvements were on the way. The Lincoln Highway Association was ecstatic. "Each improvement stimulated traffic . . . and demanded more improvements, which brought more traffic, and so on, down to the present and seemingly on to an indefinite date in the future," noted the association's promotional narrative, *The Story of a Crusade that Made Transportation History.*

San Francisco marked the opening of the San Francisco–Oakland Bay Bridge. On November 12, 1936, officials held an acetylene torch and burned asunder a heavy chain barrier as onlookers enthused. "An electric button pressed by President Roosevelt in the White House in Washington flashed the green 'Go' signal and three columns of whirring automobiles sped from each shore of San Francisco Bay over six lanes of the world's greatest aerial highway." Some 35 million commuters deserted the ferry and drove across the bridge. Though city planners constructed the bridge for both rail and motor vehicles, the car would crowd the trolley out. In Pittsburgh, seventeen hundred bridges spanned the ravines. In other cities the quest to ease traffic flow pushed turnpikes ahead. In 1937 engineers began the Pennsylvania Turnpike, excavating eight tunnels intended for an old railroad tunnel through the hills of Appalachia and constructing bridges across 250 rivers and streams. America's first express highway boasted a high speed of seventy miles an hour.

Southern California planners had also proposed elevated highways to wrap the region with a freeway system and bypasses patterned on New York's parkways. State and WPA aid helped them do so. In 1940, the same year the Pennsylvania Turnpike opened, Californians started the four-lane, six-mile Arroyo Seco Parkway, a limited-access superhighway. A year later, the parkway adopted the new word "freeway" and became the Pasadena Freeway. True to the word, the Los Angeles road builders, like their railroad ancestors, attracted commuters and developers to land farther afield. The road fattened developers' coffers and won support from speculators as Pasadena grew in tandem with the highway boom. Progress was at hand. Or was it?

Biographer Caro made this observation:

> Watching Moses open the Triborough Bridge to ease congestion on the Queensborough Bridge, open the Bronx-Whitestone Bridge to ease congestion on the Triborough Bridge and then watching traffic counts on all three bridges mount until all three were as congested as one had been before, planners could hardly avoid the conclusion that "traffic generation" was no longer a theory but a proven fact: the more highways were built to alleviate congestion, the more automobiles would pour onto them.
>
> Force the building of more highways—which would generate more traffic and become congested in their turn in an inexorably widening spiral that contained the most awesome implications for the future of New York and of all urban areas. . . . Pour public investment into the improvement of highways while doing nothing to improve mass transit lines, and there could be only one outcome. Failure.

If the sense of failure had scarcely dawned in the 1970s when Caro wrote these words, the Americans buying 4.5 million cars in the Depression decade were totally oblivious. *Collier's* reminded the nation that "last year not less than 6,225,000 Americans had jobs because of the automobile. That is something in any nation's economy." In 1938 Roosevelt lauded the presidency of General Motors as "a private office with a public trust." That same year, a report of the Bureau of Public Roads called for a study of six superhighways. The next year, in 1939, *Toll Roads and Free Roads* endorsed a fourteen-thousand-mile system of federally supported divided highways to go through and around urban America. Depression or not, the notion of a never-ending drive across the continent was instilled. Poverty or not, car registrations climbed to almost 30 million by the decade's end.

The Streamlined Sweep

The technology and motion of speed were defined in the streamlined Art Moderne style. Chrysler and DeSoto Airflow advertised an "aerodynamic" sweep that encompassed all their disparate parts, from grille and headlights to fenders, as "functionally correct for cleaving through the airstream." DeSoto advertised its 1934 pioneer design by parking it in front of a plane. Depression or not, Harley Earl's Hollywood entourage still embraced dashing automobiles. Breezing through the nation's bankruptcy with posh and zany comedies, movie stars took to their pricey roadsters. Gary Cooper piloted a Dusenberg and Clark Gable a sleek Packard Darrin with whitewalls. Chrome it up. Gadgetize the interior. The mascot of flight on the hood symbolized the spirit of the day.

Impressed, architects also followed the futuristic, swooping lines of annual models. Designers Henry Dreyfuss, Raymond Loewy, and Norman Bel Geddes moved from industry to transportation, and architects absorbed their "machine age" design to put a smile on the glum face of the Depression downtown. Stunning projects left over from the Roaring Twenties attracted the multitude to urban America. On Manhattan's Upper West Side, near Central Park, city builders adorned Manhattan apartments with picturesque names like Beresford, San Remo, Majestic, and Eldorado. A "City of Opportunity" was the theme of the ornaments on the Chanin building, which opened a year after the Crash. Towering across the sky, the glistening Chrysler Building, the auto company's apex, reigned over the cityscape for just one year before the Empire State Building, by architects Shreve, Lamb & Harmon, rose higher still in 1931.

Fine, if modest, apartments lined borough streets. For the Bronx middle class the Grand Concourse was "our borough's closest thing to a Parisian Boulevard," recalled historian Marshall Berman in *All That Is Solid Melts into Air,* describing his childhood neighborhood with its "rows of large, splendid 1930 apartment houses." They were "simple and clear in their architectural form . . . whether geometrically sharp or biomorphically curved; brilliantly colored in contrasting tones, offset with chrome, beautiful interiors played with large areas of glass, open to light and air as if to proclaim a good life that was open not just to the elite residents but to us all."

Art Deco and its Art Moderne heir also dotted other, smaller downtowns. The sleek glimmer of commercial blocks or a buoyant Horn and Hardart Automat streamlined Depression America in the auto-derived style. From Miami, with its pastel-colored Art Deco district, to downtown Tulsa, parading its oil wealth with "Okie deco," the cosmopolitan style held sway in America's cities. Eclectic Art Moderne buildings flourished in Los Angeles. The black vitrolite Darkroom camera store was a streetside favorite in the Southern California city. The Brown Derby or Zeppelin restaurants, the glistening diners, appealed. The neon-lined, "EAT"-decorated Automats flashed their message. The resplendent picture palaces, embodying the style of speed borrowed from the automobile, dazzled both large and small downtowns. Flatly ornamented and stark, the design took well to the application of the latest adornment of cube glass. Aztec, plant, or flower motifs decorated the buildings that lined the bustling sidewalks. Some eight hundred homes, hotels, and shops in Miami's Art Deco district created a design extravaganza for blocks, while smaller pedestrian cores applied the forms that fit the motor age's sense of speed.

In the suburbs, too, the architecture of the car culture made its dominance visible in design on the go. Image-laden architecture produced jaunty building shapes like the Long Island duck and the spinning chickens that flagged motorists. The first drive-in bank, along with markets, restaurants, and shoe repair stores, attracted drivers. Early off-street parking at Highland Park Village in Chicago or larger parking lots behind Rodeo Drive in Los Angeles were modest nods to the motorcar. Seedy intruders thrown together under dangling electric wires or spry designs also multiplied in an entourage of roadside emporia. "A store near your door . . . open evenings," Pep Boys Auto Parts advertised. Motor courts and tourist cabins hosted one-quarter of the nation's overnighters. For a quarter drivers could have their own "private theater box" at the first drive-in movie in Camden, New Jersey, in 1933. By mid-decade the driver on the go could pull into a drive-in parking lot and dip into Howard Johnson's twenty-eight flavors of ice cream on twenty-five roads. Drive-in eating got a bigger lift in 1938 when two California brothers, Maurice and Richard McDonald, opened the first of their chains, a San Bernardino hamburger spot, turning Henry Ford's assembly line to hamburger production.

Such Depression roadside eateries and retail outlets attracted more

Americans beyond Main Street to the concrete aprons and tattered streetscape of the auto strip. In the mid-1930s, "super" was affixed to "market" to lure shoppers farther. One "automarket" actually admitted cars inside. Parent of the mall, the mid-1930s "shopping center" was devised by planning reformers to wrest the walker from the car and make pedestrian and vehicular traffic interact more humanely. For all the would-be interaction, the inner ring of older stores felt the impact.

The signs of the automobile were ubiquitous, and they hampered Main Street. Some thirty-five thousand gas stations altered their surroundings. "One was immediately struck in walking the streets by the fact that filling stations have become in ten years one of the most prominent physical landmarks," reported the "Middletown" sociologists Helen and Robert Lynd in a celebrated 1935 study. "Milestone on a road that has no end," a Gulf station advertisement declared. "Here in stone and steel lies a monument." By 1939, U.S. Route 1 had three hundred gas stations. That year, more than a thousand billboards edged the road between Washington and Baltimore; and five hundred billboards and four hundred drive-in businesses stood between New York and Trenton.

Stable Mobile Homes

While design mated with ever more mobility in the roadside architecture of motor courts, it became architecture itself in a new form—the mobile home. Throughout America drivers were swarming to trailer colonies. "We are facing a movement of population besides which even the crusades will seem Sunday school picnics," said critic Gilbert Seldes in describing the phenomenon. These cars-cum-houses lumbered across Florida's state line, twenty-five an hour in 1937. In 1936, *Automotive Daily News* calculated 160,000 such trailers on the road. *Fortune* magazine exuberantly noted the lifestyle at one enclave of mobile homes on Biscayne Boulevard in Miami: "Such swagger maidens, such expensive rigs, a flunky serving drinks."

The mobile home was not just a sleek epitome of movement for the affluent. It also offered affordable housing for low-income Americans. Californians "blamed the trailer for dumping 50,000 children into city schools." Detroit authorities refused to allow "gasoline bedouins" to park more than an hour in their "tin can towns." Roger Babson, who had forecast the Depression, predicted that half of all Americans would live in the stationary vehicles.

Today's and "Tomorrow's" Train

Despite hard times the rail industry managed to make technological progress. Though overbuilt and disowned by Washington, encumbered with $6 billion in debt, and down some 750,000 workers, rail owners cut their expenses and dividends and forged ahead. Rail lines expanded in Chicago. Funds were spent to electrify the Pennsylvania Railroad from New York to Washington, complete Philadelphia's Thirtieth Street Station, and in 1937 link the new Newark station to the system. Many trains traded their dingy coal-firing engines for diesel power and stainless steel. Vivid streamlined models with air-conditioning dazzled Depression America. Passengers of the glittery Super Chiefs and Broadway Limiteds sped along in stylish glamor. "Tomorrow's Train Today!" said a yellow egg-shaped train seen by more than a million visitors at the Century of Progress Exposition in Chicago.

Travelers took to these lightweight, streamlined trains in early experiments with the celebrated Zephyrs, Eagles, and Rockets. Alcoa bragged about "speeds as high as 120 miles an hour." An advertisement for Raymond Loewy's Streamliner train called it "the shape of speed." Rival lines competed to create the bullet-headed smooth surfaces and sleek contours that gave the aura of Art Moderne motion. The style also defined Douglas DC-3 planes, the shining silver aircraft that heralded the competition to come.

New terminals also rose throughout the decade. In the heartland Omaha's handsome Union Station opened in 1931; two years later, Cincinnati's Union Terminal merged the old and new in an ambitious station that gave the impression of a Philco radio outside and depicted the city's history within. Harking back to Pennsylvania Station, Newark's $42 million terminal by McKim, Mead and White displayed a spacious interior above the nexus of long-distance, commuter, and subway lines. Nonetheless, though twenty-seven thousand railways were still in service, the clash with the car accelerated and the future dimmed. By the decade's end one-third of all the nation's largest carriers lay in receivership.

Los Angeles's ebullient Spanish Deco Union Station, which opened with flair and urban adroitness, closed the decade and the terminal designs. The last great gateway to a great city, it linked the Civic Center with a City Beautiful mall. The warm and suavely ornamented interior allowed passengers to get a shave at a barbershop, eat a hearty meal at an elegant Harvey House restaurant, or have a moment of repose in the palm-studded patio, courtyard, or waiting room.

So, too, the building of Rockefeller Center, which affirmed that family's faith in the urban nation in the Depression, displayed the last majestic merger of architecture and rail. Its three-block collection of high-rises housing the Rainbow Room, Radio City Music Hall, and offices was tied to the subway lines below. From the corridors that funneled the commuter, to the back door loading docks where trucks slid inconspicuously into the cellar, Rockefeller Center was a masterwork of movement and a lingering ember of integrated city planning and transit-oriented design. Urban and cohesive, Rockefeller Center was the most important civic-minded structure since Grand Central Station. On a more modest scale, the Hotel New Yorker's tunnel, joined to Pennsylvania Station, shared the gift of integrating rail into the city's world. In slighter structures, the handsome facades of small stations and the well-designed pier building for ferries continued the tradition of humanizing and beautifying public transport.

Streetcars on the Skids

Some electric streetcars also managed to trot out new wares. At the onset of the Depression, twenty-five electric railway companies formed the Electric Railway Presidents' Conference Committee, and in 1935 the much-lauded, long-lasting streamlined PCC, the Presidents' Conference Car, chugged forth. Larger yet lighter, faster yet smoother, quieter and cheaper to run, it sold rapidly. Some eleven hundred PCCs would join streetcar systems within five years. Lamentably, they still could not replace the worn staples of the fleet. Encumbered by the same municipal fees, the street railway industry was also enfeebled by low ridership in the weak economy, their rights-of-way contested by more motor vehicles.

More motorcars also meant 50 percent more traffic in major urban areas, and the blow of congestion added to the brunt of poverty. Hit by poor maintenance and declining urban growth, electric rail was facing formidable opposition. Agitation for new subways, though an issue throughout the Depression and even favored by Detroit employers, never materialized in votes to bond them. In 1932, the same year New York opened its third subway system, its first system declared bankruptcy. The following year, America's interurbans noted a loss of 60 million passengers over five years. Abandonments accelerated. Though steam rail survived, streetcar companies skidded into ever greater deficits from lost ridership, the reduced workweek, and competition from the car and bus. At the time of the Crash of 1929, 14.4 billion passengers took the trolley; by 1940 almost half had deserted steel wheels for rubber ones.

The cause of the decline of streetcars was not simply the withering economy but also the preference of drivers who wanted control of the road for themselves and of municipalities that could ill afford to take over streetcar operations from the impoverished owners. Adding to the downslide of two decades was the advancing bus. In 1932, General Motors, the manufacturer of buses and owner of the largest share of Greyhound, formed a consortium of tire, oil, and highway men to buy and shut down America's streetcar systems. Attacking the trolley mile by mile, the syndicate of General Motors, Firestone, Standard Oil, and Mack Truck, allied as National City Lines, cajoled and bought off local officials. Paired with the ethos of the era, the motor advocates menaced the streetcar's space and customers. Between 1932 and 1949, they would help persuade 100 electric systems in more than forty-five cities to scrap their street rails. Bus riders rose 20 percent. In 1935, Manhattan had replaced most of its trolleys with buses. By 1940 total public transportation ridership had shrunk by 2 billion. The magnificent rail lines fell, taking with them the private rights-of-way, the street corridors, that had insured their fast passage.

"Conspiracy," opponents would assert in later congressional hearings. "Flexible" and inexpensive, the motor lobby would counter.

Whatever the ratio of the criminal to the guileful, the streetcar had scant hope. In 1933, a decade after the first small city's transit system had fallen, San Antonio's, which served 200,000 residents, became the first big city line to fall. Commuter and freight trains joined the streetcar, and interurbans rattled into the death rites of delayed maintenance. The Depression drained the lifeblood of an invalid. The rest would be a matter of time.

The Sliding Cities

The bold traffic signal on city streets symbolized the future. The 1937 proposal to build the first freeway in Los Angeles, stamping a wide grid across valleys with no downtown, set the tone. Scant vestige of a central city was left in the design. The parking lot, an all too prominent frontispiece to L.A.'s Union Station, symbolized the premier status for cars. It was a harbinger of America's tomorrow.

Francis in William Kennedy's *Ironweed* was of the generation that watched as small towns shut down lines and trains took their last runs on rails soon overrun with weeds. Kennedy's sodden hero "remembered trolleys as intimately as he remembered the shape of his father's face, for he had seen them at loving closeness through all his early years. . . . Terrific machines," he thought, "but now they're goin'."

With the trolleys would go the cities they served. In their stead the motor suburb demanded ever more cars. Housed in places ill equipped to provide public transportation, some 13 million suburban Americans were now devoid of rail service altogether. Their cars crowded downtowns, heading in and out on the commute. New York's Regional Plan Association busied itself advocating freeways to empty the car-filled city for its own good. Los Angeles, with 90 percent of its dwellings single-family homes, lost half its mass transit patrons to motor vehicles, resulting in the need for still more cars and, in turn, the presence of more motor vehicles to deplete downtown. A *Los Angeles Times* reporter called the automobile a "Frankenstein" in 1938, "spouting exhaust smoke and reeking of burnt gasoline fumes." The "emancipation" that auto enthusiasts had promised, he concluded, "is becoming a mockery and a memory." Even the chief engineer of the Los Angeles auto club blamed the motorcar for the attrition of the American city: "sprawling, nonconformist, ugly, and inefficient."

Across the country troubled cities flattened worn buildings for parking lots. On the skids since the last decade, Detroit's once stately homes on Woodward Avenue, crowded by automobile showrooms and garages, fell for a mid-1930s widening. In the three years before 1939, officials took ninety-six buildings for parking. Imposing mansions tumbled under the wrecking ball, and other streets suffered the slow attrition of fleeing commerce and empty lots. The flight to the posh suburban Grosse Pointes of America hastened the dilapidation that made the Motor City symbolic of the motorcar's exactions.

Other advocates affirmed the virtues of urban density. "The city has seemed at times the despair of America, but at others to be the Nation's hope, the battleground of democracy," a report on the cities, the first in twenty-eight years, declared in 1937. "The faults of our cities are not those of decadence and impending decline, but of exuberant vitality crowding its way forward under tremendous pressure—the flood rather than the drought."

And, still, more complaints about the motorcar causing noise, congestion, fumes, and traffic accidents produced a fatal answer. "We must dream of gashing our way ruthlessly through built-up sections of overcrowded cities, in order to create traffic ways," said Studebaker's president. It was a foreshadowing of the decade of urban renewal ahead. In his own way John Nolen shared the sentiment. "The future city will be spread out, it will be regional, it will be the natural product of the automobile, the good road, electricity, the telephone, and the radio, combined with the growing desire to live a more natural, biological life under pleasanter and more natural conditions," he said. "Subways are evidence of an unsuccessfully planned city."

Disciples of Automotive Design

As the 1930s wore on, a solution was broached in *The Saturday Evening Post*: "If we are to have full use of automobiles, cities must be remade. . . . A waiting industry that will do wonders for prosperity will spring up when we revamp our cities and make it safe, conve-

nient, pleasant and easy to use a car on city streets." The modern
hero architects absorbed the car culture and lent their imprimatur.
The landmark 1932 International Style show at the Museum of
Modern Art displayed Le Corbusier's tower in the park girdled by
highways. His doctrine reinforced the asphalt mind-set of engineers
and planners.

Frank Lloyd Wright, doting on the motorcar's consequences, was
equally influential. "Considering this traffic problem, reflect that the
present city is yet only about one-tenth the motor city it will be. . . ,"
he wrote in "The Disappearing City" (1932), endorsing the sprawling landscape as an antidote to urban life. By reshaping the "city" as
a glorified suburb, Wright's tract echoed Henry Ford's distaste for
urban life. Out of Wright's infatuation with the automobile came his
vision of a future off the arterial. Where Le Corbusier saw vertical
towers, Wright saw the horizontal "Usonian" house, one for every
home owner. Yet the two architects provided point and counterpoint,
for both visionaries gave pride of place to the road. "Every Broadacre citizen has his own car. Multiple lane highways make travel safe
and enjoyable," Wright wrote. No palliative even in their day, the architects' motor-centric designs, when combined with exclusive zoning for single-family houses, laid the foundation for the car-bound
Levittowns to come. From the architectural salons to the streets,
from the texts to the look-alike subdivisions after the Depression, the
designs of these two elite architects made their way to the landscape
of an asphalt nation.

"The car is no longer a machine but a detachable room," wrote
one enthusiast. "Today, in many homes, it is possible to leave the
comfort of the living room, pass directly through a hallway or
kitchen into the garage, and head for the open roads without ever
being outside at all," declared another promoter. Now, even more
than in the 1920s, the garage advanced; the porch retreated, drag-
ging down standards and safety for pedestrians. A Middletown editorial saying "Sidewalk Play Is Dangerous" reflected the hazards of
design for motion.

Nothing quenched the desire for motion. It characterized the
monumental engineering of the decade. "Almost superhuman in
performance," Roosevelt had told five thousand spectators while

dedicating the George Washington Bridge at the decade's beginning. From the George Washington to the Wilshire Boulevard causeway extension in the mid-1930s and the multilane urban arterials drawn at the decade's end, engineers dreamed of the superscale expressway. Under the powerful Thomas MacDonald, the Bureau of Public Roads emerged from its back roads origins in a 1939 plan to excise curves, redraw alignments, and make blunt cut-and-fill patterns for the traffic volume of the future. Years beyond its mandate for getting the farmer out of the mud, the bureau called for a ribbon of free roads crossing the continent. In the report sent to Congress, it moved to finance a 26,700-mile intercity system.

Adolf Hitler's emerging autobahn had sparked America's vision for a transcontinental road. The parkway for speed, the highway drawn without stoplights or curves, fit the sentiment for long-distance limited-access roads. The four-lane fantasy of "Magic Motorways" was on the drawing boards for good. Forget public. Forget shared space. "What greater, nobler agent has Culture or Civilization than the great Open Road made safe and beautiful for continually flowing traffic when it is a harmonious part of the great whole?" was the doctrine. The vision of the commanding urban hub with its spokes of rail would be yesterday's geometry. For the new mapmakers entering the war era, the automobile enabled, the streetcar enfeebled. The President's Research Committee on Social Trends had warned that social policy was outward bound—"redistributing its citizens, disorganizing its cities, causing random suburban building and blight."

By adopting the Home Owners Loan Corporation, policy makers had pushed Americans outward. By favoring green fields and disowning compact cities, they had made housing synonymous with homes at the end of the road and hence car dependent. As the decade wore on, buying became cheaper than renting. More Americans could buy more houses. The countryside felt the exodus as impoverished farmers, their workforce reduced by mechanization, scattered under the onslaught of suburban taxes. The result, according to historian Mark Gelfand, was "nothing less than an officially sponsored exodus from the cities."

As the decade ended, so did reformist impulses. Radburn was

broke. The Chatham Village and the Baldwin Hills Village arcadias planned by Radburn's heirs and sixty or so New Towns would attract few followers, and greenbelt towns still fewer. Neither the utopian aspirations of the Garden Cities nor the charm of the Art Deco and streamlined apartments, neither the economy of close-packed communities nor the urbanity of multifamily designs would survive. The New Deal's furthering of the car-fed, single-family standard, its indifference to cutbacks as small towns shut down trolley lines and disheartened streetcar owners went broke, were "powder for the post-war suburban explosion," in Lewis Mumford's words.

Tomorrow on Wheels

"Who can say what horizons lie before us?" intoned the voice at General Motors's Futurama exhibit, the most popular attraction at the 1939–40 New York World's Fair. GM could. With rising net earnings, more than a quarter million employees and 2 million cars and trucks in production, the auto company's horizons were endless—as endless as "The World of Tomorrow" exhibit of the fair. GM needed only public support to further public works and highways, and the price of an exhibition was well worth it.

Five million visitors passed along the fair's "Magic Motorways," designed by Norman Bel Geddes. Beneath the perisphere and trylon that dominated the fairgrounds, Americans saw a motorized heaven linked by vast highways driving to GM's "Town of Tomorrow," complete with twenty-one single-family homes. Sedans scooted above the fairgrounds, spiraling to Ford's "Road of Tomorrow," a model expressway. Roosevelt, sharing America's enchantment with the superhighway, entertained Geddes himself.

As for *The City,* a World's Fair film doting on a swing-filled town in Greenbelt, Maryland, it actually denigrated urban life, contrasting smoky cities and urchins in gutters with the pastoral suburb. "The city and its traffic have become rival elements," the film—written and narrated by Mumford—declared, offering his images of limited access and "Townless Highways for the Motorist."

The president of Studebaker had the remedy:

In highways, then, lies a new national frontier for the pessimist who thinks frontiers have disappeared. It challenges the imagination and spirit of enterprise which always have been the distinctive marks of American life. And even the gloomiest of men admit that America never ignores the challenges of a new frontier, geographical or otherwise.

With Hitler sweeping through Europe, America was challenged not only by war in Europe but by economic disarray. In the early 1940s, the country was less concerned with a "new frontier" than finding work. Roosevelt had drawn the nation back from the abyss of economic and social catastrophe. He had invigorated the notion of conservation; he had left a legacy of the government's obligations and a heritage of public works. But the roads spread across the countryside, the housing props that pulled the nation outward, and the plans of the entrenched Bureau of Public Roads were a self-perpetuating— and perpetual—motion machine for the future. America was on the road to asphalt.

OPPOSITE: As the visionary highway of the World's Fair metamorphosed
into speed-first freeways, Americans could drive their dream machines
to their dream homes, courtesy of VA loans and FHA mortgages.
(From the collections of the Henry Ford Museum and Greenfield Village)

The Asphalt Exodus

"This is a war of engines and octanes. I salute the American oil industry. I salute the American auto industry."

—Joseph Stalin

"Everyone in the United States is waiting for the close of the war to get in a car to go some place."

—Thomas K. MacDonald

"I have been thinking about the cloudburst of new houses which as soon as the war is ended is going to cover the hills and valleys of New England with so many square miles of prefabricated happiness."

—Joseph Hudnut, *The Post-Modern House*

WORLD WAR II DID what no Depression could accomplish: it stalled the American motorist. As the nation mobilized its armed forces, highway construction ground to a halt and civilian car making all but ceased. The most motorized war in history throttled car production, lowered mileage, and braked the automobile culture. Motor vehicle manufacturers became munitions makers, and car sales plummeted by 3 million in the first year of the war. To secure oil, tires, and batteries for the "arsenal of democracy's" trucks, tanks, airplanes, and jeeps, Washington encouraged conservation. "Victory Speed 35 miles per hour," said the signs urging Americans to slow down in order to save rubber. Boy Scouts collected tons of tires, while other home front patriots heaved scrap into piles labeled "aluminum for defense fund." Though pioneering expressways like Davison and Willow Run heading to "Bomber City" Detroit opened during World War II, road building lapsed.

A nation of car owners tinkered with rebuilt engines, retreaded their tires, scraped together gas rationing coupons for two gallons a week—and took to their feet. "Citizens learned to walk again," historian Doris Kearns Goodwin writes. "Car pools multiplied, milk deliveries were cut from twice a day, and auto deaths fell dramatically." Desperate to move workers to new jobs, planners began to think in terms of human mobility as well as automobility. Government posters sloganeered life by rail and foot power, not horsepower, admonishing citizens to car pool, to "conserve everything you have, to walk and carry packages." "When you ride ALONE you ride with Hitler!" one poster admonished. "Join a car-sharing Club TODAY!"

World War II would mark the last time that catering to the car and using it to disperse the population did not constitute the nation's manifest destiny. Instead, public transportation moved the masses. For forty-five months, travel centered on getting soldiers to war on rail, and passenger trains were in the black for the first time in fifteen years. The railroad was a "vital war industry"—no longer the tool of robber barons. With more than one-third of U.S. commuters on bus and rail, the trolley and the interurban bulged with passengers. The PCCs, the Presidents' Conference Cars, were pressed into service, and elevated railway cars were taken from Manhattan to Richmond, Virginia, to serve production.

"Is This Trip Necessary?" a government sign nailed to the depot wall of a Southern waiting room cautioned casual riders. In theory, only those with the need could take the train. In fact, the trains were jammed by one and all. Even though the glut of riders took their toll, accelerating the Depression's problems of finance and upkeep, the war years marked a high point for public transportation. Transit lines remained as essential to the home front city as the city was essential to transit. Travelers packed passenger trains. With a blast of the train whistle, *Grand Central Station,* the late Depression era radio show, dramatized the great terminal's role as the "crossroads of a million private lives! Gigantic stage on which are played a thousand dramas daily!"

The cities at the center of this rail network throbbed with life, if not health. Despite the Depression's population drops and creeping slums, America's cities had managed to endure. Now they were wartime centers that drew 4 million workers and their families. A new workforce of women and African-Americans helped turn peacetime goods to armaments. War production brought prosperity and revived faltering urban economies. The funds pumped by Washington into older manufacturing cities on the East Coast (Newark, Boston, Philadelphia, New York); the Midwest (Milwaukee, Minneapolis, Chicago, St. Louis, Detroit), and the South (New Orleans) stabilized their populations.

The Spatial Shift

Nonetheless, federal policies still sent resources away from cities toward fresh fields. Partly to avoid the possibility of attacks by German bombs, partly for diversity, partly to build more easily on clear land, the government meted out war contracts to the South, Southwest, and Pacific Coast. Shipyards and airplane factories brought some 500,000 new residents to live in Los Angeles, and the polynucleated region was born. A whopping $332 million in aircraft contracts swelled San Diego's population. Boeing's aircraft industry enlarged Seattle, while shipbuilding inflated New Orleans's population 50 percent. Other war industries made Portland, Oregon, one and a half times larger and Houston one third. Production whiz Henry Kaiser shaped a fresh town of 140,000 in Vanport, Oregon, locating eight of his ten shipyards on the West Coast. Through the war years the government bankrolled the shift from transit-based towns to the suburbs, depriving the old nucleus to fuel the new fringe. It was a replay of times past—and a portent of times to come.

To Americans huddled in their hometowns throughout the war, and to GIs dreaming of return, Main Street was the abiding center of American life all the same. Cities were community hearths and the countryside their rural roots. Both still described the place called home. Forty-four percent of the nation's fresh vegetables were raised by 20 million backyard urban gardeners to help the war effort.

Throughout the nation the war engine ran at double time as it raced to stop Hitler's army advancing across Europe. Heroes in an emergency, U.S. automobile leaders gained the wealth and credibility lost in the Depression, and the forerunner of the military-industrial complex was born. In what historian John Morton Blume called "the hardening pattern of bigness," government grew bigger and bigger businesses got the bucks. Among them the biggest of all was the automobile industry. Washington handed out two-thirds of its $175 billion in contracts to the nation's top 100 corporations, 8 percent to General Motors alone. "The hand that signs the war contract is the hand that shapes the future," a Senate committee summed it. Some of these "hands" belonged to GM's William Knudsen and to home lender Jesse Jones, chief of the Reconstruction Finance Corporation. These directors of the War Production Board would indeed shape the future. As they attended their private luncheons, they lobbied for the postwar highway leading to the single-family home. From this place of privilege, such corporate chiefs would become the fathers of the 1950s Road Gang in the postwar world.

Eyeing the Interstate

Even before the war ended, plans for a highway network to help "the boys" loomed ahead. As the war machine chugged to victory, worries about the returning veterans put bureaucrats to work. Plans for an interstate system emerged. The superhighways of the 1930s were evolving into the limited-access highways of the 1950s. The cry to fix battered, congested urban roads and the clamor for toll roads like the Pennsylvania Turnpike resounded from state to state. Washington echoed the cry. In 1942 a 513-page report of the National Resources Planning Board called for a federal transportation agency that would create "a modern interregional highway system and urban express routes to accommodate the automobile of the future. . . ."

Express highways and off-street parking in urban areas figured prominently. In 1943, in the midst of its wartime boom, Portland, Oregon, summoned master builder Robert Moses, who called for a ring road. It was a long way from the vision of the river-based, greenbelted town that Lewis Mumford offered the city five years earlier. In 1944, in the flush of enthusiasm for a peacetime program, the Federal-Aid Highway Act was passed, creating a National System of Interstate Highways intended to run through cities. Though the program was underfunded, its aspirations to upgrade—i.e., widen and repave America's postwar highways, linking trucks and long-haul travelers—were imprinted; its wedge into urban areas was enlarged.

That same year, Washington's plans for peacetime housing further advanced the country's car-dependent destiny. With victory in sight, the GI Bill of Rights authorized the Veterans Administration to guarantee some 16 million veterans a housing loan to purchase the "dream houses" packaged in the *Ladies' Home Journal.* More mortgage guarantee money was channeled into the Federal Housing Administration, and, by 1946, housing starts had multiplied eightfold. The suburban explosion was ready to ignite.

The mayor of St. Louis planned a brave postwar tomorrow: "When our service men lay down their victorious arms they may pick up the implements of peacetime construction and begin the building of a greater city." St. Louis's plans for a "greater city" were, unfortunately, based on an airport and a highway infrastructure. Likewise, in Baltimore a greater city meant expressways and garages, waterworks, and slum clearance—the very items that would nullify its urbanity. In 1948, Detroit, Pittsburgh, and Baltimore built their first city parking garages and Los Angeles voters turned down a rapid transit system. Some downtowns did outline plans for resumed trolley service, bus terminals, and the trains to link the nation. "Goodbye standing room only," Pullman advertised a double-decker rail sleeper. But the agenda was a motorized one.

Coming Home

The end of war was the beginning of building America anew. "So nice to come home to," said a Buick ad. "You're a swell looking guy in civvies, too!" said the classic Rosie the Riveter as she welcomed homecoming vets in a *Time* magazine insurance ad in 1946. Other pages featured advertisements to coax postwar Americans to buy tires, fly self-propelled planes, or drive a shiny Nash. The Nash family sedan was more than an automobile, said the advertisement. It was a "Prophecy—on Wheels." It was "so big and roomy that the front seat was *sofa* size—and the back seat can be stretched out into a double bed at night." Spread out. Expand. In the decade after 1947, Americans would buy 30 million cars to help them do so. Forget austerity. Conservation was over, consumption was in. Christian Dior's "New Look" featured lavish swirls of fabric. The new look in mobility was equally expansive.

The pages of *Automotive Industries* predicted a glowing future. The car, helpmate to housing and partner with Cold War defense industries, would power the boom. Forget "freedom from want" and the New Deal dole. Never mind the "commodious . . . crowd-haulers," those Chicago trains pulling voters to whistle-stop speeches by the newly elected President Harry S. Truman in 1949. Within eight years, rail trackage was half of its 1916 peak. Airplane travel was the way to go, plus those newly engineered highways. In the first five postwar years, dealers and buyers jump-started the automobile culture with an average of 3 million car sales a year. Consciousness II, the auto as icon, had returned full-blown. "There's a Ford in your future," the carmakers had advertised midwar. The postwar nation bought it.

Americans took their pent-up dreams and drove to their green horizons. The states financed big city Detroit, New York and Chicago expressways. Toll roads were built. In a decade, Americans had doubled their 25 million automobiles. The car and road consumed four times the road and land space of a bus and twenty of rail.

Appetites reined in by the Great Depression and war controls were unleashed at every level. In urban America, though, dwellings were crammed to capacity. Ten million veterans added to the vast numbers of Americans in shacks, garages, Quonset huts, and decayed housing stock. The postwar housing crisis made the need for new homes severe.

Levitts on the Range

The large-scale builders ready to fulfill that need were on hand. Abram Levitt and his sons William and Alfred had been building subdivisions since the Depression. Speculating and spinning out their prototypes in mass production, they had constructed 2,350 units of wartime housing to serve Norfolk, Virginia. Now they had new customers and the support to assemble even more units. Building small on small lots, building cheap at the rate of five thousand a year, they opened their first postwar Levittown on Long Island in 1947. There, in what had been potato farms, twenty-five miles outside New York City, the tract housing for commuters took hold.

Levittown was the Model T of the built environment. It was assembly line architecture erected in massive numbers to coax the veteran in his car to the green fields of the East. And the prospective buyers lined up. Filled almost from day one, the wood-frame boxes spread to the spinach fields outside Philadelphia in the mid-1950s. The affordability and availability of the Levitts's prefabricated structures combined with public policy to tie Americans to the quarter-acre habit. As postwar spending took off, a nation of cities drove itself into a nation of home-owning suburbanites.

Washington subsidized the motorized exodus with FHA and VA mortgages. Five hundred dollars launched a veteran on the way to home ownership. A buyer needn't earn much more than the median $5,000 income. Buying was easy, courtesy of the federal government. A scant $30 a month (no down payment with a VA mortgage) and the key to a 750-square-foot Cape Cod house was in the hands of many of those 10 million veterans. Out to the suburbs they went, out where the homogeneous families settled to watch Ozzie and Harriet's family on the family TV. "Levittown, A Garden Community," was

the sign posted at one section of ranch models, identifying the 1949
model with Ebenezer Howard's Garden Cities. "No man who owns
his own house and lot can ever be a Communist; he has too much to
do," was William Levitt's contention. It was a Cold War update of
Roosevelt's view that "a nation of homeowners, of people who own
a real share in their own land, is unconquerable."

The look-alike promised land matched the monotonous highway
that sired it. Aided by the tools of the time—zoning laws, subdivision
dictates, deed restrictions, blueprints with the same setbacks, and dimensions—the design was a predictable and repetitive vision, made
more so, critics insisted, by the pressure of 1950s conformism. Frank
Lloyd Wright's horizontal flow of suburban space was paralleled in
the wide picture window; his carport was the signature of the ranch
house facade. His Broadacre City Plan allowed a scant five hundred
residents a square mile. The tract houses built on that model in the
maturing auto suburb sated the home owner's craving as happily as
the two-tone automobile or hardtop convertible in his garage.

If the Levittown boxes seemed minimal and unlovely to the elite—
garage to the fore opening like a maw and widening the one-story
shape, black tongue of a driveway stuck into the street—Levitt at
least filled the white middle-class landscape with schools, community
halls, and churches. Other standard subdivisions were even more
lackluster; there a few hundred homes might adjoin a supermarket,
with scant school or play space. "Little Boxes Made of Ticky-Tacky"
was the dismissive song. A "one-class, antidemocratic, socially repressive environment," planners complained; "boring," said architects. The horns honking on the way to the suburbs drowned them
out.

Levittown was a Northeastern phenomenon repeated in the South
and West. The population of the Sunbelt states, turned gunbelt states
during the war, proliferated. In Houston the public spur was federally funded aerospace and petroleum; in Los Angeles and Phoenix
the government paid for water-siphoning and other infrastructure
subsidies. Everywhere, it was government housing aid, putting dollars into developers' deepening pockets, that hastened the flight.

The oil boom made the drive even breezier. World War II, in part a
petroleum war where the pursuit of oil exhausted combatants, as-

sured America's access to fuel. "The abundance of oil begat the pro-
liferation of the automobile, which begat a completely new way of
life," asserts oil analyst Daniel Yergin in *The Prize*. "This was indeed
the era of the Hydrocarbon Man." In a quarter of a century, oil use
would double. Houston, once a Main Street city shading walkers
under arcades and deep awnings with streetcars shooting out for a
five-mile radius from downtown, now had more than a hundred subdivisions and became the classic centerless city. With cheap oil and
easy access to houses, bought at the rate of 2 million a year by the
decade's end, the consumer exodus advanced. Few noted that by
1954 the United States had burned away its best energy reserves, becoming a net importer of oil. The nation was on easy street.

Or was it? For, as congestion grew, the living, or at any rate the
driving, began to seem less easy. With three out of four Americans
now owning cars, the mid-1950s boom began to jam the roads to
home while commuters were crowding downtowns. Once more, that
old bogeyman—the crisis of car congestion—came back. Mustn't
traffic halt? officials asked. Yes, planners echoed. How? There were
the old answers. Empty the city. Disgorge its congestion. "Disgorge,"
of course, meant "dislodge." And how? Condemn "useless" buildings for parking lots, the *New York Daily News* offered. And every
decree from Washington to build roads and settle the suburbs would
support that mission.

Blowing the Brick House Down

Just before the war, John T. Howard, a planner at the Massachusetts
Institute of Technology, had divided America into the "gone" and
"going" neighborhoods of the city and the "coming" ones of the suburbs. Then he uttered a caution. "The bottleneck in city planning is
people," he wrote. "That bottleneck can be broken. But not by
splashing superhighways across the newspapers, or dreaming visions
of the ideal City of 1970. . . . Good neighborhoods—good 'old'
neighborhoods—are the blocks with which we must build." He went
unheeded. The old was ignored. At 1 million and then 2 million
housing starts a year the new rose, and soon yet one more federal
subsidy helped tear down the old blocks.

The Housing Act of 1949, designed by Congress to remedy city housing ills, initiated what would be called "urban renewal." Descended from New Deal legislation to replace slums with housing through private enterprise and create "a decent home and a suitable living environment," the act set the wheels in motion to clear the land. With money to level working-class housing—termed "slums"—but not put up public housing, with funds to builders and business districts—but not to owners—the act worked in the opposite direction: it shuffled the poor and flattened downtowns. In *The Federal Bulldozer,* a decade and a half later, Martin Anderson would describe how the federal legislation sacrificed working-class communities on the altar of development, aggravated racial and class differences, and obliterated neighborhoods.

The search to tab a neighborhood "blighted" and hence fundable, to find, as Robert Moses had it, "the blight that's right," now took precedence. Moses and his allies were back in action, coupling stump clearance and highway construction, ransacking the city for suitable sites and reducing them to rubble. Solid, if frayed, neighborhoods, two-thirds of them minority, and historic, if worn, buildings became multilane highways and public housing towers. "You can draw any kind of picture you like on a clean slate and indulge your every whim in the wilderness and lay out a New Delhi, Canberra or Brasilia, but when you operate in an overbuilt metropolis you have to hack your way with a meat cleaver," Moses declared. The modern automotive city was under construction. Hearings on Moses's Lower Manhattan Expressway and the rebuilding of the West Side Highway incited opposition and inspired him to declare the political credo of the highway age—"Nothing I have ever done has been tinged with legality"—and its supplement—"If the end doesn't justify the means, what does?" His notorious Cross Bronx Expressway, which smashed through 113 streets and 159 buildings, taking the homes of five thousand people, was the means.

The ballyhoo for "modern expressways right through and not merely around and by-passing cities [and] offstreet parking facilities of all kinds" traveled through the nation. Toll roads had carved through the country in Illinois, New Jersey, and Virginia. They soon spliced Oklahoma, Colorado, Texas, and Kentucky. In 1953,

Philadelphia, Detroit, and Pittsburgh built their first freeways direct to the suburbs from downtown. Mimicking Moses elsewhere, the Baltimores, New Orleanses, Bostons, and Philadelphias of America would pluck the meat from the federal bone to aid highways and recast neighborhoods. Reaching their peak in the mid-1950s with twelve thousand miles executed or en route, the new local roads presaged the interstate.

For cities the combination of building highways and taking homes was a disaster; for if urban renewal sounded fine in theory, it was mayhem in practice. "Negro removal" was the epithet of opponents. Beset by road building, plus the continuing arrival of the rural poor from the South and from Caribbean nations and the exodus of the rich, cities flared into that expletive "inner cities." Costing more than $10 billion, the urban renewal program would level 300,000 more homes than it raised in the next quarter century. Combined with the magnet of single-family housing policies—FHA and VA postwar programs that excluded urban and minority populations and income tax deductions for property taxes and mortgage interest—the 1949 act had monumental consequences. The outward drift seemed like an act of nature. Its hurricane force would sweep through urban centers and blow the brick house down.

The Spanning of America

The President's Advisory Committee on a National Highway Program had an even broader goal: span the nation with concrete. And, on June 29, 1956, the year of Dwight D. Eisenhower's reelection, the hero president signed the greatest peacetime public works project in the history of the world. Or so Eisenhower called it when he approved the legislation establishing the Interstate Highway System. Gas tax receipts, invisible in yearly budgets—not tolls—would funnel $50 billion annually into the Highway Trust Fund to build forty-one thousand miles of roads. The fund would become infamous, the interstate system prodigious. No river or ravine, no gorge or gully, no urban or suburban land would stand in the way of the onrushing auto age. With Boston's Route 128 under way as the nation's first loop road, other cities followed to plunge five thousand miles of free-

ways through downtowns and countryside. Before this act, less than
five hundred miles of urban freeways had been built. After it, no city
would be untouched. Urban America would empty out on the new
arteries.

The 1956 act reflected not only the urge for asphalt, the low price
of oil, and the push of the auto lobbies, but also sounded the era's
Red alert. Defense needs had powered road building since World
War I, when military leaders advocated "national defense roads." In
World War II the armed forces had promoted roads to reach military
reservations and defense industries. Now, in the heat of the Cold
War, the interstate system answered the military imperative. It was
officially known as the National System of Interstate and Defense
Highways, and the documents stressed "defense." Advocates emphasized that the roads would ease evacuation in a nuclear attack. One
pamphlet offered twin images boasting of the safety of this American
autobahn in the missile age. One photo showed the close-packed co-
ziness of a Swiss village; the other depicted a sweeping vista of concrete highway, vast and empty, waiting for evacuation. The image of
the village bore the warning "unsafe" in time of nuclear attack. The
highway was labeled "safe." For the first time, in the guise of pro-
tecting the U.S. from Communist bombs, the federal government was
ordaining roads between cities. The standards of the trucking industry—wider and pricier—would limn the route, benefiting the more
than 10 million trucks registered in the mid-1950s.

While such military follies of the age of the Atomic Café ruled the
road from Washington, builders and lobbyists exulted over the implications of the interstate for peacetime mobility. "Transportation no
longer will be a problem," one enthusiast declared. "Pedestrian and
vehicle traffic ways will be separated . . . walking will once more be
safe and pleasant," the author wrote. They might be separate, but
they were scarcely equal. "The Tiger Is Through the Gates," warned
Grady Clay, the *Landscape Architecture* editor in Louisville. "Not
long ago I saw a seven-mile interstate expressway placed on a city
map at the request of an anonymous official at a nearby Army post—
a man never identified in public debate, never quoted except indirectly." And this for "a ten- to twenty-million-dollar expressway
though a crowded city," he told his colleagues in 1958.

The U.S. city seemed to collaborate in its own demise. When mayors and urban politicians heard that half of the initial $27 billion highway funding would pass through their hands, they became cheerleaders. In 1957, the GM president, Charles E. Wilson, proclaimed, "What's good for General Motors is good for the country, and vice versa." This classic phrase of the era soured many, but its message ruled the day. Eisenhower himself began to worry about the interstate's urban repercussions, noting that "it was very wasteful to have an average of just over one man per $3,000 car driving into the central area and taking all the space required to park the car." His misgivings did not impede its progress, however. The notion of crossing the country without a stoplight was magnetic. The 90–10 percent split in financing—90 from Washington, 10 from the states—both guaranteed the interstate and also stimulated local highways. The spreading network helped buses and medium-weight trucks multiply. Truck trailers, virtually nonexistent before World War II, reached more than a million before 1960, taking over the long-haul work of the freight train. And, as the cattle and hogs of the Chicago stockyards rolled off in trucks, freight trains themselves declined. "First the freight house was closed, then the stockloading pens were abandoned, and finally the railroad station was closed," one commentator mourned. Simultaneously, throughout the 1950s, passenger cars deteriorated, service languished, and terminals grew dank and dirty, while mass transit as a whole declined.

In Europe it was otherwise. There, passenger trains were revived. Stockholm, Rotterdam, Rome, and Leningrad constructed underground subways. West Germany, England, France, and other European nations, nurtured by the Marshall Plan, began to rebuild their shattered cities with updates to old transit systems and with thirty-two new ones before 1970. Americans decimated what they had.

In, of, and on the Road

In the heyday of the highway, Americans didn't fret about the outcome. They saw the romance of the getaway, not the tedium of parking. Most famously, Jack Kerouac wrote about hitting the highway in *On the Road*, heading toward the Western sun or the Arizona dawn, hitching a ride at seventy miles an hour in a Cadillac through "Frisco," or poking "five miles in local buses." Moving briskly, hitching, or sallying forth in a "toolshack on wheels"—whatever, wherever, crossing and recrossing America—he waved the flag of freedom in his 1955 book. In *Lolita,* Vladimir Nabokov told the erotic tale of Humbert Humbert's life on the road, too, describing the highway culture through days and nights in the roadside establishments of the auto age. There were poignant pauses at "the lowly Eat," visits to a log cabin "boldly simulating the past log cabin where Lincoln was born," or "a winery in California, with a church built in the shape of a wine barrel." Seedy or colorful, these were the artifacts of a motorizing landscape.

Behind the wheel of the Chevy, Ford, or Plymouth, the ordinary father who "knew best" was using his knowledge to help mom pile the family goods into the car and head out to the American dream home. Out along the new toll roads and turnpikes, Dad would commute by car from work. At home mom was busy behind the wheel as well, foraging for food, chauffeuring junior, shopping daily at the supermarket, or visiting the Miracle Mile of shops that rose in synch with the vehicle miles on her odometer. Why go downtown anyhow when suburban services were a spin away, entertainment was on the TV screen, and serenity was in the green grass all around? "Station Wagons . . . Ho!" columnist Erma Bombeck would later call them as Americans rolled off the exit ramps to the new suburban roads.

William Manchester used the title *The Glory and the Dream* to define the postwar exodus to the 40 million homes serviced by these multiplying supermarkets, drive-in eateries, drive-in motels—drive-in everything. Drive-in movies alone tallied 1700 by 1950. In 1952, four years after the McDonald brothers automated their restaurant, the company recorded its first million hamburgers sold and the golden arch was born. That same year, Holiday Inn welcomed its first guests. The once-racy motel now attracted the same family customers who stopped at a Kentucky Fried Chicken or parked their cars in the wraparound lots at Sears and J.C. Penney. Bobby-soxers headed to the drive-in bowling alleys or fast-food franchises beneath the glass peaks and massive, curling steel signs. Churchgoers could even motor to Rev. Robert Schuller's drive-in church in Garden Grove, California, a "shopping center for Jesus Christ," opened in 1954. The auto-based suburban shopping spree swept the country. In the twenty years following 1950, the number of shopping centers grew from a hundred to some three thousand. The architecture and engineering of the motor vehicle multiplied from the four-lane roads to the eight-lane highways, cloverleaf interchanges, and toll booths on the ever smoother, straighter highway. These arrow-straight roads would send motorists to "See America First" directly, not on scenic roads but point to point from Cape Cod to the Grand Canyon. Neither topography nor urban heritage would interfere. The roads kept city dwellers from their waterways as well. They made urban habitats less scenic by cutting communities off from the Charles, the Hudson, the Potomac, and countless other rivers.

The Golden Dream Boat

The children born to the baby boomers of the "Fertility Valley" fifties would enter a golden age of consumerism which took as its axiom that "it was human nature for all of us to want good highways," as California Governor Earl Warren declared. And, as the postwar automobile regained its place at the head of the capitalist dream, each one of the babies would grow up to own a motor vehicle. "U Auto BUY Now" was the creed. Incomes rose with the speed of the lengthening chassis.

The late 1950s were the time of tail fins, of fanged grilles, and of pastel paint jobs, as Americans turned in their old cars for the latest showroom models and powerhouse engines. The GM Cadillac introduced in 1948 was inspired by the Lockheed P-38, emulating the airplane by supplanting the rounded streamlined style with the tail fin mode. Harley Earl, still at the company's design helm, said that he shaped the postwar automobile for "aerodynamic styling," incorporating passions for motion and the spread-out shape of widening ranch houses. For thirty-two years GM's "Cellini of Chrome" masterminded the design of 50 million vehicles, inspiring Ford and Chrysler as well to put an extravagant face on the country's most visible artifact. With 46 models, 32 engines, 20 transmissions, 21 colors, not to mention 9 two-tone varieties and more than 400 accessories and options, one Yale physicist estimated that "the number of distinct cars that a Chevrolet customer could order exceeded the number of atoms in the universe!" The gadgets multiplied as well. Dials, switches, wraparound windshields, fake gun ports, taillights shafted like the rockets of a plane created the road warrior look of the embryonic space age in automobiles. Wrote one commentator, "Motorists were never quite sure whether they were seated in an automobile, a land-based dreamboat or an earth-bound aircraft."

Status-seeking Americans took to their rollicking, tricked-out bombers depicted in the movie *American Graffiti*. They cruised their chrome-encrusted, late-model muscle cars down Main Street. Earl's phrase "dynamic obsolescence" would characterize this conspicuous consumption. Their increases in mileage increased fatalities, too. But that didn't dissuade contemporary Americans. From the hot rod hit at the decade's beginning, to the three-miles-a-gallon Cadillac or Thunderbird at its end, the driver's power, social standing, and spirit of adventure resided in the car. "Drive it like you hate it . . . it's cheaper than psychiatry," went a television commercial.

The Maiming of America

The view through the rear window past the fins revealed something equally obstreperous, prompting architect Victor Gruen to denounce the automobile's environment. "We pass through the avenues of horror, stretching for endless miles through the suburban areas, flanked by the greatest collection of vulgarity—billboards, motels, gas stations, shanties, car lots, miscellaneous industrial equipment, hot dog stands, wayside stores—ever collected by mankind," he wrote. Gruen's answer was the shopping center. It would "counteract the phenomenon of alienation, isolation and loneliness," he wrote. Ironically, his solution would become known for increasing that withdrawal.

The architect's Northland Center, built in Detroit in 1954, was an early mall. It was the first mall with an assemblage of open-air stores and walkways for shoppers. His Southdale Center near Minneapolis, which opened in 1956, proclaimed the covered, climate-controlled space that would become the automobile age's most celebrated architecture. Both were wrapped by parking lots that covered ever wider acreage. Gruen's later notions for whole cities hooded over with futuristic forms made him the king of planners in the auto-based environment of his day.

Earlier, Northgate in Seattle had established the open pedestrian shopping mall, while Shoppers World in Framingham, a half hour out of Boston, took its place as the first closed mall in 1951. Grand Rapids planner Kenneth C. Welch designed the latter as a space-age icon of architecture sheltering an arrangement of shops so alluring, so commodious, so accessible by automobile, and—with four thousand spaces—so parkable that his shopping "world" would be what developers would later call a "destination." A highway look-alike, the mall's ramps and elevated tiers, 100 feet wide and 675 feet long, overlooked a sunken mall beneath an all-weather dome. So walkable was it in the architect's eyes that he called it "a double-decked mainstreet."

Arthur and Sidney Shurcliffe, landscape architects with a historic consciousness, also fancied that they were pulling a page from the past by merging the up-to-date and the antique on the mall's grounds. They spoke of re-creating the essence of the New England town common, garnishing the mall with tidy bluegrass, coiling paths, and spruce and dogwood trees. Shurcliffe took special pride in the parking lot designed by town planners Adams, Howard and Greeley, with its looping thoroughfares to make for handy parking and its fast "ring roads" separating walkers and speeders.

But Gruen, molder of the world of concrete, had even grander visions. He would build total cities for the suburbs, with the artery as conduit and downtown as a complete, enclosed environment. "It will be . . . possible for the young matron to assemble her spring wardrobe and arrange for her daughter's tonsillectomy without a change of parking place," said one Westchester observer. Nothing was neglected in the pursuit of the quiet setting, the "refined aesthetics"—nothing except the failure to mitigate the fifty-acre blacktop surrounding it and the compound's role in drawing more traffic.

Together, the mall and the strip became the front guard of the automotive, suburban invasion. As 85 percent of U.S. housing went to bedroom dormitories and drivability became primary, Americans were yoked to their new marketplaces. No longer did commercial buildings line the boulevards with parking behind. Strip shopping backed off from the street to let the cars park on all sides, and the definition of the mall as an asphalt island spread. Supermarkets and gas stations, shopping centers and malls multiplied on a scale heretofore unknown.

Attacking the Ecology

As motorized America dictated this new geographic and personal space, the automobile inspired the colossal environmental alteration of the new lawn culture. In the East the green front yard was paired with a backyard barbecue pit and deck. As this combination took hold, spreading over more soil, home owners turned the tap to water the power-mowered grass fed by DDT and other pesticides and herbicides. The garage was expanded and the roof of the house elongated to cover two cars plus dad's workshop. In the arid Western lands, a whole new set of environmental strains occurred as the region grabbed the waters of the Colorado and other rivers and piped them from afar to sate the thirst of newcomers. The Western garden city became the enemy of the ecology of the desert landscape, a foe to the hill and valley topography chiseled into house lots. Mumford's "town for the motor age" had become totally subservient to it. The injunction to "come as you are in the family car" ultimately meant 300 million tons of exhaust in the 1950s, with excretions from lead and other pollutants.

Pollution had tweaked consciences throughout the early days of the automobile. As early as the 1940s, Southern Californians saw the smog. By noon the skies of Los Angeles began to look brown, unrelieved by the day's sea breezes. In the 1950s, one observer scribbled this graffiti: "I shot an arrow into the air, and it stuck." Congestion came along with the dirty air. The Long Island Expressway had a traffic jam on its first day; Route 128, America's first looped parkway, would require expansion from four to eight lanes within ten years of its completion in 1949. Protesters suggested that it was not so good for the suburbs to be isolated and financially overextended. Others feared for the fate of the family farm as the lawn crop replaced the food crop on the perimeters of cities and suburbs. Already, the farm was staggered by bigness and consolidation, its fields bisected by highways, its owners reeling from the taxes required by the services for the newcomers' homes.

As the interstates swept around them, back roads and the small towns they served became backwaters. If the farmer's goods traveled further, so unfortunately must the farm family to make its rounds; if the farmer's doctor came quicker, the farmer's children got bused further away from the old one-room school. The romance of the open road, the quiet vistas of the country highway, the lyrical curve of the scenic byway began to change. So did the pragmatic and economic viability of the land's use for agriculture. "We lost country life when we moved to tractors" was the way one farmer expressed the downside of the helpmate internal combustion machine.

"We lost city life when we moved to automobiles," city dwellers might have chorused as manufacturers abandoned their aging urban plants and installed themselves on what were formerly the outskirts. With industry moving outward, low-skilled Mexican and African-American migrant workers could find only low-wage jobs and low-income housing in the cities. Restricted from the zoned and cordoned-off suburb by "the Maginot Line of suburbia," built to keep out "undesirables," poor and minority Americans were ghettoized. The city's vacant factories and scuttled sites, poised now beside the arteries, reflected the exodus from the Newarks, the Detroits, and the Bronxes. And the phrase "white flight" joined the lexicon of urban necrology.

Ring Around America

As the red, white, and blue shield of the interstate signs stamped the nation's highways, the ring road choked the heart of urban America. The freeway grid reorganized space in the name of time and safety. Benton MacKaye's vision of a ring—a road or greenbelt like a jade collar to adorn the city and keep cars out—reincarnated in Route 128 strangled the nation's cities. The concern with capacity, sight lines, grade, and continuous flow, all part of the engineers' "high construction standards," meant sweeping hardtop whose mission was speed and motion, not accommodating topography. The slow change of level, the long distances with unobstructed sight, the "efficiency" of the engineer's design for speed—not the pleasure of the driver's trip or the neighbors' surroundings—mattered. Road builders fantasized savings in gas, savings in lives, savings in money. With a swipe of the pen, they inked out urban "obstructions." And the cloverleaf culture germinated

The Robert Moseses of other cities had clear sailing. Public land was seen as empty and "free." The water's edge was cheap, and parks had no owners to do battle for them. Freeways would cleave waterfronts from cities with impunity. The Alaska Way in Seattle, the planned Embarcadero for San Francisco, New Orleans's Vieux Carré, or Hartford's riverfront looked doomed. Parkland, owned by the government, was nobody's land, "a sitting duck," as *Landscape Architecture* editor Grady Clay put it. "Any attack on city park lands has the sanction of the American Association of State Highway Officials in its official bible," he said in describing the new codes defining the nation "Location opportunities for arterial highways" was stamped on the landscape. "And what do they consider a 'location opportunity'?" the Louisville editor asked. "The one and only park in the entire city."

In 1946 only seventy cities had parking requirements in their zoning plans. A decade later, most had them plus wider roads; and one-third of America's cities were hard topped to house the car. No wonder the downtown property fell by one-quarter in the thirteen largest metropolises. Parking lots and roads made gap-toothed wastelands of historic neighborhoods. Downtown hotels were slowly edged out by motels and picture palaces by drive-in movies; historic neighborhoods succumbed to wind-whipped high-rises and cities became cadavers. Domino by domino, demolition took over the nation's cores. The urban carnage devoured America.

When downtown trembled, its institutions fell. Once retailers were no longer fed by foot traffic, they moved out. Advertising dropped, and big city newspapers shuddered. Medical, social, and other services also abandoned downtown. The cure of urban renewal was worse than the disease of decline as city mayors struggled to clear and rebuild with big projects and vast parking linked to major arteries. In Pittsburgh it was David Lawrence and the Mellons and the "Pittsburgh Renaissance" of a "gateway center." In New Haven it was Mayor Richard Lee, who took his success at the polls as a "popular plebiscite" and proceeded to turn downtown into a "Model City" by leveling the center and letting the Oak Street Connector wipe out an urban neighborhood. In San Francisco the impoverished Buena Vista community looked like fodder for a convention center. Urban, U.S.A., seemed a graveyard of the auto age.

The Uprooting of Rail

In concert with their highway building, workmen trashed the old rails. "Down in one Texas city where I worked there was an old Interurban Trolley being dismantled," one baffled Texan recalled. "Many people confused the two—thinking urban renewal was trolley removal. Most simply don't know," he said. By the late 1940s, the number of trolley cars had shrunk to a scant 17,911. Streetcar operators made a stab at saving their systems by trying to attract the commuter from the bedroom suburbs. "Daddy Come Home Early. Ride the Street Car," a round-checked cherub coaxed in an Eastern Texas Electric Company billboard. But Daddy was driving.

By 1956, the year of the interstate act, the National City Lines's cabal of oil and automobile interests had finally bought out the last of the electric rail lines, finishing the conversion to buses in forty-five cities. By then General Motors had replaced 100-plus downed streetcar systems from Baltimore to Los Angeles, Philadelphia to Salt Lake City. Pursuing their mass transit "enemy" with vigor and no opposition from motorists and policymakers, the Medicis of motor manufacturing had supplanted the interurban and the trolley with the little-loved motor coach. Letters to local newspapers decried the new buses "for their fumes, their jerky starts and stops, their lack of room and even their slow speed." To little avail.

Aided by General Motors's body blows, transit was surrendering. When the once immutable nickel fare for the New York subway doubled to a dime in 1948, it set the model for other penniless lines to do the same, pricing themselves further into extinction. In the early 1950s, the Los Angeles mayor had tried to promote rail and Chicago to integrate a rail line into the city's first expressway, but without success. The bankrupt trolley lines were transferred to public agencies that virtually ignored them. Only a handful of big cities held on to the skeleton that had laced America. From the year after the war, when Philadelphia's quaint Fairmount Park line, eight miles of streetcars tucked within a green oasis, closed, until 1960, when Williamsport, Pennsylvania, the nation's last small city line, shut down, crews axed the old rails out of existence to let traffic flow. In a tragic waste of resources, the deed was done. Whether through the highway lobby, mass exodus—or a potpourri of policies—America had trashed its trolleys.

Draped in red, white, and blue banners to take their final trip through a jammed downtown, Denver's tired-looking electric cars saw their last. A lone trolley now waited to depart in the evening rain along New Orleans's Canal Street, one of the greatest "streetcar thoroughfares" in North America. So it went across the nation as the last of the great systems were demolished, their insides torched, their steel sold for scraps. Lost was the famous scenic trolley in Portland, Oregon, that took in a view of the Columbia River. The Oklahoma City station, a refuge for old cars, was destroyed. Even in transit-loving Chicago, Mayor Richard J. Daley shut down the State Street streetcars, and San Francisco passengers took the last rail ride over the San Francisco–Oakland Bay Bridge late in the decade. The stalwart PCC streetcars had struggled to beat out the competition, but they couldn't match the trackless, zigzagging buses and the cars that shouldered out their old routes. With six thousand of the PCCs sold, the company stopped producing new ones in 1952.

In the late 1950s, Los Angeles mourned the loss of the fabulous Big Red Cars of the Pacific Electric Railway when they made their last runs. The Southern California city's mighty railways were a shadowy trace on the map overtaken by the freeways that ran parallel to their old routes. Gangling freeways left the nation's largest municipality with no rail, while traffic swelled in the suburbanized alfalfa fields of the San Fernando Valley. The City of Angels, known as "a bottomless pit" for auto sales, was now devoting 40 percent of its land to the storage of cars and recording the worst congestion and poorest air quality in the nation.

The trains that crossed the continent also had other competition. By funding port and river improvements and subsidizing airplanes, trucks, and highways, the federal government competed with freight and passenger trains. The airline industry, ushered in by the war and nurtured by postwar administrations, began to capture long-distance travel. The trains chugging across the continent barely managed a final flourish. Diners and coaches on lines in the Northeast corridor and the Midwest still serviced passengers. But the "name trains" of ten to twenty coaches and Pullman sleepers that had carried long-distance riders to the portal of Los Angeles's Union Station into the 1950s saw the Santa Clara Freeway at the terminal's rear snatch their travelers. The trains that had swept along the coast dwindled, their whistles piercing the lonely air.

With the trains went their depots and terminals. It was death at a mature age for many of the more than eighty thousand stations that had marked the epic age of rail. For decades those splendid stopovers, from wooden "Stick Style" to monumental edifices, had lingered on in the landscape, providing centers of commerce and community pride and requiring only marginal maintenance. Now even marginal expenses were excessive. By the middle of the Depression, forty-one cities of more than half a million people had commuted by rail on 240 separate routes; by the end of the 1950s a scant twenty such metropolitan areas had one-third their number of passengers. As Americans deserted public urban transportation and urban life, sweeping shutdowns sealed the rails' fate. The classical majesty of the Baths of Caracalla that was replayed in the superb Pennsylvania Station would give no security to preserving its replica in new times. Entwined with the fate of the trains they sheltered, the magnificent public spaces of America's stations and terminals were lost.

In the transit-heavy cities of Boston, Philadelphia, and New York, commuter trains still handled more than 50 percent of the rush hour traffic. It was nothing short of a miracle. From the end of World War II, states and towns had handed out more than $156 billion for roads, but only pennies to create a scant sixteen miles of subway extensions. Since the interstate highway act, the Highway Trust Fund had spent $70 billion on highways, with only 1 percent of total expenditures, less than $1 billion, going to rail. The financial consequences were predictable. The streetcar companies updated their ads by using the Beat language of "Daddy-o, man, swingin', and endsville" to encourage the commuter to use the rails. But the "Daddy-os" were driving from the dissolving cities to the fragmented suburbs.

"This is a book for people who like cities," sociologist William H. Whyte would write almost apologetically in 1957 in the introduction to *The Exploding Metropolis*, derived from a *Fortune* magazine report on urban America. "Are Cities Un-American?" Whyte, an urban advocate, titled his introduction. He scored the extremes brought about by urban renewal's devastation of downtowns and by the deference to the automobile. "They [Americans] dislike the city's variety and concentration, its tension, its hustle and bustle." The retail core was eviscerated.

Could nothing stop the roadmongers' attack? Was there no Consciousness III on the horizon? No sense that the automobile was undermining America?

Some saw signs of opposition to its attack on the landscape. As the mechanical scythe of the highway maimed whatever it touched, sociologist Jean Gottmann coined the word "megalopolis" to describe how the car had coagulated the Northeast into an amorphous blur. The open space marred by random development marked the demise of the bucolic landscape along with the city. "Trees that President Roosevelt planted as a reforestation project have been removed for subdivision developments—yet they were eighty miles from New York City. Hay and trees can never pay as well per acre as motels, split-levels, or apartment houses," Gottmann wrote.

Older suburbs suffered along with the countryside. Rather than build or retain the close, neighborly dwellings, the garden apartments, the two-, three-, four-, and multifamily dwellings, the rental units, the boardinghouse spaces, the single-room occupancy buildings—the myriad hives called home—the single-family house was all. Atomized, unwalkable, unneighborly, such developments supported few stores or services. In the 1950s, courtyard architecture largely ended, dissolving shared space. Row houses and three-deckers tumbled, junked into weedy lots or high-rise wastelands by urban renewal. Main Street suffered the incursions of faceless, car-contoured, homogeneous design.

Traversing space now mattered more than creating place. Subsidized home owners had taken their subsidized cars from their subsidized homes on their subsidized roads to their malls. The middle-class home owners had fled the inner city. And, city space, public space had eroded in the flight to a rural dream. As John Kenneth Galbraith pointed out in *The Affluent Society,* the nation of consumers of private goods was not affluent in public ways. The publicly funded private car had established the auto age. As post-war Americans bought a million or more new houses a year and 2 million cars a year in the late fifties, their driving mileages soared. Few realized what they had incinerated on the altar of mobility. The automobile had become the master of their universe, and protest would come only slowly as the servants to speed and sprawl saw what it had wrought.

Braking the Juggernaut

> "See how the finny monster dominates your life, occupies a large room of your house, eats up about 13 percent of your income, demolishes the hegemony of your town, manufactures your smog, threatens your park, recklessly sires a profusion of billboards in an already uglified world, invites the spread of slurbs."
>
> —Samuel E. Wood and Alfred E. Heller,
> *Phantom Cities of California*

> "Today a magnificent instrument has ruptured the human environment in the name of progress. Its terror has been accepted as a fact of modern war—almost as if it were a sacrifice of war."
> —Kenneth R. Schneider, *Autokind vs. Mankind*

"HOW CLEAN IS Quincy's air?" The question would have startled me the day before I wrote it. As a novice reporter at the *Quincy Patriot Ledger* in the 1960s, my assignment was to visit a strange mechanical device installed on a rooftop near the office. The apparatus was monitoring the cleanliness of the city's air, but how could air be dirty?

Quite easily, I, like the rest of the nation, found out. The color scheme of brown to gray to yellow that mottled the nation's contaminated skies was staining America's sense of well-being. The origins of that smudge became equally obvious: "mobile sources" (cars) and "nonmobile sources" (industry). Not just the "Gasopolis" Los Angeles valleys but also pockets that once boasted pure air were polluted by the exhausts of cars and the smokestacks of industry.

An age of environmental indifference was ending; an era of environmental concern was on the rise. Consciousness was growing that the agent of mobility that menaced those azure skies was also threatening our historical and urban life. Quincy, Massachusetts, ten miles south of Boston and my newspaper's hometown, was typical of our asphalt nation. The city's architectural heritage, dating back to the days of President John Adams, had escaped the highway hit list. Unfortunately, its Buddliner rail cars had not. The South Shore commuter rail line had shut down the year before I started work, the same year the formidable Southeast Expressway opened, carrying the region's drivers in and out of downtown.

You could see the consequences in two ways. Public transportation riders were forced to take longer trips, on the one hand, and accidents and automobile fatalities rose, on the other. Lacking the train route, carless commuters, myself among them, now faced a chain of mass transit journeys—in my case, seventy-five minutes on bus, train, and yet a second bus to accomplish a trip of a meager twenty miles. In my entry-level slot as a *Patriot Ledger* obituary writer, I also saw the second effect: the drivers smashed, lacerated, and even decapitated by the guardrails on the new road.

As the auto age accelerated, so did criticism. The idealism of President John F. Kennedy's New Frontier silhouetted against the sacking of cities, the pillage of our architectural tradition, the displacement of whole populations, the destruction of 40 million acres of farmland, and the desecration of the environment, seemed to wake up the nation.

Sacred Texts

The woman who would make saving urban neighborhoods a shared cause found her inspiration in the very city streets shattered by the automobile. Crusader Jane Jacobs's passions were kindled as a local crusader trying to block Robert Moses's Lower Manhattan Expressway. As the senior editor at *Fortune* magazine who shocked her colleagues by bicycling from her Greenwich Village neighborhood to work, Jacobs turned her bike power and her neighborhood activism to political purpose. Her book *The Death and Life of Great American Cities* was a clamorous indictment. It questioned the values that had emptied cities. It scored planners who had packed the poor in public housing towers and eviscerated urban life. "Traffic arteries, along with parking lots, gas stations and drive-ins, are powerful and insistent instruments of city destruction," Jacobs wrote. "To accommodate them, city streets are broken down into loose sprawls, incoherent and vacuous for anyone afoot. Downtown and other neighborhoods that are marvels of close-grained intricacy and compact mutual support are casually disemboweled." Instead of watchful "eyes on the street," she wrote, empty passageways of hulking cars and boarded-over buildings filled cities. The modernist "tower in the park" had become the tower in the parking lot, wrote Jacobs.

Published in 1961, Jacobs's book became a classic. A year after this urban manifesto, Rachel Carson, a biologist looking at the natural habitat, illuminated the threat of another menacing intruder, DDT, on the environment. Her *Silent Spring* confirmed the intimate link between the acts of human beings and the act's effect on nature and ushered in the environmental age. Increasingly, reformers questioned the human race's mindless mastery over the landscape and cityscape. In this era of countercultural turmoil, the reformers' range grew broader, amplifying earlier critiques.

As early as 1947, Paul and Percival Goodman had insisted in *Communitas* that a city street is not "a machine for traffic to pass through but a square for people to remain within." Now, fifteen years later, Herbert Gans in *Urban Villagers* showed what urban renewal had done to the streets of Boston's West End.

As the highways rolled on, the number of belligerents increased in the mid-1960s. One of the most famous, consumer advocate Ralph Nader, "Motown's Savonarola," told General Motors and America in *Unsafe at Any Speed* that the automobile, especially the Corvair, was dangerous. And so, he argued, was the air being treated like a sewer by these vehicles. The car industry stalked and harassed the anticar crusader, publicizing their own misdeeds still further. Architect and editor Peter Blake surveyed the landscape and saw the scrap, junk, and auto graveyards of 6 million abandoned cars a year that blighted 265,000 miles of interstate and other highways. "Downtown Detroit has practically gone under now," he wrote. "Downtown Los Angeles seems to have disappeared without a trace; and other big cities are on the brink of disaster."

It wasn't just the "unsightly accumulations of scrap metal," the bad air, or the bad cars, but the artifacts of highway settlement that littered the nation. It was the pennants flapping over the tawdry strip mall and the subdivisions gnawing the countryside, consuming the land that William Whyte had bemoaned in *The Last Landscape*. These were just a handful of the outcries that informed the 1960s. In *Design with Nature,* landscape architect Ian McHarg offered his alternative: shape the earth according to its natural dictates, not the heavy hand of the highway engineer. The book had readers, but there were few applications of its theories on the soil.

Fighting the Freeway

While the omnipotent Federal Housing Administration and Federal Highway Administration continued to dictate the shape of home construction and the turf of the highway, the attack on their policies galvanized city lovers and preservationists. The ferocious eight-lane, double-decked Embarcadero Freeway, which would have severed San Francisco from its waterfront, gave birth to a revolt. Other strikes on treasured neighborhoods inspired communities to battle. Citizens in Louisville fumed as highway engineers drew plans to raise Interstate 64 aloft between the downtown and the Ohio River. Preservationists in Louisiana agitated against a 1940s plan by Robert Moses that threatened the Vieux Carré riverside district in New Orleans. "It would have been disastrous—six lanes wide, 40 feet high, a monster," said planner George Marcou as he later recalled the highway that would have imperiled the area. The proposal was defeated in 1969.

"Every major city from Boston to Los Angeles is festooned, draped—or is it strangled—with ribbons of concrete" was the cry Helen Leavitt uttered in 1969 in her *Superhighways—Superhoax*. By then the Federal Highway Administration had handed the Senate Public Works Committee a list of sixteen cities engaged in highway contests. The list was alphabetical, from *A* (Atlanta, 4 miles displacing neighborhoods); to *B* (Baltimore, with 5.5 miles of displacement of historic sites); to *C* (Cleveland, 8.8 miles of parkland, [of] historic and religious interests); to *D* (Detroit), moving along to Indianapolis, Memphis, Nashville, Newark, and Washington. "As neighborhoods are sliced in two and cemeteries are relocated, neither the quick nor the dead are safe," said the *New York Times*.

Natural areas fought to stave off the highway men as well. Franconia Notch, in New Hampshire's White Mountains, and Overton Park, in Memphis, stood in the path of the oncoming bulldozers. The Schuylkill at Philadelphia and the Brandywine at Wilmington were scuttled. No blank on the map was too much for the traffic engineers.

And worse was to come. The original 41,000-mile interstate system, by now expanded to 42,500 miles, wasn't half built before the Commerce Department was talking about another "100,000 miles of scenic roads and parkways, and a quarter of the projected mileage through places never before serenaded by the tappets of internal combustion." All to get back to nature, which was looking less natural. Despite the Highway Beautification Act of 1965, the posies placed by the roadside did little to help the greenswards gouged out for highways, the parkways mutilated by expansion, and the cities eviscerated by streets and parking lots. "But this is only one manifestation of a still larger fault: utter obeisance to the automobile," noted historian Norman Newton in his classic *Design on the Land*.

The Devastation of an Icon

For devotees of railroads and architecture alike, the cause that opened their eyes to the pillage of America was the demolition of the monumental Pennsylvania Station in 1963. Preservationists who headed New York's social register picketed. So did national figures. The protest hit the front pages. The photos of its demise followed. In 1963, not much more than half a century after its birth, the magnificent marble cavern of the great age of rail crashed into oblivion. The station's Doric columns "lie shattered in the Secaucus Meadows," mourned critic Ada Louise Huxtable. The forsaken sculptures lay in fractured heaps. So did the passenger fleet the station had served four decades earlier with some twenty thousand trains now down to a pitiful six hundred. No more would Thomas Wolfe's "great, slant beams of moted light" fall or "the calm voice of time hover along the walls and ceiling of that mighty room." When McKim, Mead and White's soaring spaces were replaced by a new Pennsylvania Station, a tacky subterranean hive, lamentation gave way to fury.

This wanton destruction became a symbol of municipal vandalism: it was the ultimate betrayal of architectural grandeur, of public space, and of public transportation. The preservation movement, for too long the hobby of upper-crust Americans doting on historic mansions and other artifacts of their class, expanded. Members of the social elite joined with residents of embattled neighborhoods to protect their cherished buildings. Concerns for the larger monument of the city as a work of collective art culminated in the National Historic Preservation Act, passed in 1966. In detailed language, Section 106 of the act required federal agencies to "take into account" the impact of new projects on historic properties. Each construction, each demolition, each license, each loan or transfer that bore Washington's stamp would now need review from the Advisory Council on Historic Preservation. The review became a cornerstone of the preservation battle.

That same year, another measure passed. With section 4(f) of the National Transportation Act of 1966, the Department of Transportation forbade its secretary to fund undertakings that damaged historic sites and parks unless "no feasible and prudent alternative" appeared and the "program includes all possible planning to minimize harm." Both laws would become tools—and mantras. The mechanisms for the antihighway movement were in place.

A hands-on appreciation of America's heritage coincided with these rules. "Gentrification," a word imported from England, was used to describe a wave of urban rejuvenation. From Society Hill in Philadelphia to Boston's South End, historic neighborhoods blossomed. Small-scale fix-ups flourished as urban pioneers applied paint to worn buildings and tiles to bruised roofs. At the end of the decade, the small seaside town of Newburyport, Massachusetts, threatened with losing its Market Square and historic Federal-era structures to urban renewal, became the first city in the country to channel the funds into revitalizing its historic landscape. Attacking Washington's role as "slum saviours" and urban renewal as "Negro removal," neighborhoods began to retaliate.

A new attitude was at hand. "U.S. Road Plans Periled by Rising Urban Hostility" was the headline in a *New York Times* front-page story. The secretary of transportation called the team approach devised in Baltimore to stop the Jones Falls Expressway "revolutionary." Highway engineers retorted that their opponents were "petunia planting esthetes, birdwatchers and do-gooders." But successes filled the preservation log. From the "Save the Sycamores" struggle, to keep the graceful trees along Cambridge's Charles River from a road widening, to the triumph in deleting the Embarcadero from the interstate system in 1965, victory was visible. Poised at the Pacific terminus of the interstate system, the wiry guts of San Francisco's aborted freeway dangled as the emblem of antihighway warriors. Manhattanites banded to fight plans for an expressway along the Hudson River, too. Pickets labeled the expressway espoused by Governor Nelson A. Rockefeller in the campaign of 1966 as "the Rocky road to ruin." Philadelphia trashed a crosstown expressway, and Transportation Secretary George Volpe helped kill the road through the Vieux Carré.

Fighting highways had transformed odd bedfellows into allies. In Seattle an unlikely coalition stopped a major freeway, the R. H. Thompson Expressway, near Lake Washington. "The Black Panthers would sit down with the society ladies," recalled activist and social

scientist Chris Leman. "It was a colorful era." Seattle's crusaders got
the issue on the ballot. By 1970 the Federal Highway Administration's so-called Stewardship Report declared that thirteen cities had
stalled their interstates. Alas, other coalitions failed to stop highways
and interstates that still perched on stilts obstructing waterfronts or
lurched through seething urban areas.

The Fires Burn

Not only did cities seethe, they shattered. Riots detonated in Harlem
in 1964, then exploded anew in Watts in 1965. They flashed across
the nation—in Cleveland, in Newark, in Milwaukee. In 1967 the
army was called to quell disturbances in Detroit, where Michigan
Governor George Romney, a former American Motors president,
listed freeway construction as a major cause. Wrapped by freeways
that isolated impoverished ghettos, the ringed-off inner cities compounded the policy mistakes of the government. One planner called
the central city a sandbox for the refuse of society. The crisis of the
cities was at Washington's door.

The transportation crisis joined the urban crisis as the long-standing havoc dealt to the nation's rail system sped up. Between World
War II and the mid-1960s, the nation had spent a meager $1.5 billion
for local public transportation, an average of $75 million a year,
while doling out $51 billion a year to motor vehicles. Federal, state,
and urban policies combined to swing the shovels to dig up the
roads, remove the old rails, and send their customers outward
bound. In Washington, D.C., loyal trolley buffs took their last out-
ings on the old streetcars in 1962. The next year, Los Angeles's electric railway service was extinct. Even buses idled in the mass transit
doldrums. The headlines in the trade magazines told the tale: "Trenton Buses Will Halt at End of Month"; "Bus Company Declared
Bankrupt in Beloit, Wis." With two hundred private transit providers
bankrupt and ridership down to 5.9 billion trips a year, a third of its
World War II high, the engines that powered urban America were
stalled.

At the beginning of the 1960s, a *Fortune* article titled "How to
Unchoke Our Cities" cited the cause of the imbalance. "The Ameri-

can consumer, in deciding between private and mass transportation, has for years and years been presented with a market heavily rigged in favor of using his own car in city traffic." In the quarter century after World War II, Washington and the states allocated $226 billion for highways for private cars and less than a quarter of that for public transportation.

In the administration of Lyndon B. Johnson, however, there were funds to spare, and money for Great Society programs to right both urban and transportation ills. There was some good news for mass transit lines. As supporters attempted to mend the skewed system, the federal government looked beyond adding roads as a solution to all problems and instead sought a mix of cars, buses, and rail. The Federal Highway Act of 1962 demanded that transportation projects within urbanized areas plan before proceeding; they must shape the land with what was called a "3C" process. Plans must be continuing, comprehensive, and cooperative. It insisted that a metropolitan planning organization coordinate the systems. That same year, the High-Speed Ground Transportation Act paved the way for upgraded Metroliner service on Northeastern routes. Two years later, in 1964, the Urban Mass Transportation Act, under the new Department of Housing and Urban Development, sent some $375 million to the states.

"Just in time, if not too late," said public transit advocates. The Urban Mass Transportation Act opened federal coffers to public transit. It allotted funds to buy equipment and to run it. Blessed with more money in the next decade, municipalities and public companies had funds to buy buses back and send bedraggled trolleys along their old tracks, and even time to dream of monorail. Big city Philadelphia, Boston, or New York could still rely on rail; San Francisco and Washington's visions for speedy lines got a push. In 1968, Pittsburgh's once formidable system shut down all but a hundred cars; two years later it was funded.

Money now went to new lines and new ideas, sometimes unfocused ones. In an era that sought to do it all, transit was reorganized. The opposition to the car was swelling. With the twenty-seven thousand electric railways of 1940 down to a paltry thirteen hundred in the late 1960s, protests sounded and city mayors pushed another transit program into law in 1970. The Urban Mass Transportation Assistance Act handed public transit its highest funding of the era, changing the urban transit map of America. The $3 billion given for five years fused with the energy of localities battling the automobile.

Smothered in the Highway Haystack

The passenger trains of America had never quite hit the depths to which surface light-rail and heavier commuter lines had fallen, yet abandonment loomed. "In autumn 1964, the news that a high-speed passenger train was running did not make the front pages in the United States—where everyone knew the passenger train was doomed," noted the *Passenger Train Journal*. Everywhere, angry and melancholy passengers, among them E. B. White, noted the decline of railroad service and its accoutrements of red-blazered porters and streamlined nostalgia. Northeasterners cheered the opening of the high-speed Metroliner service between Washington and New York, but the twenty thousand locomotives that had puffed from coast to coast in the 1930s had fallen to three hundred. By 1970, Penn Central, with only nine daily Metroliners each way, was in receivership.

That same year, the federal government created Amtrak as the National Railroad Passenger Corporation. "Wards of the state," Stephen Goddard summed it in *Getting There*. The public would cover costly passenger service while the profitable freight would be siphoned off for private operators under Conrail. It was little short of a hatchet job. Equipped with wretched cars from a ravaged system and severed from the profitable freight lines, Amtrak got short shrift. "Amtrak was intended to go gently into that good night," a veteran railroader observed. The act virtually dictated a permanent state of crisis.

So it was that, for all the fanciful drawings of supersystems, for all the modernizing with air-conditioned, lighter streetcars, the funds were a straw in the highway haystack. Though the money made public ownership of public transportation viable, it barely touched the highway handouts. In the first five years after transit's early 1960s start, funds measured one-sixtieth of the $24 billion fed to the car. In 1966 the Mayors' Task Force on Urban Design scored the New York subway as "the most squalid public environment in the United States." Graffiti, muggings, and the urban financial crisis made things worse. Transit lines were emasculated; terminals became weary shells of themselves. At L.A.'s Union Station, the famed Harvey House and cocktail lounge closed. Cars proliferated—the U.S. had 88 million by the 1960s. By the decade's end a Chamber of Commerce survey confirmed the results: urban transportation problems were either critical or getting worse. The notion of balanced transportation wasn't even on the political scales.

In 1971, Los Angeles journalist Jack Burby, back from his stint in the Department of Transportation, wrote of the mess in *The Great American Motion Sickness*. And all the symptoms of motorized "sickness" were in his book: the deaths of 56,400 people and the maiming of almost 4 million by the nation's 109 million motor vehicles in 1970; pollution and the fear of the greenhouse effect; the thirty-two cents of every food dollar going to transportation and the 13 percent of every working day spent in traffic jams caused by motorists—motorists who were, Burby noted, still in debt for their cars by some $37 billion. Ever speedier jets would be flying above the traffic congestion. Shipping, given four times as much funding as public transportation, would sail offshore from the stalled arteries. The poor were in the ghettos and the jobs were in the suburbs, and no money could bridge the two. The blighted land and the jerry-built suburbs were "dissolving slowly into ranch-style slums," Burby wrote.

Yet, awareness of the wounds to the landscape and cityscape was growing. Gas stations were now "eyesores," in the popular vernacular, and the dirty air found in Quincy, Massachusetts, as in smogged-over Los Angeles, was literally making eyes sore everywhere. "L.A. Has a Cough" was the way *Esquire* described "America's Airborne Garbage." "If we continue on our present course, such basic atmospheric contaminants as sulfur dioxide, carbon monoxide, and nitrogen oxides will increase two to four times . . . within the next thirty or forty years." The tales of Tokyo school children wearing protective surgical masks provoked columnist Art Buchwald to describe an America discovered by scientists from Venus. Surveying Manhattan, the spacemen declared that there was no life on Earth. How could there be? The planet was clearly uninhabitable because it was covered with concrete and empty of oxygen, he wrote.

Conservation Comes of Age

Never had "The Earth As Modified by Human Kind," described by the nineteenth-century conservationist Charles Perkins Marsh, been modified so rapidly. Inspired by Ralph Nader's indictment of car companies and other battles, a new body of environmentalists sought to curb the car in court. An oil spill in 1969, in which a Union Oil platform gushed out 3.3 million gallons of petroleum, incited more than a blaze in the sunbaked Santa Barbara Channel. It sparked the nation. Senator Gaylord Nelson of Wisconsin and twenty-five-year-old Denis Hayes initiated the first Earth Day, modeling it on the teach-ins used to oppose the Vietnam War. And the environmental decade began.

The federal government responded. On January 1, 1970, the National Environmental Policy Act became law, stipulating that all federal agencies "evaluate the environmental aspects of their proposed actions and consider alternatives to proposed actions." The government was given the imperative to look at the alternatives and consequences from road building. Responding to groups like Pittsburgh's GASP, Congress passed the Clean Air Act, a powerful tool for the anti-automobile movement. "Environmental wonders should be heard," Supreme Court Justice William O. Douglas said of the act. And heard they were. Acts to stop noise, acts to manage pesticides, acts to tend the coast and marine mammals issued from Congress. The Clean Water Act of 1972 prohibited paving wetlands or coastal waters, and the Endangered Species Act of 1973 protected their inhabitants. Court cases and legislation grew along with environmental organizations.

With the foundations in place, environmental stewards could take advantage of scientific studies that certified the motor vehicle's damage to human health. It seemed that the polemics rolled off the presses daily. Ben Kelley's *The Pavers and the Paved* scored the highway. In the highway's wake, any notion of a balanced transportation system was in shambles. In 1972 car crashes reached a high of

56,000. Even the conservative *Reader's Digest* headlined an article "Our Great Big Highway Bungle."

Anti-Highway Hopes

Urban missionaries rallied from city to city and plugged into the possibilities. In Boston, a hotly contested inner belt, scheduled to displace thirteen hundred households with an eight-lane highway, allied briefcase and lunch pail crusaders, academics and public housing families to fight the marauding interstate. Throughout the 1960s protests over the project churned. "Cambridge Is a City, Not a Highway" stared from signboards as protestors petitioned Washington to withhold federal funds from the inner belt, shaping a radial highway through urban neighborhoods. In 1968, a "People Before Highways" day was held. Bowing to the pressure, in 1970 Governor Francis Sargent imposed a moratorium on highway construction. The Federal Highway Act of 1973 created the nation's first "highway transfer fund," thus permitting the state of Massachusetts to trade in highway money for the splendid Southwest Corridor. The corridor, a linear greenway, unified heavy long-distance rail and a new rapid transit line and bridged two communities, the South End and the Back Bay, once severed by tracks.

The transfer fund also allowed other cities to divert highway money to mass transportation. It was a dramatic gesture to restore balance in mobility, and other localities jumped on board. Santa Clara County, not yet bearing the name Silicon Valley, looked to light-rail. Heroic efforts to tunnel under other cities were initiated and constructed. Buffalo went underground with "the biggest transit project in Buffalo since the completion of the Erie Canal," which the city planned and partly built. Baltimore authorities drafted and dug a rapid transit route from its downtown. Even Detroit proposed six rail routes totaling 148 miles under Woodward Avenue and a people mover soon rose in the central business district. Chicago, New York, Philadelphia—all the old star-shaped cities—had a slate for freshly minted transit lines it seemed. So, too, did some newer car-based sprawling cities.

In Portland, Oregon, a classic freeway fight turned into a victory that inaugurated a model for the nation. Opposing the Mount Hood freeway that would have taken three thousand homes, in 1973 the state's progressive governor Tom McCall castigated the "shameless threat to our environment and to the whole quality of life." Citizens rallied behind a land use policy that shaped a stronger downtown with an urban growth boundary to control development in the out-skirts and better transportation within. By voting for the new MAX streetcar line, Portland's citizens kept their urban core for street rail, not road, and saved downtown.

Could this new consciousness compete with the power of the auto-mobile as the economic engine of America? The gross domestic prod-uct tallied nearly twenty cents of every dollar spent on the construction and use of highways. The Bureau of Public Roads sounded like Paul Bunyan and Babe the Blue Ox in boasting that its excavations would "move enough dirt and rock to blanket Connecti-cut knee-deep; sand, gravel and crushed stone for the construction would build a mound 50 feet wide and nine feet high to circle the globe." And yet, in these quickened times a Consciousness III seemed possible, a movement to fuse 1960s activism with 1970s environmen-tal impulses. The automobile's birth in Consciousness I and its spread as icon in Consciousness II had set the course. A Consciousness III was needed now to tame the automobile and eradicate its ill effects.

The Energy Crisis

One year after the date slated for the demise of the Highway Trust Fund and the completion of the interstate system, an event occurred that threatened the very underpinnings of the automobile. An oil shortage caused by an Arab embargo on exports in 1973 doubled prices at the gas pump. It was a crisis of more than inconvenience. Motorists steamed while waiting in long lines to fuel their cars. The furor hit Washington. Within a year prices had more than tripled, and Americans lining up to fill their cars felt the jolt. The energy cri-sis was at hand.

A Rube Goldberg machine of palliatives was installed to save en-ergy. Solutions multiplied, and rationing was installed. Although the forthcoming $10 billion Trans-Alaska oil pipeline alarmed environ-mentalists, Congressional curbs on oil use looked promising. Legislation reduced speeds from seventy to fifty-five miles an hour to save gas. Funds were even siphoned from the Interstate Highway Fund for mass transit. Against the odds, Amtrak increased ridership. Gas guzzling was out and smaller Japanese cars in, forcing the Big Three to shrink their petrol imbibers. Energy-saving devices, from solar heat to insulation, were on the agenda. Energy conservationists raised corporate average fuel economy (CAFE) standards from eighteen miles a gallon to twenty-seven in ten years, and the National Energy Act was passed to "wean ourselves away" from oil. A second crisis helped bump the price of oil from $10 to more than $30 per barrel. Over the next decade the National Mass Transportation Act of 1974 would authorize $5.3 billion to local transit systems.

More Americans questioned the automobile's invincibility. Where was it writ that automobile showrooms, the stages of America, should have a new and costly product every year? Why must prices on these weighty muscle machines rise annually? Why did Americans have to spend a quarter of their income on automobiles, with more and more going to accessories? Small imports, less expensive to drive than domestic gas-guzzlers, nibbled away at the Big Three's sales. "Herbie," Hollywood's version of the adorable Volkswagen, also known as the Bug and the Beetle, and the less endearing Japanese vehicles offered low-mileage, low-frills mobility and gave Detroit stiff competition.

The Last Extinction

Yet it was not to be. The nation was more car dependent than ever before. Other plans still simmered, but trouble in the central cities often quenched their fire. New York's fiscal breakdown in the early 1970s killed the fourteen-mile segments of the Second Avenue subway line before it was finished. While Washington's subway came off the drawing board, other schemes stalled. When Los Angeles planners and politicians put mass transit on the ballot, voters pulled the no lever three times between 1968 and 1976. It would take more than token handouts, polemics, or would-be druids rolling in the Woodstock fields to halt the auto's growth.

The Gang of Three in cahoots with the highway industry made formidable foes. Their lobbies permeated American politics. With one automobile for every two people, the 1970 census showed 75 million Americans living in suburbs versus 63 million in central cities—more circling downtown than centering within it. In 1973 automobile ownership reached an all-time peak with 9.7 million cars sold that year, and the hit movie *American Graffiti* romanced the fabulous 1950s with their cruisers.

With the poor in the central cities, and the ever wealthier in the outer ring, could a new ethos move Americans? A new Westway was proposed for Manhattan, and clamorous Los Angelenos made the city close their car pool and bus lanes. With the federal government still supplying 90 percent of the cost of road building to the local share of 10 percent and federal subsidies cushioning the home building at the end of the interstate, with every aspect of development and subsidy pushing the car outward, opponents of the car culture didn't have a chance.

As public policy bolstered the suburbs, Americans in flight seemed to change their telephone area codes more speedily than the seasons. Their journey to the fringes grew. Driving rose from World War II's 250 billion miles per year to 1 trillion in 1970. In the fourteen years after 1969, the baby boom generation upped its driving 56 percent, more than three times the growth in population. Parvenu car cities in the South and Southwest still increased. Fluid, auto-oriented, exurban America pulled more industry from the towns of tradition. The benefits of a water infrastructure supplemented the highway's route to sprawling Sunbelt carburbs, and big firms fled downtown for cheap exurban space, drawing employees.

In a 1974 *Harper's Magazine* article, L. J. Davis described a typical town in mid-America: "Boise stands an excellent chance of becoming the first American city to have deliberately eradicated itself." But the statement could have applied to countless others. "Main street is virtually deserted. A few eerily patronless stores still stand on the north side, the offices above them empty, while across the street a small inland sea of parking lots stretches as far as the railroad tracks two blocks away." The new office rising a few hundred yards away encased by desolate emptiness looks as "forlorn as buffalo standing in the rain at the zoo."

Urban preservationists reacted more aggressively. The National Trust for Historic Preservation established a Main Street program to

revive downtowns. Yet, the city was still in shambles. Parking remained the Holy Grail, and in Victor Gruen's words, "for each addi-
tional automobile penetrating the heart area of a city, one visitor or
inhabitant of the same heart area is lost." As the roadside-bred franchises multiplied and prospered, they invaded downtown, and the
center, too, took on the asphalt look. Parking chewed away the center. The corner café became the fast-food chain; chatting over coffee
became a quick bite. Seventies America was more likely to construct
a Tire City, an auto parts shop, on a Chicago strip or a Starrett City,
six thousand units of housing towers, on an island than a real city. It
was more likely to build a faux Disney Main Street than a genuine
one.

The Architecture of Anyplace

Le Corbusier's vision that modern city planning would not come to
fruition until "we have killed the street" was coming true. With the
street went the public realm and its architecture. The interior court,
the marble lobby, the galleria, and all the evolving forms of architecture sped the execution. Like the automotive culture, the xenophobic
spaces reflected a withdrawn, anticivic impulse. No more would the
glow of a Chrysler Building illuminate the skyline and its shops line
the streetscape. GM's towering headquarters on Fifth Avenue drew
back from the public sidewalk and space with an aloof concrete
apron. The plazas and forecourts of American architecture pulled the
welcome mat off the sidewalk.

Downtown Minneapolis's IDS Building and Nicollet Mall, with a
pedestrian mall, skywalks, and sky-high atriums, designed in 1968
by architect Philip Johnson, tried to do otherwise. For all the winter-
weatherproofed activity and the street for buses and pedestrians, the
building's interior glass atrium did not, could not, feel really public
or welcoming. The malaise was simple: the design and management
alike said, "Keep out." Had architecture become more introverted?
Did it wing upward in ever higher towers to escape the lifeless
streets? Or did its design create those streets? Either way, John Portman's soaring glass atrium hotels above a vacant downtown Atlanta
typified America and spread.

Los Angeles's downtown was "where the action cannot be," critic

Reyner Banham noted. Instead of action, Americans had motion. At best, planners and architects were ambivalent. Some mourned the death of the pedestrian city and helped install two hundred or so pedestrian malls across the country, a sometime cure. Others seemed mesmerized or enchanted by the scale and geography of the highway, not to mention the commissions. Architect Kevin Roche described his looming Knights of Columbus building to the *New Haven Register* with a minimal apology: "It may seem out of scale with other structures in the city," he said, "but you can't put a small building near a superhighway." Like Le Corbusier, urban renewal agencies and planners worked to revive the city street by killing it. Design for drivers, not pedestrians, turned downtowns into wastelands with sky-shearing towers and street-emptying plazas.

New York's seat of government, the Empire State Plaza in Albany, completed in the early seventies, became a prototype of the highway scale. Its public space was as otherworldly as a set for the movie *Blade Runner.* The vast concrete plaza, with its block buildings, was empty on weekends save for roller skaters. The Rockefeller court architect, Wallace Harrison, designed a vast plaza above the underground garage in the center of the complex, replacing a historic neighborhood across from H. H. Richardson's landmark City Hall. In Connecticut, Constitution Plaza, "the pride of Hartford" and the insurance companies' greeting to a new world of towers, was a grim space off the arterial evacuating downtown, which died at night. Similarly, Pittsburgh's Mellon Square covered a garage with a raised rooftop park too high above the sidewalk to encourage street life.

Corporate flight, abetted by the building of interstates, had made every structure a servant to the automobile, a highway adjunct and car park alike. Courtesy of subsidies to highways, housing, and infrastructure, fifty corporations abandoned New York City between 1956 and 1980. In less than two decades after the interstate, downtown Chicago lost fourteen of its Fortune 500 companies, Pittsburgh seven, Detroit twelve, and Philadelphia six. Business headed to the exurbs or leaped cross-country to the South, West, and Southwest to new jobs and homes.

Perhaps it was failure of the real downtown or the binge home building in what columnist Erma Bombeck called septic tank suburbia that made Disneyland seem a veritable urban mecca. While Main Streets were failing, designers were proclaiming Disney's animated stage set "the new Main Street," though the "urbanity" of its pedestrian-packed environment was as much mall as Main Street.

The trailblazing plans of the day were car bred, too. The community of Irvine, California, hailed as a green model of town planning, scattered buildings at a driver's scale. The other so-called new towns—Columbia in Maryland, by the era's well-intentioned developer James Rouse, and Reston in Virginia, owned by Robert E. Simon and Gulf and Western—though celebrated for their integration and walkable communities within, didn't do much more for the vitality and variety lost with urban life. Carved into rural lands northeast and west of Washington, D.C., the clustered homes glimmered off the pages of the professional magazines, not a whit less auto dependent than before. Whether elite or standard design, the home gave up two-thirds of its space to garaging the car; affluent or poor, the community relinquished more than one-third of its streets to cars. And public transit had no part.

Accelerating Auto Dependence

In the years from 1950 to 1970, the motor vehicle population had grown four times faster than the human one. In the subdivisions being built at the rate of a million homes a year, deprived of sidewalk or crosswalk to ease movement on foot, human mobility was impaired. Zoned for exclusivity—house next to house, mall next to mall, and office park next to office park—auto-based land use had shaped a life that could not function without 2,000 pounds of steel and wheels. Traffic grew, cities shrank, and, as Americans embraced the automobile, the two-car culture was installed, with more than one automobile sitting in many of in those suburban spaces. Forget wartime posters saying "Share Your Car. Conserve Gas Tires Autos." The spatial appetite of the automobile was consuming the landscape. Even the engineers' trade magazine, *Traffic Quarterly*, noted that "On urban commuter expressways, fast, peak-hour traffic congestion rises to meet maximum capacity." The $2,432 good enough "to construct several miles of good highways" in 1907 had multiplied tenfold to $2,432,000 for a quarter mile, by the early 1970s. The cost was up to $100 million a mile projected for the Lower Manhattan Expressway.

No wonder traffic grew. *Will They Ever Finish Bruckner Boulevard?* was the title of a book published by critic Ada Louise Huxtable at the beginning of the decade. The answer was no, but no one noticed. The engineer's sway endured, and automobile historian John B. Rae, funded by the car manufacturers, still remained sanguine: signals, electronic controls, strips, reversible lanes, one-way streets, and all the old engineered etceteras would solve the problem. More lanes, more access, more exit ramps, and more double-decking, tunneling, and bridging would do the job. It was an old tune for a society in overdrive. Starved cities with dwindling tax bases from acreage lost to asphalt still watched while suburban homeowners deducted mortgage interest payments and property taxes.

As New York went broke in 1975 and Cleveland defaulted thereafter, Lewis Mumford had his usual well-chosen words: "Make the patient as comfortable as possible. It's too late to operate."

Bicentennial Revival

And yet, as the encroaching 1976 bicentennial of the American Revolution came around and the tall ships sailed into America's harbors, it seemed possible to resuscitate the patient. Preservation had kindled road-swiped communities from St. Louis's Italian Hill and New York's Little Italy to Cincinnati and Savannah. "Urban renewal" was now a nasty phrase. The patriotic celebration marked an awareness of the nation's traditions; not the least among them was common parlance in common space. Rehabilitating old warehouses was commonplace, bringing life to downtown's old bones thereafter. Seattle's Pike Place Market was rescued and prospered near the waterfront. A stone's throw from its rupturing Central Artery, Boston's Quincy Market escaped the bulldozer to earn new life in 1976. Revived by developer James Rouse, it would soon boast more visitors than Disney World, becoming a model for so-called festival marketplaces across the nation. In that same bicentennial anniversary year, architecture deemed historic won tax relief through legislation to support old buildings.

Hustling through the corridors of power in Sacramento, the capital of California, Senator James R. Mills seemed the hero of radical resolve as he led the state to introduce light-rail. With the new measures installed, surface lines invigorated the downtowns of his own San Diego and of other cities in the state. After battles in getting, battles in spending, and battles in digging, on September 1974 district train number 101 of the new BART line pulled out of the maintenance yard in Oakland and began its morning run across the bottom of San Francisco Bay to collect its first fares. A decade later nearly 200 million passengers a year, more than a third of the number of rush hour drivers, would climb aboard. BART was a visionary civil engineering feat that would become a regional backbone.

Washington's Metro opened its first subway stops in 1976. The handsome system, with stations designed by architect Harry Weiss, set standards for service and appeal. Nodes of activity planned or built around each station would make hubs of pedestrian and commercial life to support the transportation infrastructure and towns along the way.

Not many years after officials proposed to mangle yet another majestic terminal, Grand Central Station, by placing a ruinous addition atop its roof, the U.S. Supreme Court acted. Its ruling to keep the station intact insured the historic integrity of the building and established the right of local governments to affix their own landmark status. The judgment alerted would-be wreckers that states and cities could enact land use controls "to enhance the quality of life by preserving the character and desirable aesthetic features of a city." Landmark commissions multiplied to care for the nation's heritage.

The victory won for "quality of life," for "aesthetic features," and for "environmental wonders" cheered environmental stewards. The message of René Dubos's injunction in *The Limits of Growth* to "think locally, act globally" on what was now called "spaceship earth" awoke the nation. And, as legislation charged automakers to eliminate lead poisoning and reduce smog and acid rain, the crusade to slow the internal combustion engine seemed to progress. The proposal to update Robert Moses's West Side highway, by then ragged with age, had gone down to defeat in 1973. A scheme to butcher the nation's trains that was aired in antitrust hearings in 1974 further undermined the auto industry. The bicentennial's passions took hold in America. In this anniversary year the nation no longer seemed to idolize the automobile.

"The automobile," wrote Barry Commoner in *The Closing Circle*, "could be regarded as a nearly perfect technological object. Up until the point that you turn the key and start driving it. Then it becomes what? It becomes an agent for causing lung cancer as a result of asbestos coming off the brake lining. It becomes an agent for producing smog. It becomes an agent which is harmful by way of its intrusion into the environment."

Activists and economists, environmentalists and urbanists agreed. The urge to stifle the car's restless expansion, to quell its wreckage of urban and environmental values, had grown. But "ladies and gentlemen, start your engines," the anthem of America, would be hard to muffle.

OPPOSITE: Car-bred building reached ever outward as seen in this aerial view of a 6,000-acre project in Sun City, Arizona. (UPI/Corbis-Bettman)

The Three-Car Culture

"Hey, you mean we're going to walk from the car to the living room? My feet haven't touched pavement since we reached Los Angeles."

—Annie Hall

"If we are an automobile-riding, we are also an automobile-ridden people. Despite the daily offerings that Americans insert in parking meters, and the grand new parking temples rising in the centers of our cities, we seem unable to appease the motor goddess. . . . The yearly births of automobiles have for some time now been exceeding those of the human population."

—Daniel J. Boorstin, preface in *The Automobile Age*

"In Houston, a person walking is somebody on his way to his car."

—Anthony Downs

BICENTENNIAL IMPULSES NOTWITHSTANDING, in the aftermath of the sixties' antiroad activists, Americans continued driving from the old hubs to the highway's fringes. As the energy crisis receded and cheap oil flowed again, the boom years of the eighties created a counterrevolution of consumption. Conservative administrations began to constrain environmental and progressive urges. The car culture roared.

And the questions echoed: How clean could Quincy's air be if we doubled our highway mileage every decade? How could auto dependence end if Washington continued to subsidize roads and starve public transportation? The laissez-faire landscapes of Presidents Ronald Reagan and George Bush beckoned. The car ran wild. From the beginning of the 1980s, 125 million "fuel-injected" Americans drove six times the number of miles as at the close of World War II. The doubling of vehicle miles to 2 trillion before 1990—almost double the 1970s figure—negated gains made in the last decade.

Rising urban poverty meant deteriorating city centers. One writer described this "urban thanatopsis" accurately if glumly—"the city as cemetery." The great divide was not just between rich and poor but between suburb and city, and the fact that the first—the affluent suburb—still sucked in government subsidies stretched the car divide and shrank urban and environmental well-being. The great divide served to reinforce the mobility divide. Transportation was not the only social service in which Americans pulled the covers over their eyes and blanked out, of course. The equity divide segregated the rich and poor. As social and spatial polarization split the nation, cities, once ladders of opportunity and upward mobility, were abandoned.

At the beginning of his administration, President Reagan told the Detroit Economic Club that the private automobile was "the last great freedom," and thereafter attacked passenger trains. He asked for an end to the "huge federal subsidy" of $35 per train passenger, ignoring both the $42 subsidy per flyer and the auto-based subsidies at seven times mass transit's. Washington defended cheap oil in its international military policy and subsidized homes and highways in its domestic ones. The sprawling suburbs were where the federal heart beat. The populations of Philadelphia, Chicago, and New York spilled out into the suburbs, increasing the built-up acreage. Big cities shrank by hundreds of thousands.

To be sure, the house that Henry Ford had built still had enemies. In Atlanta in the 1980s, road fighters chained themselves to trees to stop the so-called Freedom Parkway from chewing through an Olmsted park to connect Jimmy Carter's presidential library. Though the two Republican presidents added pennies to the gas tax, members of the "me decade" sated their needs for more and larger cars and larger, more distant homes. Encouraged by S and L deregulation, tax breaks to nurture more suburban or second homes than transit-based urban ones, and cheap oil to feed motorists, buyers scurried outwards.

Train ridership fell. The number of motorists rose. The battle for Amtrak had few visible supporters in Washington. By 1987 the nation's 167 million cars outnumbered its 162 million drivers. In 1985, Senator Robert Dole told a tale on his wife, Elizabeth Dole, Reagan's secretary of transportation, that reflected this attitude. "My wife wakes up during the night saying, 'Amtrak, Amtrak.' That's her private view. Publicly she wants to eliminate it." The schism said something about the changing times.

Dispersal by Driving

Headlights headed now in more than two directions, not only in and out of town but also round about, shooting, darting, coiling, spiraling to corporations pushing into the hinterlands. From 1963 to 1987, nearly three of every five jobs created were located in the once rural countryside now called exurbia, and the number continued to grow. High-tech and light manufacturing plants moved to the South, to central New Hampshire, to the open space between Topeka and Kansas City, to the western counties of Wisconsin, to the northern Great Plains, and to Houston, Denver, and Dallas, where oil spurted forth.

In terms of highways, the inner belt was wrapped by a ring of outer belts that circled the old roadways. Migrating beyond what William Whyte called the "last landscape," Americans created those so-called edge cities. The new fringes, from Tysons Corner, Virginia, to Irvine, California, from Las Vegas to Phoenix, were, as ever, fattened by the federal budget—what Minnesota legislator Myron

Orfield called a "Marshall Plan sewer buildup." Whatever the name, the nation was playing leapfrog over the past, across the decaying heritage of the city and beyond the older inner suburbs that were languishing as well.

The "eighty six million separate automobile transportation systems" described by Helen Leavitt multiplied to 200 million in the mid-1990s. "Americans are individualists," according to Joel Garreau, the defender of the new exurbia. "The automobile is the finest expression of transportation-individualism ever devised," he said in a perverse echo of the dreams of the old Progressive reformers. As for the future, "The Houston Galleria is larger than downtown Amsterdam, or Cologne or Denver," and would emulate its urbanity in a few centuries or so, he insisted.

Other supposed gains were doing equal damage. Henry Ford II's solution, the seventy-three-story Renaissance Center, a soaring collection of towers designed by architect John Portman that was severed from the city by a roadway and touted as "a catalyst for the development of downtown" Detroit, proved to be symbolic. Its detached fortress, wrapped by roads and stuffed with parking, isolated the burned-out city further, draining activity from the dreary remains of the once lively Art Deco core downtown. By 1983, Renaissance Center was in default, and the city's people mover rolled through downtown like a toy train.

The architecture of the hour reflected the design for the automobile that spread America thin. Crystal Cathedral, by architect Philip Johnson in Garden Grove, California, was a 1984 glass complex for Rev. Robert Schuller's drive-in church. A logo of God on the run, it was fronted by parking, its spiritual glitz a hymn to the asphalt Almighty. The aloof towers in two-tier downtown Houston bespoke the car culture's architecture of isolation. There, the white middle class parked and headed for the interior links of buildings, while low-income blacks passed back and forth along the streets. The Hyatt-ization of the urban landscape continued as remote atrium-filled fortresses, heirs to actual Hyatt hotels, sprang up, removed from the worn downtowns around them.

The epitome of highway design occurred in Danbury, Connecticut. Coaxed out of Manhattan by a federally funded highway interchange, Union Carbide settled in the countryside. "Union Carbide Takes to the Woods," *Fortune* magazine said in 1982. Plopped among the trees, its corporate headquarters offered a literal extension of the road. The building, designed by architects Kevin Roche and John Dinkeloo let people drive off the highway via a ramp to the top of the building, park, and enter from the roof. The building's novelty was its nineteen lanes of roadway, joining infrastructure and architecture as one. For all the subsidies of the auto age, however, the firm would soon abandon this surreal structure.

Exit ramp architecture also emerged in Roche's high-tech General Foods building in Rye, on New York's Gold Coast. The building's imperial entry, designed for the corporate stretch limos, swept across a bridge to a drop-off point at the front door. It, too, changed owners as precipitously as many a strip shop or suburban mall deserted for large retail stores, the so-called big box that succeeded the earlier chains. Driving out along the interstate to the "last remnant" or "frontier," Americans seemed to reach an end point. One author called it the "last migration." For how long would or could a throwaway society trash Phoenix for the next Phoenix in Montana or in Utah? Empty out Los Angeles for the next dream city? For how long could we turn scenic landscapes into concrete scars on the landscape?

Architecture, a relentless manifesto of the way we live, registered the mastery of the automobile everywhere. Tysons Corner, a massive development in Virginia outside Washington, D.C., was the ultimate exclusive "urban village" for the upscale, a 1,700-acre road-swept pit stop, thirty-four times the size of Boston Common. "Rent here, save money and choose your neighbors," the sign at the Lincoln homes described this exclusive zone for life on wheels. Movement on foot was impossible. Disclaiming every retail maxim, Bloomingdale's faced Tiffany's across an impenetrable roadway inaccessible to the shopper without a car.

The Last Frontier

A turn of mind, if not design, was visible, however. Throughout the 1980s, a number of revived historic centers made what one political writer called a "salable package" in every large city. Modern architects took to planning along an older model, and the cosmetic of "postmodern" designs replicated the old, but alas at superscale. A "New Urbanism" appeared in architectural circles. Harking back to the plans of John Nolen and his peers, a coterie of designers aimed to shape "neotraditionalist" neighborhoods with gridded streets of close-packed homes that emulated preautomobile America. Planner Peter Calthorpe's "Pedestrian Pockets" was a more promising, more transit-oriented label for the walkable clusters drafted in the literature and on the landscape.

The Florida panhandle community of Seaside, conceived as a car-free community, became the emblem of the "New Urbanism" movement. On eighty acres of land along the Gulf of Mexico, the developer and designers created the narrow streets and wide sidewalks of an intimate shore-bound town. Seaside's benign parent, developer Robert Davis, and the godparents of its design, Andres Duany and Elizabeth Plater-Zyberk, shaped a pastel village that followed the vision of taming the car to the needs of the pedestrian. The amiable and beautiful town was made for walking beside the cobalt blue waters of the gulf. In simulation of Main Street, a crescent center of shops and apartments with a tiny post office dotted the entry. Strolling through the congenial enclave, the visitor could fancy everything old as new again. Down the road, however, it was hard to ignore the dreary surroundings. Toward Tallahassee, the garish highway landscape, the lack of public transit, and the excess of empty strip buildings accentuated the isolated nature of Seaside's experiment.

For all the idea of community, these other New Urbanist or neotraditional single-family enclaves failed to ease dependency on the automobile. Developer-driven, their architects mostly designed suburban pods in fresh fields like Kentlands, Maryland, or Laguna West, California. Such places still lacked the mass transit or the neighborhood mix to allow freedom from the automobile. In the rest of the nation it was worse, however. The million housing starts a year in the wrong place with the wrong planning and the million cars sold each month to take people there inevitably tread heavily on any notion of alternative transportation.

No wonder activities in Washington, D.C., once labeled "from the

Capitol, "became known by its highwayesque nickname "within the beltway." From the federal center, the new asphalt-encased post offices sent to the periphery of small and large towns were typical of government policies that deprived Main Street for mall. It wasn't accidental that growth fed the architecture off the exit ramp. Federal defense monies still supported sprawling, faceless places in the South and West, while the Frostbelt paid the infrastructure bill. From the mid-1970s through the 1980s, defense outlays meant that Northeastern cities sent Washington $165 billion more in taxes than they got back, and the 32 Sunbelt and Western states had a $112 billion windfall. And the trend continued.

As the "big box" phenomena spread, Home Depots replaced depots close to home. "Industrial Strength Retail," one planner called this attack on Main Street. Pasted-on facades modeled on bygone cultures, what architect Denise Scott Brown called "taste cultures," tried to compensate for real ones. In 1993 the National Trust for Historic Preservation put Vermont on its annual list of America's Most Endangered Historic Places "because sprawl was, and still is, testing the state's commitment to the preservation of its cohesive small towns and countryside."

"Where do you live?" I asked my doctor.

"Metro West," he replied.

Where, on God's earth, was "Metro West"? Everywhere, of course, and hence nowhere. Lacking name, lacking fixed geography, lacking core or center—save as an appendage to a four-wheel vehicle—the place called home lacked identity. An exit off the ramp or maybe four exits. The higher the number of exits, the smaller the centers. And that other axiom also prevailed: the more parking places, the less place.

The numbers told the story of the settlement that followed the horizontal course of the highway as the decade wore on. Los Angeles spread the same number of people as Brooklyn in seven times the space. Phoenix stretched a million residents in almost twice the square miles of long-depleted Detroit. The aerial perspectives of new developments that looked like used car lots confirmed Art Buchwald's 1970s view that extraplanetary visitors would conclude that no human life could exist on such a place.

Flames from Ashes

Here and there, old battles yielded benefits, however. From the ashes of the contested and aborted roads slated to create Boston's inner belt and Southwest Expressway arose the splendid five-mile, fifty-two-acre Southwest Corridor. Hours of community planning and bureaucratic coordination, plus a fine landscape design, produced a greenway and walkway above the train and Orange Line streetcar. Walking down the landscaped brick path now decking the railroad tracks, flanked by a vegetable garden or sports fields, pausing on a bench by a basketball game, or watching life grow around the extended rail, one could see a model for the salvation of city and community alike.

From the victory in Portland, Oregon, over a proposed freeway came yet another waterfront park. Portland's street rail would carry 40 percent of the city's workers to a lively center, and a greenbelt would control growth and update the Garden City ideal to create a showpiece for anti-automobile enthusiasts. So, too, in New York. Soho stood where a road was downed, and the defeat of Westway provided a second chance for the waterfront.

Waterfronts were revived. San Franciscans, relieved of the Embarcadero Freeway, began planning for a waterfront esplanade to be opened in the mid-1990s. Baltimore's Inner Harbor followed comebacks in Boston, San Francisco, and Seattle. Month after month, the Waterfront Center published signs of the revitalization. In their book *Waterfronts: Cities Reclaim Their Edge,* the center's founders, Ann Breen and Dick Rigby, described the national phenomena of seventy-five cities that were reinventing themselves. Along lakes, oceans, or rivers small niches were made green and public for festive moments a nice walk away from nearby communities.

In 1989 the Exxon disaster in Alaska revived the old environmental fires. The 11 million gallons of oil that spilled into Prince Edward Sound were followed the next year by the Persian Gulf conflagration. In 1990 "Partying for the Planet" celebrations were held for the twentieth anniversary of Earth Day. Environmental impulses linked to fears of the hole in the ozone and to global warming accelerated the outrage at the automobile. In 1990 the federal government, seeing the lack of progress in stopping smog, added new amendments to the Clean Air Act, ordering cities to comply or lose their funding. The nation's first oil war, fought in the Persian Gulf, promoted a new anti-auto activism.

The regulations of the Clean Air Act of 1990 enforced the control of emissions. To do the job, it encouraged means like restricted parking, giving a boost to trains and encouraging public transportation in many of America's cores. Fourteen cities that had lacked streetcars built new lines. A rise in commuter rail was recorded, too. Light-rail was on track. In 1980, after three refusals, Southern California voters had approved a 150-mile rail transit system to be paid for by a sales tax. Beginning with the Los Angeles–Long Beach Blue Line, which tracked the route of the hallowed Big Red Cars, the sleek lines headed outward. New York's subway, in the throes of decay, embarked on a $20 billion program in capital improvements. Despite administration opposition, in 1987 Congress funded mass transportation. By the 1990s, the city's vast transit and commuter rail system had been revived. New Jersey, too, undertook new public transportation work. Other cities extended old systems or tackled new ones.

Visiting the new light-rail lines was nothing short of exhilarating. They were the "comeback kid" of transportation, "Streetcars of Desire." New surface lines in Baltimore, San Diego, and St. Louis were a delight and reinforced their downtowns. They were a lightning rod, encouraging still more counties to sign on to ambitious plans to center their systems around transit-oriented development. From bonds in Portland, Oregon, to the Campaign for Sensible Transportation in Portland, Maine, residents voted for balanced transportation. In Dallas and Denver lines were planned to follow the routes of the streetcars of the past. Even Amtrak, a slow sister to Europe's spit-and-polish bullet trains, had started to clean its stations. Stop by stop, the nation's passenger rail system rehabilitated terminals. The revival of Daniel Burnham's Union Station in 1988 invigorated Washington, and half a dozen years later, the refurbishment of South Station delighted Boston. Along Amtrak's corridor, spruced-up stations made serviceable centers. Passenger-miles increased. Despite the road network's ongoing benefits to trucks, freight train profits rose.

The Cannibalizing Car

Looking more broadly at the nation, however, the picture was gloomier. Between 1930 and 1980, the miles of railway track had halved. Only 4 percent of public transportation was by rail, in stark contrast to the 35 percent of Americans who headed downtown by rail to the thriving cities in the last year of World War II. And the number even dropped a percentage point in the 1990s. In the first four years of the decade, the money put into New Jersey highways alone exceeded Amtrak's expenditures across the nation, and former Governor James Florio, chairman of America's Coalition for Transit NOW, explained the obvious: "If you cannibalize or disinvest in any system, you will have problems." In 1983 only half of Amtrak's funding had come from the fare box. A decade later, subsidies had dropped. Passengers now paid for 80 percent of their train tickets, while drivers paid less than half of their costs. The result was a fact and part of the fabric of the carbound country as the decade began.

Enough Asphalt?

It was in 1991 that I went to witness the events with which this book began. The conferences in Greenwich Village and Secaucus, New Jersey, reflected the shared sentiments that America was stuck in traffic but that there was more promising news. A crew of activists—urbanists, environmentalists, preservationists, walkers, bicyclers, mass transit supporters—had arisen, and legislation was on the agenda. The Intermodal Surface Transportation Efficiency Act, some were insisting, would help change the balance of money from road to rail. The interstate system was done. A new way must be found to support transportation of many modes, to make things "intermodal," in the language of the legislators. "We've poured enough concrete," said Senator Daniel Patrick Moynihan.

In a room barely wider than its word processor, two activists charged to fight the highway lobby were sitting and describing their work to pass this act. Harriet Parcells, the energetic head of the Campaign for New Transportation Priorities, and Bob Patten, a lanky West Coast radical who had transported his zeal in fighting for El

Salvador and Nicaragua to the cause of mass transit, were hardly sitting, though. They were pausing, poised to race off to orchestrate what seemed the most substantial shift since the interstate legislation had been enacted. Tucked in the quarters of the National Association of Railroad Passengers, they belonged to a new alliance of advocates formed to champion the kind of landscape that "sensible transportation" could provide.

That alliance, the Surface Transportation Policy Project, had joined a familiar cast of preservationists and environmentalists, neighborhood activists and architects, ranging from the ride-the-rail National Association of Railroad Passengers to the brown-boot Rails to Trails hikers, from grassroots activists like the Alliance for a Paving Moratorium to professional associations like the American Institute of Architects. With mere months and no staff to push the balance from road to rail, highway to bicycle path, billboard to beautification—with their Xerox-copied articles still warm—they were racing to drop off position papers for a new highway act.

Almost a quarter century earlier, in 1968, Secretary of Transportation Alan Boyd had proposed just such a transfer of funds. He would pool transportation money and send it to the states, not to the federal highway builders. "He had no illusions about how Congress would receive the idea," Jack Burby wrote. Now, though, illusions came true, and the bill passed. It gave choice. No more would total funds be ordained for roads. Half the money could go where a new will wanted.

A new way of working was at hand, enthusiasts insisted. Money from the deep pockets of the highway fund would finally be "flexible." Some funding for pouring concrete could go to enhancements— paths for pedestrians and bicyclists, historic and scenic amenities —and to create a balanced transportation system defined by planners, not highway engineers. Planners could frame the proper land patterns to insure movement without the automobile. The palace revolt would reverse fifty years of asphalt, said enthusiasts. Antihighway crusaders honked for the new highway bill.

Yet, I had my doubts. "So highway-bound had we become, that this version of the re-authorization to move us here and there for the next five years was taken as radical," I wrote. Yes, the act seemed, if not "almost revolutionary," then a revolution in particulars. Yes, it professed common sense. But common sense was not common coinage in the auto age. Would it do more than provide paper policy? I wondered. "Jobs, jobs, jobs," said President George Bush in creating it. What kind of jobs? I wondered.

I was ready, eager, to stand corrected. I could see the rising gains of the auto age throughout its history. And the falling benefits. I had heard the experts say that we had poured enough concrete. I had listened to engineers and drivers renounce their romance with the automobile. Had they—had we—learned? Was this asphalt nation ready for recovery?

Now, nearing the act's struggle for reauthorization, the new policies can record some positives: funding from highways to rail (in Philadelphia, Denver, St. Louis); more planning officers reviewing the schemes; more enhancements of the surroundings in place. Yet, the Highway Trust Fund remains a sacred cow. And cutbacks in urban spending reinforce anxiety. Transit funding has "probably hit its high-water mark," the head of the Federal Transportation Agency said morosely, in the mid-1990s.

Righting the transportation balance and maintaining environmental progress has faltered along with other social services. The Trojan Horse of privatization threatens to dismantle viable systems with no proof of public betterment or savings. Electric rail and railroads battle each other over crumbs, while the highway system is fattened. Yet again. Amtrak, short of funds, was down five thousand workers, and mass transit was cut in the mid-1990s. Seven times more federal funding was still going to highways than mass transit. More roads and widenings were planned from Indiana to Vermont, California to Rhode Island, while ISTEA's renewal was threatened. The end of the fifty-five-mile-an-hour speed limit seemed to mean that the sky was the limit. As Americans took to gas-guzzling cars, I wondered: would more of the same tether our lives to the automobile forever?

Possibly. But perhaps not, I thought, as the battle over the car invited combatants and the 100th anniversary of the automobile was far from celebratory in 1996. If the grassroots groups provoked a larger ground swell; if the arguments of the planners, the calculations of the economists, the sentiments of a nation in overdrive . . . if

. . . I speculated, all those deprived of freedom by the automobile allied.

"Had Enough Traffic?" a poster on the BART line read. Maybe, I thought—and think hopefully on blue-sky days when a good conversation or a bright piece of news soothes the sense of alarm that sent me to Secaucus. Possibly, I feel, when the highway bulldozer rolling across our precious heritage throughout my lifetime seems to indicate that it has slowed. Yes, I believe, we can end the auto age, in which every decision is a decision following the route of the motor vehicle. Yes, in the midst of stasis on the road, we can at least reach a consciousness of how old, how very old, how very stale the single-minded automotive solution remains. We can finally realize that we have reached the end of the automotive frontier, that the solutions are there to see. There are ways proven by the past, ways promoted by the present. We can control the motor vehicle that has cordoned off our lives and landscape. It is time for our asphalt nation to examine and energize them.

PART III

Where's
The bike
lane?

Car Free
From Dead End to Exit

None for the Road

As WE ENTER the twenty-first century, it is clear that we are not only a car-driven but a car-ridden population. The vehicle that was our rescuer is arguably our ruination, certifiably, the root of many of our ills. Yet for all our automotive follies—for all the costs, the inconveniences, the destruction—the motor vehicle remains entrenched. The reason is obvious: it is a prerequisite for mobility in America. We cannot see our personal and global dilemma or perceive an escape from it. Our lives and landscape have been fashioned to the automobile's dictates for three-quarters of a century. A rescue movement is in order.

The way to end the auto age has many courses. A change of mindset and a change of the car-based character of our nation are not effected with the turn of a page or for that matter with the thrust of a single plan or project. The compass will not turn to a new way of life during the next decade or even generation. Yet, it is a challenge of the first order. Securing the next frontier of livability step-by-step is a task that should arouse the imagination of a new generation.

Putting the car in its place and assuring human mobility and accessibility may not inspire the visions of earlier generations that got us to the moon in this century or across the continent in the last. The task is restorative and protective. Nonetheless, the outlook is broader. It resonates in the work recorded in the solutions that follow. Like the environmental and preservation movements, the inch-by-inch, row-by-row operation is conservative in its localism, traditional in its individualism, and historic in its "use-it-up, wear-it-out, make-it-do-or-do-without" mentality.

In many ways, that mindset suits the turn to the next century. As a nation, we are coming around to the power of limits and the strength of incrementalism. A generation ago we exulted in our great dams and bridges. The heroic gesture counted. Technological progress inspired. Now we are looking to our fish ladders, our solar collectors, our wetland renewal in harmony with nature. The unabashed faith in scientific "progress" is gone; the machine-fashioned change is under the microscope.

There is no question, however, that deposing the car from its dominion over the earth is a radical, even revolutionary, move. It is not only an attack, however; it is an invitation to create alternatives in our most basic decisions on how to go from here to there—and, indeed, whether this hypermobile society truly needs the endless motion that long defined its settlement and existence.

Those who enlist in this countercultural rescue movement cannot be simply automobile antagonists, however. We must be promobility advocates: pro-walking, pro-bicycling, pro-transit. We must be pro-stability as well in cultivating our own gardens. Every move we make must be examined and adjusted, then reexamined and readjusted.

To go with this outlook, we need the tools and will to install it as shown in these solutions. From the fight to "just say no" to highways, to the battle to create codes to release us from bondage to bad land use practices, to traffic calming and the depaving of the kingdom of the car, to the proper pricing of our mobility and the political fight to install mass transit, the struggle engages a new constituency. The process is as participatory as democracy itself. The smallest householder and the largest corporation, the humblest local government maneuver and the grandest federal program must figure in the sea change for a new century.

Our perch is precarious. Or so say the highway engineers. With a Vermont selectman I have taken a stand on a hill above a bridge to see just how perilous this piece of road is. For half an hour, we watch the cars from our supposedly dangerous spot. One sedan after another glides down the hill, slows a bit to squeeze through the narrow bridge, then curves out of sight as it loops gently through the tight center of the tiny town of Tunbridge and beyond. "Dangerous" to users, is it? With the prospect of an engineer's widening, it is not drivers who are at risk so much as walkers, bicyclers, and a picturesque piece of Vermont's Route 110.

For outsiders innocent of traffic engineers' codes and highwayspeak, this swath of Vermont simply looks scenic as it traces the meandering course of the White River punctuated by the picture-perfect wooden covered bridge and overhanging trees. Why clear a ten-foot area and build a massive retaining wall to add four feet of roadway at a cost of $2 million? Why even widen a road that funnels traffic through the confined streets of a historic town center? Why put a speedway through the snail-paced town, with its general store, clapboard library, and small offices? ("Use this phone," the store owner says as he offers his own.) The wider route for cars intrudes on both history and common sense.

On this temperate winter day, standing near the barren branches of winter, Paul Harwood finds it not only superfluous but quite outrageous. Worried about the vanishing country road, and the safety and walkability for nondrivers, this Tunbridge selectman and planning board member has parked his forestry truck on the hill to show the view and discuss the forthcoming "improvement." The term would be farcical if it were not so offensive, and Harwood has taken up the cudgel. To irate Tunbridge residents, the engineer's phrases "up to standard, grade, code" provoke the retort, Up to whose standard, what grade, and what kind of code that defies aesthetics, safety, and reason this way? The neighbors balked. Anti–road wideners agitated. The engineer's response was "mitigation" in the form of an ugly stone buffer topped by a chain link fence. The language and viewpoint differed, but on one thing both engineers and citizens had no dispute: the widening would allow—invite—speed.

It is not just this state that is on the National Trust for Historic Preservation's endangered list. Visit any town or neighborhood and you can find a Tunbridge where "improvement" defined as car convenience holds sway in the minds of officialdom. The definition issues from the traffic engineers' so-called green book. The bible of the road builders, this book sets out the rules supplied by the American Association of State and Highway Transportation Officials that have guided the slash-and-burn school of road straighteners for decades. Yet, for all the tree hatcheters and sidewalk swipers, the street fighters grow. And while Tunbridge awaits "official word," such advocates argue to reverse this mandate held dear to road builders.

Just Say No

The will exists, and also the way, from Tunbridge to South Pasadena, California. But how do you find other hidden routes? How do you know when or where to stop more lanes and roads? How do you leash some twenty-one new "high-priority corridors" and seven urban beltways planned for U.S. cities? How do you undo the $93 billion spent each year by local, state, and federal highway builders?

The miles of would-be new roads across farmland, the would-be widenings along suburban school routes, the would-be curbcuts and exit ramps for fifty-acre megamalls seem endless. And often arbitrary or mysterious. If Tunbridge defender Jim Wick estimates two-hundred-plus projects on the Vermont Agency of Transportation agenda in his small state, what does that say of the other forty-nine? When even New York, our most transit-friendly metropolis, faces a rush of widenings, parking garages, and car-wrapped megastores, what can Anyplace, U.S.A., expect?

Grassroots groups fight the road to nowhere or the road to Wal-Mart that generates ten thousand trips a day and hence more cars, the endless projects in the pipeline that invite more driving. They mobilize in Kansas City, where the Metropolitan Coalition for Sensible Transportation Policy draws two hundred people to battle the purchase of a $10 million right-of-way for an outer loop. They agitate in Rhode Island to fight "RIDOT," the state Department of Transportation's invasion of six miles of Kingston's seventeenth-century Ministerial Road, wrapped by stone walls and rhododendron. Thinking globally, they act locally, but the field for their labors is vast. There are big-scale bridge widenings planned for Buffalo, New York, and Charlotte, North Carolina. But the unkindest cuts may be the little ones—the exit ramp for a concrete-wrapped superstore, the widening, the extra lane that wrecks a country road, the enlarged intersection that sends traffic through city and suburbs.

And the first of many steps to be spelled out in these solutions is to "just say no" to these intrusions.

"Just say no" has become a collective maneuver. Not everyone can emulate the woman who, taking a cue from Lady Godiva's route by Coventry Cathedral, jumped on top of a car and stripped off her clothes in 1996 to obstruct the hundredth birthday celebration of the automobile in that historic city. But residents of cherished sites have learned to fight for their cause. They have adopted the tactics of their Earth Day ancestors like GASP, whose members gave out "Dirtie Gertie" certificates to polluting industries twenty years ago. Their antics, their gritty politics, their hours exploring alternatives energize neighbors, besiege officials, and establish a solid line of defense. "It's just a matter of who can speak eloquently, who can effect a compromise, who can effect the sway," says Chan Rogers, a veteran traffic engineer who's joined the anti-auto combatants. If politics is the art of the possible, victory is surpassing the entrenched and *seemingly* impossible.

Slash I-710

The anti-highway fight that stands as the most intense, and ongoing, is South Pasadena's battle with Caltrans, California's unrelenting highway department. The fight to stop the leveling of the historic city's precious cache of homes for freeway I-710 is epic and enduring. The "slash 710" buttons on lapels are a symbol at conferences across the country. And the three guardian angels of this city whom I encountered wore the longevity of their four-decade struggle like a badge. The packet they handed me overflowed with signs of their commitment. Emblazoned on the cover of a recent issue of the *South Pasadena Quarterly* was the warning: "It Begins With Construction Trucks Tearing Up The Community." Inside, "duplicity," "betrayal," and lack of "good faith" punctuate the text.

Standing on the sunny plaza of City Hall that August day, the leader of these avengers, former Mayor Alvalee Arnold, clutches a bulging notebook. She also demonstrates the ability to chat up a passing young activist treading a unicycle back and forth before us, describing her leafletting in breathless bouts of pedaling and talking. Armed with the Buddha-like presence of Gertrude Stein and the charm of her native Texas, the former mayor has lobbied, organized and demonstrated the capacity of a small but dedicated crew to withstand the most tenacious road builders in the world. After years, the highway agency has yet to vanquish this woman, this city, this landscape of historic houses, fountains, and leafy streets that refuse to be traffic corridors.

"This would be a rotary," says my guide as she drives me through South Pasadena. "This would be cutoff for a ramp." "This would be flattened." She traces the death sentence as we pass the 1500 homes, 7000 trees, and 6 historic districts marked for destruction and still in danger. The late-day sun lowers as we wind in and out of the canopied streets and past splendid houses, but the tales of meetings, of promises kept and promises broken, of campaigns that make the Iowa caucus look like a road show don't abate. At the time of my visit, the preservationists were still girding for what could be the last, or merely the latest, round to stop this juggernaut. The proposed highway expansion began near the end of World War II with Governor Earl Warren smiling, happy camper–style, baptizing the behemoth. Instead, it has become a model of longevity: "due to community resolve," as the South Pasadena City Council described it that summer. Battling still, the preservationists were matching the highway men measure for measure when I visited. "I'm not discouraged at all," said the former mayor. "I've been at this since 1958. It's coming to a climax and I'm happy."

Proliferating Pork

"But do highways ever die?" asked the Washington-based Transportation Exchange. South Pasadena's struggles continue, as do those of countless other communities trying to stave off roads. Even as the budget hackers hit Washington in the aftermath of the conservative resurgence in the 1994 elections, highways stood high on the Friends of the Earth's "Green Scissors" environmental sheet. In the first annual itemization of environmental horrors that were immune to cost cutting, the organization hit the highways. Right up there with sweetheart dams and nuclear testing sites, the roads to nowhere eluded the budget cutters. In the second list, the group identified six road projects, including an automated highway system, new interstates, and a bridge, all told, accounting for $2.5 billion in federal funds. Citizens for Appropriate Rural Roads (C.A.R.R.) was fired up to fight the extravagance of Indiana's Interstate 69 extension, the so-called Corridor 18 that would snatch farmland and front lawns for 1,200 miles for the Mid-Continent Highway. Denver earned opprobrium as "the United States' Mexico" for nineteen highway widenings that would further sully some of the dirtiest air in the nation.

While the antienvironmentalists axe away, Sauk Centre, Minnesota, the basis for the setting of Sinclair Lewis's *Main Street,* remains under assault, along with the tree-shaded residential quarters of Whitewater, Wisconsin, and the seaside vista from Route 101 in Santa Barbara. Plain folks' place or paradise, no locale is immune.

The plan for West Virginia's Corridor H stands high on the "Green Scissors" roster of boondoggles. Fortunately, the state also has Bonni McKeon, one of the anti-road gang's most imaginative advocates. And so, a few months after the resilient crusader had taken her troops to the halls of Congress, carrying mock gas pumps labeled "pork barrel" to attack the needless road championed by Senator Robert Byrd, the West Virginian sat in an antebellum hotel near Skyline Drive pouring out her message. Morning coffee and message

over, we headed for a day of talk driving along the meandering roadway flanked by chicken farms and scenic countryside. The route
from Elkins, West Virginia, to Strasburg, Virginia, was as winding as
the complicated crusade to stop the reckless widening. The landscape
only reinforced McKeon's outrage at the latest swipe at the impoverished "country homers" losing their houses to the road, as they had
earlier lost them to the ruthless coal mines.

Heading home, the activist slipped in a tape, a new recording
made by country-and-western singers to support the fight against
Corridor H. "Going down the road feeling bad," went the opening
number. While the parodies made by local fighters provided a chorus
to our trip, McKeon expressed her fury at the road slated to cost
$100 million in "Federal Money," as one song on the tape was titled.
"We get more federal money for building bigger roads. . . . So pave
the farms and countryside and maximize the dough." The letters and
faxes would pile up to stop the federal hard topping. The opposition
was engaged.

Slowly, the noise from the grassroots grows, but what about com-
prehension by the perpetrators of the concrete intrusions? "We're
turning away from widening," the secretary of transportation for
Florida declared the next summer at a high-speed rail conference.
"We're only going up to ten lanes and no further." Only ten lanes of
highway? No further? In what land is ten lanes a diminutive?

But it isn't only empty spaces that attract more highways. The
snipping and slashing at the fabric of existing neighborhoods continues. The curbcut for a drive-in ramp to a luxury hotel, the garage for
a hospital, all these needs of an auto-centric country grow. But, so
too does the counterassault. On a sunny day near Borough Hall in
Brooklyn, the local opposition is in place. Two women sit selling
"Help Save a Park" flower bulbs. Lodged beside the carts packed
with fall pumpkins and honey from bees strange to this plaza, they
enlist passersby to stop Long Island Community Hospital from de-
molishing their playground to build a parking garage. To no avail.
On the phone from Portland, Oregon, the founder of STOP (Sensible
Transportation Options for People) deplores—and battles—the plan
for a bypass. It's never ending, Meeky Blizzard said ruefully, as highway people keep the plans for roads "on artificial life supports."

Blizzard holds that "as long as we provide capacity for cars, we provide for more cars." Eternal vigilance is the price these advocates pay for stopping the "capacity" for damage.

My trips through road-wrapped America have more happy moments even in Live-Free-or-Die New Hampshire, where a Nashua official stretches out a blueprint while the voice of Rush Limbaugh issues from the office radio. The plan depicts the $2 to $3 million eleven-mile bypass to relieve Main Street's dozen or so blocks of congestion. To do so, the road would swing through some forty acres of wetland and twelve acres of floodplain, bisecting ten thousand acres of open space and natural habitat. Here, however, the alarm registered. Adroit use of the Clean Water Act spurred by John de Villars, chief of the New England regional EPA, has stopped this trespass.

The Bible Tells Us So

Be sure, however, the land-grabbing for roads doesn't end there or now. The reason? In the description of Sally Oldham, former head of Scenic America, it is the old, inflexible guidebook of the American Association of State and Highway Transportation Officials. It's the momentum to keep building. It's the huge industry of bonds, legislatures, highways, and auto lobbies. Annually, Scenic America lists its Twenty Most Important Scenic Byways—the ten most endangered and the ten most outstanding parkways—to protect them from having their graceful contours destroyed. Some methods of protection are adopted, but the threat continues: the hard toppers would kill the view, ax the tree, cut the curve. Whether on outstanding "vistas of knife-edged peaks, alpine tundra and lakes" along Seward Highway, scenic Route 7 through the Ozark and Ouachita national forests in Arkansas, or Old Stage Road in Oregon, the visual and environmental misdeeds are on the engineers' agenda.

Veronika Thiebach, an attorney for the Conservation Law Foundation, has tried in vain to assess New England's so-called traffic improvements. Consult the maps or files and you see abstractions. "It says 'reconstruction' or 'maintenance,' " says Thiebach. Although the words express the idea of fix-up, the fix-up is mostly a pretext for expansion. Though, in the case of Vermont's Tunbridge, saying no has netted only modest concessions from the state's transportation department, the struggle encouraged the Vermont Trust for Historic Preservation to issue Jim Wick's guide, "A Highway Project in Your Town: A Citizen's Guide to Your Role and Rights." At his prodding a regional transportation commission has begun to institute planning to end mindless "spot improvement." Some months later, the Conservation Law Foundation published a similar handbook for New Englanders, *Take Back Your Streets*. This hefty tract, subtitled *How to Protect Communities from Asphalt and Traffic,* sold out its first edition.

Both epistles fight the "safety issue," the bogeyman of road bureaucrats who claim that bigger is safer and faster better and that the old road with its "killer tree" will promote lawsuits. Lawyers in the field dismiss such claims of liability as the language of "misspeak." In the same way that automobile "upgrade" really means human "downgrade," lawyers insist that the engineers' "safety" means "peril." As speed limits rise, they reinforce the maxim that speed kills; that a pedestrian is ten times more likely to be killed by a car going thirty-one miles an hour than by one going fifteen miles an hour and eighteen times more likely to be killed when the car is traveling forty-four miles an hour. "You can achieve safety without tearing down trees or straightening," Thiebach says. And as for the eternal "we'll get sued," the phrase is a red herring, the Conservation Law Foundation's attorney explains. If proper notice is posted, by securing a sign or other easy measures, no one will be sued. Responding to history, responding to statistics, responding to new values, these road fighters and their manuals aim to control the automobile.

OPPOSITE: Scrambling together a copious array of activities, Princeton, New Jersey's Nassau Street would be a lawbreaker in many towns that isolate store from home and home from office through rigid zoning laws. Its well-adorned and shaded mix earns kudos from Americans questioned by Visual Preference Surveys. (Photo: A. Nelessen Associates)

Zoning for Life

JUST OFF ANOTHER country road near Winnipesaukee, New Hampshire, in a woodsy office adorned with a mix of hunting trophies and surveyor graphs, a traffic engineer is busily attacking the liturgy of his field. Chester "Rick" Chellman has rejected the Procrustean standards of traffic flow that said wider was better, cars came first, and the rule of the road dictated design.

His mission to alter the canon of his field stemmed from an assignment to set new guidelines for Florida's Seaside colony. There architects Andres Duany and Elizabeth Plater-Zyberk were beginning to implant their vision of a neotraditionalist way to re-create old towns. What better way to reproduce the dimensions of the old towns than to measure them? To do so, Chellman determined to study their

source: the narrow streets of Portsmouth, New Hampshire. He
wanted to see if traffic actually stalled on roads far, far slimmer than
any new developer would ever allow. Thus, he set out to measure the
speed and volume of traffic in the traditional brick town. With its
quirky layout and wide sidewalks, Portsmouth would seem to create
obstacles to traffic flow. Chellman found that the opposite was true.
The compact collection of small shops and historic houses, in fact,
reduced traffic. The number of cars flowing through the streets was
below the national average, and their pace was faster because of less
congestion. Even on peak days, the town's eighty-acre core produced
one-third the automobile trips of the same-sized conventional subdivision "blessed" with wide roads, large lots and lower density. The
town's "trip generation," the number of journeys from, say, store to
door by motor vehicle, was reduced compared to that set up by engineers in new, more widely spaced developments. The reason was that
more people walked to shop.

What did this mean? It meant that close-packed towns like
Portsmouth—congenial to movement on foot—could be a national
model. It meant that, if we made one of our ten to twelve trips per
household per day—one-quarter of them under a mile—without a ton
of steel, streets could shrink. It meant that, if cities fixed by boundaries of water, or revitalized by progressive politics, or bred in tidy
clusters by history could multiply, then we might cut the minijourneys
that demand the second or third car owned by 50 percent of all
households. Add bikes, too, for since half of America's trips are under
three miles, people might pedal their way to still more independence.

By duplicating the style and density of three hundred years of settlement before the car was dominant, we might live and move in harmony. By replicating the old, and still working, walk-to-work ratio,
by reducing car trips, and adding mass transit, Seaside or urban sites
could use this new-old pattern and coax residents to hoof it.

It was scarcely a new notion. But the Institute of Transportation
Engineers agreed that Chellman could incorporate these patterns in
the policies he was writing for them. "Basically," said architect
Duany, the sire of New Urbanism, "by controlling, as it were, the
next editions of more than ten central texts—some highway, some
zoning—it will become legal. That does not mean the model [for tra-

ditional neighborhoods] will change, but at least it will become legal" as national guidelines are adopted locally.

Decriminalizing Codes

Unfortunately, such walkable, mixed-use streetscapes—i.e., places with a mix of shops and houses and offices—are, in fact, not legal now. They are lawbreakers. Not only the road patterns but also the zoning codes, the tax breaks, the mortgage guarantees, and a network of laws and institutions now favor one-family, no-sidewalk development. Homes meshed with lively village centers are illegal. The codes and cultural context that shaped our most livable smaller cities and inner suburbs—our Marbleheads, our Pasadenas, our Shaker Heightses—became criminal.

Architecture critic Robert Campbell has described Antrim Street, where he lives in Cambridge, Massachusetts, as "the outlaw street." Like Portsmouth, his close-knit enclave, doors up from the ethnic shops of multicultural Inman Square, is a historic neighborhood of shoulder-to-shoulder houses, some single-, some multifamily, that breeds a friendly, foot-based community life. Street fairs and reunions of old neighbors characterize the street. This kind of neighborhood life was zoned into extinction elsewhere in the postwar boom. The codes insist on setbacks and wide spaces, require excessive parking lots and spaces to house the car, and enforce residential-only areas to curtail the corner store. In the end zoning's insistence on isolating uses—home here, office there, school or library one place, store another—have made life nearly impossible without an automobile. It is time to change this. We must bring back the corner-store culture: the walkable block, the next-door neighbor, the nearby library and school.

"Obviously, no one with a choice in the matter would want to look out his window at a 7-Eleven [store]," a *Newsweek* article titled "Bye-Bye, Suburban Dream" summarily declared in 1995. Obvious to whom? Not to the concerned parents staring at the cars whizzing down streets deprived of such walkable alternatives. Not obvious to the kids trapped as backseat passengers since it's too far or too dangerous to walk for a quart of milk or a Popsicle. Not even obvious to

Newsweek reporters, many of whom live in Manhattan, the twenty-four-hour city, or take public transit to the pedestrian-oriented inner suburbs, coaxed by the pleasure in their ambulatory life.

At a sprawlbusters conference in Washington, D.C., in the spring of 1995, as an audience oohed and aahed over slides of "then" and moaned over those of "now," Duany confirmed their distress: "Everything I am showing you on the left is what is implanted into our codes and [everything] on the right is illegal."

"The zoning process." You hear it again and again, the tales of the exhausting struggle to secure variances and cut through codes to bring fuller communities and more diverse forms of housing and activity. A devotee of urban or inner-city living and fond of the rail-connected past, New York architect Deborah Berke sent her students to Queens to see the borough where, for all its changes, dense, diverse Sunnyside Gardens endures—some few minutes' walk from the Flushing #7 line and six minutes by bus to New York City. Illegal, too, by today's standards based on housing and serving the car.

Name any older city and you have such amiable places picked by those wealthy enough to have a choice in housing. Close to the trolley or train, supplemented by bus, they may be urban or suburban, a stone's throw from city, town, or village, but their inhabitants like the neighborly mix. It is the tree-shaded clusters of myth and memory that win laurels in planner Anton Nelessen's Visual Preference Surveys. In towns like Memphis, Tennessee, and Little Rock, Arkansas, as well as Portland, Oregon, planner Nelessen has gone through a long drill of what people want, where they want it, and how to get it. Photos of many sorts of streets and houses in their own communities illuminate the screens in front of which he assembles people who get to pick and choose. The compilations of responses done in some fifty of these gatherings confirm that what people want is a car-lite landscape. What people don't want, Nelessen affirms, are places that look like strip malls. They don't want concrete islands or wide streets. What they do want are older places, the shaded sidewalks, houses with detail, Main Streets with life and texture. They want the amenities of car-free architecture on the small scale. This is what altering zoning to allow a new kind of land use can allow.

"What people really want is the housing in the mostly densely populated areas, especially the hills where the density is four or five times that of housing elsewhere," John Holtzclaw confirms the phenomena in San Francisco. An urban sociologist, he blended his background with knowledge of engineering and planning to help the Sierra Club fight California's transportation plans. "If you believe the market," says Holtzclaw, "they are Beacon Hill and North Beach," Boston and San Francisco's urbanity. We can chart the surroundings people like by the high rent and high visitation rates in Georgetown, Pike Place Market in Seattle, and Vieux Carré in New Orleans. "The Land of No," Rebecca Gratz called Fire Island in *The Living City*. It is by limiting cars or limiting ferry service that these popular "Lands of No," from Nantucket and Martha's Vineyard to the sometime automaker's retreat at Mackinac Island, Michigan, become pleasure islands. Why not create them elsewhere?

"Bring a tape measure" was the way one New England town, Camden, Maine, adopted the numbers of preautomobile building to write its new zoning ordinance. By measuring the building patterns, the setbacks from the street, the lot size, the ratio of height to width, the town established a golden rule to fill in the blanks needed and set a standard for other towns in Maine as well. The details of the distance from door to door, from house to house, and from sidewalk to street paralleled the past and, said one planner, allowed the town to "move beyond boilerplate standards"—the cul-de-sac and the sweeping arterial approach of vehicle-free building.

Such vintage, pedestrian-friendly places not only earn the elusive quality of "charm" but also make cars uncomfortable. For that is the other axiom of how to escape the auto age. Two things are mutually exclusive: sense of place and space for cars. The more parking space, the less sense of place. Reverse it and you have a graceful, easier life. Whatever the problems built into our car culture, however difficult the process of change, reducing the number of cars enlarges the richness of the environment.

Community by Consensus

Architect and planner Peter Calthorpe pauses after an intense recounting of public policy and larger planning issues. "You know," he says, looking over all the plans and amenities in his airy office in an old industrial building, "if you said to me, 'Peter, if you could do one thing, what would it be?' I think it would be granny flats."

By granny flats, Calthorpe means the old corner room adjacent to the house where grandma lived in the shelter of her family. Granny flat was also the space over the garage where not only granny but also grandchild, baby-sitter, or the artist in early career was cozily tucked in. These offsprings of the Victorian carriage house turned office, rental unit, or space for child care giver have begun to appear in both old and new constructions. Among the last is a flat above a garage in Calthorpe's Laguna West outside Sacramento. "Home Not Alone," the *Washington Monthly* titled the sociability and service of such spaces.

I once wrote of the students, singles, and dog walkers boarding in semisecret in the rambling nineteenth-century houses in my hometown as "underground boarders." Whether paying rent or bartering their work for rent, such tenants made living affordable for both owner and renter. They were also illegal, which meant that paying taxes on the income they brought in would disclose and hence destroy the possibility of having them as residents. Why be underground? I asked. Why not zone for two families, for the three-decker, or for the row house everywhere instead of "making two acres do the work of one?" as Grady Clay had it. Why not quarter, subdivide and split the space to curb the pernicious one-acre habit?

The density of the older cities and inner suburbs is not just a prerequisite for transit but for all mobility and human choice. In a house-poor nation—a nation with 75.9 percent of its elderly over sixty-five years of age living alone, a nation hard-pressed for affordable housing, a nation with dwellings too isolated for children to be independent—dense living is the geometry of humanity. Alternatives to the car-dependent large-lot one-family home are many. They range from 1960s communes, an estimated three hundred still intact, to today's cohousing crusaders, with their shared family arrangements. We need to ease their way into still more surroundings. And, in some cases, we have. Elderly men and women in group or assisted living residences, artists setting up studios in abandoned buildings, all need "legal" access to more such quarters. The bias of zoning, of mortgages, of public policy against multifamily density raises costs and denies options beyond the Ozzie and Harriet mode.

We need to reverse the destructive zoning that insists on two cars for every unit of housing and focus on the transit and walking fix that makes urban and historic communities workable. We need to revive boardinghouses, maintain SRO (single-room occupancy) dwellings, and re-create row houses, twin houses, apartments, and, don't forget, newer communal homes in which adults share space. Those who live in these and other viable forms don't need affirmation. They need duplication. In short, we do not need novel housing types to establish car-free communities; we do need to push against zoning's dead end.

"We have 238 communities each with their own zoning and funding system," Louis Gambaccini, head of Philadelphia's Southeastern Pennsylvania Transit Authority, complains about his region, and the state of the nation parallels it. "NIMBY," he went on, " 'not in my backyard,' has become 'YIMBY' ('yes, in my backyard but at a price')," i.e., fees paid to encourage pedestrian-friendly development. We need to stop bribes for sprawl; need to end a system in which innovative development means dealing with the cost of 37,000 separate negotiations in 37,000 planning departments. Consistency instead of such disparate negotiations takes an act of collective will, of enlargement state by state. It demands activism. Persuading officials, from council member to legislator, from ground up and top down, altering zoning codes to no longer defer to highway design.

We must just say yes then to alternative land use patterns to secure a multimodal choice. Widening our options for both mobility and livability is more pluralistic, more pleasurable, and, above all, possible. Looking for ways to bolster and re-create such neighborhoods, we must "retrofit" America's auto-centric wastelands to parallel the rail-linked, foot-powered past. We have seen how the highway dismantled streetcar cities and rail-linked suburbs that provided options. To right the transportation balance, we must reconnect the cities and suburbs. We must revamp them with a viable infrastructure and structure. The future of human mobility depends on reviving the built environment. To do so, we must concentrate on land use and public transportation.

Putting Transit
on Track

"HAD ENOUGH TRAFFIC?" asked a poster on California's BART, advertising the San Francisco–to–Oakland line as the way to go. Like to go back to the days when grand rail transit systems laced the nation? Want to reinstate the Big Red Cars, the railroads, the web of streetcars and buses, the many modes of movement crippled by preferential treatment given to the car? Can you go home again? Back to the days when book-toting schoolchildren and package-laden parents had mobility without automobility? Can we resurrect and reinforce mass transit?

These questions were in the air as Jeffrey M. Zupan, coauthor of

Public Transportation and Land Use Policy, addressed transportation professionals at the conference "Beyond the Open Road: Reinventing Transportation Policy for the 21st Century," held in the
wood-paneled assembly room of the New York University Law
School.

And so was his answer. Zupan, the cogent senior fellow of the Regional Plan Association of New York, had the statistics. But it was
the headline from the *Daily News* that said it all: "FOR MASS
TRANSIT NEED MASS." The slogan was no more than five words,
but it was based on a fact of human movement that has defined the
success (or lack thereof) of public transportation in America: the fact
that the average rider will walk no more than eight to ten minutes to
his or her transit stop. This truism of transportation and humanity
means that collecting enough riders to fill the trolley or bus depends
on collecting passengers who live nearby. It means shaping surroundings close or coaxing people to walk or bicycle. Land-consumptive
sprawl spreads people. It supports only the land-consuming private
car. Conversely, more close-by communities bring more people closer
to transit, hence more riders. As coins follow customers, it follows
that the more people dwelling in a smaller radius around the fare
box, the bigger the ridership. Land use is the issue.

Zupan breaks this formula into more precise figures, too. "To get
an hourly bus in the residential district, you have to have one house
per quarter acre," he said as he spelled out the specific numbers. "To
get one every half hour, it's seven an acre, and for every ten minutes,
it's fifteen an acre." That's the number of houses—with their inhabitants—who will supply the needed riders to fill a bus at thirty- or ten-
minute waits in residential areas.

Downtown defines the mass needed for mass transit in terms of the
commercial space that attracts these potential riders. "To get an
hourly bus you need to have 5 to 8 million square feet of retail space
in the retail district; for one to come every half hour, it's 7 to 17; and
for every ten minutes in the CBD (Central Business District) downtown it's more than 20 million."

Zupan's measurements are formulaic, and in every case the formula is based on two things—land use and density, the pattern of
building that pools people to live or shop in proximity to each other

and hence to transportation services. The more we congregate, the more we fill our buses. The more buses we fill, the more we get. It is a chain. The more buses we get, the better transit works and the fewer cars we need. When we house fewer cars, density can rise—and the more we fill our buses and can insert rail.

From buses, Zupan moved on to discuss streetcars. They require a still tighter web of living for good, economically viable service. To provide streetcars on surface tracks—that's light-rail with a right-of-way—transit providers need nine homes an acre or 19 million square feet of retail space. "You need, above all," he insisted, "a reasonable downtown." A Baltimore or Portland, Oregon, say, of some but not great size.

For rapid transit, or underground, unobstructed rail, it's twelve houses per acre or 50 to 70 million square feet of retail space, and only six or eight downtowns can supply that. This handful includes Chicago, New York, or Philadelphia.

A walking community and transit are intertwined: to secure transit service, you need community; to secure community, you need transit within walking distance. How do you get that closeness and congregation? Again, by organizing land use to insure density, i.e., by having enough people live less than a ten-minute walk to rail. As history shows, star-and-beam or hub-and-spoke designs have provided this in the past. Modern transit-oriented developments or pedestrian pockets do so too, building afresh on such patterns or intensifying existing nodes. By doing so, they create a balanced transportation system that must include all options from foot to rail.

Pattern Alphabet

The National Growth Management Leadership Project, an assembly of state leaders formed to refashion the buckshot pattern of growth, puts forth another formula. Patterning land use for sustainable transportation depends on three "Ds": density, designation, and design in their outline.

"Density," according to the group's guide, enforces the dictum in the headline: "for mass transit need mass." Density means that enough people live within an eight- to ten-minute walk of public transportation. Whether in a metropolitan city or a village center, building compactly by infilling or by intensifying the use of structures enlarges the bus and rail population. In big transit cities like Chicago and New York or in Montreal and Toronto people cluster near mass transit stops. There, foot traffic dominates and automobile traffic diminishes.

The second "D" means changing the land use designations that prevent accumulating the mass or density needed, that make living streets become "outlaw" streets, and that define mixed neighborhoods as "criminal." By shifting homogeneous zoning codes to multipurpose ones, by allowing commercial way stations, day care stops, services, and retail shops and restaurants, we can energize such transit stops—and enhance our lives.

The third "D," "design," means adding the amenities of trees and narrow streets to promote close living, with adroit single- or multifamily housing arrangements to insure the privacy that makes nearness not only manageable but desirable. "Livability," the Federal Transit Administration calls its program. Walkability through narrow, pleasant streets; strollability through lively shops; bicycle-rideability along pleasant paths and attractive streets—all stem from good design.

Drive-Less Design

Proof of the efficacy of rail when joined to tight settlement exists in pre-auto cities and post-auto ones, from the rail cities of Boston and New York to Chicago in the Midwest and San Francisco on the West Coast. It is written on the odometer. Simply put, shoulder-to-shoulder communities reduce vehicle-miles traveled by car. The result is that city dwellers drive eight thousand miles a year by car; mixed inner suburban ones, fifteen thousand; and those in fringe suburbs, thirty thousand.

William H. Lucy and David L. Phillips, professors at the University of Virginia, found that inner or older suburbs connected to downtown by the umbilical cord of good transit have prospered. Alexandria and Arlington, Virginia, which embraced land use policies that nestled shops and services and provided density around their transit stations more than a decade ago, now thrive along with Metro service to Washington, D.C. Designed thoughtfully, the sites were the result of good planning and good politics. They created a land boom by settling businesses and housing around the transit line in Maryland and northern Virginia, turning potential auto-dependent sites into walkable cores. Not so in Fairfax County, the next tier. In this ring, where officials snubbed the pattern of dense, mixed land uses and instead augmented roads, the centers languished.

American towns and cities have revived or installed a sampler of such livable enclaves. Labeled "transit-oriented development" or "transit sheds" (like their source in watersheds and "viewsheds"), they are patterned after stars or satellites. Webbed with tracks, they serve the stores and offices, services and restaurants—amenities—in the penumbra of the station or stop. Whether a simple station or the nerve center of a million rails, these places are the nuclei of a mass transit world.

Other crowd-pulling attractions, placed strategically by planners, reinforce the transit spine. When San Diego settled its transit offices near a stop or Portland, Oregon, sent a line to its convention hall or Baltimore to the Camden Yards baseball stadium, they boosted ridership and decreased traffic congestion. Such transit-oriented development characterizes the best and broadest plans of the day. The Regional Plan Association of New York has sketched the future growth of the region along transit lines, with nodes at rail stops. Such land use strategy dots the planning maps of Sacramento, California; of Portland, Maine; of Montgomery County, Maryland; and of many other regions struggling to install it. In North America, Toronto demonstrates its effectiveness. Europe's transportation planning—its long-tested greenbelts and control over land use—provides a germane and successful guide to how such placements encourage a natural market. No sooner had the New Jersey Transit announced a direct route from South Orange, New Jersey, to New York City's Penn Station, eliminating one transfer and cutting some twenty minutes off the trip, than the center at its station showed new signs of life. A bakery appeared. A coffee bar and real estate office opened. A dry cleaning service sprouted in one strip of storefronts. Elsewhere along the New York–New Jersey transit corridor, offices to supply day care and other services arise beside the train station. Commerce can ride rail construction as surely as it rode the highway.

Starry-Eyed for Streetcars

And perhaps it may. When Los Angelenos get starry-eyed about the restoration and opening of their funicular, a toy-sized incline railroad, a cosmic shift is in the making. The dismantled line was revived in 1996 to the delight of crowds. For a decade a wave of investment has funded light-rail and has charmed, and served, America in the process. Tourist buses across the country stick a "trolley" label on their sides, playing on streetcar chic as they drive on rubber wheels. And real trolleys spring up elsewhere. "The Future Is Quaint," said *New York* magazine, describing plans for the real thing in Manhattan. Talk about the love affair with the automobile. Here is a faithful suitor replacing it. San Diego, Sacramento, St. Louis, Baltimore, Los Angeles, and Portland, Oregon, as well as San Jose, San Francisco, and Oakland, have launched or extended lines. Commuter rail ridership has risen, notwithstanding the shrinking of mass transit funds.

Unfortunately, the downsizers attack. New York's state and city budget cutbacks have undone decades of progress; elsewhere, decimation of the public transit budget has been corrosive. Yet, even in the midst of hard times for the public sector, streetcar success stories appear and tracks fan out to combat congestion and sprawl. St. Louis had a lights-out downtown, its aged infrastructure intact but its parking lot–strewn urban core orphaned by the motorized exodus. It opened a new line linking the old Eads Bridge and Kiel Stadium. New riders headed downtown to shop, to see sporting events, and to work and outward to the airport. Voters funded extensions. Even car-comatose Secaucus, New Jersey, where this book began, has proposals for a new transfer station and light-rail. Within less than two weeks after New Jersey Transit opened its new passenger link from Manhattan, the ridership had exceeded the 1,500 expected per day by almost 3,000. New Jersey has committed $1.3 billion to a twenty-one-mile light-rail line along the state's northeastern shoreline from Bayonne to Hoboken. Dallas opened a new five-mile line in the spring of 1996, while talk of light-rail grows in Milwaukee and Dayton. The Federal Transit Administration is overwhelmed by the requests. Though few of these systems emulate the subway lines of America's great metropolises, the comprehensive networks of Montreal and Quebec in Canada, or Europe's transit cornucopia, are the first steps to spark enthusiasm.

Surface lines to counter the single-occupancy vehicle spread. Across the country, cities plan to roll on old lines (Hartford), build new ones for new needs (Salt Lake City for the 2002 Winter Olympics), or extend old ones (Cleveland). In the big transit towns, heavy-duty urban systems in hard-pressed areas have revived stations as far more than pit stops. In Chicago, renovation of the Edgewater stations and spaces began as the Chicago Transit Authority teamed with private developers on a pilot project for four station stops. Coffee shops, laundries, and other niche stores for retailing revived and succeeded there. Elsewhere in the city, the new Orange Line to Midway Airport elevated property values close to the line by 30 percent and had a ripple effect in shops supported by the South West Corridor development corporation. DevCorp North, in Douglas, Philadelphia works to rehabilitate its old El and sells fresh vegetables at its Fruitvale stop. Boosted by legislation to develop so-called arrival zones along the seventy-two-mile BART line in Oakland and San Francisco, communities have begun to transform park 'n' ride wastelands of asphalt into compact mixed-use "transit villages." BART's "Village Vision," *Planning* magazine called it. Officials plan to build housing and retail and commercial developments around the other transit stops.

"New York has been off its trolley too long," says the Port Authority sign at the dreary end of West Forty-second Street, where a new-old trolley would also travel. "Paris: Mais oui!" is the way the city's Committee for Better Transit proclaims its urge to replicate French light-rail. "New York Aussi?" The advocacy group promotes a "Liberty Loop" of streetcars from Lower Manhattan pushing out through today's auto-only Brooklyn-Battery and Lincoln Tunnels. New York, with 40 percent of the nation's mass transit and a majestic track record, knows how to capitalize on its rail and walkability. A federal study of how to reduce the city's swollen traffic included reviving the Second Avenue subway, forsaken during the 1970s fiscal crisis. An East Village, West Village, and Greenwich Village coalition is pushing for a Village Crosstown Trolley Line, the Eighth Street corridor rail; "the greatest civilizing element," says transportation planner George Haikalis.

The historic corridors for the ubiquitous trolleys of times past remain more than a memory of pre–World War II cities. They are also an endoskeleton and invitation to unearth new-old lines. Some half million Denverites celebrated the opening of their new line along its old corridor, now running five miles from downtown to an interstate, with an 8.7-mile extension approved. Such trolley revivals beguile the affluent along with the budget minded. Philadelphia has begun to refurbish a "welcome line" of streetcars downtown. In 1996, San Francisco brought back the weighty old Presidents' conference Cars (PCCs) and sent them parading down Market Street, its tourist boulevard, joining some eighteen rebuilt PCCs rolling along the refurbished Embarcadero to Fisherman's Wharf. Surveying Syracuse's restored "City Express" rail line, the *Wall Street Journal* found a "surprising" connection between the trolley and more trade. Only doubting Thomases of the rail world could have failed to perceive the logic of the connection.

A small transit-oriented gesture can spawn a whole community. In Graesham, Oregon, design guidelines were legislated to offer incentives to make spaces near transit lines pedestrian friendly by shifting entrances near sidewalks and away from parking lots. In Los Angeles bothersome automobiles ("row after row of car hoods," the mayor complained) were encouraged to settle behind or beside stores. Southern California thus has its public transit fans along with its construction problems and autophiliac observers. "Los Angeles by Trolley" may never stand beside Disneyland or Universal Studios as a tourist mecca, but the appeal of the color-coded red Metro line, the blue Los Angeles–Long Beach light-rail and the green suburban line has surprised scoffers. Palmdale station's prom night even offered tuxedoed teenagers a fear-free ride to the Biltmore Hotel downtown.

Trains: Revival and Survival

Those passenger trains that once spanned the continent exist at barely a subsistence level. Despite its troubles, Amtrak has spent a decade polishing its elegant stations. In the midst of cutbacks and travails (and subsidies to trucks and planes that undermine the viability of rail), a program to refurbish passenger stations from Los Angeles's splendid Art Deco Union Station to Boston's vibrant food-filled South Station attracts a constituency that won't die. Worn but not impossible to resuscitate, stations and terminals endure in major rail cities like San Francisco and Chicago. Alive with active, upscale commuters toting Power Books, the vast spaces of Washington's refurbished Union Station or New York's Grand Central still reflect the vitality of the age of rail. Smaller comeback stations from Newark, New Jersey, to Tacoma, Washington, add services and anchor their areas. Together, these stations form an ideal sun for a car-free solar system, the destination around which shopping, browsing, socializing, and services from food to day care can flourish.

Despite what *Passenger Train Journal* editor Carl Swanson calls the "Kill Amtrak" bill of the year, Amtrak passenger-miles managed to rise 41 percent from 1982 to 1995. The success of private freight lines made the cover of *Time* magazine as they battle against the fleet of trucks trying to add more weight and dangerous trailers. Struggles in Congress notwithstanding, Amtrak is electrifying its New York–Boston passenger train to reduce the travel time by two hours by 1999. A Portland, Maine, extension moves ahead, with New Hampshire service en route. West Coast trips have also gone beyond "cruise" status to regular service in the past decade, and Chicago remains a busy hub. From the Northwest corridor to Florida, regions have begun to plan to install or improve rail. Overnight service between cities gains fans.

Alas, it's thin porridge compared to times past, especially when one considers the overlooked potential: one-third of the passenger flights in the nation, carrying some 113 million people a year travel less than five hundred miles to their destinations. Passenger rail could easily cover those miles, not only benefiting from the former flyers but replacing drivers and freight trucks and adding commuter rail stations along the way.

Looking backward with nostalgia and fearing the incursion of cars and more parking lots for the vast hordes of visitors to Yosemite Valley, Grand Canyon, and other natural wonders have prompted plans for action. Northern California's Yosemite Valley Railroad Company has undertaken the recovery of the rail route downed half a century ago. Other trains that once carried passengers to dramatic vistas and scenic vacations move to solve the problems of pollution and congestion that a glut of cars brings to these environmental splendors.

Buses on Track

"Buses don't get no respect," *Planning* magazine observed. But the "loser cruiser" label is under attack. While streetcars are essential to guaranteeing the stability that encourages dense land use and hence an auto-free existence, buses are the way much of sprawling America must, and does, move. Architect Douglas Suisman, for one, would like to see Los Angeles's Wilshire Boulevard, where the Big Red Cars once traveled, packed with buses. The street's possibilities for revival by improved transportation captivate Suisman, who is the author of *The Boulevards of Los Angeles*. He envisions the buses that ply Wilshire Boulevard promoting commercial stops and terminals—"transit sheds" that create nodes for easier, walkable living for the poorer neighborhoods. As means of movement in themselves, or as precursors of surface streetcar lines, regular buses can encourage transit-oriented land patterns.

While America's buses are, by and large, stuck in traffic, sharing roads with cars, Curitiba, Brazil's model for public transportation, has designated lanes for buses. By setting aside the land and funding the system, the city has succeeded in making bus service as reliable as rail. Closer to home, some highways, like those in Houston, offer exclusive, hence speedy, rights-of-way to buses. On a larger scale, San Francisco's buses move rapidly through town. While underfunded and sporadic, American buses have earned a bad rap for poor service, they can provide an alternative. More comfort, more reliability, more dependable service could benefit the neediest—and the nation.

Such niche lines as the Hop in Boulder, Colorado, circulating at five-minute intervals between downtown, the university campus, and a pedestrian mall, all for a quarter, are success stories. Los Angeles's DASH and Foothill Transit Zone serve communities, supplementing the Metropolitan Transit Authority bus lines that go down arterials. Though eighty percent of riders on fifty-three DASH buses on five routes own cars, supervising transportation planner Phil Akers calls buses imperative to the "schizophrenic spider web of origins and destinations" that make his city work. To Akers "the land use thing is so completely out of control" that he looks to buses along freeways to take advantage of the highway system. Like other rubber wheel proponents, Akers sees money spent on rail as undermining buses, without acknowledging the need for many modes—many flowers—to bloom.

Bus and rail are complementary, not competitive, and the tendency to cut back on the former to fund the latter instead of allying the transportation-deprived against their mutual enemy, the automobile, does a disservice to both. Funding commuter lines should not drain feeder or basic bus lines. When Los Angeles rail builders removed buses, they shortchanged their constituency, giving some bus riders long and impossible hikes to grab the Blue Line streetcar. When Washington, D.C., rightly nourished its Metro subway line, it wrongly skimped on Metrobus services or tried to privatize them. Like the foolish feuding between Amtrak and streetcar systems, the battle between the underdogs of mobility typifies a car-dominated system too oppressed to bombard the true villain of the piece. From Chicago and Boston to smaller cities, the wave of transit downsizing robs Peter to pay Mammon.

Similarly, the quest for "efficiency" through privatization is a menace, luring communities to sell off transit systems to private contractors. Dedicated to private gain, these profit-makers drain what is left of mass transit's life by maintaining what they deem the profitable commuter runs while cutting back the "off-hour" rides that link city neighborhoods. Moreover, the budget-cutters who hawk this public service not only fractionalize the system, slighting both rich and poor, but in the end also lose money.

"When you examine the real numbers, you realize that the privateer's claims for savings from Denver to Southern California to Miami are inflated," says transportation planner and economist Elliott Sclar. "More often than not, the figures reveal that privatization is a money-losing proposition for all but the privatizers." In the end, the balkanizing of public transit wrecks the chance for cooperating lines and slows moving us quickly and safely from points A to B.

When they are centralized, convenient, and consistent, buses can begin drawing in far-flung places if the system follows the maxims for density in transit-oriented development. Affluent, suburban Bellevue, Washington, transformed its strip into a core of stores and offices framing a bus stop and corridor for riders going downtown. Old lines, like San Francisco's well-oiled bus service, and new ones, like Seattle's polished underground system, serve cities. In more spread-out or rural areas, buses are the only source of mass mobility. The bus remains the essential vehicle in rural and exurban regions and the vital connector in urban ones. Its function as a connector—bus to train, bus to trolley—is imperative in underpopulated and populated places alike.

"Rural Mayday" systems, as the Surface Transportation Policy Project calls them, are hard to assemble. In some places, vans take the rural elderly to hospitals, tourists to national parks, and students to campuses, reducing car traffic. Dial-a-ride and other paratransit operations serve nondrivers in wheelchairs, but for the 30 percent of the nation in rural environments, it is a struggle to gain mobility. "Vulnerable and underserved populations," Joycelyn Elders describes her parents in small-town Schaal, Arkansas, and the elderly have become the subject of more concern. "You could have a doctor on every corner in Schaal and my parents still would not have access to health care. Why?" she asked. "Because they do not have any way to get there to see the doctor." It is "far cheaper to train a bus driver than it is to train a doctor," Elders went on, "yet the town has neither."

Connecting Door to Door

"Intermodal" is the new word for linkages between modes of transportation. In cities like Chicago, Toronto, and New York that integrate bus and rail, 70 to 90 percent of all trips downtown are car-free. "Intermodal" denotes the concern with connections to interlock the geography of life and end the car-bred sprawl that scatters settlement and denies movement for a multitude. It sums up the motto of advocates for human mobility: "Let many flowers bloom." Buses and vans can collect inner-city residents and drive them to work sites; when frequent and efficient, they can link to rail and provide coherent service. A seamless web that hooks buses, vans, cabs, and cars in a multifaceted—"multimodal" in the jargon—system supplies mobility for all segments of the population.

Down by the waterfront, Americans already take some 60 million trips a year on the ferry. New York City boasts a half dozen. The ferry to Staten Island, shared by automobiles along with pedestrians in early days, became so packed with people that its management excluded cars until recently, when a pro-automobile mayor reversed the policy. Other ferries have gradually surfaced along waterways to serve congested communities. The SeaBus in Vancouver and the Seattle and Boston ferries expand, while those connecting small islands and points of land in Portland, Maine, and New Orleans serve both commuting and vacationing needs. Transforming city commutes into a peaceful journey, ferries offer freedom from traffic and a direct route.

In a nation where 53 percent of the population lives within two miles of public transportation, the connection of bus and streetcar, foot and ferry, train and bicycle in so-called intermodal linkages could return us to such once scorned means of circulation. More shuttles and vans could roll through the inner and outer rings of the metropolis, taking inner-city residents to work, the elderly to the opera, youngsters to school.

Some cities seek the solution to the problem of work on the fringes by supplying transportation for transit-starved, inner-city employees with vans as well as buses. Frank J. Wilson, New Jersey's transportation commissioner, testified before Congress that "for many, public transportation is the difference between welfare and work," and he is working with the state's Department of Human Services on a ride brokerage program linking people and jobs through public transportation. Meanwhile, programs to shuttle workers on buses and vans gain advocates.

"Ridership on our bus service is going up on every level," says Tim Davis, chief executive officer of Summit County, Ohio. The success persuaded him to push for rail between Cleveland, Akron, and Canton, in the northeastern quadrant of his Rust Belt state. Mass transit even won a vote for a sales tax, he says, and remains vital. "If we're only creating $8 jobs and you have to buy a $15,000 car to get to an $8 job, how do you do it?" His reply is a hub-and-spoke line to assemble and disperse workers. The rail plans have gone slowly, however. The $150 million to redo the rail line from Cleveland to Canton in eighteen months competes with the $329 million, nineteen-mile Interstate 77, which will take from ten to fifteen years, far more than the train, to complete. Still, Davis plugs on locally and with Washington. "They're going to get tired of seeing us," he laughs.

Other innovations multiply. Some communities already have dispatchers to connect callers to vans that loop through neighborhoods. Jitneys, the independent fixed-route taxis that roam streets in Mexico City, Puerto Rico, and other places, live a subterranean existence in poorer American neighborhoods, where gypsy drivers roam the streets. The jitneys reflect the demand for inventive alternatives. With chits for public transit linkages and cabs, the safety net for those without automobiles, could well serve the system. The new field of transportation demand management offers call-a-ride, connect-a-ride strategies to decrease traffic and travel. Replacing the door-to-door flexibility of the automobile, these alternatives to one-car-per-person are diverse. Ride sharing, telecommuting, and car and van pooling, along with flextime, figure in their options.

Car sharing is an innovative expedient that reduces the need for extra automobiles per household. A neighborhood car can serve a street. Companies, too, have spare automobiles, supplying cars to let parents take a midday trip in case of an emergency. Some businesses have supplemented cars with free in-house child care facilities. Other companies give travel allowances and rebates to those who come by alternate transportation.

Blossoming in some seventy European cities, car co-ops form a new network. Berlin's Stattauto, now spreading to the United States, works by using reservations. Cars sit on fourteen lots throughout the city, and borrowers make reservations and pick up keys in safe-deposit boxes. Experiments in shedding the automobile altogether ensued from car cooperatives in Germany. When householders in Bremen decided not to use their cars for a month, the majority abandoned their cars for good. Berlin created a car-free node of housing with no space for the automobile. Sprinkled throughout America, informally and formally, the pattern grows. Earthworks in Jamaica Plain, Massachusetts, and the Eugene Car Co-op in Oregon follow the Berlin model.

Car rental is the American version, a standby for urbanites on vacation or for weekend trips. Even in the auto-dependent Southwest, Phoenix residents rent cars by the hour, a serviceable way to lessen car ownership. Alternatives, from companies that offer a free ride home during emergencies to the station car or car pool, encourage more than the single-occupancy vehicle. So, of course, do services from letter carriers, pizza deliverers, in-town messengers, and retail store and copy service drop-offs. Though not total solutions, a legion of carriers may diminish driving or allow two- or three-car households to shed a car. Again, all of these solutions work best, or work mostly, where compact living provides alternate transportation. Here, too, a close-in kind of living, a land use shift, can bring the density needed for the walking, biking, transit-friendly world that can support alternatives to the car.

Above all, the network of public transportation must be seamless. "A station in every backyard" is the phrase Auto-Free New York uses to describe access to public transportation. The methods range from walker-friendly neighborhoods to upgraded feeder buses and bus lanes. Transit agencies should cooperate, not combat one another, to create a unified system. A train pass system should integrate all modes. "One fee fits all" should be the motto for moving from shuttle to bus to train. Taxis should get more than a grudging okay for all their ties to the car culture, since they serve the poor along with the rich. Cabs do contain the need for the car. To many, park-and-ride facilities are a last resort, since the space to park automobiles can create a wasteland and work against human mobility.

Whatever turns transit into mass transit seems a cure. Yet proclaimed antidotes like the High Occupancy Vehicle (HOV) lane heal little. The idea of shrinking traffic by putting three-passenger cars in their own lane works in theory and sometimes in fact. Often, however, adding the HOV lane is an entry for traffic engineers to hard top. A road is widened. If, or when, the lane fails to attract enough multipassenger cars, commuters complain. The extra lane is opened for two-passenger cars. ("Two people in a car is not an HOV lane; it's a date," say opponents.) Worse yet, the lane reverts to use by the standard single-occupancy vehicle. The New York/New Jersey/Connecticut Tri-State Campaign calls it "the camel's nose under the tent." "Backsliding," a report for the Chesapeake Bay Foundation, "Re-Thinking HOV," describes this conversion. A truly helpful high-occupancy vehicle is mass transit in a lane of its own. The conversion of old single-occupancy vehicle lanes to multi-occupancy lanes, not the building of new ones, is an alternative. Otherwise, HOV means "Help Out Vehicles."

Work options like flextime and telecommuting stand high on the list of solutions. Telecenters, described as urban villages, where workers share space away from the office, have opened from Oberlin, Kansas, to Steamboat Springs, Colorado. Home offices to save driving win praise. Sit behind your computer, your phone, your fax, on-line, at home, say supporters of this solution. Peer out at the green grass through the window. This reduces vehicle miles. The car stays in the garage or vanishes, right? Yes and no. Futurists who project the rising number of telecommuters fail to acknowledge how small a number of telecommuters exist (3 percent of the population), how small a percentage of miles are traveled by the commuter, and, most important, how large a percentage of miles are spent performing errands in sprawling suburbs. So stay-at-homes still pass their days performing the personal trips that run mileage into five digits. We need to solve the land use, density issue before telecommuting can help.

Rewinding the Transit Clock

More transit, or even more forms of transit, is not the only answer, of course. Better transit is. High-tech, super-speed rail is appealing, but upgrading the existing stock, car by car, is essential. While we can anticipate and strive for France's TGV and German and Japanese bullet trains, longer rail lines and better accommodations on conventional trains assure the constituency for them. The successes of European and Japanese rail, the happy chapters in the mass transit saga, stemmed from the maxim to keep "innovation to the minimum." The Japanese, who secured great achievements with American technology in the 1960s, coupled the best of what worked rather than going for the untried. Good service means frequency and ease of connections, supported by passes, free and easier transfers between modes, and other financial incentives to encourage ridership.

Building or extending ordinary rail lines takes long enough. My own wait for Amtrak's Boston to New York speedup project began with word of the project two decades ago. Between delays in funding, planning, and technical or public input, fifteen years is the minimum for a high-tech advance.

Instead, rail services need to offer and advertise a civilized commute. Make the public aware of what exists. Enhance the travel environment, not the razzle-dazzle. Be on time. Make the connections work. Provide short headways between trains (i.e., little waiting), updates on train arrivals, safety in door-to-door connections. Smooth rail beds, good seats and good meals might help. "Making Transit Irresistible," Rutgers professor John Pucher calls it. And why not copy the utopia of free rides or free fare zones from Seattle and Portland, Oregon? By shortening transfer times and supplementing evening arrivals with taxis, escorts, and community policing as GoBoulder does, plus using neighborhood patrols for walkers, we can raise mass transit ridership.

The Ultimate Draw

Portland, Oregon, is everyone's case study for adroitness and conviction in the blending of myriad options to form new land use patterns that promote mass transit and curb the car. From the day almost a quarter century ago when Portland halted the Mount Hood Freeway to replace it with a park, this Northwestern city has led a movement that blends regional planning, transportation, and clean air goals. In 1973, the state created an inviolate greenbelt around the city. A realization of Ebenezer Howard's Garden Cities and Lewis Mumford's dream, this urban boundary maintained the center—the mass—by creating a barrier against sprawling development. Only farm and forest use could go in this ring. Within the circle, zoning densities could return to close, traditional pre-sprawl norms, thus quadrupling the amount of land for multifamily units and almost halving the size of the single-family lot.

Lined by trolleys, downtown Portland was revived to become a transit-friendly pedestrian place. The downtown plan, based on light-rail, has become the symbol of success. Fare-free zones bring walkers striding a dozen abreast along city streets in the center. In the outskirts, mass transit, not the freeway, has become the armature of growth. Spearheaded by the Thousand Friends of Oregon, the developments have moved the community from "just say no" to this political and communal "just say yes." The group has minted the awkward acronym LUTRAQ (for land use, transportation, and air quality) as a goal for other regions.

Eight states—Vermont, Maine, Rhode Island, New Jersey, Minnesota, Florida, Georgia, and Washington—have revamped their planning and zoning laws to preserve green carpets of open space and to channel new growth into the cities and towns that support trolley systems. The greenbelts bear many names: "urban growth boundaries," "urban service areas," and "community development boundaries." Greenbelts, in which building is restricted and open space reserved, have helped Europe's town centers prosper. Canada, Australia, and European countries have lessons to teach doubting Thomases. Amending the political process to adopt the larger model of these greenbelts or open spaces and to restrict development on the far-flung fringes is essential on a large scale. Combining that with the zoning and code adjustments already mentioned, new standards for the road and highway, and regulations to throttle the megastores that destroy downtowns and Main Streets, are a must.

Just as zoning alone is not enough, so transportation planning alone won't do. As Mumford said in *Botched Cities*, "Zoning, properly speaking, is the legal agent of intelligent city planning." "Zoning without city planning is a nostrum; and city planning without not merely an initial control of land—which every municipality has in its unplanned areas—but a continuous supervision over its actual development and uses—is merely a branch of oratory or mechanical drawing." Regional planning that tackles the bigger picture is the building block of constructing a "there there" for our transportation systems.

Because the Intermodal Surface Transportation Efficiency Act demands input in transportation planning, it has allowed the pursuit of design to move beyond developers and road operatives to include the larger public.

Some of these Metropolitan Planning Organizations (MPOs) required by the act have begun to make sure that the road ahead has a shape and destination. So-called currency legislation in places like Florida, Washington, Oregon, and Georgia stipulates that builders strike a balance between transportation capacity and growth. Other mandates use public policy to place public buildings—from a post office to government offices—around nodes of transportation. Such injunctions are too few and far between, but the principle holds. "Land use is the bottom line," as Fred Williams of the Federal Transit Administration puts it, bringing us back to the axiom around which all solutions revolve. The goal is balanced, not car-based, transportation; human mobility, not just automobility. To achieve this goal, we must find public ways of revering and safeguarding the land.

The Centering of America

"MAIN STREET IS almost all right," architects Robert Venturi and Denise Scott Brown observed years ago. The clear-eyed estimate is not exactly O. Henry's ode to the "ragged purple dream, the wonderful, cruel, enchanting, bewildering, fatal, great city." Yet, Main Street is icon and starting point enough, a symbol of what Lewis Mumford called "centers of gravity." From the mighty urban fountainheads to the villages and hamlets, the town and community hearts, here is where we need to look to reinforce walkability and livability. For every move that enhances these cores bolsters the human mobility that can redefine our days.

Every city, thriving or dying, is always in transition, "a city in the making," as the French architect Bernard Tschumi once said of New York. The question is how to make that transition spiral upward, to reverse the outmoded and pernicious policies that drive us outward. And to do so quickly.

Reversing the Spatial Equation

"Centering" is what potters call the process of shaping a stable vessel. Place the clay on the wheel and spin. Shape the wet earth, all the while balancing and resisting the outward pull. Keep the slippery clay poised—centered—and you will find the object whole and workable. Let the spin of the wheel pull it outward and the mass will crash. So it is with centering our gritty cities, our Mark Twain towns and villages, our suburban centers. Resist the pull, and you have the enduring center: foundation for walking, for mass transit, for life released from four wheels.

"Last one out turn out the lights" went the doomsayers of the American city when motorized flight drained downtown. We must turn on the lights by reviving Main Street to bring people back. "The street," writes San Francisco planner Allan B. Jacobs, "is a political space. It's on Elm Street that neighbors discuss zoning or impending national initiatives, and on Main Street, at the Fourth of July parade as well as the anti-nuclear march, that political celebrations take place." To loosen the grip of the automobile, we must strengthen and redeem the settled city street. The old nerve centers are our targets for revitalization with not only the "Ds" of designation and density but also with the "D" of design on the large and the small scale through microcosmic adjustments and macrocosmic public policy.

The National Trust for Historic Preservation calls its Main Street program "300 Places Proud." Since 1980, when it set up shop, the trust has helped join the public and the private sectors to restore the nation's heritage of small towns and hamlets, urban and close-in suburban walking cores. Trying to make communities whole, generating vitality, the trust has begun to counter the pull of the big box discount store off the arterial by urging merchants to consider whole streets, to design and green storefronts and sidewalks, and to stage celebrations and special events. Stressing self-help and public aid, the trust orchestrated $40 million in private investment to revitalize the downtown of Franklin, Tennessee, and save it from gutting by the sprawling Nashville suburbs. In Saratoga Springs, they staved off a sprawling mall by shaping a district that incorporates an $8 million library downtown and 250 trees planted by volunteers. All told, the organization's Main Street Center has dropped into Main Street and made it work, offering technical assistance to revitalize more than twelve hundred towns and cities. The trust has netted 102,000 jobs and attracted $5 billion in investments to this urban landscape.

The agenda is not reinventing streetscapes but retrofitting them with the amenities that make for the welcoming corner café, the handshaking world that keeps Main Street's walkers from driving to the mall. The trust is not alone. Mayors, aldermen, selectmen and neighborhood representatives, city planners and consultants like Partners for Livable Places have tried to encourage local cooperation and funds from merchants and community members for streetscape makeovers. The café-ing of America brings foot traffic to the city and inner suburb neighborhoods. Even in an era that fails to recognize their worth and economic value, our cores have begun to revive themselves.

"Social conditions, the local economy, city fiscal problems and a leadership vacuum on 'quality of life' issues have produced conditions that make New York appear to be a city in decline," the century-old Municipal Art Society observes. "We sense, however, a change in the air." New York, "the city that never sleeps," differs from other cities and the urban boroughs nearby. Yet, all centers contain a collection of smaller parts, a salad of neighborhoods, that can be revitalized as Main Streets. Civic art is not "tying tidies on poles and putting doilies on the cross-walks," Charles Mulford Robinson declared in 1904. "Town planting" is threefold. It is devoted "to the replanning of existing cities and towns, to the planning of new towns, and to a scientific plating of new sections of existing towns." For almost a century since Robinson's words, we have devoted ourselves to having the "new" and to replanning for the motorcar. Now it is time to use his values, to rework the "existing towns" mangled by the automobile.

The lessons of Robinson's pre-auto neighborhood have spread to historic enclaves. But even at the aging "new" town of Reston, Virginia, designed at the end of the road for the car, the landscape architectural firm of Sasaki Associates has retrofitted the town center for pedestrians. Sasaki Associates shaped a public square with shops and restaurants, outdoor tables, and noontime concerts—for a social setting beyond Reston's roots as a single-use home-dwelling town.

The incremental movement of Americans to the sidewalk parallels and accompanies this slow retrofitting and reurbanizing. Such centers of life are what planner Randall Arendt calls "landmarks of the heart," memorable and dear to those raised in them, and the ways to save and enhance them are legion. As we preserve, we reinforce the stitching of our urban centers. Large or small, these streets and historic structures promote human interaction and, hence, elicit mobility beyond car door to mall door.

Village by Fill

City Comforts is the title of David Sucher's eclectic handbook on "how to build an urban village." The former Seattle city planning commission member has used his perception and his camera to recount ways to reclaim our "almost all right" or even not-so-right spaces through design. His "God-is-in-the-details" approach shows how a plethora of design decisions—from excluding parking lots to inserting benches—transform car sheds into people sheds. The Main Street design devices vary, but they similarly eschew the void of what Richard Register has called "carchitecture."

"Blankness seems to be an innate human horror," as Sucher writes. These vacuous spaces are corollaries of the car culture. Instead of empty or abused asphalt, architects can subdue the presence of the car with amenities. Soften walls, screen the parking lot with display cases, shield the view, or, better still, eradicate the automobile.

"Infill" and "retrofit" are the words used for reweaving the torn fabric of the city and restoring the density that makes public transportation viable. To revive the sometimes wasted center, a fill-in-the-gaps style is essential. The new can help, but only in harmony and service to the old. Context is all. Restoration means preservation, endorsing the old, not the new. We need to connect the dots between the empty spaces gutted by the car, to connect the pods off the highway. We need, in the new language of urbanists, to transform the so-called brownfields, the vacant lots of our cities, instead of obliterating the greenfields of our countryside.

The squalid outskirts of urban America and the ravaged inner cities are the concern of policy makers. With 100,000 brownfield sites in the nation, by EPA estimates, the cleaning of polluted urban land has primacy. Infill or rehabilitation in the most desolate spaces can provide jobs and homes close to the transit infrastructure ready to serve them and rally urban neighborhoods as well. The move to fill these empty, sometimes toxic or Superfund, sites with their crumbling industrial plants has earned them a constituency trying to woo business nearer to a dense center.

Rather than splice and dice the greenfields with more corporate pullouts to the fringes, some 450 agencies and businesses in Minneapolis and St. Paul have joined in the Voluntary Investigation and Compliance Program. The Twin Cities's program lists a thousand potential waste sites. Adding some six new properties a week to the rescue list, officials have attacked the problems by, say, removing contaminated soil from a dump for a new medical center or reusing an abandoned factory. They thus create productive property at the center rather than watch business disperse to "green," i.e. clean, sites on the fringes. Other communities explore the means to ease the rescue of these damaged lands. In Akron, for instance, a Goodyear factory could be retooled for a high-tech replacement by indemnifying against future pollutants through insurance companies.

Soothing the "Here"

The old we need to honor, then, need not be a landmark. Infill means caring for what we have. It means tackling even the forlorn strip malls of the 1950s and 1960s. Not long after Seattle banned parking lots in front of such malls, half a dozen Safeway grocery stores agreed to park cars behind. The streetscape was reurbanized. At one "restored" Safeway in North Seattle, the car-free sidewalk that lines the street now promotes walkability for shoppers and access for retirees who stroll out from nearby apartments. When Taco Time put parking behind one restaurant, business rose 20 percent higher than the chain's asphalt-encased norm. Resisting a "cars-first" policy requires consistency and resolve. "Being tough as nails has produced good environments," says Seattle landscape architect Richard Untermann. The best places have the stiffest rules and not, incidentally, the most appealing and prosperous streetscape.

Ban drive-ins. Build wide sidewalks for walkers and scenic paths for bicyclists. Keep parking to a minimum. Eliminate curbcuts, which let cars intrude on the sidewalk. Place trees along the way. Station the bollard, an architectural post, to keep out traffic. The bench, the fountain, sculpture provide respite. Eradicate the car-filled setback for stores. Place stores below, apartments above. Untermann describes his forward-thinking state as a place where "you haven't an apartment that doesn't have a ground floor with mixed uses." Such amenities, and such approaches harking back to zoning changes, can fit into what Untermann calls a "centers strategy." It asks, "How do you do things that are relatively easy?" Microcosmically, of course. One day at a time. Macrocosmically, too, in a ten-year scheme orchestrated both locally and regionally, privately and politically. Rezoning, Main Street programs, palliatives of design, broader planning—all count. "If we do a number of things right, it will happen," Untermann maintains. And, in Seattle and other cities it has done so.

The River Beats the Road

Nowhere did highways hit cities harder than where the river or sea met the road. The water's edge, where ships landed and city life began, was split from its urban origins by concrete, steel, and onrushing traffic. In recent years, however, cities have begun to capitalize on their waterfronts as shared space for amusement and recreation, as well as sites for industrial life. Crowd-pulling "blue spaces" like Pike Place Market in Seattle or riverside promenades like

New York's Battery Park multiply. Seventy-five waterside revivals fill the encyclopedic record of renewal compiled by Dick Rigby and Ann Breen, consultants and founders of the Waterfront Center, who have displayed prizewinning rejuvenations in *Cities Reclaim Their Edge.*

"I say to people, 'What's up on the waterfront is not unlike the City Beautiful movement,' " says Breen. Old riverside towns from Pine Bluff, Arkansas, to Hudson, Wisconsin, link walkable waterfronts to their historic center and revitalize both. Cincinnati is making a heroic effort to undo the quintessential spaghetti highway junction by the Ohio River. Faced with a grim beachfront, Fort Lauderdale has planned their waterfront design to pull back the cars and stud the sidewalks with palm trees and undulating walks. "Someday we're going to look back and see this great investment in parks and public grounds," says Breen. "You name it. It's all over."

"If I could swim in the Hudson, I would not need to go by train and bike to Long Beach, or Jones Beach by car, or Bermuda by plane," as economist and bicycling activist Charles Komanoff puts it. If we could have more of the urban swimming pools of the Scandinavians, the tree-lined canopies of European boulevards, the well-kept parks found throughout the Continent, along with the European core of commitment to infrastructure, and if we could support, as Europeans do, institutions of education and well-being in the name of equity, we would draw the nation back from the abyss carved by the car culture.

Despite their wear and tear—and the fear of social evils—older neighborhoods are often a mere step away from achieving the vitality and mobility of the past. To address their physical state alone does not suffice, however. Clearly, we need to address the myriad ills of a society in which the affluent have left "The Other" behind in the flight to bedroom communities. We need guardians in the political process to act as advocates for education, health, and quality of life for all races and incomes, equity in our national policy as well as in our transportation practice.

These boulevards of broken dreams do have prospects and could figure in that policy. However scattered and sidewalkless, the old arterials could mimic Main Street. Just off these bedraggled but transit-friendly streets of an earlier America lie the compact neighborhoods and congenial homes whose owners can still amble to school, to the library and other civic buildings, to services and stores. Here, new immigrants generate vibrant and walkable neighborhoods. The urban shops of a Latino open-air market along downtown Los Angeles's Broadway, of Asian markets in San Francisco, or of Russian ones in Brighton Beach show the life brought by a new wave of immigrants fighting for survival on too often vehicle-dominated streets. As planner Allan Jacobs says in *Great Streets,* streets are made for "symbolic, ceremonial, social and political roles, not just those of movement and access." Three decades ago, in the dark days of an earlier auto age, San Franciscans voted to spend $24.5 million on Market Street. Today, a new trolley skirts a revived boulevard. Elsewhere, tree plantings and street narrowings, the mending of storefronts, and the restoring of gaps have salvaged boulevards from their car-based concessions.

Such good streets are inevitably secure streets. The human presence has created the essential "eyes on the street," and neighborhoods now contribute the community patrols and formal protection to supplement the improvements in lighting and other physical upgrades that make people feel safe. To be sure, feeling safe, being centered, demands all our resources. Urban issues to insure the centering that lessens the grip of the automobile are complex and go far beyond the physical, ranging from racism and crime to lack of education and the ills of poverty, drugs, and multigenerational destitution. Like the revamping of cities themselves, these issues must be addressed and corrected. They demand social, cultural, and educational attention that has long been lacking.

Cities have already revived to counteract the negative stereotypes. The city of play and amenity draws Americans to downtown on rail and foot to sip and loll and indulge in zones for walking. The First Nights that draw transit riders from the periphery to celebrate the New Year, the celebrations and ethnic festivals make cities a lively recreation. The longstanding cultural and educational institutions of such communal "living rooms" on the large and small can revive our centers, excluding the car. Such places more than fulfill the pure commercial maxim of the realtors: "location, location, location." That is what centering with strong public transportation does. Main Street is more than almost all right. It is home for the individual mobility that allows those who cherish true freedom and quality of life to patch together an America no longer in servitude to the automobile.

The De-Paving
of America

THE EARLY SPRING still chills the air as Tom Samuels strides through North Toronto's narrow Balliol Street. The lanky pedestrian advocate seems more at home walking these neighborhood streets than in the office of the Better Transportation Coalition, where his restless foot taps up and down as he charts the work that has made his agency an ombudsman for the city's citizens. Through the coalition, and his own energy, Samuels drew 1,500 citizens to an antiroad rally not long before my meeting with him. From the coalition's small, packed office along the trolley line, he helped champion large-scale transportation planning and a concern for safe streets.

This day, however, the grassroots activist is here to show the results of the door-to-door politics that changed one neighborhood raceway into a model for controlling cars. "Traffic calming" is the name for this work of taming a thoroughfare to make a crossable road. The concept, now common, was developed in Holland a generation ago, based on the principle that the street belongs to more than cars. The Dutch *Woonerf,* literally "living yard," describes the shaping of the streetscape to make it the province of human beings.

By whatever name, traffic calmers—pedestrian advocates, planners, bicyclists, landscape architects—use design to debrutalize the road. By de-paving and seeding, by creating curves, bumps, and plantings, and by widening the sidewalk, they slow the pace of the moving vehicle. Dominance is returned to the walker.

One Street's Story

A match in dynamism to Samuels, Zynet Onen is a dark-haired attorney who, galvanized by the danger of her children's trip to school, marshaled her Toronto neighborhood and the political system to calm the street in her community by such means. Onen sits in her sunlit kitchen relating how she brought these skills to her neighborhood. It was a long saga of leafleting and persuading, and the morning wanes as she recalls the phone calls, the meetings, the letters, the after-work hours spent taming this space. Then we are off.

A walk through the pleasant, tree-lined neighborhood and we arrive at Balliol Street. The quiet is a testimony to the residents' success in disarming the road. Cozy English Tudor brick houses edge the street this late morning. We walk, passed by the occasional slow-moving vehicle. The traffic is light, the surroundings calm.

The residential street fighters did not simply barricade either end of the street to create a car-free zone. Neighborhood protectors here as elsewhere resist the urge to kick the car onto someone else's street. They espouse a policy of what Samuels calls "aggressive coexistence," aiming to one day reduce the motor vehicle's reign in the entire neighborhood. Calming a roadway is an art, not something accomplished by arbitrary decree.

Grass over a small section of road, plant a tree. Create a bend in the road to slow down speed by cutting off the driver's sight line. Swell the sidewalk out at corners. Set a median in the middle. Throttle movement at the entry where cars and people intersect. Surface the street with bumpy pavement. All are traffic calmers. Raise the road, and you have the speed table, or speed level; a less jarring intrusion than the speed bump, it is an encumbrance but not a threat to motorists. By such means Balliol Street's cheek-to-jowl residences and other neighborhoods are returned to the tranquility of their earlier origins.

Consider the street corner. The radius of its curve determines the speed of the automobile. A turning radius of fifteen degrees is the pedestrian advocate's norm, not the usual wide swoop of King Car. Surprisingly, parked vehicles are equally helpful to the pedestrian; they actually limit and slow passing motor vehicles. Short blocks are high on the agenda. The shorter the block, the easier for walkers to cross the street. Given long blocks, pedestrian advocates call for mid-block crossing places. And, of course, longer pedestrian lights.

The tactics to ease the pedestrian's way are as endless as the human imagination and range from the amenities of benches and light fixtures to the vigilante pothole, endorsed by those on private streets who want to keep out cars with rough roads. Historian Clay McShane writes that his father's recurrent attempts to keep the street in front of their home ill paved during his childhood gave him "an important perception of the functions of streets." Regard the car as a guest, not the owner, and the goal evolves. Honor the street as a public room—the shared and valuable resource of its inhabitants—and you make a transformation in a neighborhood or even a city.

For Tom Samuels, now head of Toronto's Safe Routes to School, traffic calming has broadened into an effort to enhance safe routes and create "eyes-on-the-street" neighborhoods for school children. "It's not only about redesign of streets, it's about designing better transportation." Samuels's latest strategy is the "walking school bus." No bus at all, but a band of parents was organized to go from door to door as guardians for the local school children, most of whom live under a ten-minute walk from their classrooms. Not only was the way safer, but the group trip also inspired a sense of community, Samuels says.

In Chicago's Edgewater neighborhood, the noise and pollution from the 100,000 commuters who swing through residential streets to avoid rush hour congestion on Lake Shore Drive and the surrounding arteries aroused another community effort. The lively ward whose close-packed housing holds a mix of nationalities and whose streets resound with seventy different languages worked through its alderman to slow drivers or discourage them from its streets. "Sometimes you have to force the issue," says Doug Fraser in the office of Alderman Mary Ann Smith. Rotaries and other devices were set up not to exclude but to inform, the planner says, to tell motorists that "there are children playing, there are people talking and walking on the sidewalk. You're going to have to show it some respect."

The Walkers' Movement

Though Europe is the source for the "de-vehicularization" movement, retrieving streets and downtowns from auto strangulation has an honorable history in America. Veteran urbanists like William Whyte and Bernard Rudofsky, author of *Streets for People,* have had a role in planning for pedestrians; Simon Breines and William J. Dean's *The Pedestrian Revolution* offered plans for streets without cars. The zeal with which pedestrian advocates follow these tenets recalls the early historic preservation movement. Spend a few days in Boulder at the Annual Pedestrian Conference, begun in 1980, and one hears the intensity in the crusade for lengthening the duration of stoplights, ending curbcuts, and widening sidewalks. As my stay in Secaucus revealed, the fervor of the stop-the-bulldozer movement resounds as these advocates blast the lack of pedestrian crossings and indict "WALK" lights that turn to an intimidating "DON'T WALK" too fast. Zealous walkers grow apoplectic at expressways, malls, and parking lots unapproachable by foot.

Whatever the device, wherever the place, pedestrian advocates increase. There are some twenty grassroots groups, allied as America-Walks, promoting walkers' rights. The Intermodal Surface Transportation Efficiency Act has installed one pedestrian-bicycle planner in every state, and a "ped-net" allows computer communication. The orange barricades I saw in Phoenix or the staple striped white lines on town and suburban streets no longer suffice. The work extends from Portland, Oregon, where Meeky Blizzard of STOP itemizes the range of bumps and vegetation for her "Skinny Streets" program, to Portland, Maine, modifying its first street.

Beyond fixing bad streets, pedestrian advocates try to plan ahead and prevent them from opening. WalkBoston, a group of activists for a foot-friendly city, stopped the hardtoppers from putting ten lanes between the downtown and the waterfront in its "Big Dig" project to bury the Central Artery. In its ongoing promotion of safety laws, WalkBoston's guide "Walkable Communities" sets a speed limit of twenty miles an hour for pedestrian comfort. "Walkers avoid high speed streets with good reason," the guide insists, since the majority of pedestrian fatalities occur on streets where vehicles move at thirty-five miles per hour or more.

Thirty million people use transit every year and everyone walks, the Surface Transportation Policy Project likes to remind us. While the Federal Highway Administration registers a scant 7.2 percent of the population as walkers, a more realistic accounting recognizes that most journeys include a walk; hence, most travelers are walkers. These walkers are looking to take back the street.

A Thread of Greenways

Moving at a veteran walker's clip through the city he helped shape on pedestrian principles, octogenarian Edmund Bacon, author of the classic *Design of Cities,* led me through a chilly Center City Philadelphia as I began this book. The man who called modern architecture "the great amputation" linked movement on foot to an even larger scale—the connections of parks and regional walking spaces that comprise a "greenway." A planner for half a century, Bacon worried that "people think in fragments, not wholes." Taking a holistic approach to city, suburb and countryside, a generation ago he developed the concept of the greenway.

At the time of our visit, in the early 1990s, such urban and suburban paths for bicyclers and walkers had won support from 72 percent of the population of Philadelphia, according to a Louis Harris poll. Greenways and trails for providing pleasure and mobility have proliferated. The eleven-mile suburban Minuteman Commuter Bikeway, heading west from Boston-Cambridge's red line Alewife stop to Bedford, typifies the history and purpose implicit in its name: here the commuter can supplant an automobile trip on the local scale with a bicycle ride. Elsewhere, projects range from easy walking or bicycling trips to grandiose visions of town-to-town, city-to-city hikes, both North and South and across the continent.

The legacy of Olmsted parkways is a model and the spaces designed by his firm still provide walkable routes in older cities and suburbs, literally in his Boston "Emerald Necklace" chain and metaphorically in the plans his sons' firm drew. The worn but viable green routes of early planners encourage new connectors, like Gwynns Falls Trail in Baltimore, to stretch into longer corridors for non-automotive commuters and weekenders. Commuters comprise more than a third of weekday users of the old Pinellas Trail near Florida's west coast and the Burke-Gilman Trail in Seattle. Similarly, Benton MacKaye's prototypical Appalachian Trail lives on along back roads and mountains from Maine to Georgia. Its urban descendants find its continuous band of wilderness an exemplar and work to make the trail usable for travel without a car.

The urban offspring of the Appalachian Trail, the East Coast Greenway, bills itself as "A Trail Connecting Cities," aiming to assemble a path from Maine to Florida. Formed in 1991 to link two-thousand-plus miles, the nonprofit organization has drawn a map of local urban, suburban, and rural trails already opened, with plans to connect them to new ones. The envisioned route through "the heart of cities" to existing greenways would encompass New York City's water edges, Boston's Minuteman trail, the edges of city rail, and the rural spaces of the group's own Kingston, Rhode Island, base. "We see this as the spine greenway," says Karen Votava, a former city planner of Manhattan's open spaces who runs the organization. An interurban parallel to the Appalachian Trail and an "emerald corridor," it would link with existing pieces of the Farmington Canal Railroad (Hartford), urban greenways in New York City through the Bronx, the National Scenic Historic Trail (Delaware to New Jersey), and Olmsted's Mall in Washington, D.C., eventually reaching Florida. The patched-together trail would provide mobility not only to hikers but also to elders and young roller bladers, wheelchair users, and equestrians. Says Votava, "It's really an alternate transportation system."

Crossing the continent east to west, the American Discovery Trail, another ambitious project, would complement this vision to "make trails for all Americans within fifteen minutes." Myriad local trails would tie into a "super national scenic network," says Tim Provencal in the American Hiking Society's Baltimore headquarters. The group's dream of the nation's first cross-country foot route takes the Lincoln Highway's scheme of spanning the nation from sea to shining sea and uses it to slow the pace and change the focus of American movement.

Everywhere, greenway mileage accumulates, from St. Paul's Mississippi River edge and the Texas Trails Network to San Francisco's Bay and Ridge trails. Boulder's longstanding pedestrian and bicycle route, which winds through a graceful landscape in the city, has heirs across the country in the remakes of once dreary routes by rivers, roads, or railroad tracks. The trend for small towns to make plans and install trails grows, from Connecticut's greenways to Raleigh, North Carolina, Cheyenne, Wyoming, and smaller towns.

Bicycle paths multiply along streets as well as the trails cross-country. "Bicycle facilities, both on- and off-road, continue to expand from Fairbanks to Fargo to Fort Lauderdale," says Massachusetts bicycle coordinator Josh Lehman. Bicyclists are being afforded more space to operate safely in a growing number of communities and along rural roads, too. Florida especially has become "trail-friendly." Michigan, home of the car, "is way up there in miles of rail trails," he says. Rails-to-Trails has almost $700 million of conversions through ISTEA funds to be matched 80 to 20 percent by localities. This organization has already converted more than 750 lines of former railroad track to paths and corridors across the country, thereby saving open space and sometimes providing new routes of mobility. For all their sad commentary on mistreatment of the nation's passenger trains, such pedestrian and bicycle linkages can, and have, changed the pattern of land use in our suburbs and our cities. Hopefully, a pattern of rails with trails could bring the best of both worlds.

Two Wheels at Work

The most zealous of the human-power champions to cross these paths and trails are the bicyclists. Their number is legion, and their politics diverse, from the kids with their first two-wheelers to radical activists. Political, polemical, indefatigable, they pedal double-time in the auto-free cause. Lodged together in planning departments with advocates for pedestrians, the bicyclists sometimes compete, sometimes share their too slim funds to make the landscape fit for human mobility. Like the bus and rail partisans scrapping among themselves, both should be well-funded allies. The 12 million bicyles regularly bought every year—equal to the number of motor vehicles—offer a legion for balanced transportation. "One Less Car" says the 1970s motto of Transportation Alternatives.

Bicyclists everywhere have energized the volunteer world with their "pedal power." Launched in 1992 to emulate the swarms of bicyclists who overwhelm the roads in China, the colorful crusaders, under a banner reading "Critical Mass," swarmed up San Francisco's Market Street to show their might. The phrase has spread to other cities, where bicyclists infuse their own streets with a "critical mass" of riders and an array of guerrilla tactics. In Austin, bicyclers took over the streets from cars, creating a fracas that led to arrests. In Edmonton, Alberta, three protesters were hauled off in a paddy wagon when a hundred residents, cyclists, and environmentalists blocked the opening of a scenic road that had been closed to car commuters.

Bicyclists use less incendiary tactics to push for sustainable transportation and public space. Activists in Washington and other major cities make their impact felt in both pro-bicycle and anti-automobile activities. Washington's Auto-Free D.C. and New York City's Transportation Alternatives work to free their cities' park systems from cars. Avid bicyclists head the list of grassroots crusaders against the automotive infrastructure and for auto-free zones. They fight to rope off lanes on roads and work to secure separate bikeways and greenways. In community meetings they agitate for admission to mass transit and for lockers at park-and-ride lots; in offices they push employers to provide showers and locker space. And their influence grows. Every bike rider not only removes a car from the road but also frees a park-and-ride space; a bike rack costs $250, a parking lot $20,000 per space to build.

Between the endless road of the automobile and the limited span of the walker, the bike route could be the lane of first resort for commuters or college students. Using bicycles for errands and visits—for the 49 percent of trips three miles or less—could bring mobility to riders and free up seven-eighths of the parking space of an automobile. Car-free, livable college campuses from those at Santa Barbara and Davis, California, to those of the Midwest are positive proof of the benefits of miles switched from horsepower to pedal power.

Even "pickup truck" country has its share of avid bicyclists, says Bud Melton, president of Texas Trails Network and a bicycle shop owner who has worked with leaders in Dallas to secure trails and connectors to local streets. Allied with equestrians in the state that has the highest population of horses per capita, the activists have facilitated trails to shopping centers, schools, and libraries. "Our region is going through a metamorphosis," he says.

Bicycling magazine begins its list of "The Best Cities for Cycling" with this thought: "In biology, an indicator species is a group of plants or animals whose health foretells the vitality of the surrounding environment." Bicyclers are indeed an urban indicator. Toronto heads the list, with 7 percent of central city dwellers riding to work. It is a paltry number in comparison to cities outside North America but more than the 1 or 2 percent in the U.S. The top ten cities register miles of lanes and lists of ideas to encourage bicyclers: central bicycle stations in key locations (Portland, Oregon) and bicycle swaps (Tucson). Some cities win praise for even stronger measures: Eugene, Oregon, for reducing the car spaces required of builders, and Ottawa for replacing parking stalls with bicycle racks. Because of automobile congestion, Seattle falls under the heading "paradise lost," says the magazine. (Others say that automobile congestion promotes riding.)

John Dowlin, a founding father of bicycling advocacy ("when you keep at it, people call you that," he says) and the bicycle parking project coordinator for the Bicycle Coalition of the Delaware Valley, which he initiated, sees an expansive future for pedal power. "What the spinning wheel was for Gandhi and India, the bicycle could be for the world's cities," he says. Dowlin remembers the reply when he first proposed putting police on bicycles in the seventies. "Imagine trying to handcuff a guy and holding on with your legs," the police guffawed. Today, more than five hundred police departments have bicycles and each one replaces a car.

Save Paradise, Rip Up a Parking Lot

Taking back the street and gaining dominance for human mobility can mean shrinking streets and de-paving on the large scale, too. The urge to make places accessible to walkers may also involve digging up asphalt. Boulder, Colorado, and Burlington, Vermont, banished cars for walkers, and their longtime pedestrian malls survive. Born out of the desperation of the 1970s, others of the two hundred pedestrian zones planners installed have remained as ragtag as the depleted Main Streets they tried to revive. Some, like the pedestrian mall in Oak Park, Illinois, reintroduced cars, only to become an equally lackluster vehicular zone, suggesting that the failure was not in the car-free fad. Some new pedestrian-only places, like CityWalk and Las Vegas's Fremont Street, are not so happy hybrids; others have more promise and vitality.

Designers have shaped Miami Beach's pedestrian mall and Sacramento's car-free surface rail route. Weekend traffic bans liberate Cambridge's Harvard Square and Memorial Drive from traffic; New York's Auto-Free activists do so more intermittently with Central Park and Prospect Park. Simon Breines, an architect as well as the author of *The Pedestrian Revolution* of twenty years ago, hasn't relented in his labors. His latest blueprint to resuscitate the declining fortunes of Lower Manhattan calls for a people-first zone with wide sidewalks to create what he calls "Wall Street City."

The area around the White House qualifies as a pedestrian zone. After attacks on the White House frightened security forces, barriers were installed. Fears that roping off Pennsylvania Avenue would cause congestion never materialized. There was little impact on traffic (if you shrink it, they will go), and roller bladers, bicyclists, and walkers now use the space on weekends. Even the Secret Service has begun patrolling nearby streets on mountain bicycles.

Reclaiming the earth from pavement is a high priority. Builder

Richard Register, who coined the word "de-paving," did so at a pioneer garden in Berkeley, California. His parking lot in an Italian neighborhood transformed into a vegetable garden may be the best-known green space of its size in America. It was here that the proselytizing builder-writer launched his movement to dig up asphalt, and today, twenty years later, continues the work with de-paving the parking lot behind a housing project. The most heroic de-paving, however, may be in the smallest state in the nation. In withered downtown Providence, Rhode Island, officials chopped up acres of highway that obscured the Woonasquatucket River and restored its watery course. It was asphalt removal on a super scale. Poised at the foot of the city's historic capitol, architect William Warner's Waterplace Park has revived the area.

For all the grandeur of ripping up highway, the sum of rescuing small parts of city sidewalk can be more impressive. We are all walkers. We are better walkers when it is safer and easier to go by foot. If streets constitute 40 percent of downtown, they belong to us, the walking public. "The sidewalk is a far larger space than all the open space downtown," says urban designer Evan Rose, voicing the premise on which San Francisco installed a program to widen the walker's turf and improve downtown.

Standing beside a stack of the city's plans that materialized into "Destination Downtown: Streetscape Investments for a Walkable City," the planner explained how setting up design guidelines for sidewalk environments reinforces "public space as democracy." Here, with the four-way red light crossings known as "pedestrian scrambles," or "cluster crossers," the city has put people before cars. Their new Downtown Pedestrian Network and Downtown Open Space Networks improve the streetscape and enhance the path between tourist attractions like Chinatown and Market Street.

Bolstering walking, the ultimate human transportation, reinforces and is reinforced by all the other solutions. George Haikalis, who founded Auto-Free New York, looks to rail. "Of course, the ultimate traffic-calming carrot is a transit system," he says. But his mantra comes back to ripping up roads, not building them. "If you build it they will come. . . . If you shrink it, they will shrink. . . . If you tear it down, they'll disappear," he says.

De-Paving the Wilderness

Some road rippers not only aim to give human beings the right of way, but to give animals and the environment their place. The de-pavers who reclaim the most mileage live not in the cities or suburbs but in the so-called wilderness that sometimes seems equal parts roads and woods. The ROAD-RIP Alliance has taken on the charge of reducing roads through the wilderness, aiming to curtail the work of what may be the largest road-building agency in America, a quali-fication based on how many roads dissect national forests. Embattled road rippers keep their eyes on the Forest Service, whose turf ranges from the relatively small Finger Lakes region's 14,500 acres to the granddaddy Toiyabe National Forest, with 1.3 million acres overlap-ping Nevada and California. Altogether the Forest Service has 370,000 miles of road in 156 national forests. With 300,000 square miles of land, the Forest Services averages more than a mile of road per acre.

"Road truthing" is how the environmentalists and antiroad builders describe the struggle to make sure that such roads don't grow. To stop the invasion of the landscape, they stake out illegal roads and legislate against them, adding another ecological notch on the belt of those who would free the asphalt nation. "Not One More Road," says the T-shirt of the Alliance for a Paving Moratorium. Stop paving, says the alliance's director, Jan Lundberg. "We must go backward and forward to no car," he says.

OPPOSITE: "Pay at the pump" may be a hard sell, but this and other ways of charging the driver for car costs could help bring an end to motor vehicle de-pendency. Other industrial nations have achieved a far more balanced system than has the United States by adopting such methods. (Photo: Sol Libsohn. Photographic Archive at the Ekstrom Library, University of Louisville)

Righting the Price

WE ARE NOT only stuck in traffic, we are stuck in spending money that promotes more of the same. By underpricing and oversubsidizing the automobile, the highway and sprawl, we have made this lifestyle the overwhelming option and diminished the alternatives. History has shown us how the government's bankrolling of car costs and car-based land use has made the automobile look economical and become essential. Our subsidies, not only ourselves, have ruled.

So it is that people are *not* "voting with their gas pedals," *not* victims of a born-to-lose "love affair," *not* opting for exurban flight out of pure passion or even a clear preference. They are responding to a rigged market. They are reacting to price supports for ring roads, beltways, and free parking, responding to taxes and infrastructure that promote far-flung highways and suburban homes. "Driving's not just a free lunch," says one activist, "it's a free lunch you're getting paid to eat." And whether through selfishness, ignorance, or indifference, we devour our landscape and cityscape, aggravate our lives, and destroy our environment.

We know that every year we "invest" $25 billion of federal taxes in auto-dominated transportation. Add to this the amount from state and local agencies. We have seen the direct costs and indirect ones, the incalculable sums spent in the wrong way, in the wrong place, for the wrong way of life. It is time to price them correctly—to right the imbalance toward sustainable transportation.

We have seen the true costs for our lives behind the wheel; we know the folly of rebuilding roads to breed more traffic. We need to do the tabulating for every project as Worldwatch did. These environmental watchdogs looked to Eugene, Oregon. They calculated that $10 million spent in highway money for a parkway there might go to commuter bicycles equipped with baskets, lights, locks, helmets, and rain gear for the ninety-three-thousand citizens of the city who were more than eleven years old. Or that the $300 million for a new interchange to be built on an interstate highway in Springfield, Virginia, could instead build two thousand off-street paved bicycle paths in urban areas.

Extend these figures. Calculate that the same number of people who spend an hour driving sixteen lanes of highway can travel on a two-track rail line. Consider that a subway train uses one-sixth the energy per passenger used by a single driver in an automobile, while cutting pollution costs. Then broaden the comparisons. In its campaign against raiding transit funds, Orange County, California, used a cost-benefit equation to determine public transit's savings. County officials estimated, for example, that depriving the elderly of vans could put them in nursing homes at $35,000 a year per person.

We need to make such calculations, to develop that awareness. We need to change our mindset and reset the cash register. Remember the quote "We 'invest' in highways. We 'invest' in airports. But we 'subsidize' trains"? More than simply remember, we should alter it. Officials attack rail and other public transportation for "losing money," when, in fact, these civic necessities no more lose money than schools and police. Never should we accept the phrase "money-losing public transportation" without considering the costs of sprawl, of pollution, of congestion, of commuting—of the money-losing car. We know what should be done ("for mass transit need mass"), but how to do it is more difficult.

Making Money Talk

Standing before an audience concerned with repossessing the auto-centric society, transportation planner Jeffrey Zupan was pessimistic. "What then can you do in the suburbs?" he asked. Build out? Just try it, he said. Use infill and new zoning? Maybe. Connect the dots? Not over the dead bodies of the NIMBYs.

You can change travel behavior, however, he declared. You can put transit, walking, bicycling in place slowly, Zupan went on more optimistically. It's a matter of "pricing."

"Money," said Zupan, "talks."

Money does talk. Just how loud is the sticker shock? Given the truer accounting presented earlier—the personal cost of $6,000 per car per year, plus a cost to society beyond $3,000—how do we change? How can we stop paying to send developers outward from the walkable center? How can we charge more to the motorist who pollutes than to the one who doesn't contribute to dirty air? How, in sum, do we change the "stop" or "go" signs of public policies that benefit the car culture?

The gas tax, now at an all-time low in real dollars, is the first thought that comes to most Americans. "If I were the dictator of the world I would raise the price of gas," says one carbuster. With gas cheaper in real dollars than it was two decades ago, America's petroleum taxes don't even make a semblance of paying the car's way. While cheap U.S. gas encourages driving, in Europe, Canada and Australia motorists pay $2 to $4 in taxes per gallon, restraining driving and boosting the health of cities and economic well-being. Combine true pricing with good transit and you lessen car dependency.

In Europe, high gas taxes are the approach of first resort. In America, however, such taxes have been the argument of first reproach in the political arena. The trust fund built with money from the gas pump remains the golden piggy bank for the highway. Yet, the gas tax need not remain a political sacred cow. When California charged motorists ten cents more a gallon for cleaner gas, the complaints were few. If that ten cents went to mass transit, it would do more good. "The principle is simple: an increase in the gas tax is not an increase in taxes but in the fee for using the highways," writes John E. Hirten, executive director of RIDES for Bay Area commuters in San Francisco, put it aptly. "Freeways are not free." Many agree.

There is a constituency that deplores the money spent on the military to support oil wars, that laments environmental mayhem, that grieves for farmland lost and city land deserted, that worries about the excesses of the auto age. Conservatives and liberals alike, these people are not insignificant in number. Money wasted on welfare for automobiles is a nonpartisan concern.

The issue is social marketing, raising consciousnesses. If increasing the gas tax sounds untenable, is it more implausible than giving funds to dig Chrysler out of an early grave? In the late 1970s, the idea of offering a tax credit to restore old buildings was considered wacky. The slow and painful installation of such tax credits by the Rehabilitation Investment Tax Credit of 1978 spurred the salvation of segments of our towns and cities. A revolution occurred, or an evolution: it took time but it changed. Is raising the gas tax a more extreme measure than mandatory recycling, a runaway success in many communities, or environmental and preservation regulations that have changed the physical and political landscape? Sea changes do occur: antismoking, civil rights, the women's movements—the list is long.

Funneling Funds

The jobs, jobs, jobs rationale for the highway no longer suffices in the face of short funds and the traffic that roads generate. Fees that transfer money to public transportation undercut the automobile, and communities may vote, and have voted, funds or bond dollars for mass transit and levied a sales tax on its behalf. In 1989, San Francisco voters approved Proposition B, authorizing spending sales tax money for transportation projects and establishing the Transportation Authority of the City and County. The Downtown Pedestrian Project got money from this source to fix the streetscape. St. Louis keeps voting money for its thriving light-rail. Whatever supports mass transit and walking to it eventually reduces car ridership.

The pay-as-you-go promoters have many means of forcing the car to pay its own way. Congestion pricing, for one, has strong supporters. The report "Curbing Gridlock: Peak Period Fees to Relieve Congestion" from the Transportation Research Board consists of many volumes. Exponents argue for charging more on roads and bridges during peak periods of congestion, i.e., during rush hours. The technology exists to do the job smoothly. According to a Strategies Unlimited report, by 2004 more than a third of road tolls will be collected electronically. Such fees send motorists to drive at other times and places, or not at all, say economist Anthony Downs and others. The Federal Highway Administration has funded five pilot programs to see how they work. Never mind pilot studies. When Singapore installed the system more than a decade ago, congestion was relieved and pollution with it.

Then there are the odometer optimists. Their position is that the more vehicle miles traveled, the more money should be paid. A surcharge of a nickel a mile would cut the car's travel 10 percent, and hence its smog, all the while reducing congestion 30 percent, the Environmental Defense Fund has calculated. The vehicle-mile penalty lays blame in the right place: the car is pollution, congestion; driving is the problem, is its message.

Then there are horsepower penalizers. They argue for a tax based on the automobile's size. Let the gas-guzzlers, those hypertrophic energy hounds that consume more, pay more. Hence, we could at least reduce the number of oil gluttons, the Mercedeses, the muscle cars, and make all cars pay their way. A parallel carbon tax, based on the amount of carbon dioxide from the burning fuel, was proposed at the Earth Summit in Rio de Janeiro in 1992. Pricing by weight and distance works well. It could penalize trucks, which do ten times the damage done to roads by the automobile. By recording their weight and mileage at inspection stations, we could charge them fees that represent the subsidies they receive, thus easing road costs and benefiting freight rail.

There are many means of reducing driving. In New York City, according to one estimate, a comprehensive roadway pricing system that included smog fees, a weight-distance tax, congestion fees, higher gasoline taxes, and other fees and fines could reduce the 18 billion miles driven there each year and raise as much as $12 billion annually. Electronic toll collection could raise $75 million on the bridges, now free, spanning the East River and $300 million on those over the Harlem River. In the future, motor vehicles could be equipped with pollution monitors that record their exhausts, ring up carbon monoxide discharges and collect smog fees. Cameras and sensors at toll booths could note the miles driven so as to establish weight-distance charges. Highways with imaging could bill cars and the even more injurious trucks for the abuse they inflict on the road. Until such sensors are developed, officials could measure emissions or calculate weight-distance at test centers that give inspection stickers.

There are many ways to shortchange the car at the cash register. A report for the California Transit Association proposed a registration fee. Even small solutions can nibble away at the problem. The list is long—whether paying through annual excise taxes and registration fees or paying at the gas pump; whether charged by the mileage driven or at the toll booth. Stop subsidizing cars and solo driving goes down and alternatives emerge. End highway building and mass transit advances in central cities.

If we have the will, the devices to reprice the automobile can and will follow. To switch funds from motor vehicles to alternate means sounds heroic, but the Intermodal Surface Transportation Efficiency Act made a modest start. Adding toll charges to highways or bridges and spending the money on congestion-relieving services like mass transit also has precedents in, say, San Francisco and New York. So, too, tolls on old highways (forget building new ones) could be collected and reapportioned for mass transit, and even non-toll roads could charge their users. Some agencies craft ingenious linkages, like the Congestion Mitigation and Air Quality program run by the Department of Transportation and the EPA, which gives Rhode Islanders free public transit when high ozone levels are anticipated. There are many scenarios to eliminate auto dependence and enhance the environment.

"There are hardware and software treatments," says historian Kenneth Jackson, author of *Crabgrass Frontier.* "Any tax has to be equitable; it has to hurt the very people who are doing most of the driving," he goes on. "We say we believe in a free market. If you really believe in the free market, let's do it. If we have a ball game, and traffic comes, and we police it, let's charge it to the car, not the property tax, the way we do now." Examine every activity for its hidden—its automotive—financial exactions and make the buyer pay. "Unbundle car costs," is how Charles Komanoff and Brian Ketcham sum up these processes. Separate the car costs into the sorts of injury inflicted. Give reparations for highway damage to communities. The solutions are numerous. The equitable and economical way is to assign the costs. Market-based and specific, full-cost pricing is the way.

"Least-cost" transportation planning is the phrase from the electric utility industry gaining currency. It means giving more money to people for reducing demand than by adding highways. In states like California and Washington, the process works like this. Chokeville faces a bottleneck, the usual suspect: too much traffic to get from here to there. This time, though, a balance sheet is put on the table. On one side, the cost of building a bridge or widening a road is assigned a dollar figure. The total includes not only construction costs but also the environmental, social, and other costs arising from the trips the facility will generate in the future. On the other side is a list of other ways to go: "transportation demand management," in the jargon, or "management options," as economist Todd Litman puts it in his comprehensive *Transportation Cost Analysis.* The list of options is long, from assisting bicycle riding and walking to installing pricing mechanisms like the tolls discussed here. The community agrees on the numbers to assign to each cost on each list and then makes a choice.

Litman frames the congestion-cost question this way:

If you ask people, "Do you think that traffic congestion is a significant problem that deserves significant investment?" most would probably answer yes.

If you ask them, "Would you rather invest in road capacity expansion or use lifestyle changes, such as increased urban density and more use of walking, bicycling, car pooling, and public transit, to solve congestion problems?" a smaller majority would probably choose the road improvement option.

These are essentially how choices are framed by conventional transportation plans.

"But," he goes on, "if you presented a more realistic description of choices by asking, 'Would you rather spend a lot of money increasing road capacity to provide only moderate and temporary reductions in traffic congestion,' " thus increasing personal, municipal, social, and environmental costs and urban sprawl, or would you like to create a public transportation system over the next few decades to avoid these problems? "the preference for road building would probably disappear."

Where might our transportation money go? Anyplace, from land-banking zones to stay available for mass transit; to calming streets or subsidizing transport for poor communities. The money saved by the public transportation system of Curitiba, Brazil, with its much-admired designated bus lanes, has helped build an opera house and civic buildings in this model community.

Government Angels

The Intermodal Surface Transportation Efficiency Act (ISTEA), heralded for switching money from roads to public transportation, has dipped into the Highway Trust Fund, created to feed only the car and the road. The 50 percent of federal funds that the act allows localities to transfer to nonhighway uses, however, is too small. We should have total choice of where our transport dollars go; public transportation options should equal—if not far outweigh—private ones. Let Congress allow more swaps; let *us* do more to push Congress to do so. Metropolitan planning organizations, now theoretically empowered to shape balanced transportation designs, need their hands strengthened. The planning principles of the act need bolstering from state to state. On the local level, where the road fighters are noisiest, we must also have more states with mini-ISTEAs, emulating the flexibility of Maine's Sensible Transportation Policy. Transferring highway money to other options, that state promotes alternatives to the road. Kicking the tires of the highway culture is a must. Citizen activists must mix a range of gestures from organizing communally and acting politically, to initiating lawsuits and agitating visibly, which can effect a change in road building.

We must put a dollar figure on what the highway costs. A life cycle costing on capital projects like highways would show how much really comes out of our pockets and goes into roadbuilding. Long-term costs, not just for construction, should go into our reckonings, like the nutrition labels on the cereal box. Overcome the throwaway ethic that makes traffic engineers build new roads at double time, while we neglect the infrastructure we have. A cost-benefit analysis should take the long view and add the price of operations, maintenance, and congestion imposed on other transportation systems over their lifetimes, not just at their installation.

Take the price of parking. With 95 percent of Americans who drive to work parking at no cost and 99 percent of those taking all other trips given a free space, charging for parking is essential. Add the fact that shoppers who pay for parking tend to walk more and the solution is obvious: charge for or limit parking spaces. Take away this car perk.

No one says that it will be easy. Grown congressmen set a new standard for tantrums, even columnist George Will observed. After "acrimonious debate they voted against doing away with their special parking privileges at (Dulles) National Airport, 53 to 44." Why shouldn't we hold downsizing politicians accountable for their parking subsidies?

As he sat in the massive Department of Transportation building, Fred Williams of the Federal Transit Administration pondered the parking spaces given to Washington employees and shook his head. "Here we are spending billions to give us clean air, and here we are giving away free parking." By and large free to employees, the true cost of parking those cars is $10 a day. And the Internal Revenue Service requirement that every dollar of free employee parking over $165 a month be taxed as regular income confirms this.

"Cashing out" is another device for doing away with the free parking privilege. If drivers get a "free" parking space, actually worth so many dollars, then nondrivers are entitled to the value of that space in cash. We now pay $85 billion in benefits for free parking. That's $1,000 in free space for each of our 85 million employees. Let businesses give rebates to those who arrive on foot or bike. Let them pay for transit passes and the savings mount even more. Studies show that solo driving also goes down 20 to 40 percent. At four Los Angeles sites, a charge for parking shrank the number of solo drivers 26 percent.

Bankers Brake Against Sprawl

Not only can we stop subsidizing the car, we can stop subsidizing its roving habits. We must no longer underwrite the sprawl that demands driving and requires the space to park two or three cars. Instead, we must support compact communities. In 1995, California's Bank of America did just that. The bank and a coalition of environmentalists criticized the underwriting of exurban housing. They attacked homes located at the metropolitan fringes as nothing but a sieve for infrastructure money. Their solution was to make builders or homeowners in the outskirts pay a surcharge for living in spread-out, large-lot developments. The bank, green groups and low income housing champions itemized the damage done to wetlands, the increase in miles traveled, and the loss of farmland. They asked those who aided and abetted such a process to pay for the cost of sprawl. It was, observed Paving Moratorium director Jan Lundberg, "as if business people and farmers had donned Earth First! caps."

Proposals for breaks in mortgage insurance for home owners who give up their motor vehicles altogether have also surfaced. In the early 1990s, Jack Kemp, then secretary of the Department of Housing and Urban Development, proposed national and local banking policies that favored such mortgage benefits for families not burdened with the $6,000 annual cost of a car (and not adding $3,000 in external costs to the surrounding community). "Location efficient" policies grew based on the fact that the car-free home owner is more solvent. "Affordable housing is one-car housing," was one slogan. "No-car housing" should be the next step.

And why not institute other policies to favor trips within a downtown area, which cost about one-sixth as much as outlying trips? Or support policies that encourage a four-mile trip in the central city, the equivalent of a thirteen-mile trip through the suburbs? For that matter, what about subsidies for suburban home owners? The property tax and mortgage insurance deductions that make living cheaper for suburban or even vacation home owners than for central city renters are another sacred cow. It is time to consider the long-standing policy that established these inequities. It is essential to reverse disinvestment at the core, in nearby inner suburb communities and in vacant central lands. Clamp down on pricing policies that support so-called rim cities, metroburbs, or carburbs and you rewrite the biased transportation equation.

The ripple effect of such car-based, sprawl-breeding economic policies touches every approach to de-vehicularize America. Cities have long depended on the property tax to support services. As the worth of their housing and commercial stock has declined, their financial underpinnings have dwindled. Alternative approaches can and have been tried. Spurred by litigation, the states of Texas, Michigan, and New Jersey have ended old policies spreading taxes for the entire state to rich and poor according to their needs, not merely their wealth or location. The same legislative approach could be applied to police and fire and all social services.

For the center's survival, earmark money for infill, mixed-use zoning, or open spaces. Credit states and localities for land growth boundaries and compact communities. Restrict the decentrifugal force of developers by assessing fees for the services they require. Edward Blakely, of the University of California at Berkeley, proposes vouchers for those who move into cities and incentive zones for their development. Send Superfund money to sites in dense urban neighborhoods to bring industry downtown. Add housing and parks to the picture. The list is long. Funding a survival kit of educational, economic, racial, and social tools to restore the cores of America is a formidable task. We need to redress a half century of pushing aside housing for the ill-fed and ill-clothed sending their resources to green lawns for the affluent. We can have centers that are transit friendly, walkable, and less costly. We can live better. At the core of commitment to balanced transportation lies a commitment to national well-being on many fronts.

Is this extravagant? Perhaps on the surface. But in the long term, shifting the pattern of land use is a lucrative proposition. Already, some besieged communities have begun to charge developers for roads and infrastructure. Their ad hoc fees often merely send speculators or industrial developers shopping at the next town out. We need direction for states, regions, and the entire nation. This is where public policy, the political process, enters. It is federal policy that can keep the village post office in the center; it is state or regional planning that can reward builders for retrofitting walker-friendly places and not subsidize miles of road and infrastructure.

The financial options are myriad. Hand out a bonus for building on wasted brownfields and depaving asphalt ones; penalize building on greenfields. Reward reduced horsepower and charge for suburban lawn mower power. Pricing devices would further change the routine of auto-dependent Americans. Would Americans switch to public transit, to car pooling, to so-called trip chaining—running several errands on one route—or to some mix of these? Would they share a car in a car co-op as Germans do, or devise an American solution? They can decide.

Transferring money is a two-handed process. You cannot use the stick without feeding the consumer the carrot of better mobility or indeed more stability. While you take back from the blown-up budget of the car culture, you give to public transportation and level the playing field. Support mass transit, and its use rises. Conversely, deprive it, and it shrinks. New York transit advocates watched twenty-one years of rail improvement and ridership growth go down when the price of a token rose twenty-five cents to $1.50 in 1996. "Fouled in the fairness game" was one response. Not only transit, though, but bicycling, walking, breathing, living life as a stationary human being released from the assault of the automobile. It is time to use financial policies to do so, to make a car-free existence irresistible.

Anti-Asphalt Activism

There is only one way to ease the auto age into this new era. This is activism: a local activism looking out the front door; a regional and statewide activism attacking moribund highway-based plans; a national activism reaching to Washington to reduce the vehicle-first policies promoted by long-entrenched forces. And it is a personal activism, an activism that shifts and focuses our own lives to favor the foot, the bike, the public vehicle.

It is we who choose whether to run our odometers into the trillions, whether to ignore the diminishing advantages and rising outrages of the car culture. We can choose to do otherwise: to picket a congressman or call and write a legislator at any level; to fight a Wal-Mart or install a speed bump; to attend a community meeting or follow a state planning process. The routes are numerous and the stewards multiplying.

From weary commuters and shop-and-drop wheel spinners to environmentalists and preservationists, from advocates for walking and biking to local and national politicians, the community is wider than any of these groups realize as they travel in their own orbits. For all the might of the roadmongers, malcontents in our autocentric environment multiply. And we must list and enlist ourselves among them.

We must, also, examine the world around us and think through our lives and landscape. We must probe why we put the pedal to the metal in our two- and three-car households to get from our marooned homes to our stranded offices. We must question why we travel at all, why we run—or rather drive—in circles. One doesn't have to adopt a Luddite mentality or the "voluntary simplicity" of environmental purists to consider our restless lives and to wonder what accounts for America's belief scheme based on hypermobility. It is time to question the dream of mobility that has set us on an odyssey to nowhere. Where is it written that dwellers in the next century will find more contentment in an asphalt nation than in "a greened and pleasant land"?

Suppose we didn't have pockets emptied by car costs and a world sullied by their toxins. Suppose we didn't have traffic jams for the rich and cars on blocks and broken-down buses for the poor. Suppose we had an easier, fuller way to live. How better to live on traffic-calmed streets with grassy medians and leafed-over sidewalks, to stroll or bike down greenways, to traverse car-free Main Streets. It is time to create a living space for humans and a healthy planet habitat. It is essential to revive and absorb the walkable, bustling wonders of city life.

Not subsidy but substitution is the means to that often misused word "sustainability." To save our lives—our species—we must tread lightly on the earth. Like the scales of justice, our mobility money must be blind to the historic avarice of the car culture; our culture must consider the balance of motion and the stillness of stable surroundings.

I conclude, then, with the conviction that brought me to this book, that we must alter our notions of mobility—and our lives. The routes are many, but the long journey begins with a single step—the walker's step toward the political process in favor of foot power, not horsepower. "In balance" is the word of the transportation moderate. Balance is sensible, but achieving a balance has, in fact, failed in the glut of automotive responses; we need a radical reassessment lest the auto excesses of the better part of the twentieth century accelerate in the next.

This is not a proposal for nostalgia. It is a search for a creative forward motion to shape the way we transport ourselves and hence live. It is a quest for the connecting of lives released from mobile steel cages and a questioning of the notion that the American existence is "I move, therefore I am." Instead we must endorse the value and excitement of both passage and rootedness at the end of the rail, not the road. We need no longer find new frontiers off the exit ramp; we can find them on old lands renewed and human mobility restored. The way to stop the auto age begins with affirming the value of place and the role of transportation in easing our access to it. The mission is to evoke the very root of transportation in the word "transport" that can carry us to a loftier place and state of being.

Notes

Chapter 1: Bumper to Bumper

14 **8 billion hours a year we spend stuck in traffic:** Intermodal Surface Transportation Efficiency Act (ISTEA) video, 1994.

14 **200 million motor vehicles:** American Automobile Manufacturers Association, "World Motor Vehicle Data," 1995. Statistics show 146,314,296 passenger cars and 47,722,186 commercial vehicles (the latter including minivans, pickups, and sport-utility vehicles for personal use).

14 **of the day's 80 million car commuters:** Federal Highway Administration, July 1996.

14 **ten forty-hour weeks behind the wheel:** Conservation Law Foundation, August 1996.

14 **our three-plus daily trips on errands:** Federal Highway Administration, *Nationwide Personal Transportation Study,* 1990–92 (hereafter cited as NPTS).

15 **Seattle's traffic, for example, rising 121 percent in the past decade:** Institute for Transportation and the Environment, 1993.

15 **"ENJOY YOUR HOLIDAY!" it says:** *New York Times,* September 4, 1994.

15 **generated by increased roads:** Todd Litman, *Transportation Cost Analysis: Techniques, Estimates, and Implications* (Vancouver: Victoria Transport Policy Institute, 1996), pp. 5–16.

15 **public transportation (modal convergence):** Anthony Downs, *Stuck in Traffic* (Washington, D.C.: Brookings Institution, 1992).

15 **"actually slow things down":** Thomas Bass, "Road to Ruin," *Discover,* May 1992.

15 **quadruple in the next twenty years:** ISTEA video.

16 **"our highway 287 is a parking lot":** presentation at New York University conference "Beyond the Open Road: Reinventing Transportation Policy for the 21st Century," March 3, 1995.

16 **"number of licensed drivers":** Downs, *Stuck in Traffic,* p. 10.

16 **vehicles for every household:** NPTS. Figures show 36 percent of American households owning one car, 35 percent two, and 20 percent three or more, totaling 1.77 per household.

19 **attest to their imperative:** American Automobile Manufacturers Association.

19 of the Federal Highway Administration: *NPTS.*

20 from a "mistake": *Boston Globe,* December 12, 1992.

20 "security issue," said the company: *Boston Globe,* October 19, 1994.

20 ten to twelve thousand miles of travel per car per year: Federal Highway Administration, July 1996.

20 and one-fifth own yet a third: *NPTS.*

21 panic in New Jersey: Ralph Schoenstein, *American Health,* March 1994.

22 households own a car: Edward Wiener, statistician in the Department of Transportation, interview and fact sheets, July 18, 1994.

22 twice as many miles as the norm: *NPTS.*

23 hurt working women? Rosenbloom's study asked: Sandra Rosenbloom and Elizabeth Burns, "Do Environmental Measures and Travel Reduction Programs Hurt Working Women?" Drachman Institute for Land and Regional Development Studies, University of Arizona, October 1993.

23 a "national issue": Child Care Action Campaign newsletter, May–June 1995.

23 "a hungry person talks about food": Juliet B. Schor, *The Overworked American: The Unexpected Decline of Leisure.* (New York: Basic Books, 1991), p. 20.

24 internal combustion machine in the early twentieth century: Virginia Scharff, *Taking the Wheel* (New York: Free Press, 1991).

24 Mr. and Ms. America's comings and goings: David Elkind, *Ties That Stress: The New Family Imbalance* (Cambridge, Mass.: Harvard University Press, 1992), p. 272.

25 watched four times as much television: Peter Calthorpe, *The Next American Metropolis* (New York: Princeton Architectural Press, 1993), p. 9.

25 "probably the biggest losers": Clay McShane, *Down the Asphalt Path: The Automobile and the American City* (New York: Columbia University Press, 1994), p. 190.

26 Federal Highway Administration and the Justice Department: James Gerstenzang, "Cars Make Suburbs Riskier Than Cities, Study Says," *Los Angeles Times,* April 15, 1996; and interview with author Alan Durning, May 15, 1996.

27 "It was cold": National Public Radio, June 1, 1992.

27 there are many such prisoners: *Passenger Transport,* March 29, 1993.

29 get equal treatment: *CityWatch,* February–March 1993.

30 far too extreme: Peter Freund and George Martin, *The Ecology of the Automobile* (Montreal: Black Rose Books, 1993).

31 has no access: *New York Times,* September 3, 1995.

32 architect Daniel Solomon has put it: Daniel Solomon, *ReBuilding* (New York: Princeton Architectural Press, 1992), p. 19.

32 on snacks you can eat with one hand: *World Watch,* October, 1991.

34 **a pioneer plea:** K. H. Schaeffer and Elliott D. Sclar, *Access for All: Transportation and Urban Growth* (New York: Penguin Books, 1975).

Chapter 2: The Geography of Inequity

36 **"the 'have-nots' in our system":** "Americans in Transit: A Profile of Public Transit Passengers." newsletter of American Public Transit Association (APTA), Washington, D.C., December 1992.

36 **incomes of less than $15,000:** *Profile,* APTA newsletter, 1990.

36 **minorities among them.** Federal Highway Administration, *Nationwide Personal Transportation Study* (NPTS).

36 **those who . . . "take the early bus":** *The Nation,* September 16, 1996.

37 **"the 'loser cruiser,' " says planner Anton C. ("Tony") Nelessen:** Annual APTA conference, Boston, August 27, 1994.

37 **put it this way:** Surface Transportation Policy Project (STPP) bulletin, Washington, D.C., June 7, 1994.

37 **at one end to buffer bumps:** STPP, "Transportation, Environmental Justice and Social Equity Conference Report," 1995.

39 **"of the overlooked arts in economic development":** APTA, 1994 meeting.

40 **mobility are regressive:** Mark Allan Hughes, Ford Foundation, N.Y., "The New Metropolitan Reality: Where the Rubber Meets the Road," 1993.

41 **distributed through a region:** Sandra Rosenbloom, *Travel,* 1993, p. 8.

42 **households without an automobile:** "Getting There: Urban Transportation in Context," Susan Hanson in *The Geography of Urban Transportation,* second ed., ed. by Susan Hanson (New York: Guilford Press, 1995), p. 14.

42 **high entry fee to find work:** Jacob Weisberg, *New York,* May 30, 1994.

43 **such pokey trips:** APTA, *Profile* and *Access to Opportunity: Linking Inner City Workers to Suburban Jobs,* August 27, 1994; also, Charles Lave and Richard Crepeau. *NPTS,* "Travel by Households Without Vehicles," 1990.

43 **weighted to drivers:** Michael Cameron, Environmental Defense Fund, *Efficiency and Fairness on the Road: Strategies for Unsnarling Traffic in Southern California,* 1991.

44 **for every seven handed to the car:** APTA, 1996.

44 **more than a quarter century:** "The Importance of Cities to the National Economy," Elliott D. Sclar and Walter Hook in *Interwoven Destinies: Cities and the Nation,* ed. by Henry Cisneros, (New York: W. W. Norton, 1993), p. 19.

44 **buses which deposited them:** *New York Times,* August 8, 1994.

45 **sit on their stoops:** Ben Goldman, "Not Just Prosperity: Achieving Sustainability with Environmental Justice," report for National Wildlife Federation, December 1993; "Communities at Risk: Regional Transportation Issues in the Bay Area: The Concerns of Communities of Color and Low In-

come Neighborhoods," report for Environmental Defense Fund and National Economic Development and Law Center, March 1990.

45 **room at Harlem Hospital Center:** *Fordham Environmental Law Journal,* Spring 1994.

46 **maintain their community:** *Bronx News,* August 12, 1995.

48 **said D.C.'s** *Auto-Free News: Auto-Free News,* Winter 1994.

48 **the city's transit agency:** STPP, *Equity.*

53 **"Strides?"** Alan Pisarski, *NPTS.*

53 **these two last categories:** *Statistical Abstracts,* 1993.

Chapter 3: The Landscape of the Exit Ramp

56 **"itself is sculptured," he wrote:** *Historic Preservation,* May 6, 1994.

57 **"enjoyable," the architect imagined:** Frank Lloyd Wright, "Broadacre City: A New Community Plan," *Architectural Record,* April 1935.

57 **"No Slum. No Scum":** Frank Lloyd Wright exhibition, Museum of Modern Art, spring 1994.

57 **"of motorized humanity":** Richard Ingersoll, "Death of the Street," in *Roadside America: The Automobile in Design and Culture,* ed. by Jan Jennings (Ames: Iowa State University Press, 1990), p. 151.

58 **"the end of one's own motion":** Richard Sennett, *The Fall of Public Man* (New York: Vintage Books, 1978, paperback edition), pp. 14–15.

58 **acreage of Manhattan's grid:** Mark Fink, "Towards a Sunbelt Urban Design Manifesto," *Journal of the American Planning Association,* summer 1993.

59 **in his semantics:** Joel Garreau, *Edge City: Life on the New Frontier* (New York: Doubleday, 1991), pp. 1 and passim.

61 **the next two decades:** *Arizona Republic,* February 18, 1994.

61 **described the ring beyond "suburbia":** William Sharpe and Leonard Wollock, with comments by Robert Bruegmann, Robert Fishman, Margaret Marsh, and June Manning Thomas, "Bold New City or Built-Up 'Burb'? Redefining Contemporary Suburbia," *American Quarterly,* March 1994.

62 **classic definition in his** *The Image of the City:* Kevin Lynch, *The Image of the City* (Cambridge, Mass.: MIT Press, 1960), 19th printing 1988.

62 **Kunstler called the "geography of nowhere":** James Kunstler, *The Geography of Nowhere* (New York: Simon and Schuster, 1991).

62 **historic structures fell:** Jane Holtz Kay, *Lost Boston* (Boston: Houghton Mifflin, 1980).

63 **if they were nasty children:** Kay quoting William Whyte in the *Boston Globe,* July 30, 1989.

63 **a consumer of some seven spaces:** Kenneth A. Small, *Urban Transportation Economics* (Chur, Switz.: Harwood Academic Publishers, 1992), p. 82.

64 **to the actual structure:** Litman, *Transportation Cost Analysis,* 3.4-2.

64 "form follows parking requirements": Donald Shoup in Litman, *Transportation Cost Analysis,* 3.4-2. In terms of buildings, the garage to park the worker's car can require as much space as a floor of the office that houses its driver.

64 two-thirds in Los Angeles: Martin Wachs, "Policy Concerns," in *The Geography of Urban Transportation,* second ed., ed. by Susan Hanson (New York: Guilford Press, 1995), p. 270.

66 "storefronts," writes critic Richard Longstreth: Richard Longstreth, *Cultural Resources Management,* National Park Service, 16, no. 6.

67 "are the problem, it is cars": Solomon, *ReBuilding,* p. 43.

67 the "DNA of design": Anton C. Nelessen, American Public Transit Association, 1994 annual.

67 to drive and park the car: *Trainrider,* summer 1994.

69 "Architecture for speed reading": Chester H. Liebs, *Main Street to Miracle Mile: American Roadside Architecture* (New York: Graphic Society Book; Boston: Little, Brown, 1984), p. 39.

71 "turns the street into a utility": Calthorpe, *The Next American Metropolis,* p. 38.

73 designer Gregory Tung has observed: Gregory Tung, "Streetlights and Civic Imagery," *Places,* September 1992.

74 "an indefensible euphemism": Stanley L. Hart and Alvin L. Spivak, *An Elephant in the Bedroom: Impacts on the Economy and Environment* (Pasadena, Calif.: New Paradigm Books, 1993), pp. 69–70.

Chapter 4: The Road to Environmental Ruin

80 a "mobile source of pollution": Henry J. Glynn and Gary W. Heinke, "Air Pollution," in *Environmental Science and Engineering* (Englewood Cliffs, N.J.: Prentice-Hall, 1989), p. 47.

80 polluting life of the automobile: "Moving into the Future," *Environmental Forum,* July 8, 1991.

80 "the internal combustion machine: Union of Concerned Scientists, *Steering a New Course: Transportation, Energy, and the Environment,* 1991.

80 "threat in many U.S. cities": Natural Resources Defense Council, *Amicus Journal,* 1992.

80 concluded the following year: *Worldwatch,* February 1993.

81 temperatures were rising: There are many sources for this statement and the statistics following on environmental damage, including Union of Concerned Scientists, *Steering a New Course,* Steven Nadis and James J. MacKenzie, *Car Trouble* (Boston: Beacon Press, 1993); and various EPA and other scientific reports.

83 "doing business with us": Karen Browning, spokesperson for the Nature Conservancy, June 15, 1995.

83 **than to our homes:** "Driving Beyond the Limit," *Amicus Journal*, spring 1991.

83 **per square mile of wooded wilderness:** T. A. Pettigrew, transportation development engineer, National Forest Service, April 1995.

85 **poured off the drawing boards:** Intelligent Vehicle Highway Systems (IVHS) conference in Boston, spring 1994.

85 **a cover article on the electric car in *Audubon* stated:** Stephan Wilkinson, "The Automobile and the Environment: Our Next Car?" *Audubon*, May–June, 1993.

87 **climb the mount:** National Tire Institute, summer 1996.

88 **a firestorm of protest:** Hank Dittmar, "A Broader Context for Transportation Planning," *American Planning Association Journal*, winter 1995.

88 **hard to recycle:** A. T. Kearney, "Scrap Tire Use/Disposal Study, 1992 Update," for the Scrap Tire Management Council.

89 **legal procedures in Holtzman's office:** interview and clippings from *Santa Rosa Press Democrat* and *San Francisco Chronicle*, summer 1992 to summer 1993.

92 **economic injury cause disquiet:** *Transportation Research News*, July 8, 1993.

92 **"when it is snowing":** L. Evans, *Traffic Safety and the Driver* (New York: Van Nostrand Reinhold, 1991), p. 88.

92 **can we continue to deny:** Garrett Hardin quoted in *Amicus Journal*, summer 1993.

93 **to do their assessment:** Environment and Forecasting Institute, *The Economics of the Automobile*, 1994. Translated by Frank Goetzke.

94 **and are often left to rot:** Tire Institute, July 1996.

94 **four-fifths of this to motor vehicles:** Eno Transportation Foundation, 1994.

95 **"so we can pray":** *Boston Globe*, August 29, 1994.

95 **one-fourth of the pollution:** National Academy of Sciences, "Oil in the Sea," 1985.

95 **polluters as defined by the Clean Air Act:** *New York Times*, July 27, 1995.

95 **amount of fifty such spills:** Friends of the Earth, July 1996.

95 **into drains and sewers each year:** Conservation Law Foundation, *Conservation Matters*, summer 1994.

95 **water virtually forever:** "December Almanac," *Atlantic*, December 1993.

95 **40 percent of the nation's waterways:** Nadis and MacKenzie, *Car Trouble*, p. 17.

97 **"the main culprit in that rout":** Jim Armstrong, "Lost in Space," *Orion*, spring 1996.

97 **five years before 1991:** National Environmental Law Center, report to members, winter 1993.

97 **threat of environmental concerns:** "Impacts of Environmental Regulations on Highway Maintenance," *Transportation Review News*, July 8, 1993.

98 the lawn mower alone: *Boston Globe*, June 8, 1994.

98 billion cars was one prediction: *Worldwatch*, January–February 1994.

98 Action Institute, began: *Paving Moratorium Update*, May–July 1992.

99 motto for the first Earth Day: Charles Komanoff, "Transportation: Undoing Automobile Dependence," *The Workbook*, twentieth anniversary issue, summer 1994, published by the Southwest Research and Information Center in Albuquerque, New Mexico.

99 "is also only one of degrees": Norbert Wiener, "The Short History of Progress," in *A Documentary History of Conservation in America*, ed. by Robert McHenry and Charles Van Doren (New York: Praeger, 1972), pp. 148–49.

Chapter 5: Harm to Health and Breath

102 sophisticated level of testing: *New York Times*, January 23, 1994.

102 Dummies have no physiology: *Discover*, May 1996.

102 to the forty-three-thousand fatalities: National Safety Council, *Accident Facts*, 1995.

102 deaths per 100,000 population: Freund and Martin, *The Ecology of the Automobile*, p. 37.

103 "dying in a traffic crash": John D. Graham, *Auto Safety: Assessing America's Performance* (Dover, Mass.: Auburn House, 1989).

103 same days driving and getting into accidents: Hart and Spivak, *An Elephant in the Bedroom*, p. 61.

103 the gunshot deaths in the city: Alan Durning, author of study for the Federal Highway Administration and the Justice Department, interview.

103 responded to safety concerns: Graham, *Auto Safety*, p. 228.

103 by greater driver risks: Litman, *Transportation Cost Analysis*, 3.3–5.

104 less severity per 100,000 people: Charles Wright, *Fast Wheels: Slow Traffic* (Philadelphia: Temple University Press, 1992).

104 "injury to occupants": John D. Graham, "Injuries from Traffic Crashes: Meeting the Challenge," *Annual Review of Public Health*, 1993.

104 according to those who treat them: Dan Dyrek, physical therapist and researcher, assistant professor, Massachusetts General Hospital Institute of Health Professions.

104 called the traumas: Preston Lerner, "Road Kill," *Washington Monthly*, December 1993.

104 safety hardware unknown: *Transportation Research News*, March 4, 1995.

105 noise level should: Todd Litman, "Environmental Policies for Cities in the 1990s," OECD, 1990, 3.11–1.

106 increased employee turnover: Raymond Novaco, *Urban Ecology*, no. 1 (1995).

109 risen 8 percent: *Science News*, December 24 and 31.

109 only car-free locale in town: *Boston Globe,* January 9, 1995.

110 "severe lesions on their lungs": Greenpeace 92, "L.A.'s Lethal Air."

110 one national air quality standard: Environmental Protection Agency, *Clean Air Report,* November 4, 1993.

111 regularly exceed federal guidelines: Harvard University conference, "Clean Air and Public Health: Health Effects and Economic Costs of Air Pollution in the Northeast," July 11–12, 1995.

111 "Worse than thought": *Science News* 144, 1993.

111 leniency in enforcement: *Providence Journal,* September 24, 1994.

113 dizziness and stomach distress: "Implementing the Clean Air Act," *Conservation and the Environment,* September 20, 1993.

113 "assessing the least risk": Harvard conference "Clean Air and Public Health."

Chapter 6: The Cost of the Car Culture

116 "to get here": "The Green Alternative," presentation at *Boston Globe* conference "Shaping the Accessible Region," April 1994.

118 to hardtop the nation: Department of Transportation, Surface Transportation Policy (hereafter cited as STPP). Project newsletter, *Progress,* October 1994.

119 $30 million a mile for new roads: Tri-State Transportation Campaign conference "Beyond the Open Road" at New York University.

119 "high-priority corridors" and seven beltways: STPP, *Progress,* July 1996.

119 "Old think," says: STPP, *Progress,* August 1994.

119 a mile simply to repave: Conservation Law Foundation, *Road Kill.*

119 "last bits and pieces": *New York Times,* October 1, 1993.

119 roads across the continent: Department of Transportation, summer 1996.

119 more at a later date: Charles Komanoff and Brian Ketcham, "Win-Win Transportation: A No-Losers Approach to Financing Transport in New York City and the Region," July 1992, unpublished manuscript on file with KEA Associates, New York.

119 highway capacity slows traffic: *Discover,* May 1992.

120 "to the central district by car": Elmer Johnson, "Taming the Car and Its User: Should We Do Both?" bulletin of the American Academy of Arts and Sciences, November 11, 1992.

120 pay only 40 percent: James E. Vance, Jr., *Capturing the Horizon: The Historical Geography of Transportation Since the Sixteeth Century,* 2nd ed. (Baltimore: Johns Hopkins University Press, 1990), p. 525.

120 $6,000 in internal, or user, costs: Bureau of Labor Statistics, 1995.

120 external, or social, costs per car per year: Estimates go much higher; see below.

120 and operating of roads: Litman, *Transportation Cost Analysis;* and James J.

MacKenzie, Roger C. Dower, and Donald Chen, *The Going Rate: What It Really Costs to Drive* (Washington, D.C.: World Resources Institute, 1992).

120 **1.77 cars per household:** *NPTS.*

120 **$9,400 by some estimates:** Environmental Defense Fund, Berkeley.

121 **in hidden costs:** Komanoff and Ketcham, "Win-Win Transportation."

121 **60 percent of our road costs:** MacKenzie, Dower, and Chen, *The Going Rate;* Litman, *Transportation Cost Analysis,* p. vii.

121 **pays for the commute:** Donald C. Shoup, "Cashing Out Employer-Paid Parking," Department of Transportation, Federal Transit Administration, 1992.

121 **to finance the automobile:** Johnson, "Taming the Car and Its User."

121 **according to the Federal Highway Administration:** Litman, *Transportation Cost Analysis,* 3. 5–6.

121 **in lost productivity:** Komanoff and Ketcham, "Win-Win Transportation."

121 **from Chicago alone:** Report from the Chicago Metropolitan Planning Council, September 1994.

122 **gathering his resources:** Ivan Illich, *Energy and Equity* (New York: Harper and Row, 1974).

122 **to pay for a car:** *New York Times,* August 22, 1994.

122 **behind the wheel driving to the office:** Foy, "The Green Alternative," conference "Shaping the Accessible Region."

123 **four thousand manufacturing facilities and eighteen thousand dealerships:** American Automobile Manufacturers Association, "America's Car Companies."

123 **"driven to work":** David Morris, Institute for Local Self-Reliance.

123 **sold in the United States are imported:** MacKenzie, Dower, and Chen, *The Going Rate.*

124 **goes to the car:** Peter Miller and John Moffett, *The Price of Mobility: Uncovering the Hidden Costs of Transportation* (New York: Natural Resources Defense Council, 1993).

124 **at $50 billion annually:** American Lung Association, 1996.

124 **lost in 1995 alone from motor vehicle fatalities:** National Safety Council, 1995.

124 **on traffic management issues:** Conservation Law Foundation, *Road Kill.*

124 **going to the car:** Freund and Martin, *Ecology of the Automobile,* p. 10.

124 **fees like the property tax:** Charles Komanoff and Margaret Sikowitz, *Crossroads: Highway-Finance Subsidies in New Jersey,* Tri-State Transportation Campaign, April 1995.

125 **"True Cost of the Automobile":** Presentation and document at Annual Pedestrian Conference, Boulder, Colorado, October 2–5, 1991.

126 **fire department runs, and 16 percent of its paramedic services:** Hart and Spivak, *An Elephant in the Bedroom.*

126 apply to the Denver: Litman, *Transportation Cost Analysis,* 3.8–3.
126 San Francisco city budgets: Hart and Spivak, *An Elephant in the Bedroom.*
126 5 percent of its total budget: Komanoff and Sikowitz, *Crossroads.*
127 the next to pay the debt: Richard B. Norgaard, "Sustainability and the Economics of Assuring Assets for Future Generations," policy research working papers of the World Bank, January 1992.
127 part of our national wealth: *Newsweek,* May 16, 1994.
127 "too much chasing after wealth": Donald Worster, *The Wealth of Nature* (New York: Oxford University Press, 1993).
128 in Southern California: Michael Cameron, *Valuing the Health Benefits of Clean Air,* Environmental Defense Fund, 1994.
128 for wheat, corn, soybeans, and peanuts: bulletin of the Foundation on Economic Trends in Surface Transportation Policy Project, December 1992.
129 "making Japan more competitive": Walter Hook, publication of the Institute for Transportation and Development, summer 1994.
129 15 to 18 percent: Michael Replogle, *Transportation Conformity and Demand Management: Vital Strategies for Clean Air Attainment,* Environmental Defense Fund, April 30, 1993, p. 22.
129 more than five times as much gas: Replogle, *Transportation Conformity and Demand Management,* p. 23.
129 spend more for maintenance: John Pucher and Stefan Kurth, "Making Transit Irresistible: Lessons from Europe," "Passenger Transport," American Public Transit Association (APTA) newsletter, 1995.
129 the same amount spent on road construction: David Aschauer, "Transportation Spending and Economic Growth," APTA study, September 1991.
129 American infrastructure efforts: Felix Rohatyn, *New York Review of Books,* June 25, 1992.
130 half of which is imported: Eno Transportation Foundation, 1994.
130 trade deficit with Japan: Hook.
130 $56 billion this decade: David Burwell, *Environmental Forum.*
130 transportation, plus hidden costs. Eno Transportation Foundation, 1994.
130 opportunity cost, a minus: Mark Hanson, "Automobile Subsidies and Land Use," *American Planning Association Journal,* winter 1992.
130 a large land loss: Litman, *Transportation Cost Analysis,* 3.7–1
130 seven spaces apiece to move and park: Small, *Urban Transportation Economics* (UTE), p. 82.
130 $1,200 to that of an apartment: Patrick Hare, "Affordable Housing Is One-Car Housing," paper at Annual Pedestrian Conference, Boulder, Colorado, October 2–5, 1991.
130 to an $85 billion lure: MacKenzie, Dower, and Chen, *The Going Rate,* p. 10.
130 open space, and scenic values: American Farmland Trust.

131 **ten times the rate of cars:** *Asheville (North Carolina)* "Kokopelli News," spring 1994.

132 **that has grown by half:** Scott Bernstein of *Neighborhood Works,* Chicago, in STPP bulletin, June 7, 1994.

132 **shreds an acre for every built one:** Natural Resources Defense Council, "The Price of Mobility," October 1993, p. 52.

132 **built at 5 units to the acre:** Todd Schafer and Jeff Faux, eds., *Reclaiming Prosperity* (Armonk, N.Y.: M. E. Sharpe, 1996).

132 **drive twelve times as much:** G. Bruce Douglas, quoted in Elliott D. Sclar and Walter Hook, "The National Economy," in *Interwoven Destinies: Cities and the Nation,* ed. by Henry G. Cisneros (New York: Norton, 1993), p. 58.

134 **war among the states to end:** Melvin L. Burstein and Arthur J. Rolnick, "Congress Should End the Economic War Among the States," Federal Reserve Bank of Minneapolis, annual report, special issue, 1994.

134 **Georgetown, Kentucky, plant:** *New York Times Magazine,* September 5, 1993.

135 **that have reigned throughout history:** Elliott D. Sclar, "Back to the City," *Technology Review,* August–September 1992.

135 **to underused architecture:** Constance E. Beaumont, *Historic Preservation in Wisconsin: An Assessment of Issues and Opportunities,* State Historic Society of Wisconsin, May 13, 1993, pp. 8–9.

135 **slid 10 percent:** Constance E. Beaumont, *How Superstore Sprawl Can Harm Communities: And What Citizens Can Do About It,* National Trust for Historic Preservation, 1994, p. 104.

Chapter 7: Model T, Model City

142 **"Cities grow in splendour":** Charles Mulford Robinson, *City Planning* (New York: G. P. Putnam's Sons, 1916), p. 3.

142 **historian James J. Flink has observed:** James J. Flink, *The Car Culture* (Cambridge, Mass.: MIT Press, 1975), p. 40.

142 **social and physical landscape:** James J. Flink, "Three Stages of American Automobile Consciousness," *American Quarterly,* October 1972, vol. 24, no. 4, pp. 451–73.

142 **miracle of mass production:** John B. Rae, *The American Automobile: A Brief History* (Chicago: University of Chicago Press, 1965), p. 59.

142 **rose from 8,000 to 469,000:** Rae, *The American Automobile,* p. 33.

143 **in this arsenal of betterment:** Flink, *The Car Culture,* p. 40.

143 **9 million motor vehicles:** Philip P. Mason, *A History of American Roads* (Chicago: Rand McNally, 1967), p. 53.

144 **appalled planner Charles Eliot:** Mel Scott, *American City Planning Since 1890* (Berkeley: University of California Press, 1969), p. 23.

144 **on the plan for Minneapolis:** Minneapolis Plan by Hugh Ferris, 1916, photo in "Common Ground," University of Minneapolis.

144 **Philadelphia's streetcar franchises:** Lincoln Steffens, *The Shame of the Cities* (New York: McClure, Phillips, 1904), pp. 144–49.

144 **machine politicians downtown:** Steffens, *The Shame of the Cities,* p. 234.

145 **addressed urban issues:** Jon Alvah Peterson, "The Origins of the Comprehensive City Planning Ideal in the United States, 1840–1911" (thesis, Harvard University, 1967).

145 **one Chicago art historian:** Jon Peterson, "The City Beautiful Movement," in *Introduction to Planning History in the United States,* ed. by Donald Krueckeberg, Center for Urban Policy Research, p. 45.

146 **the colossus of the day:** Rae, *The American Automobile,* 65–66.

146 **"everywhere in the work itself":** Allan Nevins and Frank Ernest Hill, *Ford: Expansion and Challenge, 1915–1933,* vol. 1 (New York: Charles Scribner's Sons, 1957).

146 **the scenario seemed likely:** Nevins and Hill, *Ford,* chapter 1.

147 **improve their sanitation:** Joel A. Tarr and Gabriel Dupuy, eds., *Technology and the Rise of the Networked City in Europe and America* (Philadelphia: Temple University Press, 1988).

147 **in the decade before World War I:** Stephen B. Goddard, *Getting There: The Epic Struggle Between Road and Rail in the Twentieth Century* (New York: Basic Books, 1994), p. 19.

147 **opening hours of the auto age:** Howard Lawrence Preston, *Dirt Roads to Dixie: Accessibility and Modernization in the South, 1885–1935* (Knoxville: University of Tennessee Press, 1991).

148 *New York Times:* Clay McShane, "The Automobile: A Chronology," draft, 1996.

148 **Charles Beard cautioned in 1912:** Charles A. Beard, *American City Government: A Survey of Newer Tendencies* (New York: Century, 1912), pp. 243–444.

148 **or lay new ones, he suggested:** Scott, *American City Planning Since 1890,* p. 136.

148 **"A New Type of City House":** R. Stephen Sennott, "Chicago Architects and the Automobile," in *Roadside America,* ed. by Jennings, p. 169.

148 **with a built-in garage:** McShane, "The Automobile."

148 **wider lots to allow automobiles:** Edward Bassett in proceedings of the Seventh National Conference on City Planning, in Marc A. Weiss, *The Rise of the Community Builders: The American Real Estate Industry and Urban Land Planning* (New York: Columbia University Press, 1987), p. 61.

148 **one woman driver observed:** from *Suburban Life,* 1907, in John Stilgoe, *Borderland, Origins of the American Suburb* (New Haven: Yale University Press, 1988), p. 273.

149 Olmsted wrote back testily: letter to Charles G. Strater, Library of Congress, Manuscript Division, September 13, 1906.

149 said the script below the drawing: Thomas W. Brunk, *The Grand American Avenue, 1850–1920*, ed. by Jan Cigliano and Sarah Bradford Landau (San Francisco: Pomegranate Artbooks, 1994), p. 89.

149 was downed for a parking lot: Peterson, "The City Beautiful Movement," p. 151.

149 bothered residential streets: Robinson, *City Planning*, p. 223.

149 mounted antispeeding campaigns: Michael H. Ebner, *Creating Chicago's North Shore, a Suburban History* (Chicago: University of Chicago Press, 1988), p. 176.

149 the situation with alarm: Carole Rifkind, *Main Street: The Face of Urban America* (New York: Harper and Row, 1977), p. 223.

149 to be exactly the opposite: McShane, *Down the Asphalt Path*, p. 217.

149 built new railroad stations: Scott, *American City Planning Since 1890*, p. 139.

149 some planners warned: Scott, *American City Planning Since 1890*, p. 126.

149 automobiles overrun downtowns: Kenneth T. Jackson, *Crabgrass Frontier: The Suburbanization of the United States* (New York: Oxford University Press, 1985), p. 168.

149 the motorcar was the means: Bruce E. Seely, *Building the American Highway System: Engineers as Policy Makers* (Philadelphia: Temple University Press, 1987), pp. 38–40.

150 "from twenty miles away": Mark S. Foster, "Transforming the Use of Urban Space," *Journal of Urban History*, May 1979, pp. 371–72.

150 Society of Automobile Engineers organized: Rae, *The American Automobile*, p. 30.

150 "scientific" means to construct them: Mason, *A History of American Roads*, p. 50.

151 "Let's build it before we're too old to enjoy it": Lincoln Highway Association, *The Story of a Crusade That Made Transportation History* (New York: Dodd, Mead, 1935), p. 2.

151 the first census of roads: John A. Jakle and Keith A. Sculle, *The Gas Station in America* (Baltimore: Johns Hopkins Press, 1994), p. 49.

151 "wiggle worm" roads: Seely, *Building the American Highway System*, p. 49.

151 further split the rich and poor: Rae, *The American Automobile*, p. 29.

152 the envy of the world: Vance, *Capturing the Horizon*, p. 488.

152 opened more than five hundred miles of lines a year: George W. Hilton and John F. Due, *The Electric Interurban Railways in America* (Palo Alto, Calif.: Stanford University Press, 1960), p. 36.

152 its peak, at 72,911 cars: Jackson, *Crabgrass Frontier*, p. 171.

152 with 100,000 people: Spencer Crump, *Ride the Big Red Cars: How Trol-*

leys Helped Build Southern California (Corona del Mar, Calif.: Trans-Anglo Books, 1970), p. 61.

152 **a more populous world:** Mark S. Foster, *From Streetcar to Superhighway: American City Planners and Urban Transportation, 1900–1940* (Philadelphia: Temple University Press, 1981) pp. 17 and passim.

153 **"wilderness" line of Portland, Oregon:** *Massachusetts Historic Atlas.*

153 **streetcar fused the nation:** Rifkind, *Main Street,* pp. 54–55, 131, 140.

153 **from these "electric parks":** William D. Middleton, *The Time of the Trolley,* 4th ed. (Milwaukee: Kalmbach Publishers, 1975), pp. 85–88.

153 **"to stick," wrote one reporter:** Middleton, *The Time of the Trolley,* p. 86.

153 **trolley for women only:** photo, Bettmann Archive.

153 **rolled on twenty-six-thousand lines:** Middleton, *The Time of the Trolley,* p. 103.

153 **looked back in awe:** K. H. Schaeffer and Elliott D. Sclar, *Access for All.*

153 **and they won some support:** Clay McShane, "Roots of Modern Traffic Control, 1897–1933," paper presented to the Nineteenth International Congress of History of Science, Zaragoza, Spain, 1993, p. 17.

153 **"people in great cities":** Foster, *From Streetcar to Superhighway,* p. 38.

154 **ridership accelerated:** Charles W. Cheape, *Moving the Masses: Urban Public Transit in New York* (Cambridge, Mass.: Harvard University Press, 1980), p. 213.

154 **elevated-subway system in 1909:** Vance, *Capturing the Horizon,* p. 404.

154 **America's greatest metropolis:** Middleton, *The Time of the Trolley,* pp. 352–59.

155 **"picture of human destiny":** Robert A. M. Stern, Thomas Mellins, and David Fishman, eds., *New York 1900* (New York: Rizzoli, 1983), pp. 41, 247–48.

156 **awnings framed communities:** Liebs, *Main Street to Miracle Mile,* p. 12.

156 **pulsating with civic improvements:** Ebner, *Creating Chicago's North Shore,* p. 128.

157 **the century's first two decades:** Foster, *From Streetcar to Superhighway,* p. 15.

157 **hinged to tomorrow's transportation:** Daniel Bluestone, "Detroit's City Beautiful and the Problem of Commerce," *Journal of the Society of Architectural Historians,* September 1988.

157 **"Detroit has all the ages before it":** Susan L. Klaus, "Efficiency . . . Economy . . . Beauty: The City Planning Reports of Frederick Law Olmsted, Jr.," from Olmsted's 1905 Detroit report, published with follow-up in 1915, *APA Journal,* autumn 1991, p. 30.

157 **another fulsome Olmsted plan:** report of the Pittsburgh Civic Commission, 1910.

157 **traffic through integrated planning:** Beard, *American City Government,* pp. 364–66.

157 Croly wrote in *Architectural Record:* Stern, Mellins, and Fishman, eds., *New York 1900,* p. 32.

158 became known as zoning: Werner Hegemann and Elbert Peets, *Civic Art* (New York: Architectural Book Publishing, 1922).

158 "living conditions in America": Theodora Kimball Hubbard and Henry Vincent Hubbard, *Our Cities To-day and To-morrow: A Survey of Planning and Zoning in the United States* (Cambridge, Mass.: Harvard University Press, 1929), p. 181.

158 Conference on City Planning in 1913: Sennott, "Chicago Architects and the Automobile."

159 artifacts to embrace the motorcar: Jan Jennings, "Housing the Automobile," in *Roadside America,* ed. by Jennings, p. 103.

159 adorned for the motorcar: Peterson, p. 324.

161 Baltimore's Roland Park: Hegemann and Peets, *Civic Art,* pp. 194–279.

161 Apartments in Santa Monica: Stefanos Polyzoides, Roger Sherwood, and James Tice, *Courtyard Housing in Los Angeles* (New York: Princeton Architectural Press, 1992), p. 9.

161 to care for their grounds: pamphlet, collection of Sidney Brower, Roland Park.

161 described it in 1904: Jackson, *Crabgrass Frontier,* p. 95.

161 infancy of the motorcar: Ebner, *Creating Chicago's North Shore,* p. 115.

161 precedent and were expanded: Sarah Amy Leach, presentation on Rock Park and Potomac Creek, 1913–1936, American Society of Landscape Architects annual meeting, November 9, 1992.

162 into city streets: Robert M. Fogelson, *The Fragmented Metropolis: Los Angeles, 1850–1930* (Berkeley: University of California Press, 1993).

162 to match the urban East: Foster, *From Streetcar to Superhighway,* p. 14.

162 "theatric splendor," one person complained: Peterson, "The City Beautiful Movement," p. 423.

163 America for the motorcar: McShane, "Roots of Modern Traffic Control," pp. 203–13.

163 first limited-access highway: McShane, "The Automobile," p. 39.

163 "railroads to worry about": "Motorist's Paradise," *House Beautiful,* no. 36 (August 1914).

163 by "cross-town traffic," one planner said: Hegemann and Peets, *Civic Art,* p. 190.

164 "almost completely fled," he said: Brunk, "Woodward," *The Grand American Avenue,* p. 89.

164 along America's crossways: John A. Jakle and Keith A. Sculle, *The Gas Station in America* (Baltimore: Johns Hopkins University Press, 1994), pp. 112 and 131.

164 three years later: McShane, "Roots of Modern Traffic Control," p. 23.

165 pay for highway growth: John Chynoweth Burnham, "The Gasoline Tax

and the Automobile Revolution," *Mississippi Valley Historical Review*, December 1961.

165 in collecting fees: Ebner, *Creating Chicago's North Shore*, p. 175.

166 "bed, board and shelter": James Belasco, *Americans on the Road: From Autocamp to Motel, 1910–1945* (Cambridge, Mass.: MIT Press, 1979), p. 4.

166 "by the route the crowd takes": Belasco, *Americans on the Road*, p. 22.

166 car and road maintenance: Seely, *Building the American Highway System*, p. 211.

167 track went bankrupt: Glen E. Holt, "The Changing Perception of Urban Pathology: An Essay on the Development of Mass Transit in the United States," in *Cities in American History*, ed. by Kenneth T. Jackson and Stanley K. Schultz (New York: Alfred A. Knopf, 1992), p. 337.

167 the millions more on foot: Foster, "Transforming the Use of Urban Space."

Chapter 8: From Front Porch to Front Seat

170 2 million car buyers a year: John B. Rae, *The American Automobile: A Brief History* (Chicago: University of Chicago Press, 1965), pp. 85–87.

170 more than 26 million: Rae, *The American Automobile*, p. 87.

170 in value of production: Rae, *The American Automobile*, p. 88.

170 by the decade's end: Mark Rose, *Interstate: Express Highway Politics, 1939–1989*, rev. ed. (Knoxville: University of Tennessee Press, 1990), p. xiii.

170 on the installment plan: Foster, *From Streetcar to Superhighway*, p. 464.

170 to match her hair: Frederick Lewis Allen, *Only Yesterday: An Informal History of the 1920s* (New York: Harper & Row, 1976), p. 291.

170 classes "gasoline rabies": McShane, "Roots of Modern Traffic Control," p. 30.

171 "to be seen in one": Robert S. Lynd and Helen M. Lynd, *Middletown: A Study in Contemporary American Culture* (New York: Harcourt, Brace and World, 1929).

171 to the customized Cadillac: Paul C. Wilson, *Chrome Dreams: Automobile Styling Since 1893* (Radno, Pa.: Chilton Book, 1976), p. 116.

171 freedom of the auto age: Robert C. Twombly, *Frank Lloyd Wright: An Interpretive Biography* (New York: Harper & Row, 1973), p. 97.

171 "unsettling influence": Nevins and Hill, *Ford*, vol. 1, p. 381.

171 in *This Side of Paradise*: Allen, *Only Yesterday*, p. 75.

172 "joy ride to destruction": Michael L. Berger, "The Car's Impact on the American Family," quoting Blaine A. Brownell, in *The Car and the City: The Automobile, the Built Environment, and Daily Urban Life*, ed. by Martin Wachs and Margaret Crawford (Ann Arbor: University of Michigan Press, 1991), p. 66.

172 **system swelled tenfold:** Charles Hosmer, *Preservation Comes of Age,* 3 vols. (Charlottesville: University Press of Virginia, 1981).

172 **a third by rail:** Belasco, *Americans on the Road,* p. 103.

172 **"works of man," he wrote:** "The Wilderness and Its Place in Forest Recreational Policy," from *Journal of Forestry,* April 1918, in Robert Gottlieb, *Forcing the Spring: The Transformation of the American Environmental Movement* (Washington, D.C.: Island Press, 1993), p. 33.

173 **"dream of engineer saviors":** *Fortune,* March 1937, p. 105.

173 **closed roofs as with open ones:** Allen, *Only Yesterday,* p. 83.

173 **by the decade's end:** Rose, *Interstate,* p. xiii.

173 **5 million cars a year:** Rae, *The American Automobile,* pp. 85–87.

173 **fueled the auto boom:** Jakle and Sculle, *The Gas Station in America,* p. 50.

173 **artifacts and company colors:** Daniel Yergin, *The Prize* (New York: Simon and Schuster, 1991), p. 210.

174 **as we know them:** Yergin, *The Prize* (New York: Simon and Schuster, 1991), pp. 211–18.

174 **motor-poor Germany in 1918:** McShane, "Roots of Modern Traffic Control," p. 19.

174 **1 million trucks were registered:** McShane, "The Automobile," p. 62.

174 **goods from rail:** Goddard, *Getting There,* p. 86.

174 **trolley's finances declined:** Hilton and Due, *The Electric Interurban Railways in America,* p. 228.

175 **"the slowest troop train":** Yergin, *The Prize.*

175 **a billion dollars a year:** McShane, "The Automobile," p. 72.

175 **backbone of the auto boom:** Flink, *The Car Culture,* p. 141.

176 **"Omaha and New York City":** Robert E. Grese, *Jens Jensen: Maker of Natural Parks and Gardens* (Baltimore: Johns Hopkins University Press, 1972), pp. 107–9.

176 **period's "pavement-minded" outlook:** Ebner, *Creating Chicago's North Shore,* p. 17.

176 **ridership peaked at 15 billion:** Jackson, *Crabgrass Frontier,* p. 171.

176 **47 billion passenger-miles per year:** John B. Rae, *The Road and Car in American Life* (Cambridge, Mass.: MIT Press, 1971), p. 89.

177 **"corporate business" and was penalized:** David J. St. Clair, *The Motorization of American Cities* (New York: Praeger, 1986), p. 100.

177 **"alternative but to drive":** Mark S. Foster, "The Automobile and the City," in *The Automobile and American Culture,* ed. by David L. Lewis and Laurence Goldstein (Ann Arbor: University of Michigan Press, 1991), p. 35.

177 **the trolley business:** Nevins and Hill, *Ford,* vol. 1, p. 107.

178 **"Kicks on Route 66":** Michael Wallis, *Route 66: The Mother Road* (New York: St. Martin's Press, 1990), p. 65.

178 **tepees dotted Lawrence, Kansas:** Richard Guttman, presentation, Old South Meeting House, Boston, February 16, 1995.

178 **"ugliness of cheap commerce"**: Daniel M. Bluestone, "Roadside Blight and the Reform of Commercial Architecture," in *Roadside Architecture,* ed. by Jennings, p. 172.

178 **"dirty loading docks"**: Bluestone, "Roadside Blight and the Reform of Commercial Architecture," ed. by Jennings, p. 181.

178 **"industrial slums"**: Foster, *From Streetcar to Superhighway,* p. 99.

179 **the Holland Tunnel**: *New York Times,* June 27, 1994.

179 **assembly line in 1925**: Clay McShane, "The Automobile," p. 72.

179 **textbook had been published**: McShane, "Roots of Modern Traffic Control," p. 43.

179 **of banning it**: McShane, "Roots of Modern Traffic Control," pp. 31–33.

180 **"pastures into precious property"**: Jackson, *Crabgrass Frontier,* p. 176.

180 **older America's socializing space**: J. C. Nichols, "Subdivision: The Realtor Must Anticipate the Future Needs of His City," *National Real Estate Journal,* Oct. 24, 1921.

181 **store the automobile**: Jan Jennings, "Housing the Automobile," in *Roadside Architecture,* ed. by Jennings, p. 103.

181 **fashioned through the mid-1930s**: Norman T. Newton, *Design on the Land* (Cambridge, Mass.: Harvard University Press, Belknap Press, 1971), p. 483.

182 **for wider regional plans**: William H. Wilson, "Moles and Skylarks," in *Introduction to Planning History in the United States,* ed. by William Krueckeberg, Center for Urban Policy Research.

182 **59 percent rise in the suburban population**: William Worley, *J C Nichols and the Shaping of Kansas City* (Columbia, Mo.: University of Missouri Press, 1990), p. 232.

182 **became "sending" them**: Jackson, *Crabgrass Frontier,* pp. 175–76.

182 **parked cars from downtown**: Scott L. Bottles, *Los Angeles and the Automobile: The Making of the Modern City* (Berkeley: University of California Press, 1987), p. 81.

182 **as many as 550 cars**: Sennott, "Chicago Architects and the Automobile," in *Roadside America,* ed. by Jennings, p. 166.

182 **only suburban shops**: McShane, "The Automobile," p. 72.

183 **driver in front**: Peter G. Rowe, *Making a Middle Landscape* (Cambridge, Mass.: MIT Press, 1991), p. 114.

183 **tucking cars to the rear**: Reyner Banham, *Los Angeles: The Architecture of Four Ecologies* (London: Penguin, 1990), p. 87.

183 **single-family homes**: McShane, "The Automobile," p. 83.

183 **"monument of the Motor Age"**: Banham, *Los Angeles,* p. 84.

183 **to let traffic flow**: McShane, "The Automobile," p. 66.

183 **Monument for more parking**: McShane, "The Automobile," p. 69.

183 **stop in the flight**: Francis R. Kowsky, "Delaware Avenue," in *The Grand American Avenue,* ed. by Cigliano and Landau, pp. 57–59.

184 **scene in *Only Yesterday***: Allen, *Only Yesterday,* p. 226.

184 just three years: Rifkind, *Main Street,* p. 218.

185 by leaps and bounds: Hubbard and Hubbard, *Our Cities To-day and To-morrow,* passim.

185 tripled their office space: Jackson, *Crabgrass Frontier,* p. 174.

186 parking caused complaints: Maggie Valentine, "Of Motorcars and Movies," in *Roadside America,* ed. by Jennings, 136–38.

186 pumps sprouting along sidewalks: Liebs, *Main Street to Miracle Mile,* p. 16.

186 bungalows, and Spanish missions: Liebs, *Main Street to Miracle Mile,* p. 99.

186 a subway entrance's facade: Cervin Robinson and Rosemarie Haag Bletter, *Skyscraper Style: Art Deco New York* (New York: Oxford University Press, 1975), pp. 98–104.

187 acquired seven railroads: Allen, *Only Yesterday,* p. 13.

187 impoverished transit ride: Rebecca Read Shanor, *The City That Never Was* (New York: Viking, 1988), p. 82.

187 faith in urban progress: Robinson and Bletter, *Skyscraper Style,* p. 11.

188 "its present astounding rate," said one: Paul J. Barrett, *The Automobile in Urban Transport* (Philadelphia: Temple University Press, 1983), p. 132; Hubbard and Hubbard, *Our Cities To-day and To-morrow,* p. 192.

188 Chicago Motor Club in 1924: Barrett, *The Automobile in Urban Transport,* p. 139.

188 by widening streets: Foster, *From Streetcar to Superhighway,* p. 93.

188 merely multiplied: Hubbard and Hubbard, *Our Cities To-day and To-morrow,* pp. 214–17.

188 closed communities: Donald L. Miller, *Lewis Mumford, a Life* (New York: Weidenfeld and Nicolson, 1989), p. 195.

189 "tide of city congestion": Benton MacKaye and Lewis Mumford, "The Fourth Migration," in *Planning the Fourth Migration: The Neglected Vision of the Regional Planning Association of America,* ed. by Carl Sussman (Cambridge, Mass.: MIT Press, 1976) p. 53.

190 channel the car's speed: Rose, *Interstate,* p. 270.

191 in the *Boston Evening Transcript:* Newton, *Design on the Land,* p. 333.

191 "destructive of natural beauty": Hubbard and Hubbard, *Our Cities To-day and To-morrow,* p. 12.

191 policing, and upkeep: Arthur Shurcliffe, "The Effect of the Automobile on the Landscape, *Landscape Architecture,* August 1921.

192 120 cities lacked rail: Hubbard and Hubbard, *Our Cities To-day and To-morrow,* p. 219.

192 car in the nation: McShane, "The Automobile," p. 126.

192 places were on its list: Hubbard and Hubbard, *Our Cities To-day and To-morrow,* pp. 210–28.

192 in the old Erie Canal: McShane, "The Automobile," p. 160.

193 "Selling Transportation": *Metro,* American Public Transit Association, August 9, 1994.

193 "and lessened values": Foster, *From Streetcar to Superhighway*, p. 74.

193 for the chaos downtown: Foster, *From Streetcar to Superhighway*, p. 76.

193 won few new fans: Foster, *From Streetcar to Superhighway*, pp. 73–90.

193 "health from fumes": Foster, *From Streetcar to Superhighway*, pp. 63, 109–12.

193 interfering street trees: McShane, "The Automobile," p. 62.

194 "and eliminate curves": Seely, *Building the American Highway System*, p. 81.

Chapter 9: Driving Through the Depression

196 "dependent upon it": President's Research Committee on Social Trends, in Michael L. Berger, "The Car's Impact on the American Family," in *The Car and the City*, ed. by Wachs and Crawford, p. 72.

196 stood in breadlines: William E. Leuchtenburg, *Franklin D. Roosevelt and the New Deal* (New York: Harper & Row, 1963), p. 1.

196 reached six thousand: T. H. Watkins, *The Great Depression: America in the 1930s* (Boston: Little, Brown, 1993), p. 63.

196 didn't inspire confidence: Flink, *The Car Culture*, p. 113.

197 he observed in 1930: Watkins, *The Great Depression*.

197 "car" was issued: Wilson, *Chrome Dreams*, p. 136.

197 the company boasted: *Fortune*, August 1933.

197 200 million miles a year: Flink, *The Car Culture*, p. 160.

197 grew by 3 million: Frederick Lewis Allen, *Since Yesterday: The 1930s in America* (New York: Harper and Row, 1939), p. 213.

197 paying on the installment plan: St. Clair, *The Motorization of American Cities*, p. 9.

198 vehicle out the door: Robert Heide and John Gilman, *Popular Art Deco: Depression Era Style and Design* (New York: Abbeville, 1991), p. 162.

198 oil for their automobiles: Foster, *From Streetcar to Superhighway*, pp. 124–25.

198 "two cars in every garage": Rae, *The American Automobile*, p. 106.

198 to ease unemployment: Goddard, *Getting There*, p. 149.

198 was passed: Kenneth S. Davis, *FDR: The New Deal Years: 1933–1936* (New York: Random House, 1993), p. 121.

199 street or highway projects: Foster, *From Streetcar to Superhighway*, p. 166.

199 500,000 miles of road: Rose, *Interstate*, p. 10.

199 roads and construction: Rae, *The Road and Car in American Life*, pp. 31–39, 74.

199 double to 1,367,000 miles: Seely, *Building the American Highway System*, p. 88.

199 the federal highway program: Gary T. Schwartz, "Urban Freeways and the

Interstate System," *Southern California Law Review* 49 (March 1976), p. 415.

199 streetcars were paupers: Foster, *From Streetcar to Superhighway*, p. 127.

199 for trains were loans: Goddard, *Getting There*, p. 147.

200 250,000 foreclosed mortgages: Jackson, *Crabgrass Frontier*, p. 193.

200 industry and suburban home sales: Leuchtenberg, *Franklin D. Roosevelt and the New Deal*, p. 135.

200 "planning a new world": Joseph L. Arnold, *The New Deal in the Suburbs: A History of the Greenbelt Town Program, 1935–1954* (Columbus: Ohio State University Press, 1971), pp. 49–50.

201 flight to the road's end: Arnold, *The New Deal in the Suburbs*, p. 68.

201 in four no bath or shower: *Fortune*, January 1935.

201 urban housing solution: Mark I. Gelfand, *A Nation of Cities: The Federal Government and Urban America, 1933–1965* (New York: Oxford University Press, 1975), pp. 60–61.

201 compared to suburbs: Foster, *From Streetcar to Superhighway*, p. 116.

201 less than 1 percent: Scott, *American City Planning Since 1890*, p. 378.

201 "megalopolis" to come: Joseph Interrante, "The Automobile and the Spatial Transformation of American Culture," in *The Automobile and American Culture*, ed. by Lewis and Goldstein.

201 Flink and others have concluded: Flink, *The Car Culture*, p. 181.

202 fire towers, and phone lines: William Manchester, *The Glory and the Dream* (Boston: Little, Brown, 1973), pp. 284–85.

202 into his social policy: Otis L. Graham, Jr., *Toward a Planned Society: From Roosevelt to Nixon* (New York: Oxford University Press, 1976), p. 37.

203 erosion evolved admirably: Sussman, ed., *Planning the Fourth Migration*, p. 52.

203 of a federal presence: T. H. Watkins, *Righteous Pilgrim: The Life and Times of Harold L. Ickes, 1874–1952* (New York: Henry Holt, 1990), pp. 37–38.

203 "core in us all": Phoebe Cutler, *The Public Landscape of the New Deal* (New Haven: Yale University Press, 1985), pp. 1–8.

203 complained George Horace Lorimer: "The Wilderness and Its Place in Forest Recreational Policy," in Gottlieb, *Forcing the Spring*, p. 33.

204 a "green retreat": Gottlieb, *Forcing the Spring*, p. 17.

205 from Harlem to Long Island: Cutler, *The Public Landscape of the New Deal*, p. 24.

205 in *The Power Broker:* Robert A. Caro, *The Power Broker* (New York: Alfred A. Knopf, 1974), p. 508.

205 across the continent: Seely, *Building the American Highway System*, p. 103.

205 replied to critics: Bruce Radde, *The Merritt Parkway* (New Haven: Yale University Press, 1993), p. 78.

206 "greatest aerial highway": quoting *California Highways and Public Works*

Magazine, in Mark H. Rose, *Historic American Roads* (New York: Crown Publishers, 1976), p. 105.

206 speed of seventy miles an hour: Vance, *Capturing the Horizon,* p. 517; Rae, *The American Automobile,* p. 139; Rae, *The Road and Car in American Life,* p. 180.

206 became the Pasadena Freeway: McShane, "The Automobile," p. 101.

207 the highway boom grew: Jackson, *Crabgrass Frontier,* p. 167.

207 were totally oblivious: Jackson, *Crabgrass Frontier,* p. 187.

207 "any nation's economy": Kenneth R. Schneider, *Autokind vs. Mankind* (New York: W. W. Norton, 1971), p. 80.

207 "with a public trust": Graham, *Toward a Planned Society,* p. 46.

207 around urban America: Schwartz, "Urban Freeways and the Interstate System," pp. 422–23.

208 "through the airstream": Heide and Gilman, *Popular Art Deco,* p. 148.

208 higher still in 1931: Robinson and Bletter, *Skyscraper Style,* passim.

208 "but to us all": Marshall Berman, *All That Is Solid Melts into Air: The Experience of Modernity* (New York: Penguin, 1988), p. 295.

209 in America's cities: Robinson and Bletter, *Skyscraper Style,* p. 199.

209 to the motorcar: Rowe, *Making a Middle Landscape,* p. 135.

209 first drive-in movie: Liebs, *Main Street to Miracle Mile,* p. 154.

209 on twenty-five roads: Seely, *Building the American Highway System,* p. 163.

210 lure shoppers farther: Liebs, *Main Street to Miracle Mile,* p. 25

210 admitted cars inside: Liebs, *Main Street to Miracle Mile,* p. 22.

210 interact more humanely: Richard Longstreth, *Cultural Resources Management,* National Park Service, vol. 16, (6).

210 altered the streets: David Morris, *Self-Reliant Cities: Energy and the Transformation of Urban America* (San Francisco: Sierra Club, 1982), p. 19.

210 New York and Trenton: McShane, "The Automobile," p. 99.

210 twenty-five an hour in 1937: Allen, *Since Yesterday,* p. 229.

211 "into city schools": *Fortune,* March 1937.

211 ultimate nonmoving vehicle: Allen, *Since Yesterday,* p. 229.

211 and forged ahead: Goddard, *Getting There,* pp. 147–49.

211 Thirtieth Street Station: Leuchtenberg, *Franklin D. Roosevelt and the New Deal,* p. 133.

211 "120 miles an hour": *Fortune,* January 1935.

212 and the future dimmed: *Electric Railway Journal,* summer 1994.

212 lay in receivership: Goddard, *Getting There,* p. 155.

212 beautifying public transport: Robinson and Bletter, *Skyscraper Style,* p. 107.

213 the brunt of poverty: St. Clair, *The Motorization of American Cities,* p. 9.

213 votes to bond them: Robert Fogelson, "Downtown Spatial Politics," presentation at Faneuil Hall, Boston, May 6, 1996, and to author.

213 over five years: Vance, *Capturing the Horizon,* p. 294.

213 wheels for rubber ones: Foster, *From Streetcar to Superhighway,* p. 383.

213 **rose 20 percent:** Foster, *From Streetcar to Superhighway,* p. 117.
213 **its trolleys with buses:** McShane, "The Automobile," p. 93.
214 **later congressional hearings:** Bradford C. Snell, *American Ground Transport,* 1974 testimony to Congress.
214 **line to fall:** McShane, "The Automobile," p. 254.
214 **downtown set the tone:** Fogelson, *The Fragmented Metropolis,* pp. 164–85.
214 **rail service altogether:** Jackson, *Crabgrass Frontier,* p. 171.
214 **to deplete downtown:** Fogelson, *The Fragmented Metropolis,* p. 183.
215 **"mockery and a memory":** Foster, *From Streetcar to Superhighway,* p. 130.
215 **buildings for parking lots:** McShane, "The Automobile," p. 99.
215 **declared in 1937:** Schneider, *Autokind vs. Mankind,* p. 163.
215 **Studebaker's president:** McShane, "The Automobile," p. 100.
215 **"more natural conditions":** Foster, *From Streetcar to Superhighway,* p. 143.
215 **"unsuccessfully planned city":** Foster, *From Streetcar to Superhighway,* p. 156.
216 **"cities must be remade":** Snell, *American Ground Transport,* 1974 testimony to Congress.
216 **"and enjoyable," Wright wrote:** Wright, "Broadacre City."
216 **wrote one enthusiast:** Peter Marsh and Peter Collett, *Driving Passion, The Psychology of the Car* (Boston: Faber and Faber, 1987), pp. 12, 148–55.
217 **"Sidewalk Play Is Dangerous":** Flink, *The Car Culture,* p. 155.
217 **at the decade's beginning:** Rebecca Shander, *The New York That Never Was,* p. 147.
217 **26,700-mile intercity system:** Rose, *Interstate,* pp. 10–12.
217 **was the doctrine:** Schneider, *Autokind vs. Mankind,* p. 84.
217 **"suburban building and blight":** Mark I. Gelfand, *A Nation of Cities: The Federal Government and Urban America, 1933–1965* (New York: Oxford University Press, 1975), pp. 80–81.
217 **buy more houses:** Jackson, *Crabgrass Frontier,* p. 205.
218 **"exodus from the cities":** Gelfand, *A Nation of Cities,* pp. 24–25.
218 **"explosion," in Lewis Mumford's words:** Miller, *Lewis Mumford,* p. 364.
218 **New York World's Fair:** Rose, *Interstate,* p. 1.
218 **"The World of Tomorrow" title:** Allen, *Since Yesterday,* p. 283.
218 **twenty-one single-family homes:** Jackson, *Crabgrass Frontier,* p. 187.
218 **entertained Geddes himself:** Seely, *Building the American Highway,* p. 170.
219 **"for the Motorist":** Benton MacKaye and Lewis Mumford, "Townless Highways for the Motorist," *Harper's Weekly,* August 1931.
219 **than finding work:** Mason, *A History of American Roads,* p. 53.

Chapter 10: The Asphalt Exodus

222 **first year of the war:** Rae, *The American Automobile,* p. 161.
222 **"for defense fund":** photos, Wright Museum, Wolfeboro Falls, New Hampshire.

222 road building lapsed: Scott, *American City Planning Since 1890,* p. 395.

222 took to their feet: Rae, *The Road and Car in American Life,* p. 154.

222 "auto deaths fell dramatically": Doris Kearns Goodwin, *No Ordinary Time* (New York: Simon and Schuster, 1994), pp. 358–59.

222 tool of robber barons: John Morton Blum, *V Was for Victory; Politics and American Culture During World War II.* (New York: Harcourt Brace, 1976), p. 3.

222 to serve production: Scott, *American City Planning Since 1890,* p. 392.

223 workers and their families: Blum, *V Was for Victory,* p. 102.

223 San Diego's population: Scott, *American City Planning Since 1890,* p. 373.

223 population 50 percent: Blum, *V Was for Victory,* p. 93.

224 half times larger: Scott, *American City Planning Since 1890,* p. 403.

224 on the West Coast: Blum, *V Was for Victory,* p. 113.

224 help the war effort: Roger Swain, *Groundwork* (Boston: Houghton Mifflin, 1994), p. 50.

224 the automobile industry: Blum, *V Was for Victory,* p. 141.

224 General Motors alone: Mary Beth Norton et al., *A People and a Nation: A History of the United States,* 3rd ed. (Boston: Houghton Mifflin, 1990), p. 796.

224 committee summed it up: Blum, *V Was for Victory,* p. 90.

224 shape the future: Blum, *V Was for Victory,* pp. 112–13.

224 manufacturers paved the way: Helen Leavitt, *Superhighway—Superhoax* (New York: Doubleday, 1970), pp. 151–53.

225 from state to state: Rae, *The Road and Car in American Life,* pp. 180–82.

225 urban areas figured prominently: Marion Clawson, *New Deal Planning* (Baltimore: Johns Hopkins, 1981), p. 160.

225 five years earlier: Martha J. Bianco, "Mumford Versus Moses: Paradigms of Growth in Portland, Oregon," presentation, Society for American City and Regional Planning History, Knoxville, October 14, 1995.

225 urban areas was enlarged: Schwartz, "Urban Freeways and the Interstate System," pp. 416–18.

225 veterans a housing loan: Jackson, *Crabgrass Frontier,* p. 204.

225 the *Ladies' Home Journal:* Jackson, *Crabgrass Frontier,* p. 232.

225 nullify its urbanity: Jon C. Teaford, *Rough Road to Renaissance: Urban Revitalization in America, 1940–1985* (Baltimore: Johns Hopkins University Press, 1990), pp. 41–43.

226 "double bed at night": *Time,* February 4, 1946.

226 of its 1916 peak: Goddard, *Getting There,* p. 175.

226 25 million automobiles: Rae, *The Road and Car in American Life,* p. 192.

227 decayed housing stock: Scott, *American City Planning,* p. 452.

227 Levittown on Long Island in 1947: Scott, *American City Planning Since 1980,* p. 457.

227 Cape Cod house was in the hands of: Jackson, *Crabgrass Frontier,* p. 205.

227 social critics complained: Thomas Hine, *Populuxe* (New York: Alfred A. Knopf, 1986), p. 43.

228 Howard's Garden Cities: Barbara Kelly, *Expanding the American Dream* (Albany: State University of New York Press, 1993), p. 34.

228 William Levitt's rebuttal: Kelly, *Expanding the American Dream,* p. 49.

228 pressure of 1950s conformism: Marc A. Weiss, *The Rise of the Community Builders* (New York: Columbia University Press, 1987), p. 159.

228 "repressive environment," planners complained: Scott, *American City Planning Since 1890s,* p. 458.

228 "boring," said architects: Hine, *Populuxe,* p. 52.

229 oil use would double: Yergin, *The Prize.*

229 classic centerless city: Richard Ingersoll, "The Death of the Street," in *Roadside America* (Ames: Iowa State University Press, 1990), p. 154.

229 the consumer exodus advanced: Bernard J. Frieden and Lynne B. Sagalyn, *Downtown, Inc.* (Cambridge, Mass.: MIT Press, 1990), p. 11.

229 *Daily News* offered: *Passenger Transport,* American Public Transit Association, 50th anniversary issue.

230 starts a year: Frieden and Sagalyn, *Downtown Inc.,* p. 11.

230 and obliterated neighborhoods: Martin Anderson, *The Federal Bulldozer* (Cambridge, Mass.: MIT Press, 1964).

230 public housing towers: Anderson, *The Federal Bulldozer,* p. 7.

230 "way with a meat cleaver," Moses declared: Leavitt, *Superhighway—Superhoax,* p. 53.

230 traveled through the nation: Bianco, "Mumford Versus Moses."

231 suburbs from downtown: McShane, "The Automobile," p. 120.

231 presaged the interstate: Rae, *The Road and Car in American Life,* pp. 180–81.

231 the next quarter century: Chester Hartman, *Yerba Buena: The Transformation of San Francisco* (Totowa, N.J.: Rowman and Allanheld, 1984), p. 9.

232 urban freeways had been built: Schwartz, "Urban Freeways and the Interstate System," p. 419.

232 "national defense roads": Rose, *Interstate,* p. 106.

232 registered in the mid-1950s: McShane, "The Automobile," p. 125.

232 its author wrote: Leavitt, *Superhighway—Superhoax,* pp. 2–3.

233 work of the freight train: Rae, *The Road and Car in American Life,* p. 112.

233 as a whole declined: Goddard, *Getting There,* pp. 202–03.

233 what they had: Vance, *Capturing the Horizon,* p. 418.

234 seventeen hundred in 1950: Liebs, *Main Street to Miracle Mile,* p. 157.

234 golden arch was born: Liebs, *Main Street to Miracle Mile,* p. 213.

235 to some three thousand: Rowe, *Making a Middle Landscape,* p. 109.

235 smoother, straighter highway: William Manchester, *The Glory and the Dream* (Boston: Little, Brown, 1973), p. 428.

235 the "Fertility Valley" 1950s: Jackson, *Crabgrass Frontier,* p. 235.

235 Governor Earl Warren declared: Schneider, *Autokind vs. Mankind,* p. 48.

235 with the tail fin mode: Michael Sorkin, "War Is Swell," in *World War II and the American Dream: How Wartime Building Changed a Nation,* ed. by Donald Albrecht (Cambridge, Mass.: MIT Press, 1995), p. 237.

236 "atoms in the universe": Marsh and Collett, *Driving Passion,* pp. 38–39.

236 "an earth-bound aircraft": Marsh and Collett, *Driving Passion,* pp. 115–17.

236 mileages and in fatalities: McShane, "The Automobile," p. 123.

236 resided in the car: Wilson, *Chrome Dreams,* p. 252.

236 went a television commercial: Wilson, *Chrome Dreams,* pp. 115–17.

236 "collected by mankind," he wrote: Bluestone, "Roadside Blight and the Reform of Commercial Architecture," in *Roadside Architecture,* ed. by Jennings, p. 181.

236 "isolation and loneliness": Rowe, *Making a Middle Landscape,* p. 142.

237 beneath an all-weather dome: *Preservation News,* August 9, 1994.

237 "a double-decked mainstreet": Victor Gruen, in *Architectural Forum,* 1951, in Rowe, *Making a Middle Landscape,* p. 126.

237 said one Westchester observer: Sharon Zukin, *Landscapes of Power,* p. 171.

238 drawing more traffic: Bluestone, "Roadside Blight and the Reform of Commercial Architecture," in *Roadside Architecture,* p. 183.

238 "the air, and it stuck": Mark S. Foster, "The Automobile's Role in Shaping a City," in *The Car and the City,* ed. by Wachs and Crawford, p. 188.

239 internal combustion machine: Norton et al., *A People and a Nation,* p. 885.

239 Americans were ghettoized: Peter L. Abeles, "Planning and Zoning," in *Zoning and the American Dream: Promises Still to Keep,* ed. by Charles M. Haar and Jerold S. Kayden (Chicago: Planners Press, 1989), p. 137.

240 editor Grady Clay put it: Grady Clay, "The Tiger Is Through the Gates," *Landscape Architecture,* spring 1959, an issue entitled "New Highways: Number One Enemy?"

240 the thirteen largest metropolises: Frieden and Sagalyn, *Downtown, Inc.*

241 "simply don't know," he said: Scott Greer, *Urban Renewal and American Cities* (New York: Bobbs Merrill, 1965), p. 39.

241 Salt Lake City: Jackson, *Crabgrass Frontier,* pp. 170–71.

241 "and even their slow speed": Schaeffer and Sclar, *Access for All,* pp. 45–46.

242 to let traffic flow: McShane, "The Automobile," pp. 185, 190.

242 made their last runs: Hilton and Due, *The Electric Interurban Railways in America,* p. 220.

242 to their old routes: Banham, *Los Angeles,* p. 35.

243 air quality in the nation: Flink, *The Car Culture,* p. 142.

243 freight and passenger trains: Rae, *The Road and Car in American Life,* pp. 190–91.

243 Union Station into the 1950s: Bill Bradley, *The Last of the Great Stations* (Pasadena: Interurban Press, 1992), p. 32.

243 snatch their travelers: Bradley, *The Last of the Great Stations,* p. 7.

243 one-third their number of passengers: Rae, *The Road and Car in American Life,* p. 278.

244 of the rush hour traffic: St. Clair, *The Motorization of American Cities,* p. 11.

244 going to rail: Morris, *Self-Reliant Cities,* p. 23.

244 "its hustle and bustle": William H. Whyte, Jr., "The Exploding Metropolis," introduction to *The Exploding Metropolis,* ed. by William H. Whyte, Jr. (Berkeley: University of California Press, 1993), p. 7.

244 "or apartment houses," Gottmann wrote: Jean Gottmann, *Megalopolis, the Urbanized Northeastern Seaboard of the United States* (New York: Twentieth Century Fund, 1961), p. 329.

245 2 to 3 million cars a year: Manchester, *The Glory and the Dream,* p. 819.

Chapter 11: Braking the Juggernaut

249 to wake up the nation: Philip Shabecoff, *A Fierce Green Fire* (New York: Hill and Wang, 1993), p. 153.

249 Moses's Lower Manhattan Expressway: Whyte, "The Exploding Metropolis," p. xv.

249 "support are casually disemboweled": Jane Jacobs, *The Death and Life of Great American Cities* (New York: Vintage, 1961).

250 "gone under now," he wrote: Peter Blake, *God's Own Junkyard* (New York: Holt, Rinehart and Winston, 1964), p. 185.

250 "on the brink of disaster": Blake, *God's Own Junkyard,* pp. 23–24.

251 "Newark, and Washington": Ben Kelley, *The Pavers and the Paved* (New York: Charles Scribner's Sons, 1971), p. 94.

251 "the dead are safe": *New York Times,* in Leavitt, *Superhighway—Superhoax,* p. 69.

251 "tappets of internal combustion": *Audubon,* November 1986.

251 noted in his classic *Design on the Land:* Newton, *Design on the Land.*

252 "critic Ada Louise Huxtable mourned": Ada Louise Huxtable, *Goodbye History Hello Hamburger* (New York: Preservation Press, 1986), p. 51.

252 down to some six hundred: Goddard, *Getting There,* p. 215.

253 "planning to minimize harm": Christopher J. Duerksen, *A Handbook on Historic Preservation Law* (Washington, D.C.: Conservation Foundation and National Center for Preservation Law, 1983), pp. 239–41.

253 its historic landscape: Jane Holtz Kay and Pauline Chase-Harrell, *Preserving New England* (New York: Pantheon, 1986), p. 120.

253 "birdwatchers and do-gooders": *New York Times,* November 13, 1967.

254 stalled their interstates: Schwartz, "Urban Freeways and the Interstate System," pp. 444–49.

254 the refuse of society: Teaford, *Rough Road to Renaissance,* p. 202.

254 railway service was extinct: McShane, "The Automobile," pp. 282, 387–88.

254 down to 5.9 billion trips: Jack Burby, *The Great American Motion Sickness* (Boston: Little, Brown, 1971), p. 122.

255 "in city traffic": Teaford, *Rough Road to Renaissance,* p. 166.

255 for public transportation: Dennis R. Judd, *The Politics of American Cities: Private Power and Public Policy,* 3rd ed. (Glenview, Ill.: Scott, Foresman, 1988), p. 291.

255 to dream of monorail: Teaford, *Rough Road to Renaissance,* p. 235.

255 all but a hundred cars: McShane, "The Automobile," p. 385.

255 in the late 1960s: *Electric Railway Journal,* summer 1994.

256 the urban transit map of America: Elliott D. Sclar, "The Policy Setting" (Washington, D.C.: Economic Policy Institute, 1989).

256 "train was doomed": *Passenger Train Journal,* June 12, 1994.

256 fallen to three hundred: Manchester, *The Glory and the Dream,* p. 8.

256 "wards of the state": Stephen B. Goddard, *Getting There: The Epic Struggle Between Road and Rail in the Twentieth Century* (New York: Basic Books, 1994), p. 228.

256 veteran railroader observed: Joseph Silien at the 1994 convention of the American Public Transit Association and to author.

257 the $24 billion fed to the car: *Passenger Transport.*

257 "in the United States": *New York Times,* March 26, 1993.

257 or getting worse: *Metro,* birthday issue, 1993.

257 "into ranch-style slums," Burby wrote: Burby, *Motion Sickness,* pp. 2–22.

258 concrete and empty of oxygen: Leavitt, *Superhighway—Superhoax,* p. 270.

258 the car in court: Shabecoff, *A Fierce Green Fire,* p. 103.

258 "alternatives to proposed actions": Duerkson, *Handbook on Historic Preservation Law,* p. 215.

258 the anti-automobile movement: Gottlieb, *Forcing the Spring,* pp. 125–26.

258 the critical act: Shabecoff, *A Fierce Green Fire,* p. 103.

259 a high of fifty-six thousand: McShane, "The Automobile," p. 157.

260 car-based sprawling cities: Teaford, *Rough Road to Renaissance,* pp. 236–37.

260 "quality of life": Bianco, "Mumford Versus Moses."

260 "feet high to circle the globe": Kelley, *The Pavers and the Paved,* pp. 3–5.

261 to local transit systems: Elliott D. Sclar, "The Policy Setting."

262 than centering within it: Emma Rothschild, *Paradise Lost: The Decline of the Auto-Industrial Age* (New York: Random House, 1974), p. 27.

262 with their cruisers: McShane, "The Automobile," pp. 160–61.

262 1 trillion in 1970: Norton et al., *A People and a Nation,* p. 883.

262 three times the growth in population: Urban Land Institute.

263 "heart area is lost": Schneider, *Autokind vs. Mankind.*

264 "building near a superhighway": Fred Powledge, *Model Cities* (New Haven: Yale University Press, 1968).

264 died at night: Newton, *Design on the Land*, p. 53.

265 new jobs and homes: Teaford, *Rough Road to Renaissance*, p. 211.

266 "rises to meet maximum capacity": Small, Winston, and Evans, "Road Work," *Traffic Quarterly*, 1962, p. 393.

266 by the early 1970s: Schneider, *Autokind versus Mankind*.

266 solve the problem: Rae, *The Road and Car in American Life*, pp. 302–6.

267 other cities in the state: Secaucus conference, June 5, 1991, and correspondence to author, August 1992.

267 "features of a city": Duerksen. *Handbook on Historic Preservation Law*, p. 17.

Chapter 12: The Three-Car Culture

270 almost double the 1970s figure—negated any gains: Urban Land Institute.

270 "the city as cemetery": Teaford, *Rough Road to Renaissance*, p. 202.

270 auto-based subsidies: Frank N. Wilner, *The Amtrak Story* (Omaha: Simmons-Boardman Books, 1994).

271 its 162 million drivers: Mark Alan Hughes, "The New Metropolitan Reality: Where the Rubber Meets the Road in Antipoverty Policy," study done for Public Finance and Housing Center: The Urban Institute, December 1992.

271 about the changing times: Wilner, *The Amtrak Story*, p. 5.

271 the number continued to grow: Georgia Institute of Technology study by Arthur C. Nelson, *Boston Globe*, April 1, 1994.

272 a few centuries or so: Garreau, *Edge City*, p. 242.

272 proved to be symbolic: Frieden and Sagalyn, *Downtown, Inc.*, p. 221.

273 said in 1982: *Fortune*, December 13, 1982.

273 in every large city: Judd, *The Politics of American Cities*, p. 397.

275 $112 billion windfall: Neil Pierce, in David Morris, *Self-Reliant Cities: Energy and the Transformation of Urban America* (San Francisco: Sierra Club, 1982).

275 this attack on Main Street: Robert Yaro, Municipal Art Society, July 8, 1995.

275 "towns and countryside": Richard Moe, presentation at conference, "Alternatives to Sprawl," National Trust for Historic Preservation, Brookings Institute, and Lincoln Institute of Land Policy, Washington, D.C., March 22, 1995.

277 commuter rail was recorded, too: F. K. Plous, "Off the Road, Vehicles," *Planning*, September 1994.

277 reinforced their downtowns: Jane Holtz Kay, "Streetcars of Desire," *Architecture*, August 1993.

278 miles of railway track had halved: George H. Douglas, *All Aboard: The Railroad in American Life* (New York: Paragon House, 1992), p. 395.

279 "would receive the idea": Burby, *The Great American Motion Sickness,* p. 130.

280 "taken as radical," I wrote: *New York Times,* June 9, 1991.

280 "probably hit its high-water mark": *Passenger Transport,* January 1995.

Chapter 13: None for the Road

289 twenty years ago: Gottlieb, *Forcing the Spring,* p. 126.

290 federal highway builders: Eno Foundation, 1990.

291 air in the nation: Alliance for a Paving Moratorium newspaper, summer 1995.

294 sold out its first edition: Conservation Law Foundation, *Take Back Your Streets: How to Protect Communities from Asphalt and Traffic.*

294 Jim Wick's guide: Jim Wick, "A Highway Project in Your Town: A Citizen's Guide to Your Role and Rights," Vermont Trust for Historic Preservation.

294 is traveling forty-four miles an hour: Stephen H. Burrington, "Restoring the Rule of Law and Respect for Communities in Transportation," draft, 1996.

Chapter 14: Zoning for Life

296 still more independence: Federal Highway Administration, bicycling and walking study, final report, 1995.

297 are adopted locally: Andres Duany, presentation at conference "Alternatives to Sprawl."

298 declared in the mid-1990s: *Newsweek,* May 15, 1995.

300 titled the sociability and service: *Washington Monthly,* July 8, 1993.

300 sixty-five years of age living alone: *NPTS.*

301 the nation parallels it: American Public Transit Association, Boston conference.

Chapter 15: Putting Transit on Track

304 New York University Law School: Jeffrey M. Zupan at Conference "Beyond the Open Road: Reinventing Transportation Policy for the 21st Century," New York University Law School, March 3, 1995.

306 in fringe suburbs, thirty thousand: Peter Calthorpe, *The Next American Metropolis.* Princeton, N.J.: Princeton Architectural Press, 1993.

306 good transit have prospered: William H. Lucy, "Suburban and City Income Decline, 1960 to 1990," study draft, 1994, and to author, July 27, 1995.

307 the centers languished: William H. Lucy and David L. Phillips, Market Tests of Sustainable Communities.

308 "The Future Is Quaint": *New York*, January 16, 1994.

308 by almost three thousand: *New York Times*, June 17, 1996.

309 or extend old ones (Baltimore): Committee for Better Transit, *New York Streetcar News*, and *Passenger Train Journal*, passim.

309 "Village Vision": *Planning*, January 1995.

309 French light-rail: *New York Streetcar News*, May–June 1995.

310 1970s fiscal crisis: *New York Observer*, August 21, 1995.

310 or beside stores: *Preservation News*, July 8, 1995.

310 extension approved: *Metro*, September–October 1994.

310 Biltmore Hotel downtown: *Passenger Train Journal*, July 1995.

311 from 1982 to 1995: *National Association of Railroad Passengers*, September 1995.

312 adding commuter rail along the way: U.S. Department of Transportation, Origins and Designations chart.

314 "are inflated": Elliott D. Sclar, *Selling the Brooklyn Bridge: The Privatization of America*, draft, 1996.

314 to gain mobility: Surface Transportation Policy Project newsletter, *Progress*, October 1995.

315 downtown are car-free: Susan Hanson, *The Geography of Urban Transportation* (New York: Guildford Press, 1995), p. 88.

315 two miles of public transportation: *NPTS*.

317 no space for the automobile: *Rain*, summer 1994.

318 back to wider highways: Christopher K. Leman, Preston L. Schiller, and Kristin Pauly, "Re-Thinking HOV: High Occupancy Vehicle Facilities and the Public Interest," report for Chesapeake Bay Foundation, August 1, 1994.

318 Steamboat Springs, Colorado: Robert Cevero, "Why Go Anywhere?" *Scientific American*, September 1995.

318 3 percent of the population: Hanson, ed., *Geography*, p. 3.

319 from Seattle and Portland, Oregon: John Pucher and Stefan Kurth, "Making Transit Irresistible: Lessons from Europe," APTA, March 1995.

320 town centers prosper: *Wall Street Journal*, May 3, 1995.

321 "of intelligent city planning": Lewis Mumford, *American Mercury*, in *Zoned America*, by Seymour I. Toll (New York: Grossman, 1969), p. 147.

Chapter 16: The Centering of America

324 "celebrations take place": Allan Jacobs, *Great Streets* (Cambridge, Mass.: MIT Press, 1993), p. 5.

326 car door to mall door: David Sucher, *City Comforts: How to Build an Urban Village* (Seattle: City Comforts Press, 1995).

327 sites on the fringes: *Planning,* June 1995.

330 "movement and access": Jacobs, *Great Streets,* p. 4.

Chapter 17: The De-Paving of America

335 "functions of streets": McShane, *Down the Asphalt Path,* p. xvii.

337 likes to remind us: STPP newsletter, *Progress.* April 1996.

337 of the population as walkers: Federal Highway Administration, in *NPTS.*

337 **Louis Harris poll:** Freund and Martin, *The Ecology of the Automobile,* p. 36.

338 in Seattle: Florida Bicycle/Pedestrian Commuter Center newsletter, reprinted in WalkBoston newsletter, winter 1996.

341 $20,000 per space to build: *Passenger Transport,* October 2, 1995.

341 49 percent of trips three miles or less: *NPTS.*

341 with this thought: *Bicycling,* November 12, 1996.

342 calls "Wall Street City": *Metropolis,* May 1995.

Chapter 18: Righting the Price

346 city who were more than eleven years old: *World Watch,* May–June 1994.

346 all the while cutting pollution costs: Odol Tunali, "A Billion Cars: The Road Ahead," *World Watch,* January–February 1996.

346 cutting pollution costs: campaign for New Transportation Priorities.

346 nursing homes ($35,000 a year per person): Frederick Williams, researcher at Federal Transit Administration, summer 1994.

348 insignificant in number: Paul M. Weyrich and William S. Lind, *Conservatives and Mass Transit: Is It Time for a New Look?* (Washington, D.C.: Free Congress and Research Foundation, 1996).

349 according to a Strategies Unlimited report: *Transportation Research,* July 8, 1995.

350 $12 billion annually: Charles Komanoff, " 'Auto-Fee' New York City: A Roadway Pricing Primer," in *Auto-Free Press,* July–August 1994.

350 proposed a registration fee: *Passenger Transport,* April 12, 1993.

350 argued in *Urban Transportation Economics:* Small, *Urban Transportation Economics,* pp. 126–27.

353 given a free space: *NPTS.*

353 "Airport, 53 to 44": George Will, *Boston Globe,* June 3, 1994.

354 "donned Earth First! caps": Alliance for a Paving Moratorium newspaper, summer 1995.

355 to the surrounding community: Bank of America, *Beyond Sprawl: New Patterns of Growth to Fit the New,* 1995.

355 thirteen-mile trip through the suburbs: Conservation Law Foundation, November 1995.

355 **their wealth or location:** Lincoln Institute of Land Policy, *Landlines*, July 1995.

356 **for their development:** presentation by Edward Blakely at Lincoln Institute of Land Policy, Cambridge, Mass., July 10, 1992.

356 **budget whackers' cutbacks:** American Public Transit Association, May 25, 1995.

As the crushing weight of the problems caused by the automobile increases, Americans become more invigorated by the growing awareness of solutions to tame the motor vehicle. (Photo: Frank Staub. Picture Cube.)

Bibliography

ABBEY, EDWARD. *Desert Solitaire.* New York: Ballantine, 1991.

ALBRECHT, DONALD, ed. *World War II and the American Dream: How Wartime Building Changed a Nation.* Cambridge, Mass.: National Building Museum/ MIT Press, 1995.

ALLEN, FREDERICK LEWIS. *Only Yesterday: An Informal History of the 1920s.* New York: Harper and Row, 1976.

——. *Since Yesterday: The 1930s in America.* New York: Harper and Row, 1939.

ANDERSON, MARTIN. *The Federal Bulldozer.* Cambridge, Mass.: MIT Press, 1964.

ARNOLD, JOSEPH L. *The New Deal in the Suburbs: A History of the Greenbelt Town Program, 1935–1954.* Columbus: Ohio State University Press, 1971.

BACON, EDMUND N. *Design of Cities.* Rev. ed. New York: Penguin Books, 1974.

BANHAM REYNER. *Los Angeles: The Architecture of Four Ecologies.* Rev. ed. London: Penguin, 1990.

BARRETT, PAUL J. *The Automobile in Urban Transport.* Philadelphia: Temple University Press, 1983.

BEARD, CHARLES A. *American City Government. A Survey of Newer Tendencies.* New York: Century, 1912.

BEAUMONT, CONSTANCE E. *How Superstore Sprawl Can Harm Communities.* Washington, D.C.: National Trust, 1994.

BELASCO, JAMES. *Americans on the Road: From Autocamp to Motel, 1910– 1945.* Cambridge, Mass.: MIT Press, 1979.

BEL GEDDES, NORMAN. *Magic Motorways.* New York: Random House, 1940.

BENDIXSON, TERENCE. *Without Wheels: Alternatives to the Private Car.* Bloomington and London: Indiana University Press, 1975.

BERMAN, MARSHALL. *All That Is Solid Melts into Air: The Experience of Modernity.* New York: Penguin, 1988.

BLAKE, PETER. *Form Follows Fiasco.* Boston: Little, Brown, 1974.

————. *God's Own Junkyard*. New York: Holt, Rinehart and Winston, 1964.

BLUM, JOHN MORTON. *V Was for Victory: Politics and American Culture During World War II*. New York: Harcourt Brace, 1976.

BOLOTIN, NORMAN, AND CHRISTINE LAING. *The World's Columbian Exposition*. Washington, D.C.: Preservation Press, 1993.

BOTTLES, SCOTT L. *Los Angeles and the Automobile: The Making of the Modern City*. Berkeley: University of California Press, 1987.

BREINES, SIMON, AND WILLIAM J. DEAN. *The Pedestrian Revolution: Streets Without Cars*. New York: Vintage Books, 1974.

BUEL, RONALD A. *Dead End: The Automobile in Mass Transportation*. Englewood Cliffs, N.J.: Prentice-Hall, 1972.

BURBY, JOHN. *The Great American Motion Sickness*. Boston: Little, Brown, 1971.

CALLOW, ALEXANDER B., JR. *American Urban History*. 2d ed. New York: Oxford University Press, 1973.

CALTHORPE, PETER. *The Next American Metropolis*. New York: Princeton Architectural Press, 1993.

CHEAPE, CHARLES W. *Moving the Masses: Urban Public Transit in New York, Boston, and Philadelphia, 1880–1912*. Cambridge, Mass.: Harvard University Press, 1980.

CHICAGO HISTORICAL SOCIETY. "Prairie in the City." Catalogue. Chicago: Chicago Historical Society, 1991.

CLAWSON, MARION. *New Deal Planning*. Baltimore: Johns Hopkins University Press, 1981.

CRUMP, SPENCER. *Ride the Big Red Cars: How Trolleys Helped Build Southern California*. Corona del Mar, Calif.: Trans-Anglo Books, 1970.

CUTLER, PHOEBE. *The Public Landscape of the New Deal*. New Haven: Yale University Press, 1985.

DOUGLAS, GEORGE H. *All Aboard: The Railroad in American Life*. New York: Paragon House, 1992.

DOWNS, ANTHONY. *Stuck in Traffic*. Washington, D.C.: Brookings Institution and Lincoln Institute of Land Policy, 1992.

————. *New Visions for Metropolitan America*. Washington, D.C.: Brookings Institution, and Cambridge, Mass.: Lincoln Institute of Land Policy, 1994.

DUERKSEN, CHRISTOPHER J., ED. *A Handbook on Historic Preservation Law.* Washington, D.C.: Conservation Foundation and National Center for Preservation Law, 1983.

EBNER, MICHAEL H. *Creating Chicago's North Shore, A Suburban History.* Chicago: University of Chicago Press, 1988.

ENO FOUNDATION. *Transportation in America.* 13th ed. Lansdowne, Va.: Eno Foundation, 1995.

EVANS, L. *Traffic Safety and the Driver.* New York: Van Nostrand Reinhold, 1991.

FINCH, CHRISTOPHER. *Highways to Heaven.* New York: HarperCollins, 1992.

FINDLAY, JOHN M. *Magic Lands: Western Cityscapes and American Culture After 1940.* Berkeley: University of California Press, 1992.

FISHMAN, ROBERT. *Bourgeois Utopias: The Rise and Fall of Suburbia.* New York: Basic Books, 1987.

FLINK, JAMES J., *The Car Culture.* Cambridge, Mass.: MIT Press, 1975.

————. *The Automobile Age.* Rev. ed. Cambridge, Mass.: MIT Press, 1990.

FOGELSON, ROBERT M. *The Fragmented Metropolis: Los Angeles, 1850–1930.* Rev. ed. Berkeley: University of California Press, 1993.

FORD, LARRY R. *Skyscrapers, Cities and Buildings: Skid Rows and Suburbs.* Baltimore: Johns Hopkins University Press, 1994.

FOSTER, MARK S. *From Streetcar to Superhighway: American City Planners and Urban Transportation, 1900–1940.* Philadelphia: Temple University Press, 1981.

FREUND, PETER, AND GEORGE MARTIN. *The Ecology of the Automobile.* Montreal: Black Rose Books, 1993.

FRIEDEN, BERNARD J., AND LYNNE B. SAGALYN. *Downtown, Inc.* Cambridge, Mass.: MIT Press, 1990.

GARREAU, JOEL. *Edge City: Life on the New Frontier.* New York: Doubleday, 1991.

GELFAND, MARK I. *A Nation of Cities: The Federal Government and Urban America, 1933–1965.* New York: Oxford University Press, 1975.

GILLETTE, HOWARD, JR., AND ZANE L. MILLER, ED. *American Urbanism, A Historiographical Review.* New York: Greenwood Press, 1987.

GLYNN, HENRY J., AND GARY W. HEINKE. *Environmental Science and Engineering.* Englewood Cliffs, N.J.: Prentice-Hall, 1989.

GODDARD, STEPHEN B. *Getting There: The Epic Struggle Between Road and Rail in the Twentieth Century.* New York: Basic Books, 1994.

GORDON, DEBORAH. *Steering a New Course: Transportation, Energy, and the Environment.* Cambridge, Mass.: Union of Concerned Scientists, 1991.

GORE, ALBERT. *Earth in the Balance.* New York: Penguin, 1993.

GOTTLIEB, ROBERT. *Forcing the Spring: The Transformation of the American Environmental Movement.* Washington, D.C.: Island Press, 1993.

GOTTMANN, JEAN. *Megalopolis, the Urbanized Northeastern Seaboard of the United States.* New York: Twentieth Century Fund, 1961.

———. *Since Megalopolis.* Baltimore: Johns Hopkins, University Press, 1991.

GRAHAM, JOHN D. *Auto Safety: Assessing America's Performance.* Dover, Mass.: Auburn House, 1989.

GRAHAM, OTIS L., JR. *Toward a Planned Society: From Roosevelt to Nixon.* New York: Oxford University Press, 1976.

GREER, SCOTT. *Urban Renewal and American Cities.* New York: Bobbs Merrill, 1965.

GRESE, ROBERT E. *Jens Jensen: Maker of Natural Parks and Gardens.* Baltimore: Johns Hopkins University Press, 1972.

HAAR, CHARLES M., AND JEROLD S. KAYDEN, EDS. *Zoning and the American Dream: Promises Still to Keep.* Chicago: Lincoln Land Institute, Planners Press, 1989.

HANSON, SUSAN. *The Geography of Urban Transportation.* New York: Guildford Press, 1995.

HART, JOHN FRASER, ED. *Our Changing Cities.* Baltimore: Johns Hopkins University Press, 1991.

HART, STANLEY L., AND ALVIN L. SPIVAK. *The Elephant in the Bedroom: Impacts on the Economy and Environment.* Pasadena, Calif.: New Paradigm Books, 1993.

HAYS, SAMUEL P. *Beauty, Health, and Permanence: Environmental Politics in the United States, 1955–1985,* Cambridge, Mass.: Cambridge University Press, 1987.

HEGEMANN, WERNER, AND ELBERT PEETS. *Civic Art.* New York: Architectural Book Publishing, 1922.

HEIDE, ROBERT, AND JOHN GILMAN. *Popular Art Deco: Depression Era Style and Design.* New York: Abbeville, 1991.

HEIMANN, JIM. *Car Hops and Curb Service: A History of American Drive-In Restaurants, 1920–1960.* San Francisco: Chronicle Books, 1996.

HILTON, GEORGE W., AND JOHN F. DUE. *The Electric Interurban Railways in America.* Palo Alto, Calif.: Stanford University Press, 1960.

HINES, THOMAS H. *Burnham of Chicago.* New York: Oxford University Press, 1974.

HOSMER, CHARLES. *Preservation Comes of Age.* Vols. 1 and 2. Charlottesville: University Press of Virginia, 1981.

HUBBARD, THEODORA KIMBALL, AND HENRY VINCENT HUBBARD. *Our Cities To-day and To-morrow: A Survey of Planning and Zoning in the United States.* Cambridge, Mass.: Harvard University Press, 1929.

ILLICH, IVAN. *Energy and Equity.* New York: Harper and Row, 1974.

JACKSON, JOHN BRINCKERHOFF. *A Sense of Place, a Sense of Time.* New Haven: Yale University Press, 1994.

JACKSON, KENNETH T. *The Crabgrass Frontier: the Suburbanization of the United States.* New York: Oxford University Press, 1985.

JACOBS, ALLAN. *Great Streets.* Cambridge, Mass.: MIT Press, 1993.

JACOBS, JANE. *The Death and Life of Great American Cities.* New York: Vintage Books, 1961.

JACKLE, JOHN A., AND KEITH A. SCULLE. *The Gas Station in America.* Baltimore: Johns Hopkins University Press, 1994.

JENNINGS, JAN, ED. *Roadside America: The Automobile in Design and Culture.* Ames: Iowa State University Press, 1990.

JUDD, DENNIS R. *The Politics of American Cities: Private Power and Public Policy.* 3rd ed. Glenview, Ill.: Scott, Foresman, 1988.

KAY, JANE HOLTZ, WITH PAULINE CHASE-HARRELL. *Preserving New England.* New York: Pantheon, 1986.

KEARNS GOODWIN, DORIS. *No Ordinary Time.* New York: Simon and Schuster, 1994.

KEATS, JOHN. *The Insolent Chariots.* Philadelphia: J.B. Lippincott Co., 1958.

KELLEY, BEN. *The Pavers and the Paved.* New York: Charles Scribner's Sons, 1971.

KELLY, BARBARA. *Expanding the American Dream.* Albany: State University of New York Press, 1993.

KOUBA, DENNIS, ED. *Passenger Transport.* Fiftieth Anniversary Edition. 1993.

KRUECKEBERG, DONALD A. *The American Planner: Biographies and Recollections.* New York: Methuen, 1983.

KRUECKEBERG, DONALD A., ED. *Introduction to Planning History in the United States.* New Brunswick, N.J.: Center for Urban Policy Research, Rutgers University, 1983.

LEAVITT, HELEN. *Superhighway-Superhoax.* New York: Doubleday, 1970.

LE CORBUSIER: FREDERIC ETCHELLS INTRODUCTION. *The City of To-morrow, and Its Planning.* New York: Payson & Clarke Ltd., 1929.

LEUCHTENBURG, WILLIAM E. *Franklin D. Roosevelt and the New Deal.* New York: Harper and Row, 1963.

LEWIS, DAVID L., AND LAURENCE GOLDSTEIN, EDS. *The Automobile and American Culture.* Ann Arbor: University of Michigan Press, 1991.

LIEBS, CHESTER H. *Main Street to Miracle Mile: American Roadside Architecture.* Boston: New York Graphic Society Book/Little, Brown, 1984.

LINCOLN HIGHWAY ASSOCIATION. *The Story of a Crusade That Made Transportation History.* New York: Dodd, Mead, 1935.

LYNCH, KEVIN. *The Image of the City.* Cambridge, Mass.: MIT Press, 1988.

MACKENZIE, JAMES J., AND MOHAMED T. EL-ASHRY, EDS. *Air Pollution's Toll on Forests and Crops.* New Haven: Yale University Press, A Wild Resources Institute Book, 1989.

MADDOX, DIANE. *Built in the U.S.A.* Washington, D.C.: Preservation Press, 1985.

MANCHESTER, WILLIAM. *The Glory and the Dream.* Boston: Little, Brown, 1973.

MARCUSE, PETER. "The Myth of the Benevolent State: Towards a Theory of Housing." Papers in Planning 8, 1978. Columbia University, Graduate School of Architecture and Planning, New York.

MARLING, KARAL ANN. *The Colossus of Roads: Myth and Symbol along the American Highway.* Minneapolis: University of Minnesota, 1984.

MARSH, PETER, AND PETER COLLETT. *Driving Passion, The Psychology of the Car.* Boston: Faber and Faber, 1987.

MASON PHILIP P. *A History of American Roads.* Chicago: Rand McNally, 1967.

MASSEY, DOUGLAS S., AND NANCY A. DENTON. *American Apartheid: Segregation and the Making of the Underclass.* Cambridge, Mass.: Harvard University Press, 1993.

MCHENRY, ROBERT, AND CHARLES VAN DOREN, EDS. *A Documentary History of Conservation in America.* New York: Praeger, 1972.

MCSHANE, CLAY. *Down the Asphalt Path: The Automobile and the American City.* New York: Columbia University Press, 1994.

MIDDLETON, WILLIAM D. *The Time of the Trolley.* 4th ed. Milwaukee, Wis.: Kalmbach Publishers, 1975.

MILLER, DONALD L. *Lewis Mumford, a Life.* New York: Weidenfeld and Nicolson, 1989.

MORGAN, TED. *FDR, a Biography.* New York: Simon and Schuster, 1985.

MORRIS, DAVID. *Self-Reliant Cities: Energy and the Transformation of Urban America.* San Francisco: Sierra Club, 1982.

MUMFORD LEWIS. *The Highway and the City.* New York: Mentor Books, New American Library, 1963.

NABAKOV, VLADIMIR. *Lolita.* New York: Vintage Books, 1989.

NADER, RALPH. *Unsafe at Any Speed.* New York: Grossman, 1965.

NADIS STEVEN, AND JAMES J. MACKENZIE. *Car Trouble.* Boston: World Resources/Beacon. 1993.

NATIONAL SAFETY COUNCIL. *Accident Facts.* Itasca, Ill.: NSC, 1994.

NEVINS, ALLAN, AND FRANK ERNEST HILL. *Henry Ford.* Vols. 1–3. New York: Charles Scribner's Sons, 1957.

NEWMAN, PETER, AND JEFFREY KENWORTHY. *Cities and Automobile Dependence.* Aldershot Hants, England: Avebury Technical, 1991.

NEWTON, NORMAN T. *Design on the Land.* Cambridge, Mass.: Belknap Press, Harvard University Press, 1971.

NOLEN, JOHN, ED. *City Planning.* New York: D. Appleton and Company, 1916.

———. *New Towns for Old.* Boston: Marshall Jones Co., 1927.

NORTON, MARY BETH, DAVID M. KATZMAN, PAUL D. ESCOTT, HOWARD P. CHUDACOFF, THOMAS G. PATERSON, AND WILLIAM M. TUTTLE, JR. *A People and a Nation: A History of the United States.* 3rd. Ed. Boston: Houghton Mifflin, 1990.

PETERSON, JON ALVAH. *The Origins of the Comprehensive City Planning Ideal in the United States, 1840–1911*. Ph.D. dissertation, Harvard University, April 1967.

PORTERFIELD, GERALD A., AND KENNETH B. HALL, JR. *A Concise Guide to Community Planning*. New York: McGraw-Hill, 1995.

POWERS, RON. *Far from Home*. New York: Random House, 1991.

PRESTON, HOWARD LAWRENCE. *Dirt Roads to Dixie: Accessibility and Modernization in the South, 1885–1935*. Knoxville: University of Tennessee Press, 1991.

PUSHKAREV, BORIS S., AND JEFFREY M. ZUPAN. *Public Transportation and Land Use Policy*. Bloomington: Indiana University Press, 1977.

RAE, JOHN B. *The American Automobile: A Brief History*. Chicago: University of Chicago Press, 1965.

———. *The Road and Car in American Life*. Cambridge, Mass.: MIT Press, 1971.

RIFKIND, CAROLE. *Main Street: The Face of Urban America*. New York: Harper and Row, 1977.

ROBINSON, CERVIN, AND ROSEMARIE HAAG BLETTER. *Skyscraper Style: Art Deco New York*. New York: Oxford University Press, 1975.

ROBINSON, CHARLES MULFORD. *City Planning*. New York: G.P. Putnam's Sons, 1916.

———. *Modern Civic Art or the City Made Beautiful*. New York: G.P. Putnam's Sons, 1904.

ROSE, MARK H. *Historic American Roads*. New York: Crown Publishers, 1976.

———. *Interstate Expressway Highway Politics, 1941–1956*. Lawrence: Regents Press of Kansas, 1979.

ROTHSCHILD, EMMA. *Paradise Lost: the Decline of the Auto-Industrial Age*. New York: Random House, 1974.

ROWE, PETER G. *Making a Middle Landscape*. Cambridge, Mass.: MIT Press, 1911.

ST. CLAIR, DAVID J. *The Motorization of American Cities*. New York: Praeger, 1986.

SCHAEFFER, K. H., AND ELLIOTT SCLAR. *Access for All: Transportation and Urban Growth*. New York: Penguin Books, 1975.

SCHAFER, TODD, AND JEFF FAUX, EDS. *Reclaiming Prosperity.* Economic Polity Institute. Armonk, N.Y.: M. E. Sharpe, 1996.

SCHAFFER, DANIEL, ED. *Two Centuries of American Planning.* Baltimore: Johns Hopkins University Press, 1988.

SCHNEIDER, KENNETH R. *Autokind vs. Mankind.* New York: W. W. Norton, 1971.

SCHOR, JULIET B. *The Overworked American: The Unexpected Decline of Leisure.* New York: Basic Books, 1991.

SCLAR, ELLIOTT *Selling the Brooklyn Bridge: The Privatization of America,* manuscript Draft, 1996.

SCOTT, MEL. *American City Planning Since 1890.* Berkeley: University of California Press, 1969.

SEELY, BRUCE E. *Building the American Highway System: Engineers as Policy Makers.* Philadelphia: Temple University Press, 1987.

SENNETT, RICHARD. *The Fall of Public Man.* New York: Vintage Books, 1978.

SHABECOFF, PHILIP. *A Fierce Green Fire.* New York: Hill and Wang, 1993.

SMALL, KENNETH A. *Urban Transportation Economics.* Chur, Switz.: Harwood Academic Publishers, 1992.

SMERK, GEORGE M. *Urban Transportation: The Federal Role.* Bloomington: Indiana University Press, 1956.

SOLOMON, DANIEL. *ReBuilding.* New York: Princeton Architectural Press, 1992.

STEFFENS, LINCOLN. *The Shame of the Cities.* New York: McClure, Phillips, 1904.

———. *The Struggle for Self-Government.* New York: McClure, Phillips, 1906.

STERN, ROBERT A. M., et al. *New York 1900.* New York: Rizzoli, 1983.

———. *New York 1930.* New York: Rizzoli, 1987.

———. *New York 1960.* New York: Rizzoli, 1995.

STILGOE, JOHN. *Borderland, Origins of the American Suburb.* New Haven: Yale University Press, 1988.

———. *Metropolitan Corridor: Railroads and the Amreicna Scene.* New Haven: Yale University Press, 1983.

SUCHER, DAVID. *City Comforts: How to Build an Urban Village.* Seattle, Wash.: City Comforts Press, 1995.

Sussman, Carl, ed. *Planning the Forth Migration: The Neglected Vision of the Regional Planning Association of America.* Cambridge, Mass.: MIT Press, 1976.

Swain, Roger. *Groundwork.* Boston: Houghton Mifflin, 1994.

Tarr, Joel A., and Gabriel Dupuy, eds. *Technology and the Rise of the Networked City in Europe and America.* Philadelphia: Temple University Press, 1988.

Taylor, George Rogers, and Irene D. Neu. *The American Railroad Network, 1861–1890.* Cambridge, Mass.: Harvard University Press, 1956.

Teaford, Jon C. *The New American City.* 2d ed. Baltimore: Johns Hopkins University Press, 1993.

————. *Rough Road to Renaissance: Urban Revitalization in America, 1940–1986.* Baltimore: Johns Hopkins University Press, 1990.

Toll, Seymour I. *Zoned America.* New York: Grossman, 1969.

Twombly, Robert C. *Frank Lloyd Wright: An Interpretive Biography.* New York: Harper and Row, 1973.

U.S. Department of Transportation. *Urban Transportation Planning in the United States, an Historical Overview.* Washington, D.C.: U.S. DOT, 1992.

Vance, James E., Jr. *Capturing the Horizon: The Historical Geography of Transportation Since the Sixteenth Century.* 2d ed. Balitmore: Johns Hopkins University Press, 1990.

Wachs, Martin, and Margaret Crawford, eds. *The Car and the City: The Automobile, the Built Environment, and Daily Urban Life.* Ann Arbor: University of Michigan Press, 1991.

Wallis, Michael. *Route 66: The Mother Road.* New York: St. Martin's Press, 1990.

Ward, Colin. *The Child in the City.* New York: Pantheon, 1978.

————. *The Child in the Country.* London: Robert Hale Ltd., 1988.

Warner, Sam Bass. *Streetcar Suburbs: The Process of Growth in Boston 1870–1900.* Cambridge, Mass.: Harvard University Press and MIT Press, 1962.

————. *The Urban Wilderness: A History of the American City.* New York: Harper and Row, 1972.

Watkins, T. H. *The Great Depression: America in the 1930s.* Boston: Little, Brown, 1993.

———. *Righteous Pilgrim: The Life and Times of Harold L. Ickes, 1874–1952.* New York; Henry Holt, 1990.

WATSON, ANN Y., RICHARD R. BATES, AND DONALD KENNEDY, EDS. *Air Pollution, the Automobile, and Public Health.* Health Effects Institute, Cambridge. Washington, D.C.: National Academy Press, 1988.

WEISS, MARC A. *The Rise of the Community Builders: The American Real Estate Industry and Urban Land Planning.* New York: Columbia University Press, 1987.

WHYTE, WILLIAM H., JR., ED. *The Exploding Metropolis.* Berkeley: University of California Press, 1993.

WILNER, FRANK N. *The Amtrak Story.* Omaha, Neb.: Simmons-Boardman Books, 1994.

WILSON, PAUL C. *Chrome Dreams: Automobile Styling Since 1893.* Radnor, Pa.: Chilton Books, 1976.

WILSON, RICHARD GUY, DIANNE H. PILGRIM, AND DICKRAN TASHJIAN. *The Machine Age in America, 1918–1941.* New York: Brooklyn Museum in association with Harry N. Abrams, 1986.

WORLEY, WILLIAM S. *J.C. Nichols and the Shaping of Kansas City: Innovation in Planned Residential Communities.* Columbia: University of Missouri Press, 1990.

WRIGHT, CHARLES L. *Fast Wheels: Slow Traffic.* Philadelphia: Temple University Press, 1992.

YERGIN, DANIEL. *The Prize: The Epic Quest for Oil, Money and Power.* New York: Simon and Schuster, 1991.

Index